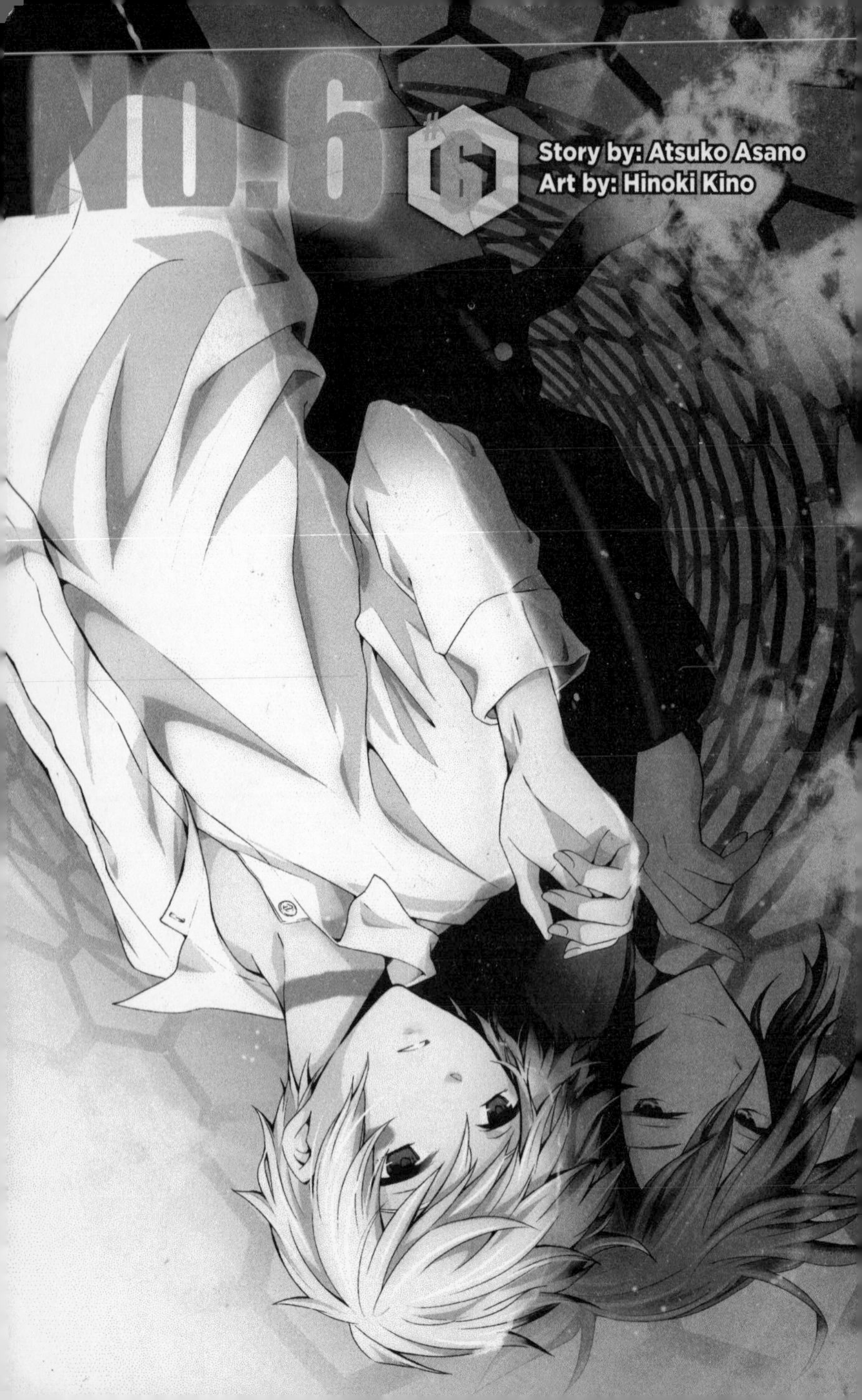
NO.6
#6
Story by: Atsuko Asano
Art by: Hinoki Kino

NO.6

#6

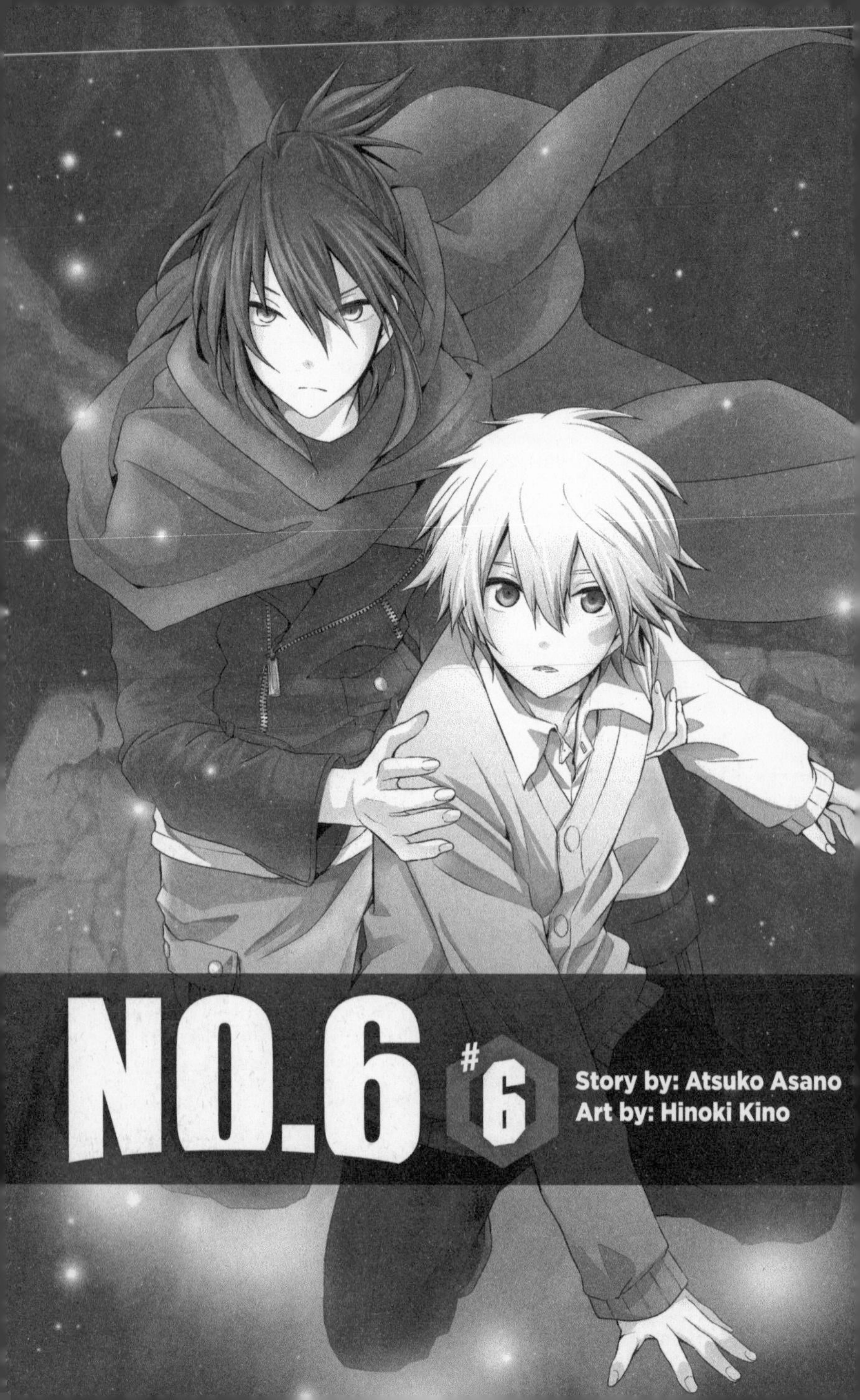
NO.6
#6
Story by: Atsuko Asano
Art by: Hinoki Kino

STORY and CHARACTERS

Shion was raised as a privileged elite in the holy city of No. 6. As the Public Security Bureau was arresting him on charges of murder, a boy named Rat, whom Shion helped during a storm four years earlier, stepped in to save him. Together they escaped No. 6 and fled to West Block, a place of violence and chaos. Shion was infected by a mysterious parasitic bee, but survived, living together with Rat in West Block. After hearing that his childhood friend Safu had been detained and taken to the Correctional Facility, Shion decided to go free her. With assistance from Dogkeeper and Rikiga, Shion and Rat allowed themselves to be captured during the West Block massacre known as the Manhunt, gaining entrance to the Correctional Facility. Surrounded by blood and shrieks, Shion pressed on. Following Rat's lead into the depths of the underground, they finally encountered a mysterious group of people.

Chronos

The top-class residential area, open only to elite citizens.

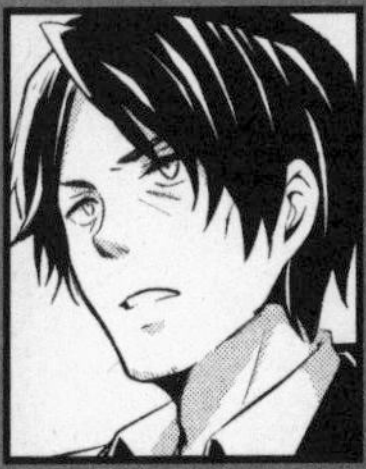

YOMIN

He's doubted No. 6 since his wife and child died.

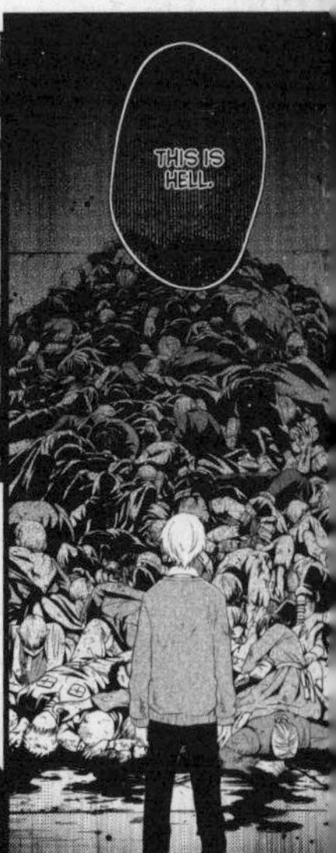
THIS IS HELL.

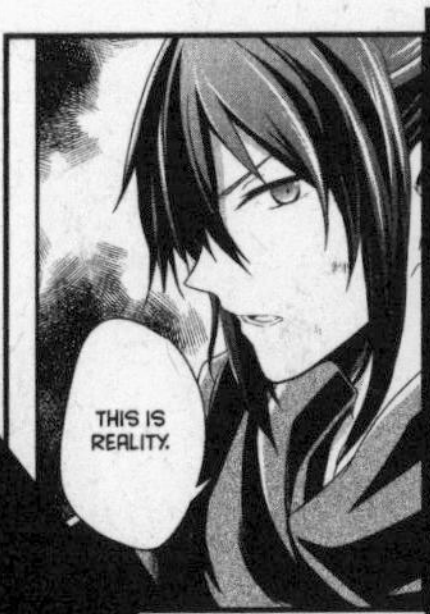
THIS IS REALITY.

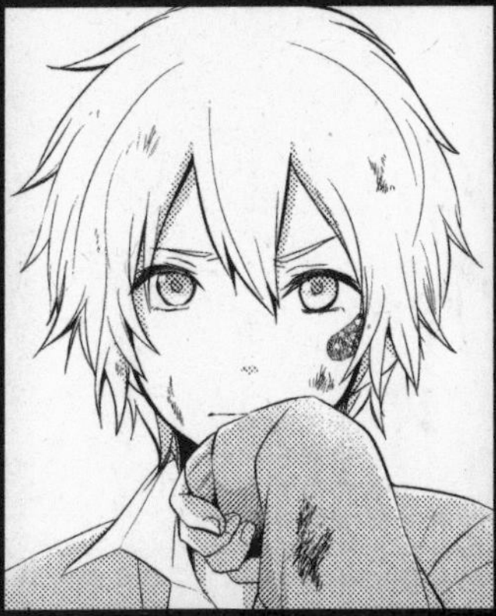

SHION

A former elite candidate, he was a kind, gentle youth, but as his life has grown harsher, he has begun to change.

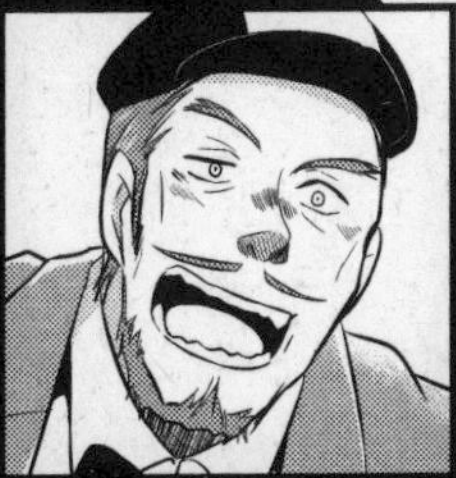

RIKIGA

A former journalist who now publishes a porno magazine in West Block. An old friend of Karan.

Inside No. 6

Upper Class

The center of the city, with the Moondrop (City Hall) at its apex.

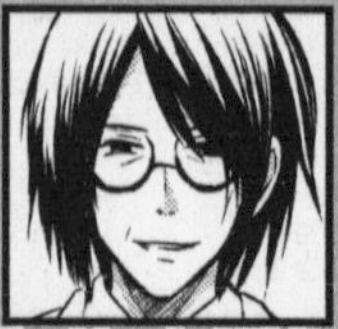

The Man in White
An ambitious research scientist.

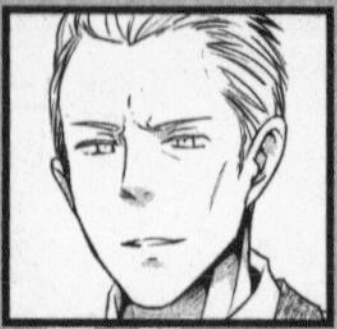

The Mayor
The most powerful man in No. 6.

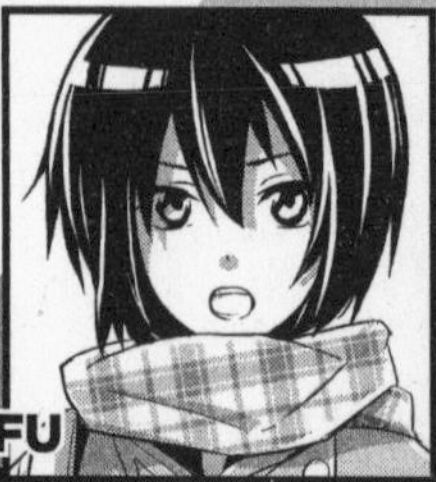

SAFU
A childhood friend who loves Shion. An elite researcher who specializes in neuroscience.

Arrested

The Correctional Facility

The prison for criminals from No. 6. Located in West Block.

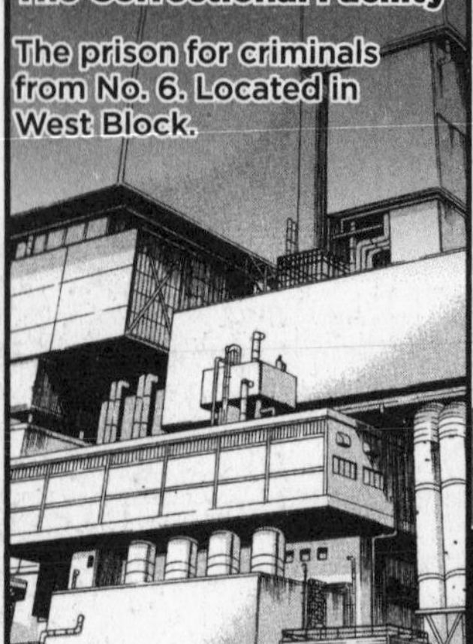

Lost Town

The lower-class residential area for the city's disenfranchised.

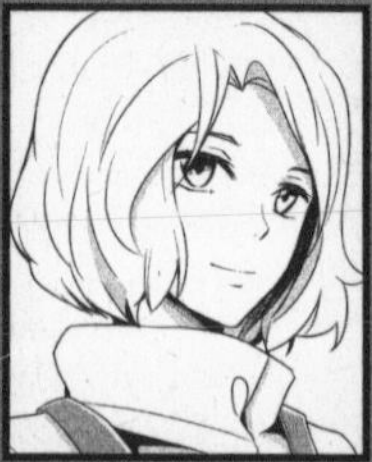

KARAN
Shion's mother. Operates a bakery in Lost Town.

The Outskirts

West Block

The dangerous special zone outside the walls of the city.

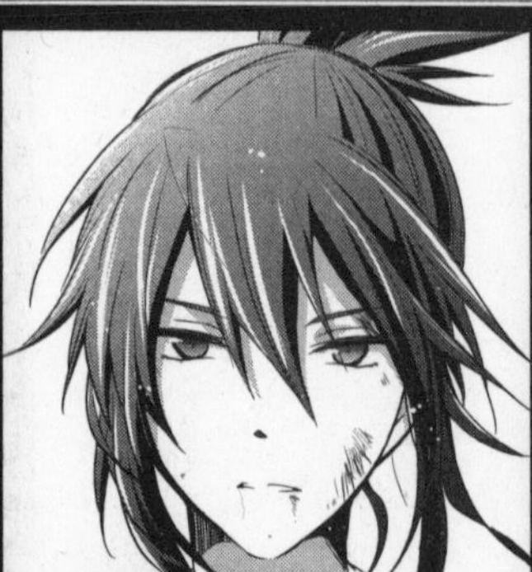

RAT
Four years ago, Shion saved his life in Chronos. In return, he helped Shion escape from No. 6.

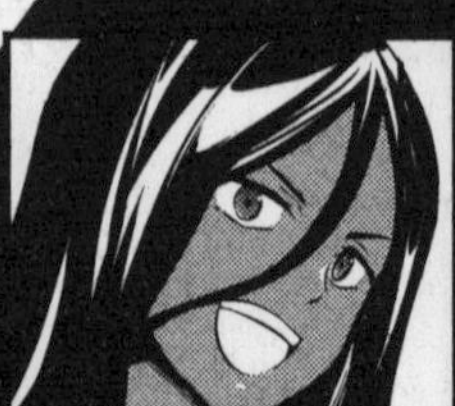

DOGKEEPER
Lives with dogs and operates a dilapidated hotel. Also gathers information for a price.

NO.6

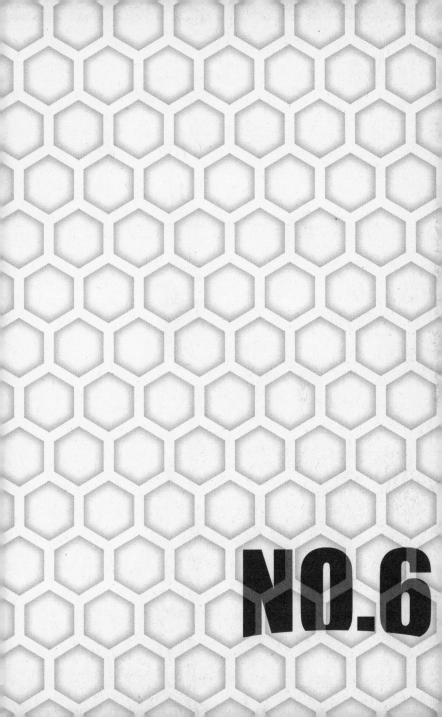

Chapter 20: A Prayer for Him

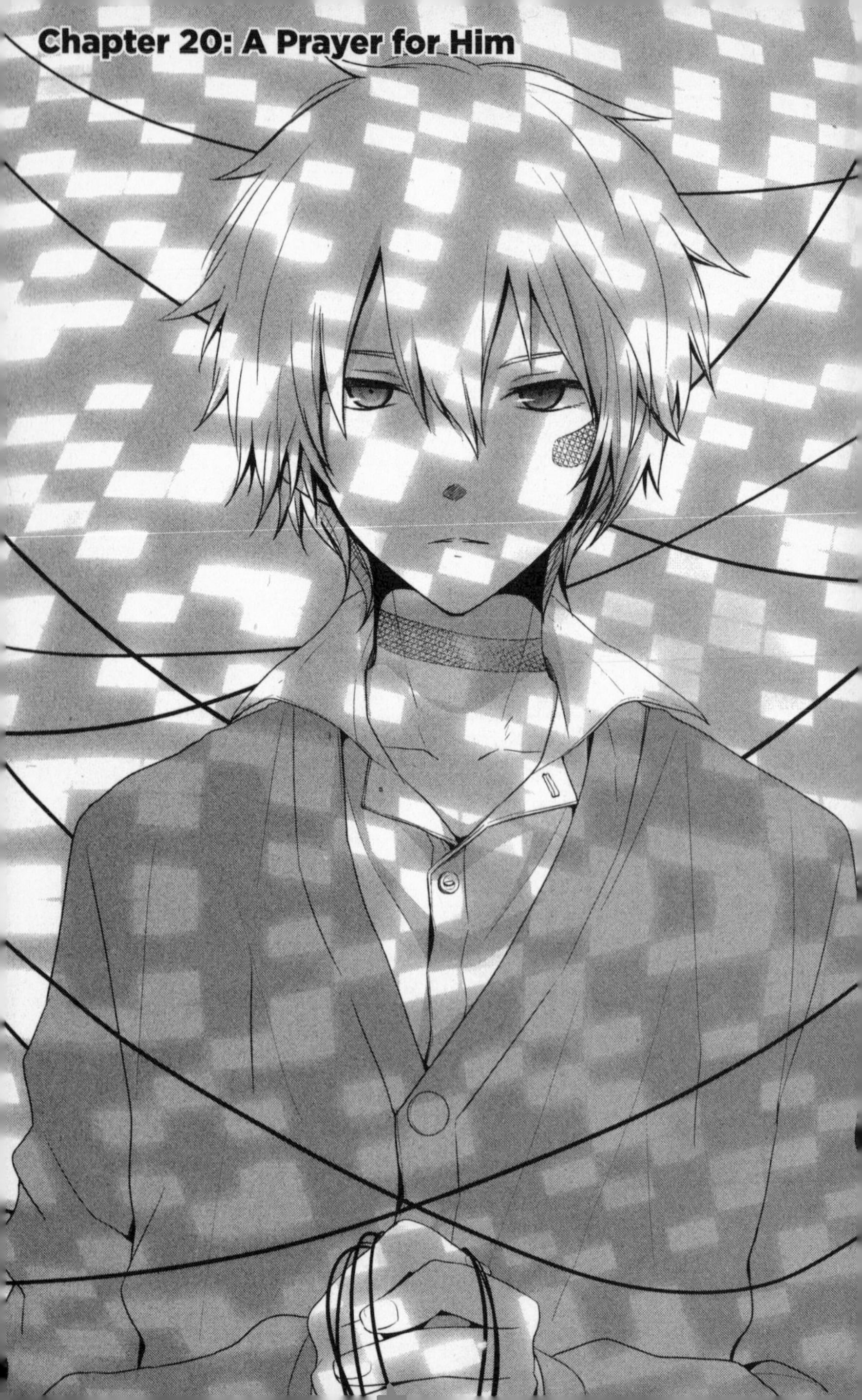

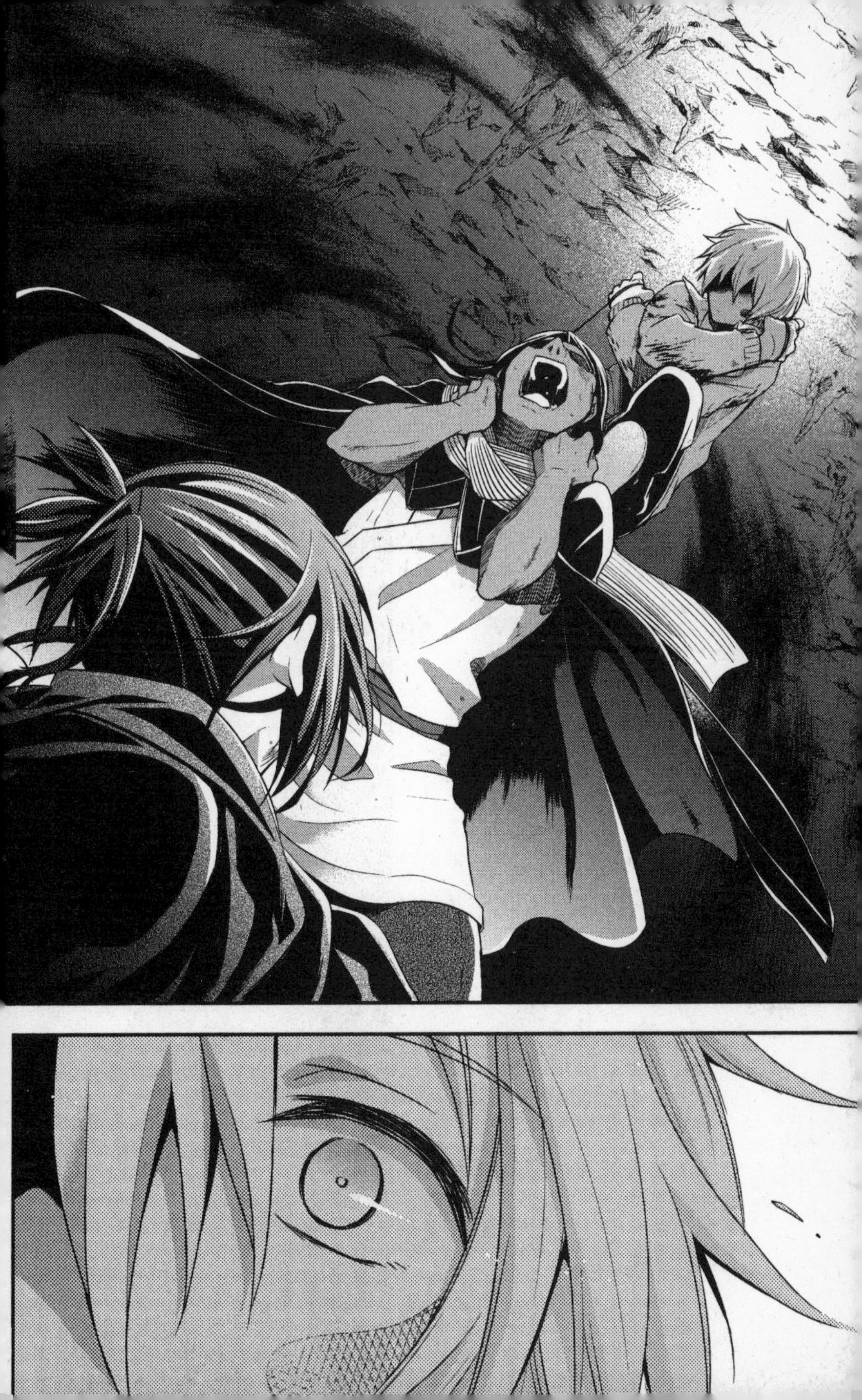

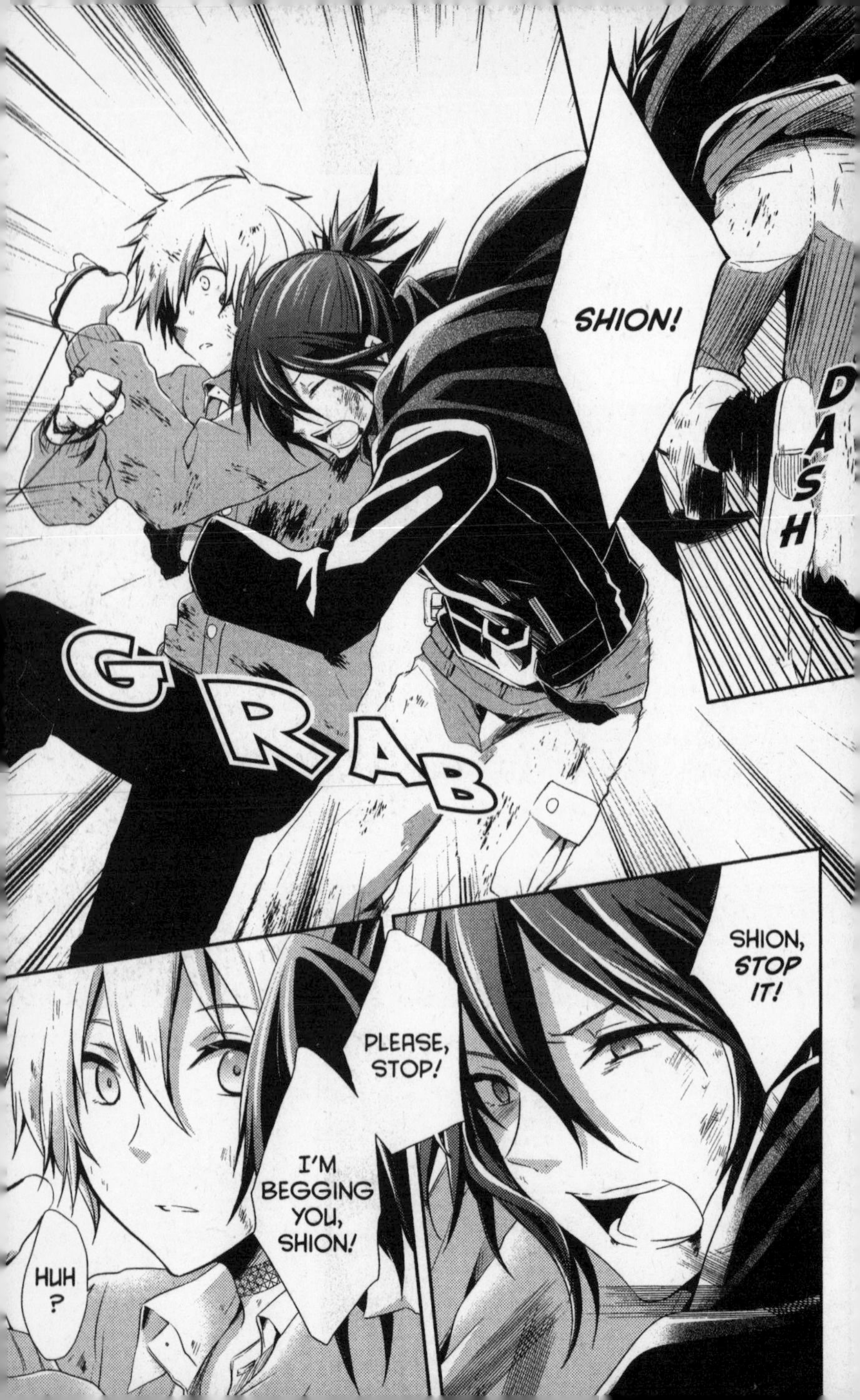
SHION!
DASH
GRAB
SHION, STOP IT!
PLEASE, STOP!
I'M BEGGING YOU, SHION!
HUH?

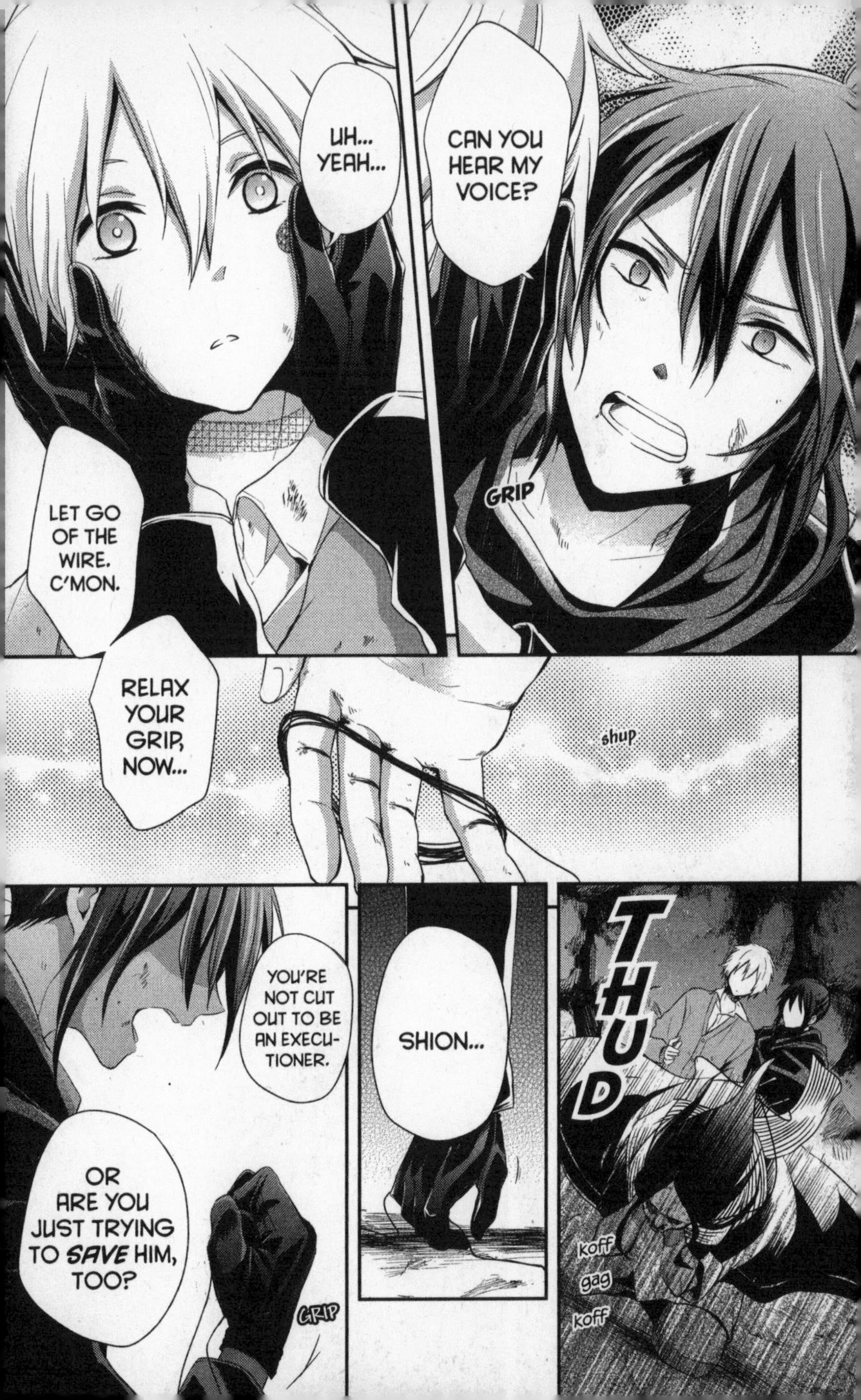
CAN YOU HEAR MY VOICE?
GRIP
UH... YEAH...
LET GO OF THE WIRE. C'MON.
shup
RELAX YOUR GRIP, NOW...
THUD
koff
gag
koff
SHION...
YOU'RE NOT CUT OUT TO BE AN EXECU-TIONER.
OR ARE YOU JUST TRYING TO *SAVE* HIM, TOO?
GRIP

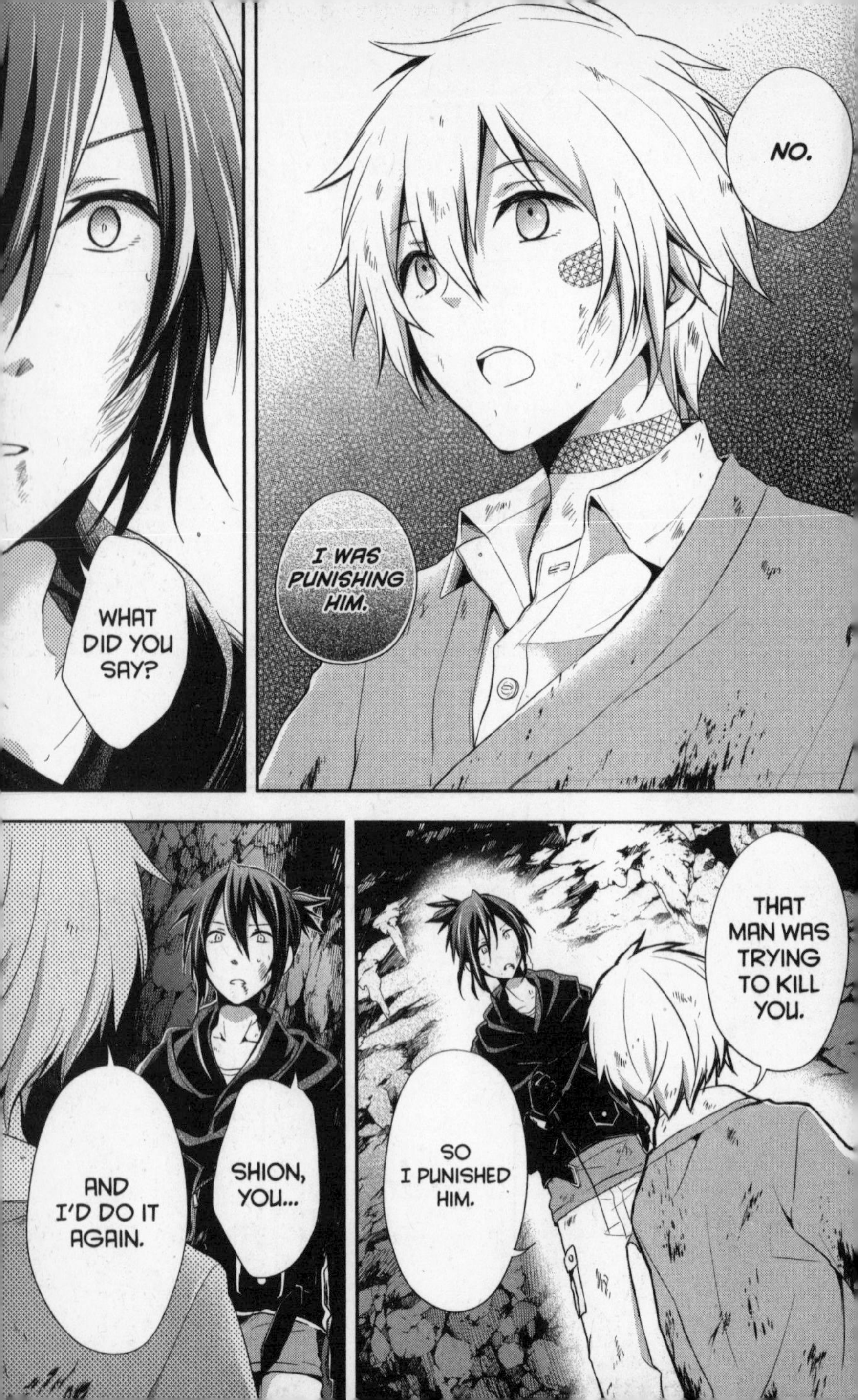
NO.
I WAS PUNISHING HIM.
WHAT DID YOU SAY?
THAT MAN WAS TRYING TO KILL YOU.
SO I PUNISHED HIM.
SHION, YOU...
AND I'D DO IT AGAIN.

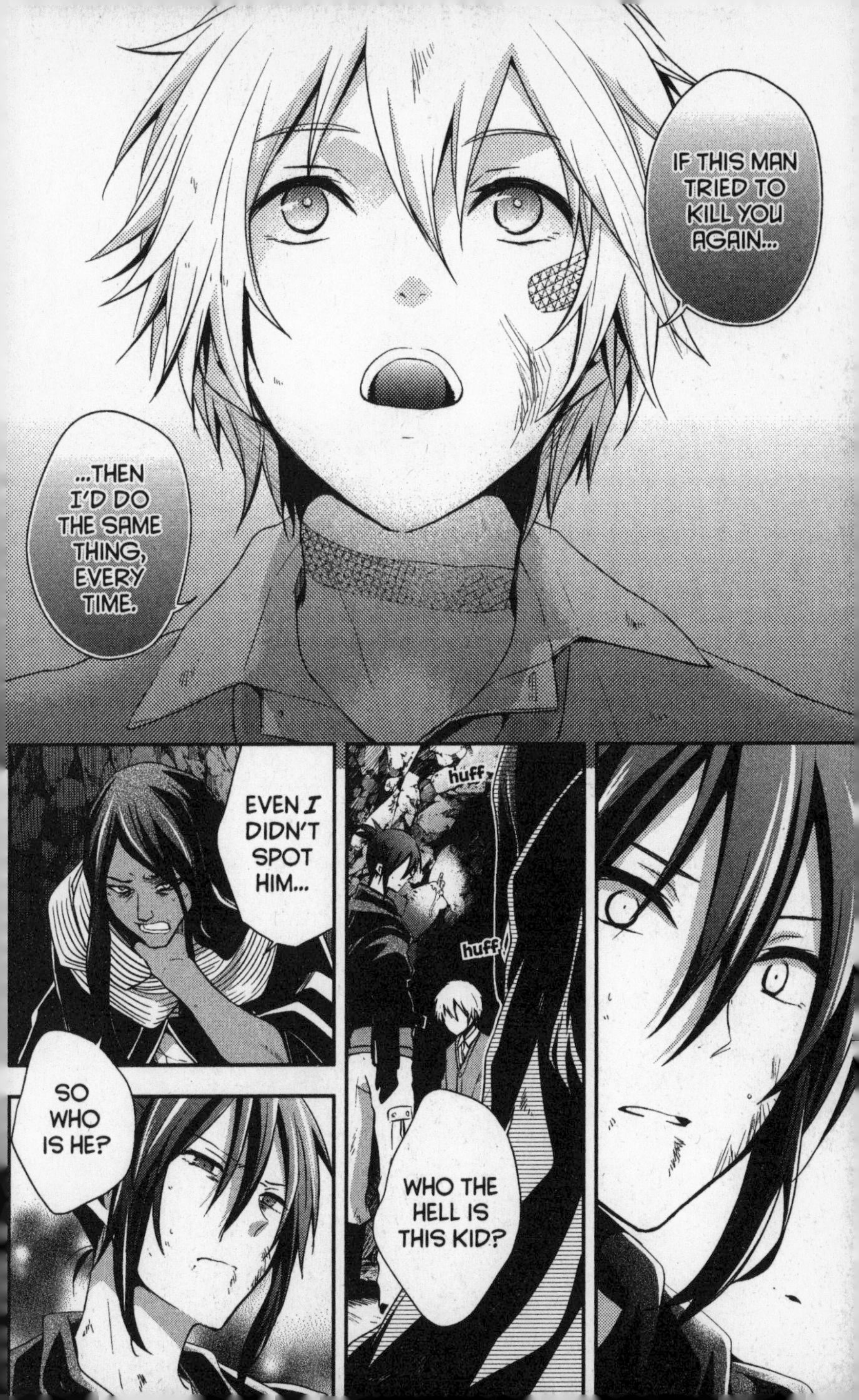
IF THIS MAN TRIED TO KILL YOU AGAIN...
...THEN I'D DO THE SAME THING, EVERY TIME.
huff
huff
WHO THE HELL IS THIS KID?
EVEN *I* DIDN'T SPOT HIM...
SO WHO IS HE?

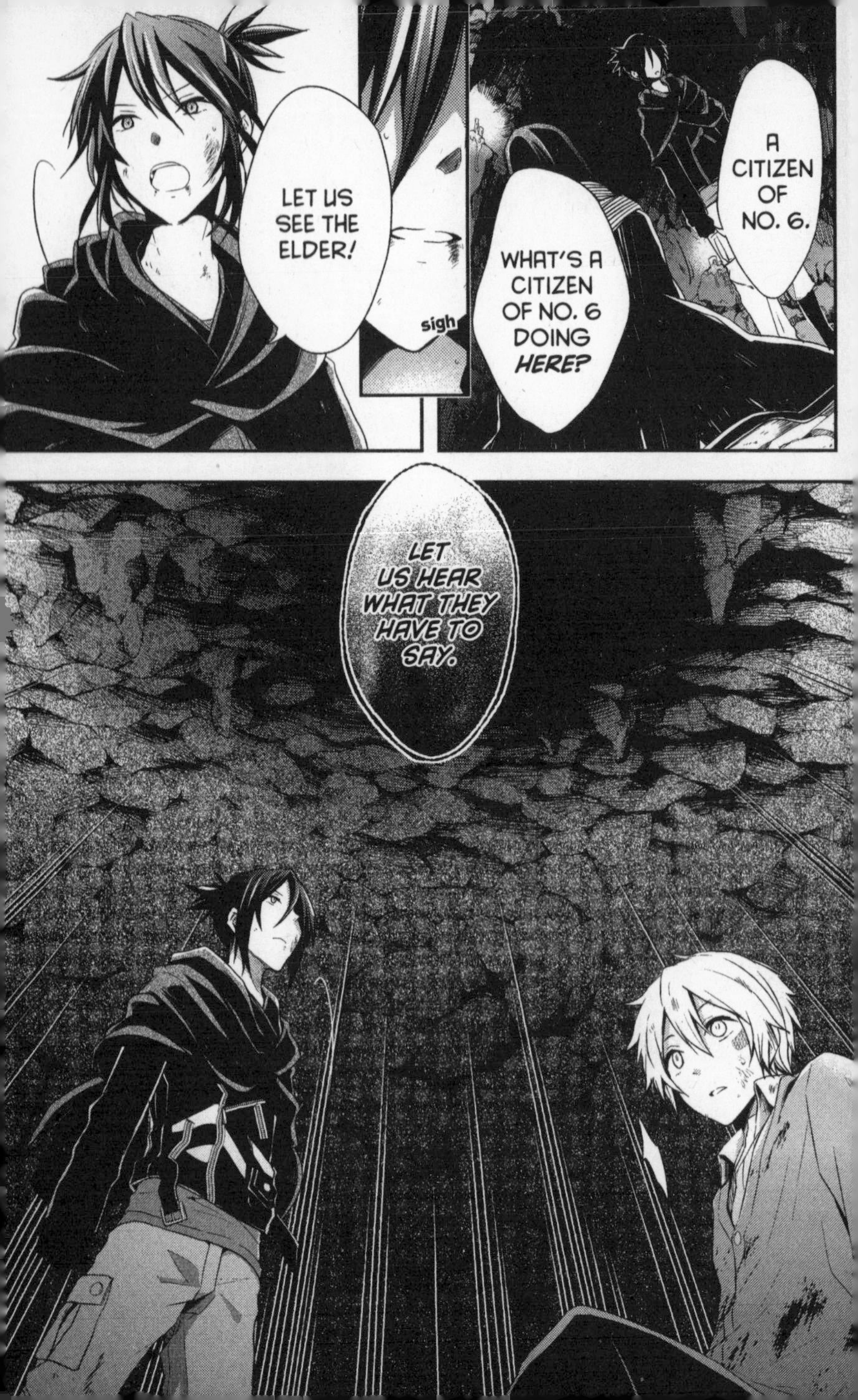
A CITIZEN OF NO. 6.
WHAT'S A CITIZEN OF NO. 6 DOING *HERE?*
sigh
LET US SEE THE ELDER!
LET US HEAR WHAT THEY HAVE TO SAY.

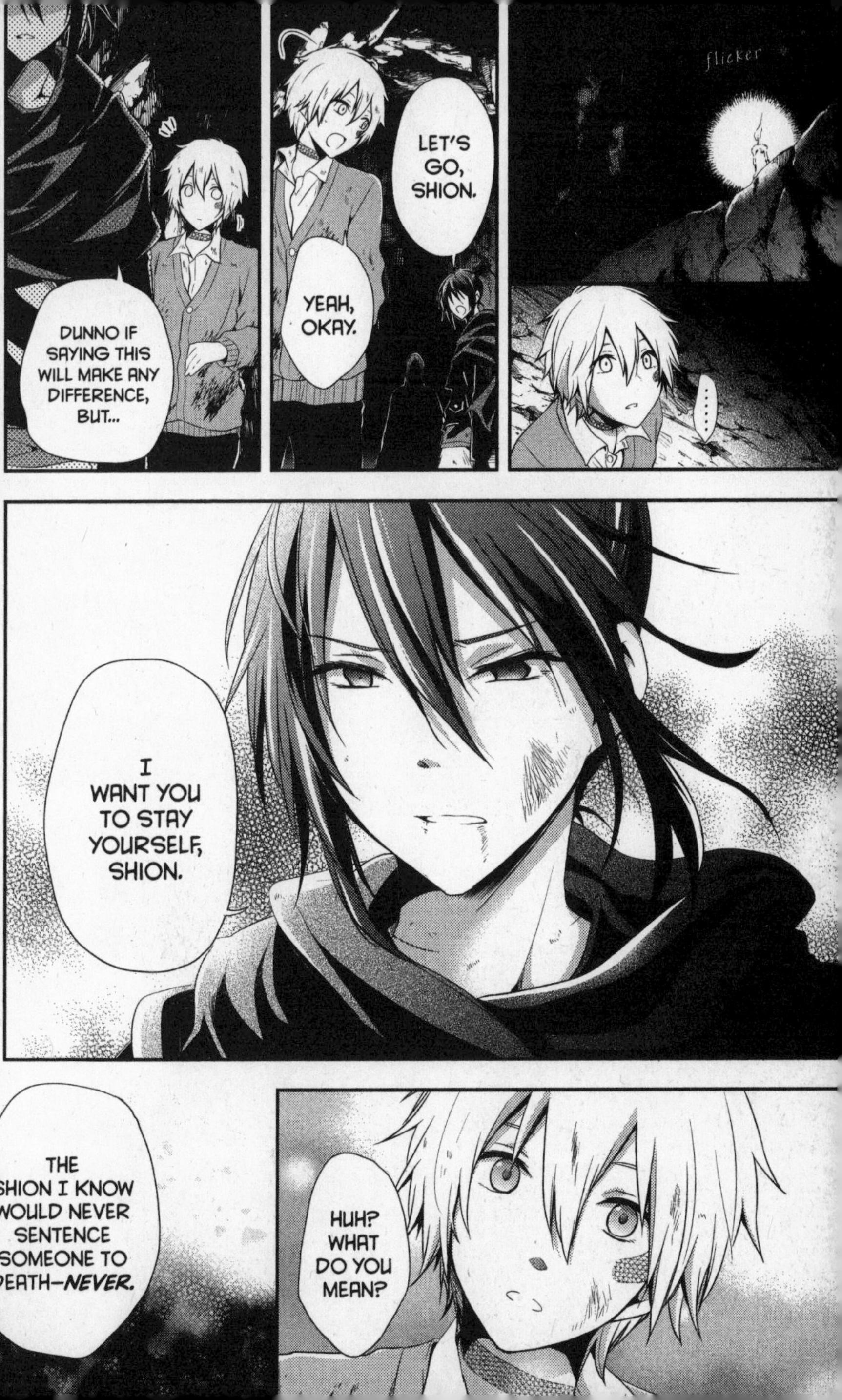
flicker
......
LET'S GO, SHION.
YEAH, OKAY.
DUNNO IF SAYING THIS WILL MAKE ANY DIFFERENCE, BUT...
I WANT YOU TO STAY YOURSELF, SHION.
HUH? WHAT DO YOU MEAN?
THE SHION I KNOW WOULD NEVER SENTENCE SOMEONE TO DEATH—*NEVER.*

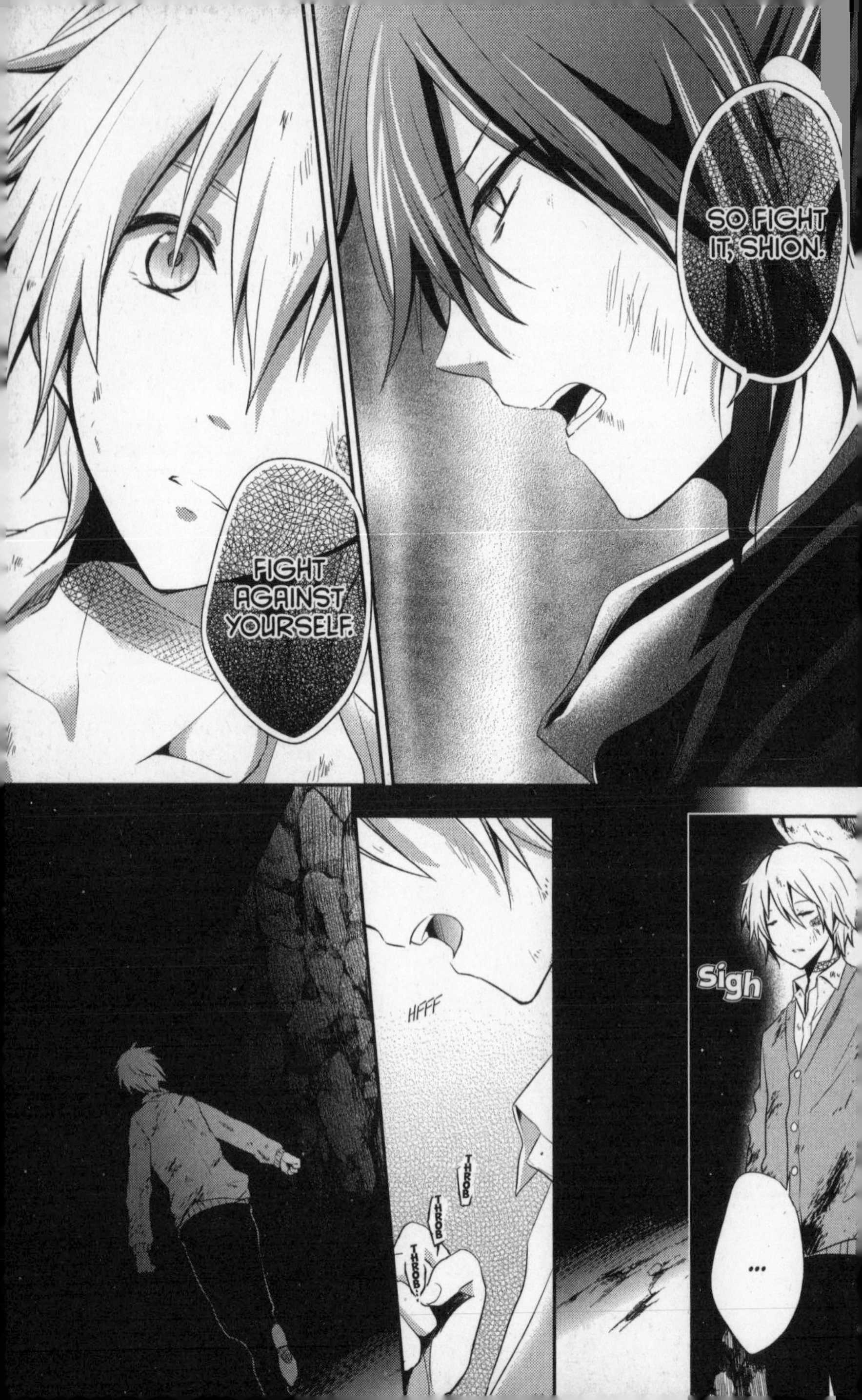
SO FIGHT IT, SHION.
FIGHT AGAINST YOURSELF.
Sigh
...
HFFF
THROB
THROB
THROB...

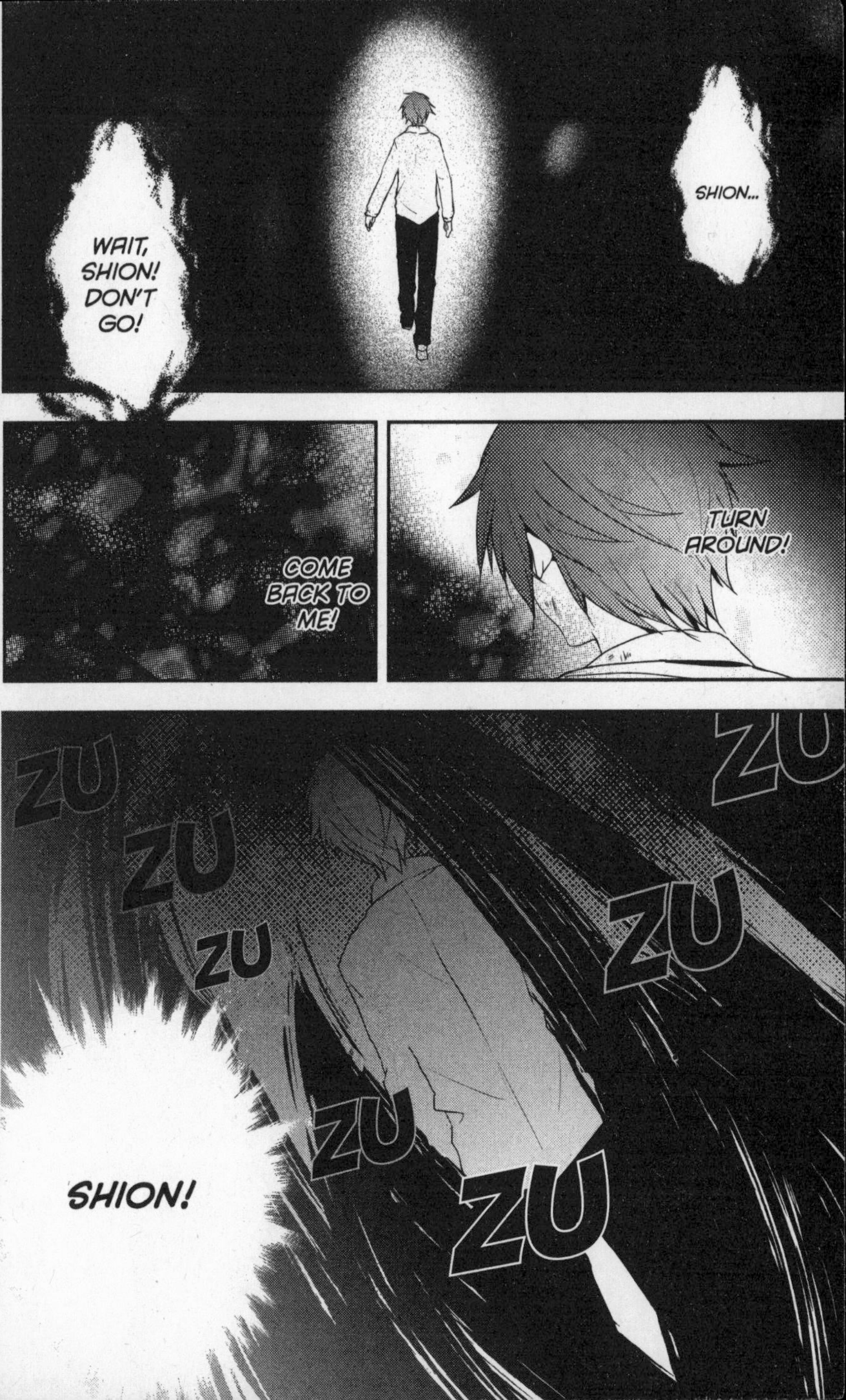
SHION...
WAIT, SHION! DON'T GO!
TURN AROUND!
COME BACK TO ME!
ZU
ZU
ZU
ZU
ZU
ZU
ZU
SHION!

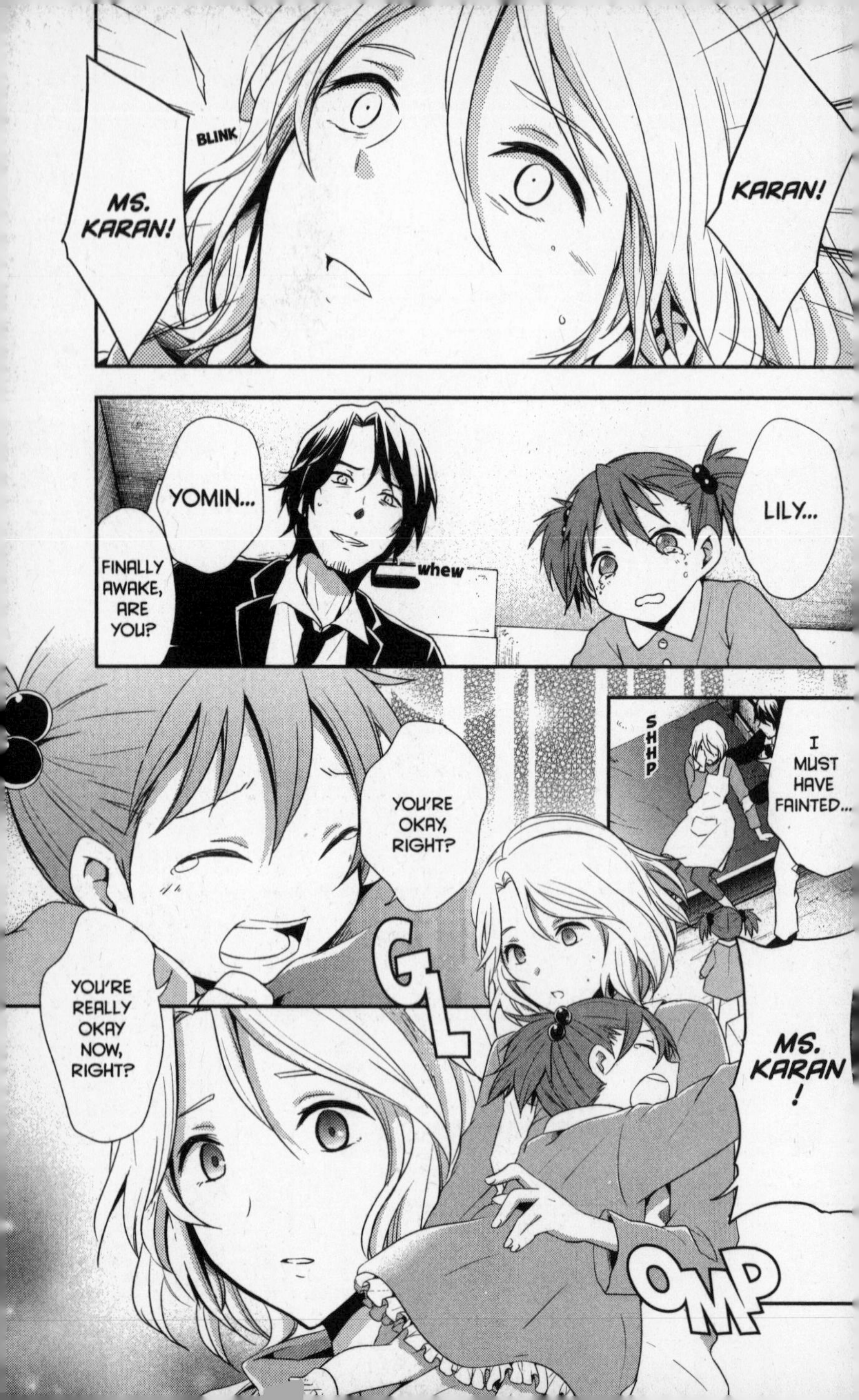
KARAN!
BLINK
MS. KARAN!
LILY...
whew
YOMIN...
FINALLY AWAKE, ARE YOU?
I MUST HAVE FAINTED...
SHHP
YOU'RE OKAY, RIGHT?
MS. KARAN!
GL
YOU'RE REALLY OKAY NOW, RIGHT?
OMP

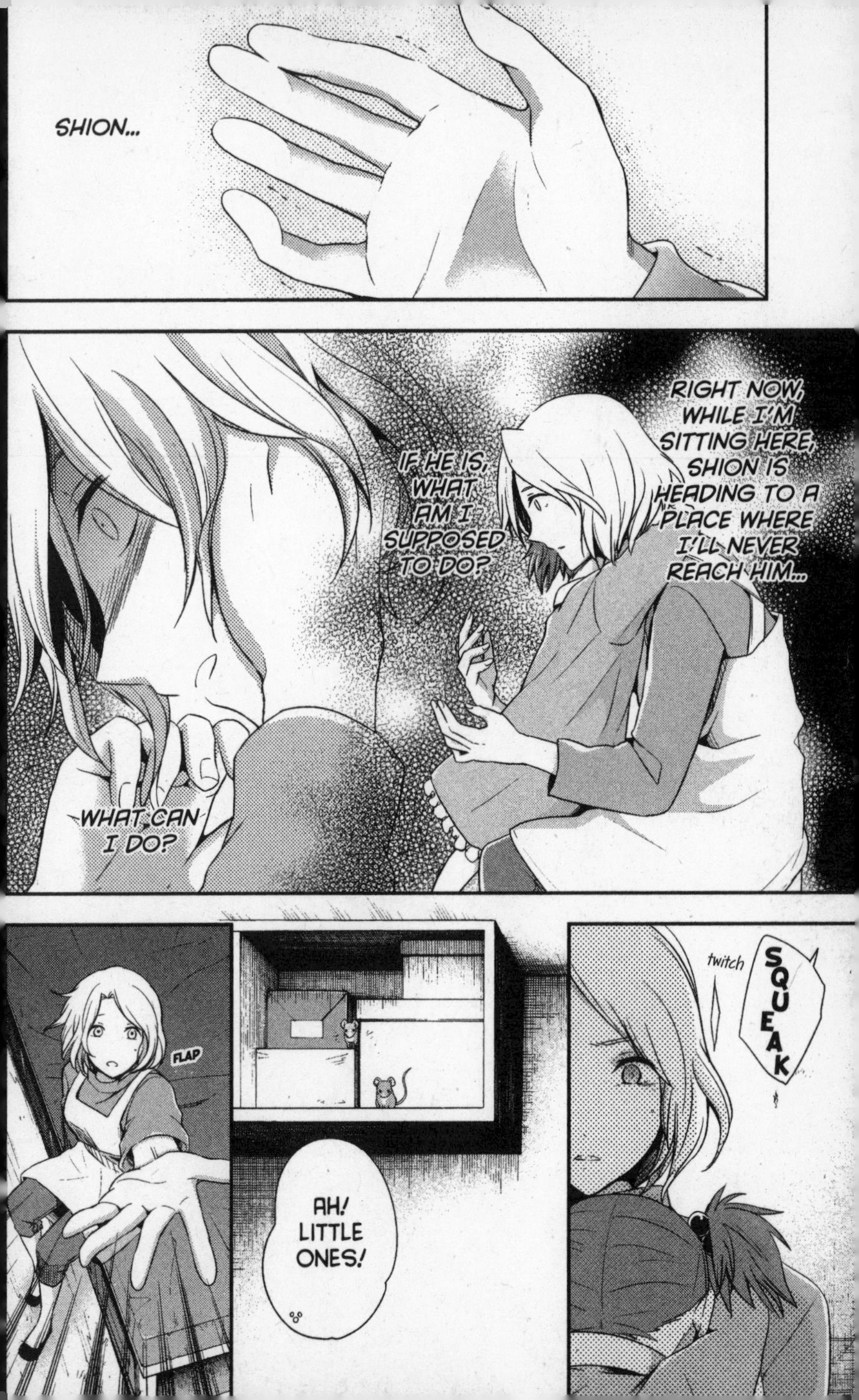
SHION...
RIGHT NOW, WHILE I'M SITTING HERE, SHION IS HEADING TO A PLACE WHERE I'LL NEVER REACH HIM...
IF HE IS, WHAT AM I SUPPOSED TO DO?
WHAT CAN I DO?
twitch
SQUEAK
AH! LITTLE ONES!
FLAP

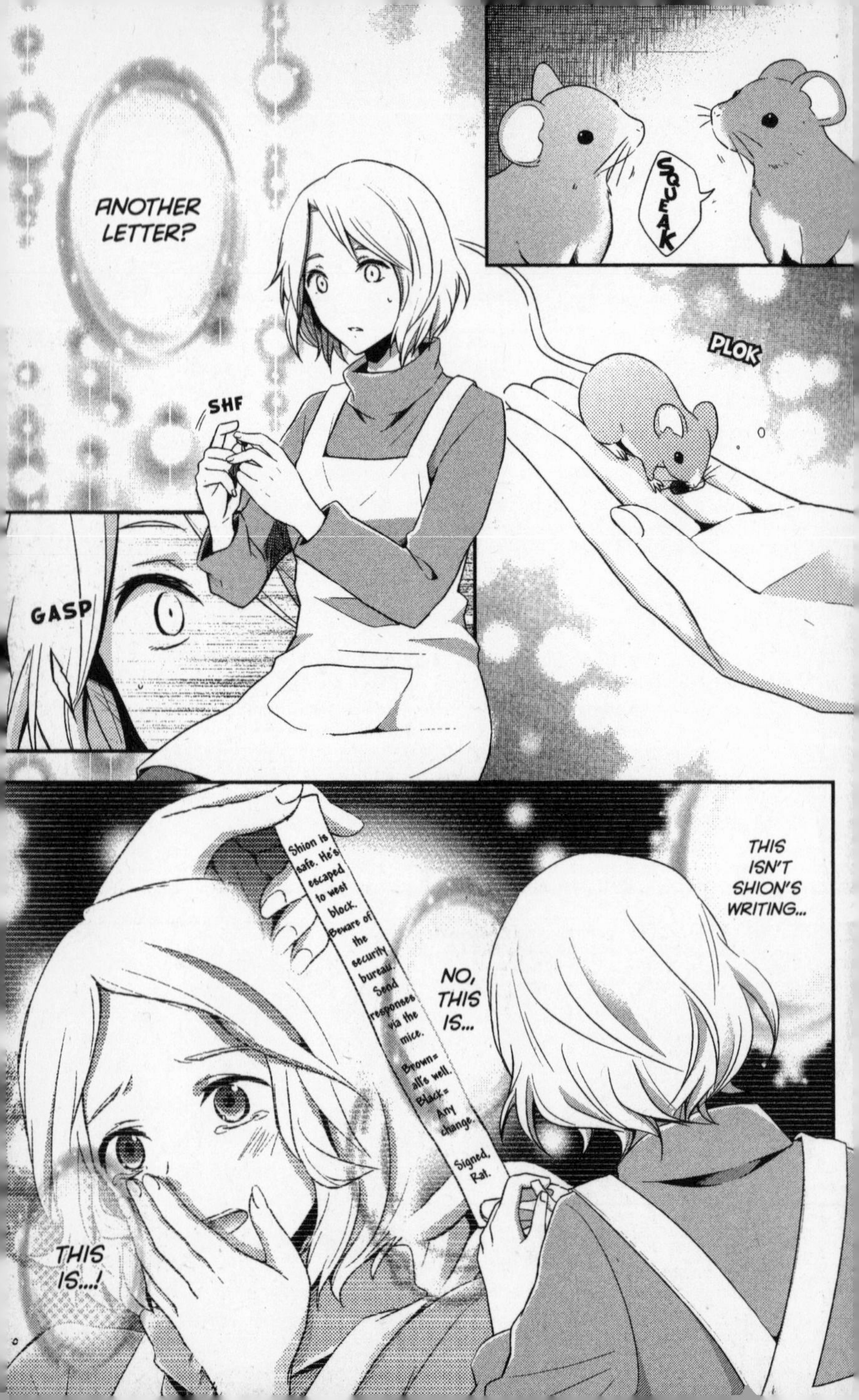
SQUEAK
PLOK
ANOTHER LETTER?
SHF
GASP
THIS ISN'T SHION'S WRITING...
NO, THIS IS...
Shion is safe. He's escaped to west block. Beware of the security bureau. Send responses via the mice.
Brown= all's well. Black= Any change.
Signed, Rat.
THIS IS...!

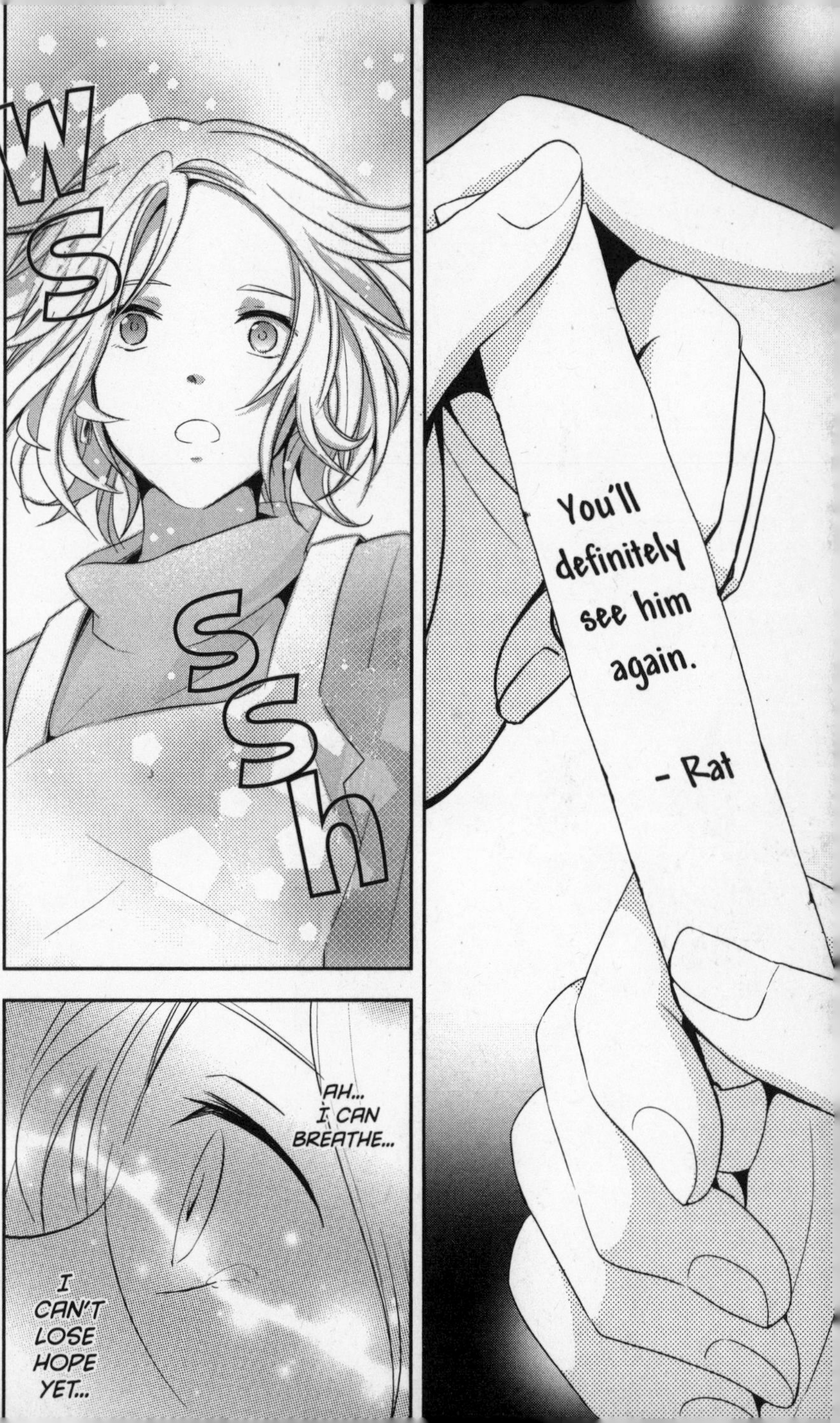
You'll definitely see him again.
- Rat
WSSSh
AH... I CAN BREATHE...
I CAN'T LOSE HOPE YET...

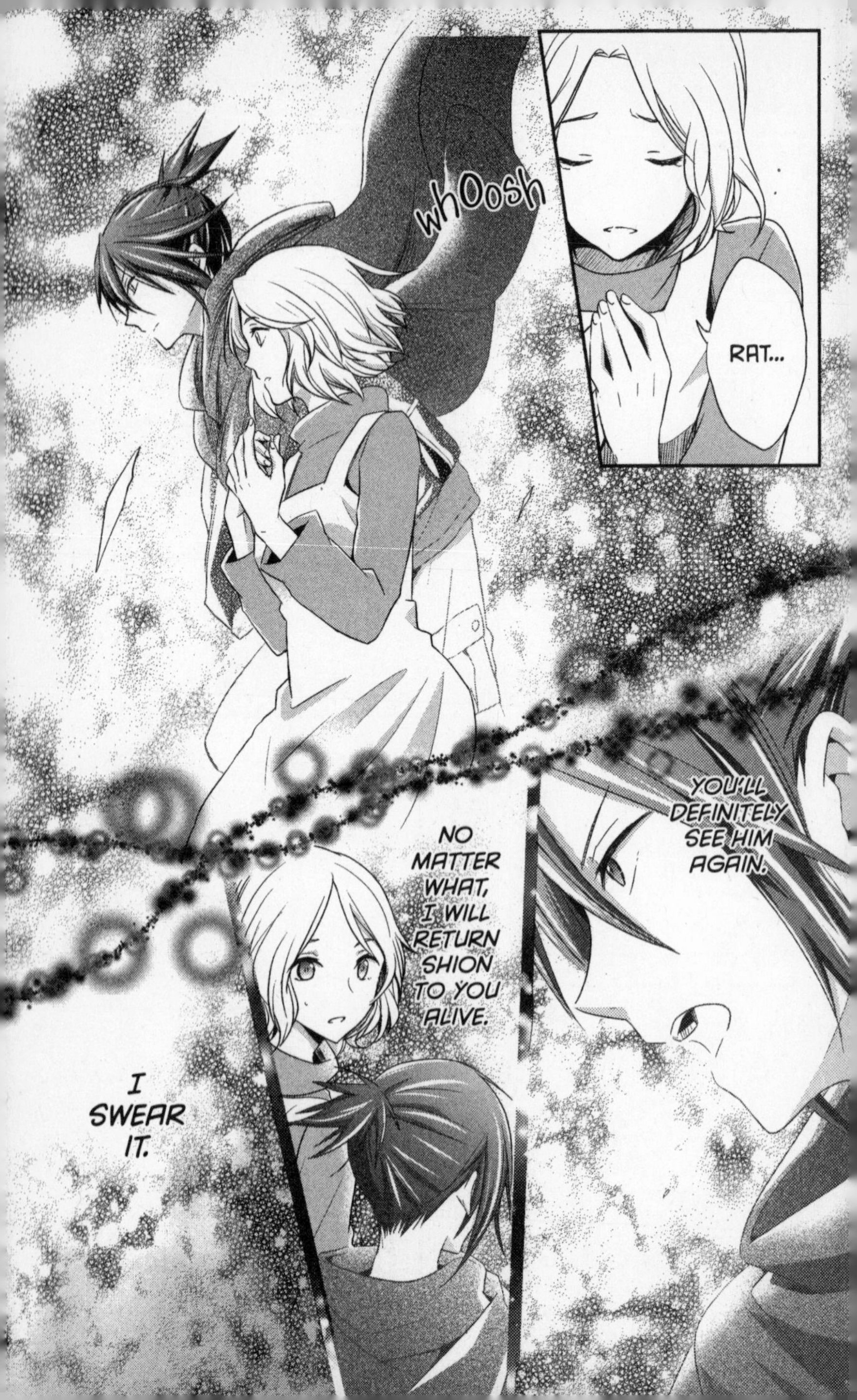
RAT...
whOosh
YOU'LL DEFINITELY SEE HIM AGAIN.
NO MATTER WHAT, I WILL RETURN SHION TO YOU ALIVE.
I SWEAR IT.

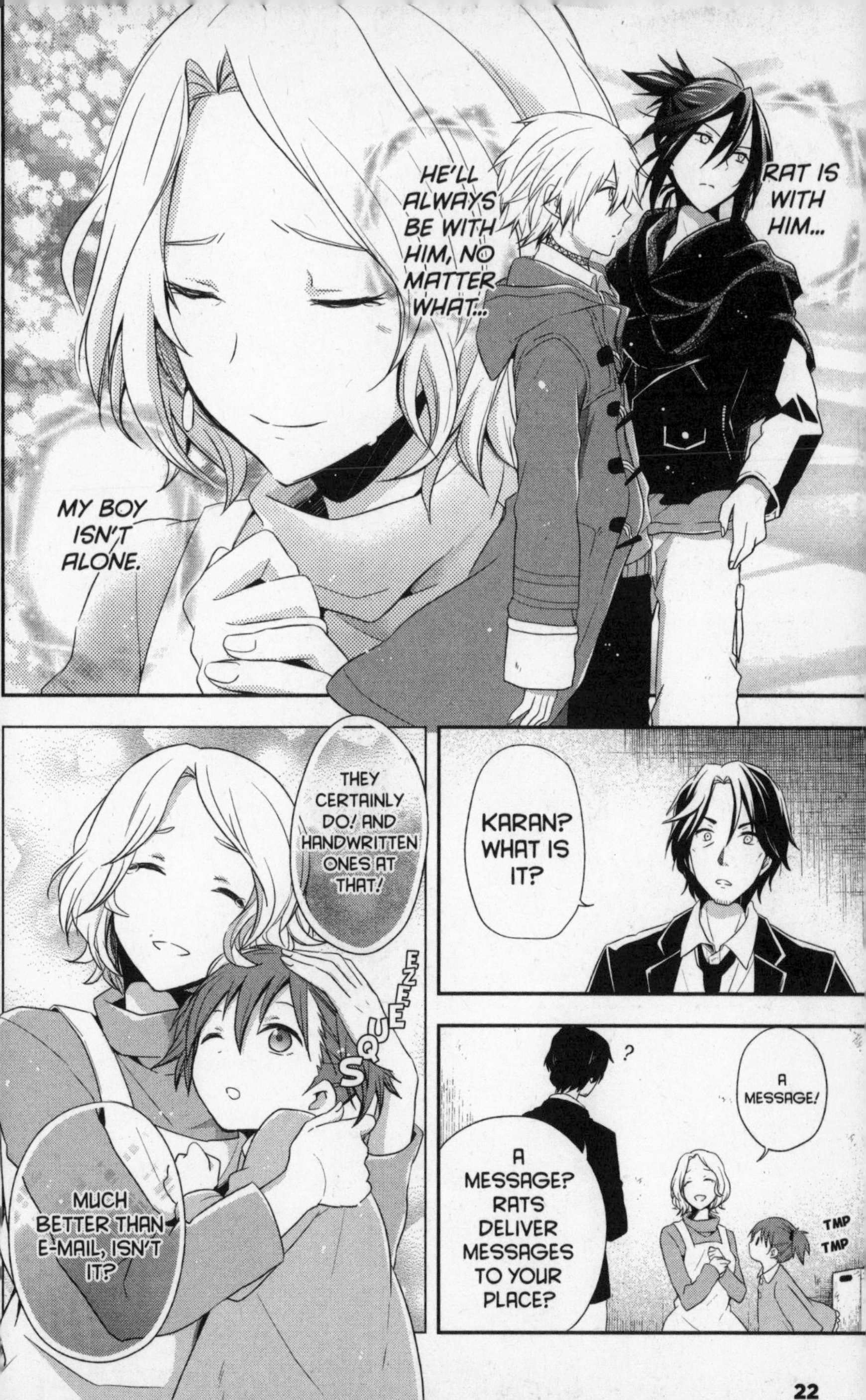
RAT IS WITH HIM...
HE'LL ALWAYS BE WITH HIM, NO MATTER WHAT...
MY BOY ISN'T ALONE.
KARAN? WHAT IS IT?
?
A MESSAGE!
A MESSAGE? RATS DELIVER MESSAGES TO YOUR PLACE?
TMP TMP
THEY CERTAINLY DO! AND HANDWRITTEN ONES AT THAT!
SQUEEZE
MUCH BETTER THAN E-MAIL, ISN'T IT?

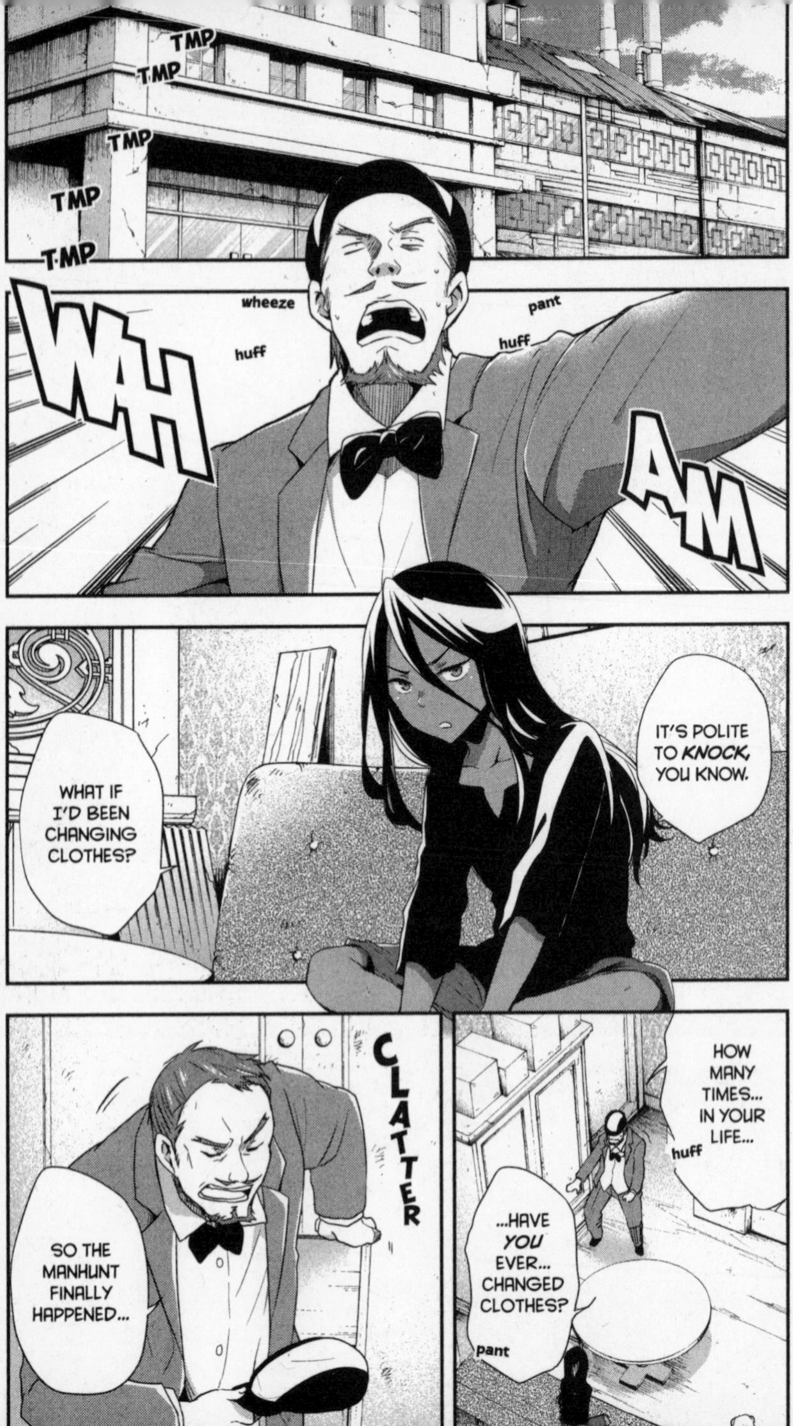
TMP
TMP
TMP
TMP
T-MP
WAH
AM
wheeze
huff
pant
huff
IT'S POLITE TO *KNOCK,* YOU KNOW.
WHAT IF I'D BEEN CHANGING CLOTHES?
HOW MANY TIMES... IN YOUR LIFE...
huff
...HAVE *YOU* EVER... CHANGED CLOTHES?
pant
CLATTER
SO THE MANHUNT FINALLY HAPPENED...

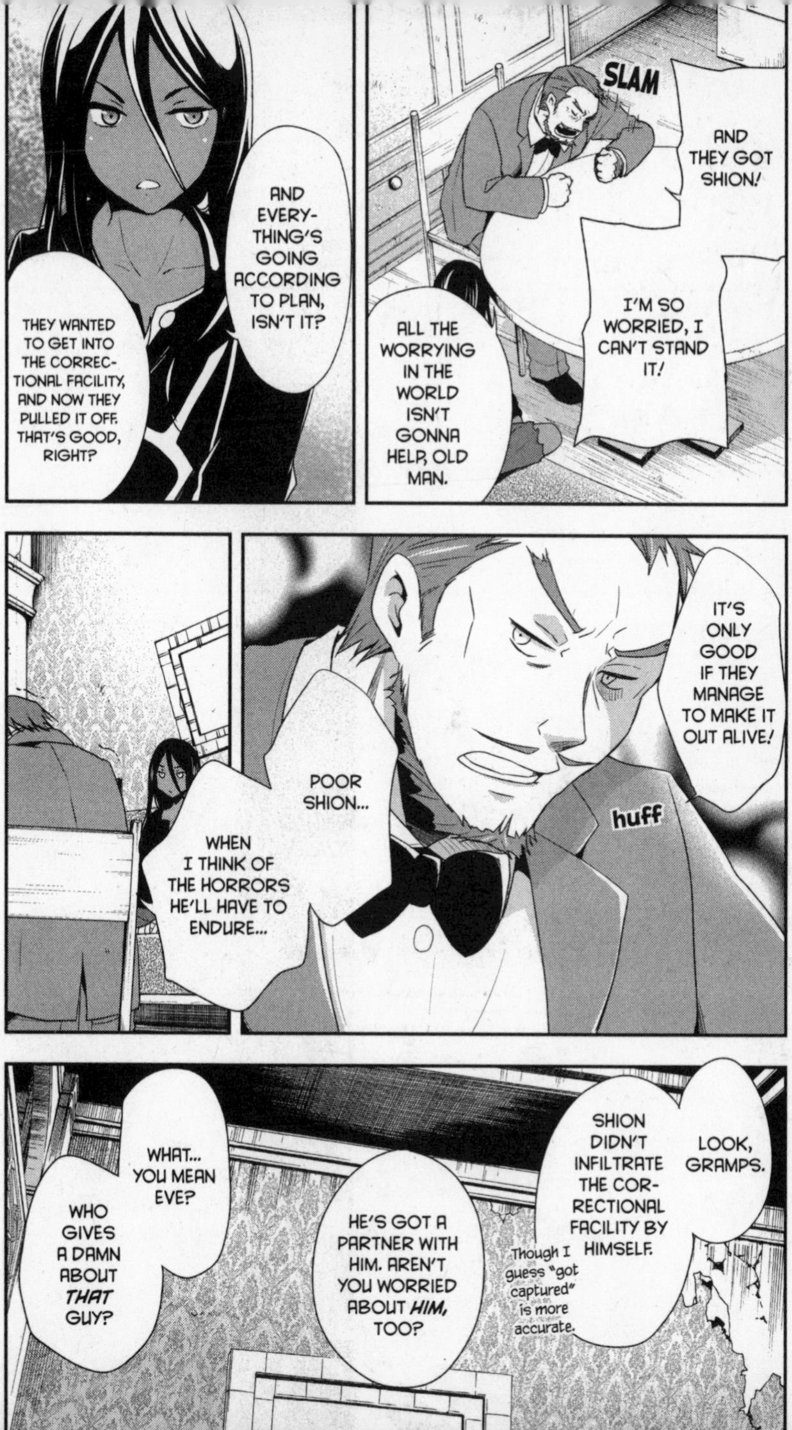
SLAM
AND THEY GOT SHION!
I'M SO WORRIED, I CAN'T STAND IT!
ALL THE WORRYING IN THE WORLD ISN'T GONNA HELP, OLD MAN.
AND EVERY-THING'S GOING ACCORDING TO PLAN, ISN'T IT?
THEY WANTED TO GET INTO THE CORREC-TIONAL FACILITY, AND NOW THEY PULLED IT OFF. THAT'S GOOD, RIGHT?
IT'S ONLY GOOD IF THEY MANAGE TO MAKE IT OUT ALIVE!
huff
POOR SHION...
WHEN I THINK OF THE HORRORS HE'LL HAVE TO ENDURE...
LOOK, GRAMPS.
SHION DIDN'T INFILTRATE THE COR-RECTIONAL FACILITY BY HIMSELF.
Though I guess "got captured" is more accurate.
HE'S GOT A PARTNER WITH HIM. AREN'T YOU WORRIED ABOUT *HIM,* TOO?
WHAT... YOU MEAN EVE?
WHO GIVES A DAMN ABOUT *THAT* GUY?

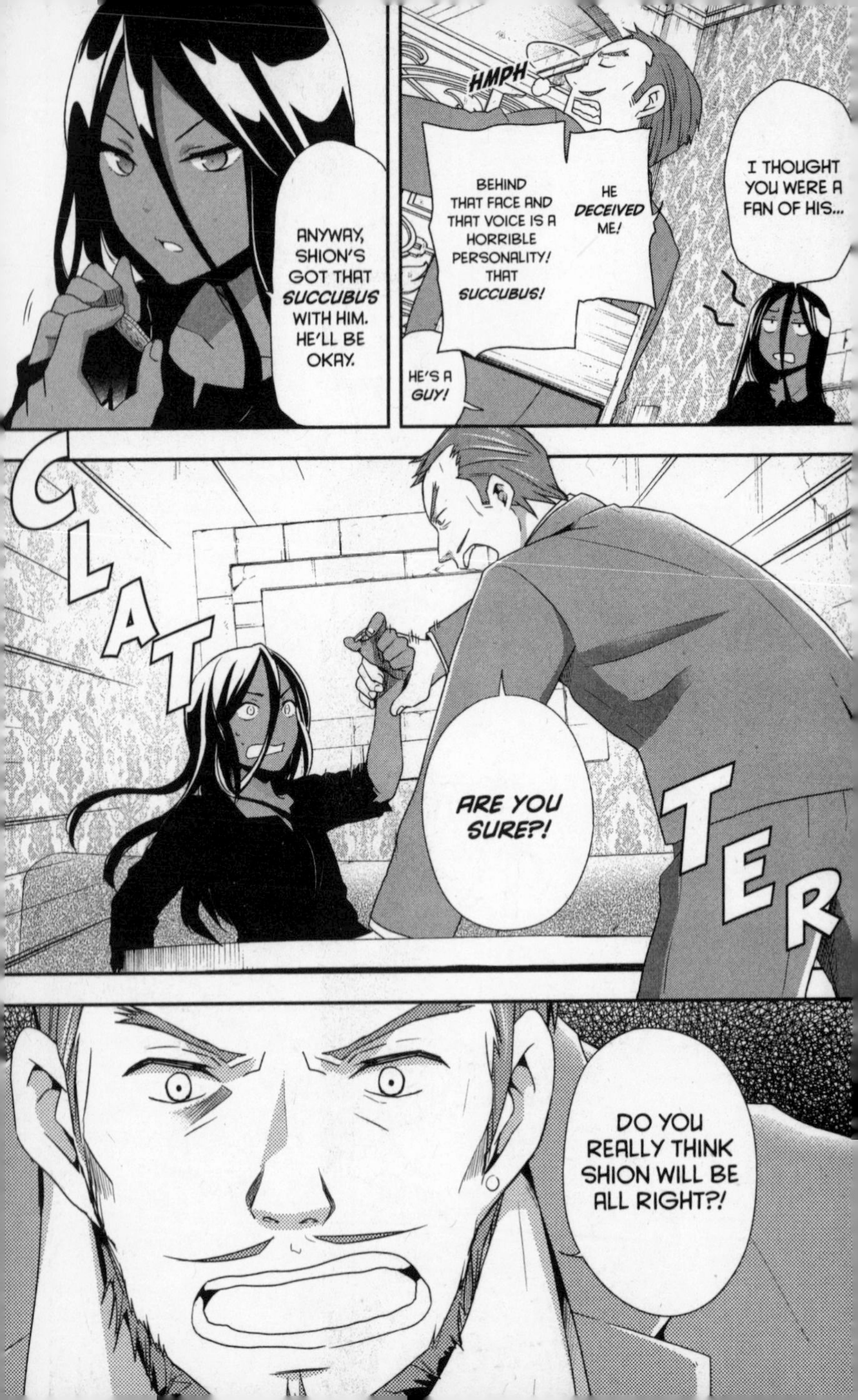

HMPH
I THOUGHT YOU WERE A FAN OF HIS...
HE DECEIVED ME!
BEHIND THAT FACE AND THAT VOICE IS A HORRIBLE PERSONALITY! THAT SUCCUBUS!
HE'S A GUY!
ANYWAY, SHION'S GOT THAT SUCCUBUS WITH HIM. HE'LL BE OKAY.
CLATTER
ARE YOU SURE?!
DO YOU REALLY THINK SHION WILL BE ALL RIGHT?!

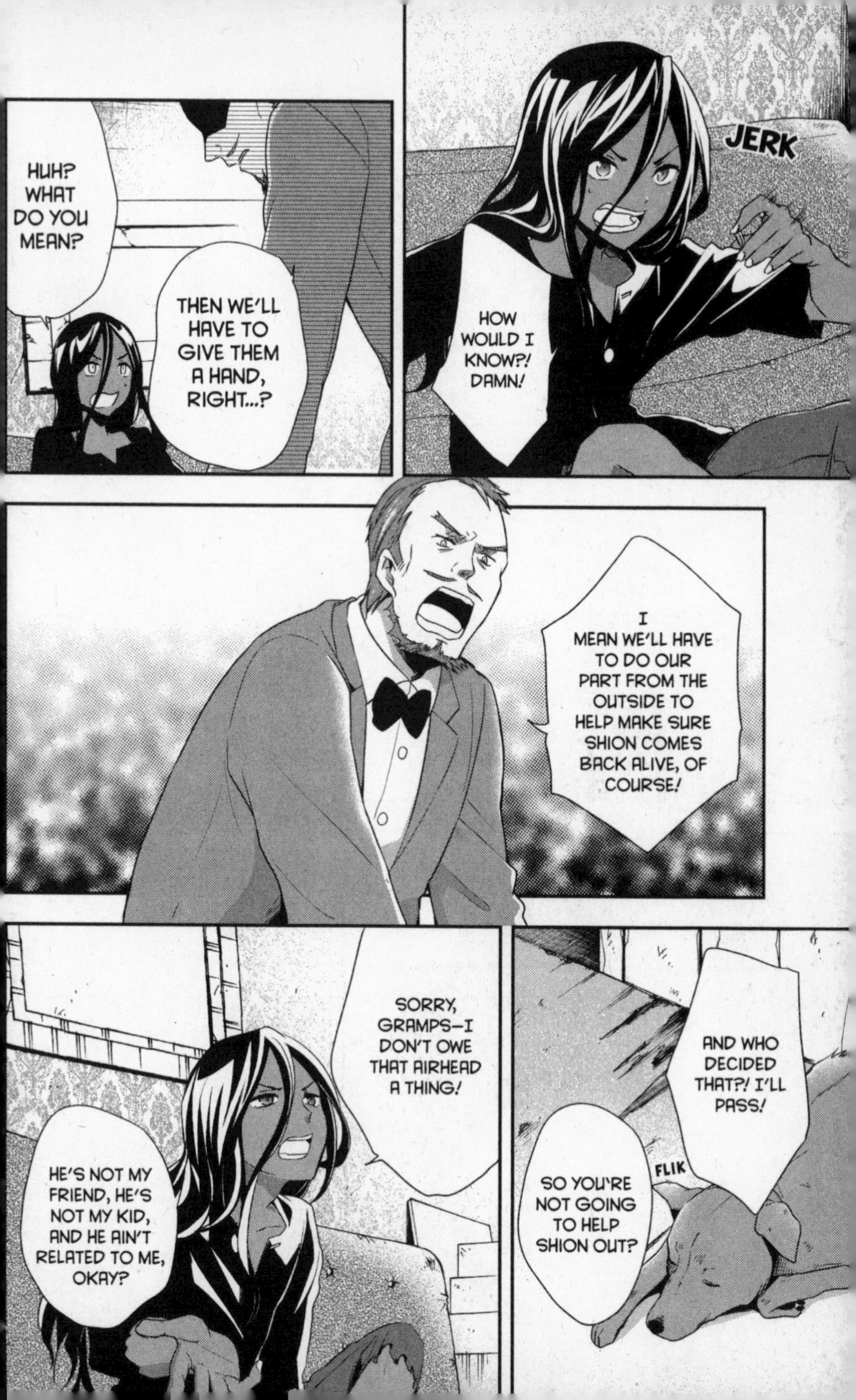
JERK
HOW WOULD I KNOW?! DAMN!
THEN WE'LL HAVE TO GIVE THEM A HAND, RIGHT...?
HUH? WHAT DO YOU MEAN?
I MEAN WE'LL HAVE TO DO OUR PART FROM THE OUTSIDE TO HELP MAKE SURE SHION COMES BACK ALIVE, OF COURSE!
AND WHO DECIDED THAT?! I'LL PASS!
FLIK
SO YOU'RE NOT GOING TO HELP SHION OUT?
SORRY, GRAMPS—I DON'T OWE THAT AIRHEAD A THING!
HE'S NOT MY FRIEND, HE'S NOT MY KID, AND HE AIN'T RELATED TO ME, OKAY?

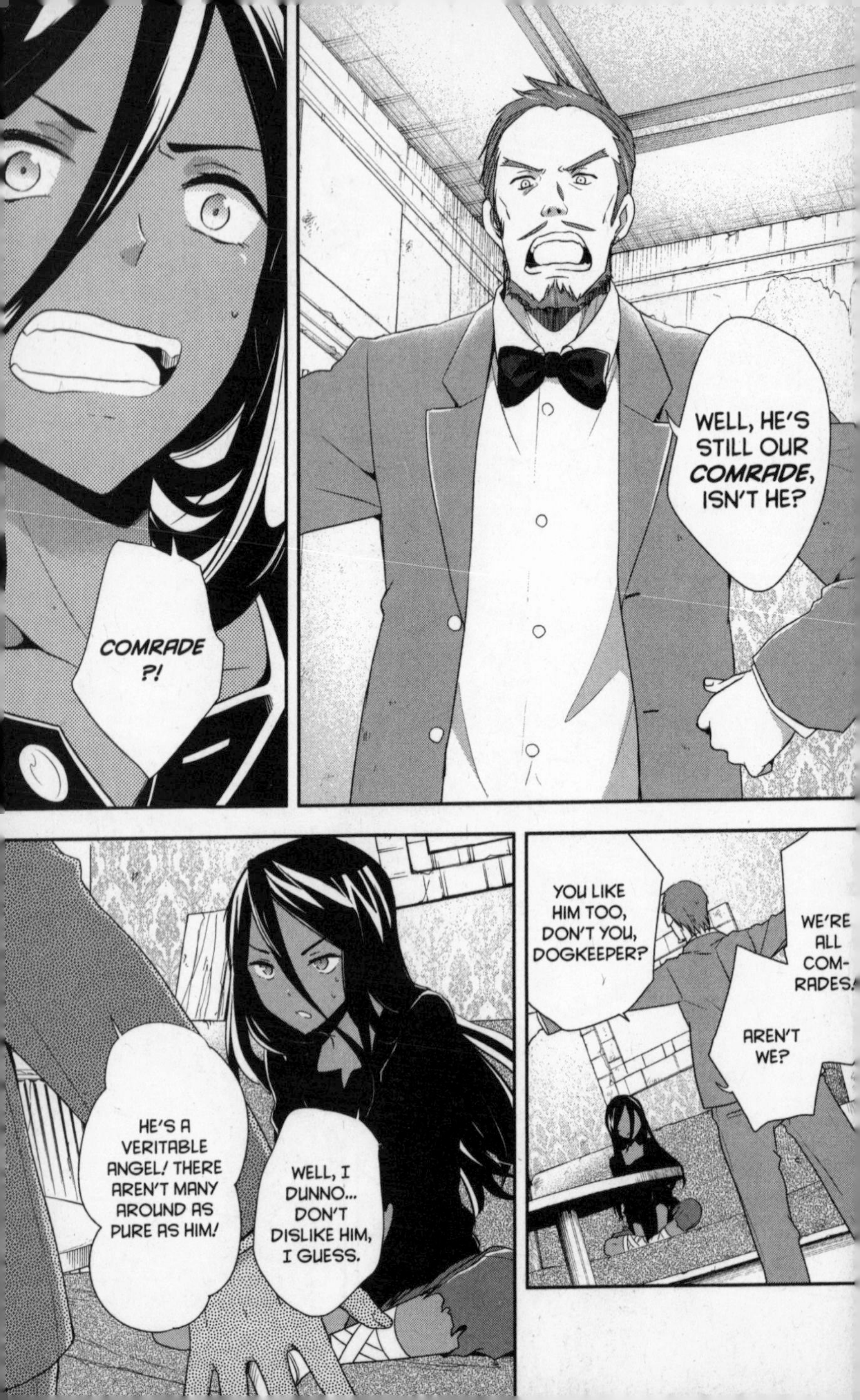
WELL, HE'S STILL OUR *COMRADE*, ISN'T HE?
COMRADE ?!
WE'RE ALL COM-RADES.
AREN'T WE?
YOU LIKE HIM TOO, DON'T YOU, DOGKEEPER?
WELL, I DUNNO... DON'T DISLIKE HIM, I GUESS.
HE'S A VERITABLE ANGEL! THERE AREN'T MANY AROUND AS PURE AS HIM!

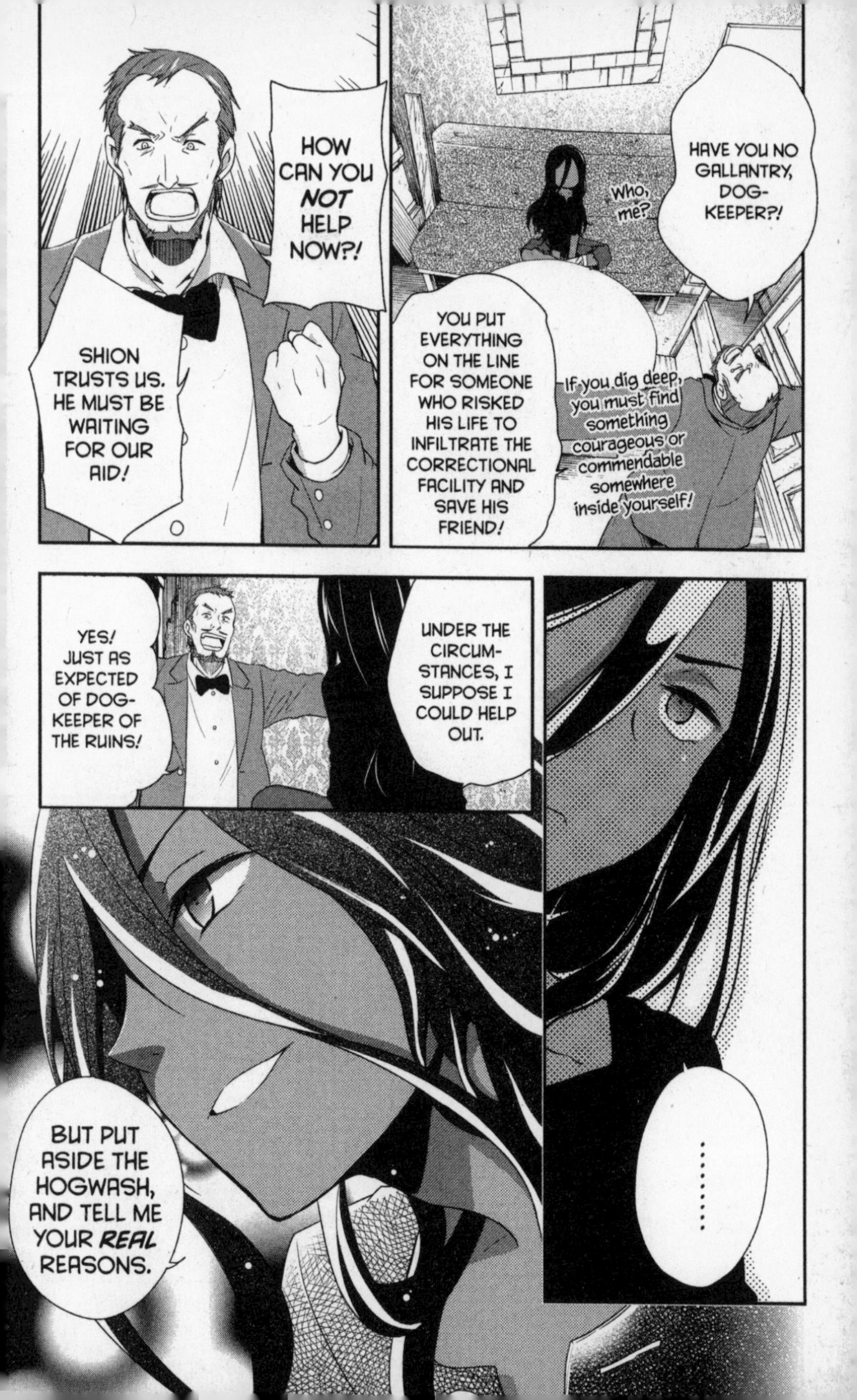
HAVE YOU NO GALLANTRY, DOG-KEEPER?!
Who, me?
If you dig deep, you must find something courageous or commendable somewhere inside yourself!
YOU PUT EVERYTHING ON THE LINE FOR SOMEONE WHO RISKED HIS LIFE TO INFILTRATE THE CORRECTIONAL FACILITY AND SAVE HIS FRIEND!
HOW CAN YOU *NOT* HELP NOW?!
SHION TRUSTS US. HE MUST BE WAITING FOR OUR AID!
......
UNDER THE CIRCUM-STANCES, I SUPPOSE I COULD HELP OUT.
YES! JUST AS EXPECTED OF DOG-KEEPER OF THE RUINS!
BUT PUT ASIDE THE HOGWASH, AND TELL ME YOUR *REAL* REASONS.

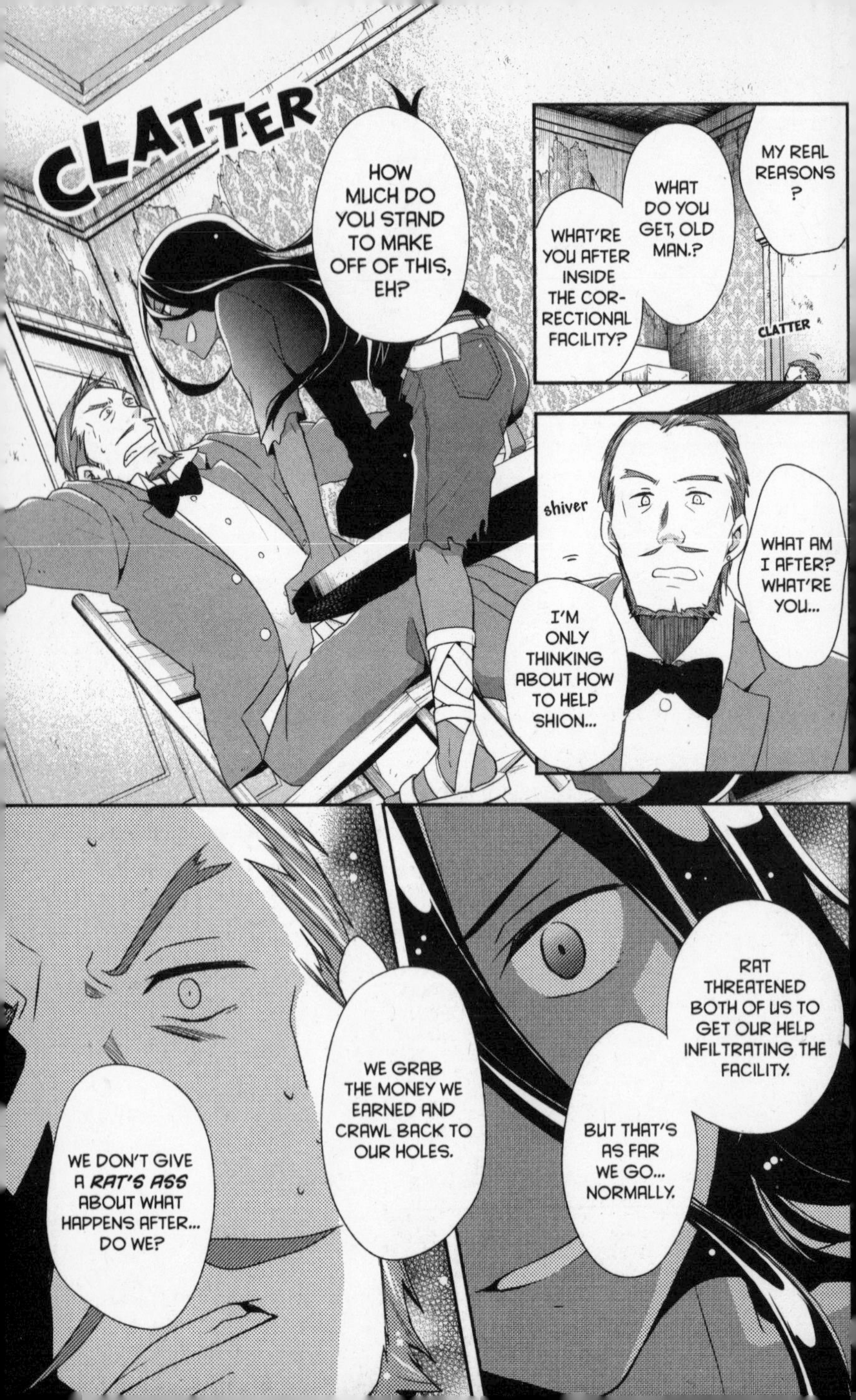
MY REAL REASONS?
WHAT DO YOU GET, OLD MAN.?
WHAT'RE YOU AFTER INSIDE THE COR-RECTIONAL FACILITY?
CLATTER
WHAT AM I AFTER? WHAT'RE YOU...
shiver
I'M ONLY THINKING ABOUT HOW TO HELP SHION...
HOW MUCH DO YOU STAND TO MAKE OFF OF THIS, EH?
CLATTER
RAT THREATENED BOTH OF US TO GET OUR HELP INFILTRATING THE FACILITY.
BUT THAT'S AS FAR WE GO... NORMALLY.
WE GRAB THE MONEY WE EARNED AND CRAWL BACK TO OUR HOLES.
WE DON'T GIVE A *RAT'S ASS* ABOUT WHAT HAPPENS AFTER... DO WE?

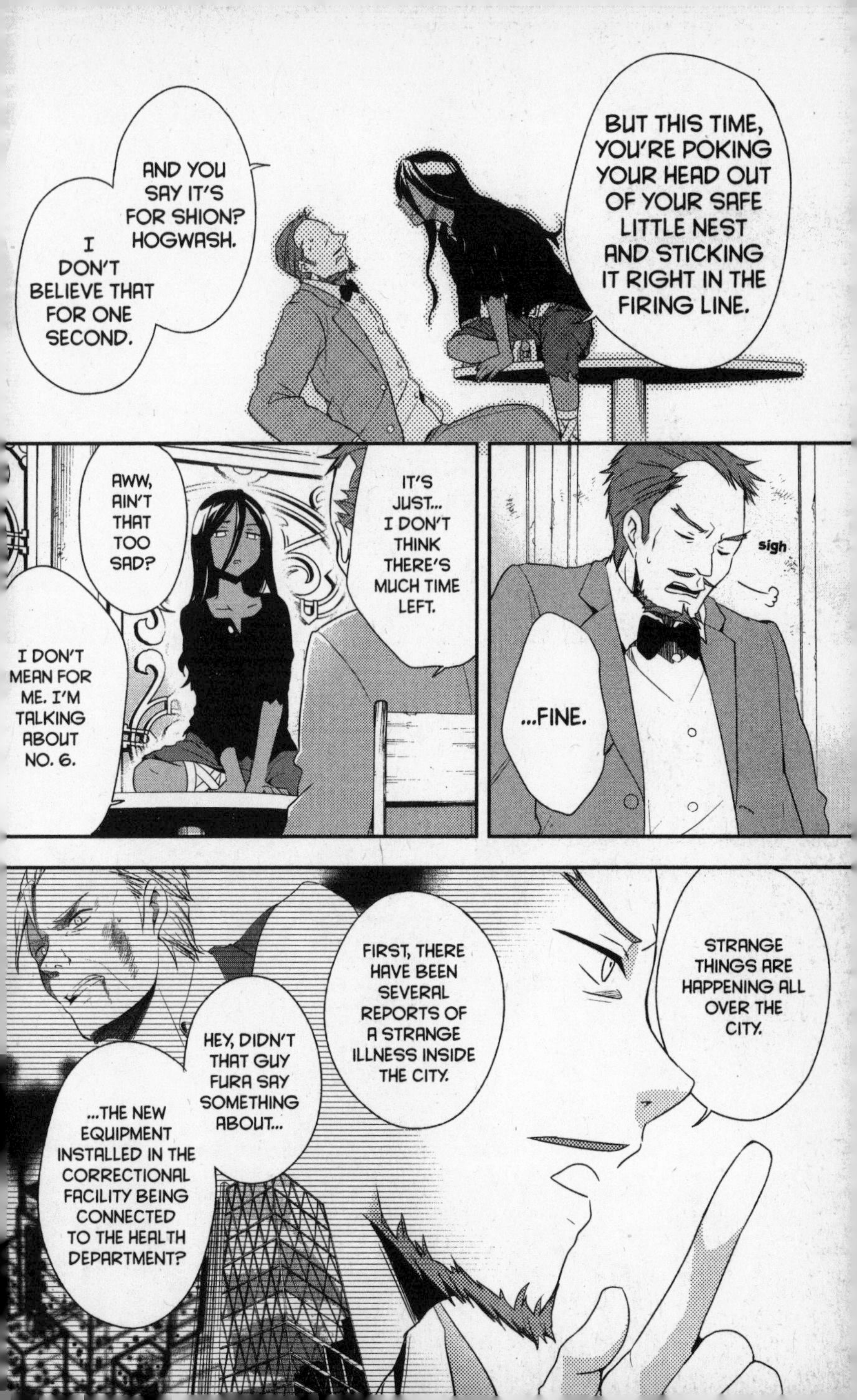
BUT THIS TIME, YOU'RE POKING YOUR HEAD OUT OF YOUR SAFE LITTLE NEST AND STICKING IT RIGHT IN THE FIRING LINE.
AND YOU SAY IT'S FOR SHION? HOGWASH.
I DON'T BELIEVE THAT FOR ONE SECOND.
sigh
...FINE.
IT'S JUST... I DON'T THINK THERE'S MUCH TIME LEFT.
AWW, AIN'T THAT TOO SAD?
I DON'T MEAN FOR ME. I'M TALKING ABOUT NO. 6.
STRANGE THINGS ARE HAPPENING ALL OVER THE CITY.
FIRST, THERE HAVE BEEN SEVERAL REPORTS OF A STRANGE ILLNESS INSIDE THE CITY.
HEY, DIDN'T THAT GUY FURA SAY SOMETHING ABOUT...
...THE NEW EQUIPMENT INSTALLED IN THE CORRECTIONAL FACILITY BEING CONNECTED TO THE HEALTH DEPARTMENT?

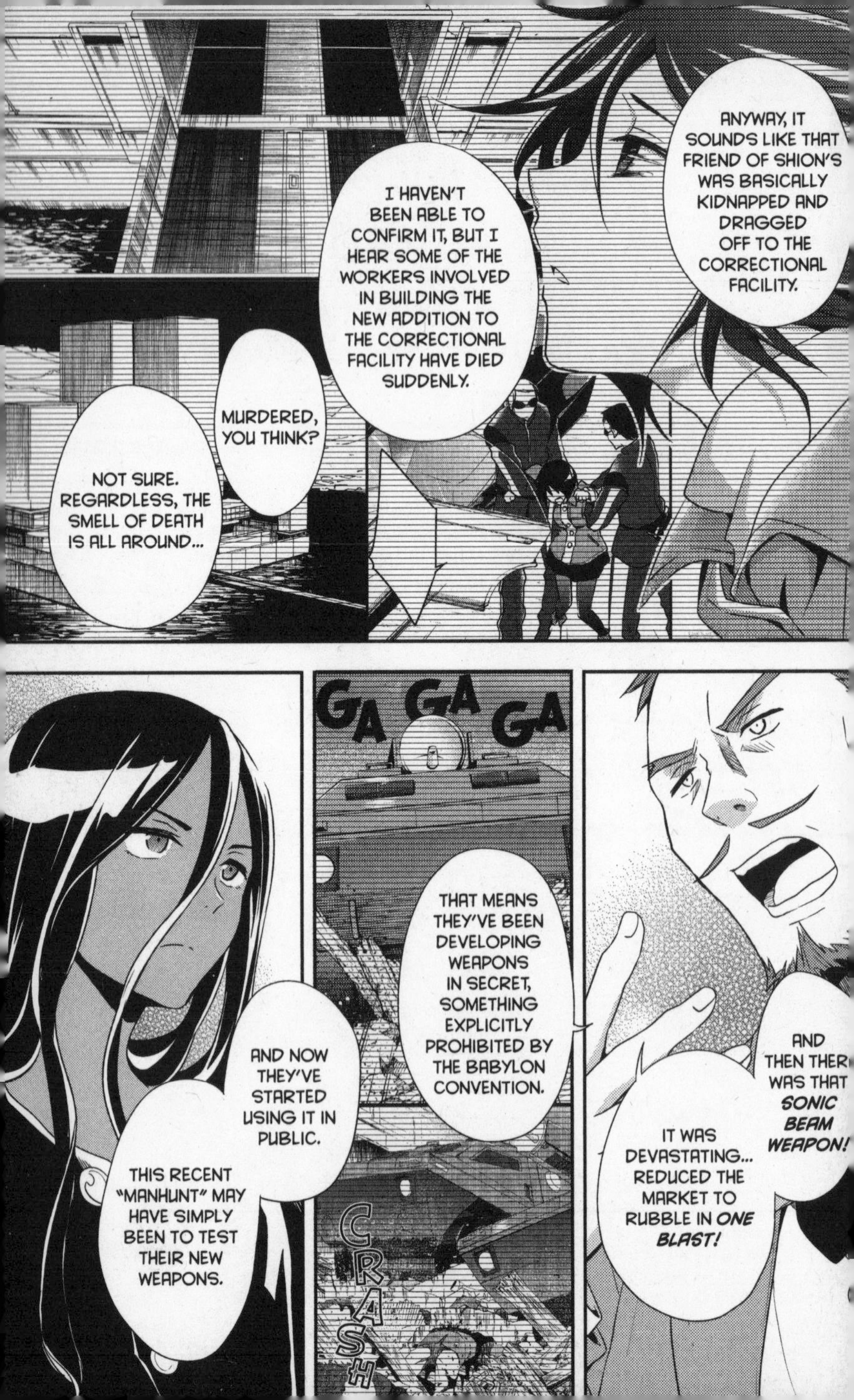
ANYWAY, IT SOUNDS LIKE THAT FRIEND OF SHION'S WAS BASICALLY KIDNAPPED AND DRAGGED OFF TO THE CORRECTIONAL FACILITY.
I HAVEN'T BEEN ABLE TO CONFIRM IT, BUT I HEAR SOME OF THE WORKERS INVOLVED IN BUILDING THE NEW ADDITION TO THE CORRECTIONAL FACILITY HAVE DIED SUDDENLY.
MURDERED, YOU THINK?
NOT SURE. REGARDLESS, THE SMELL OF DEATH IS ALL AROUND...
AND THEN THER WAS THAT *SONIC BEAM WEAPON!*
IT WAS DEVASTATING... REDUCED THE MARKET TO RUBBLE IN *ONE BLAST!*
GA GA GA
THAT MEANS THEY'VE BEEN DEVELOPING WEAPONS IN SECRET, SOMETHING EXPLICITLY PROHIBITED BY THE BABYLON CONVENTION.
CRASH
AND NOW THEY'VE STARTED USING IT IN PUBLIC.
THIS RECENT "MANHUNT" MAY HAVE SIMPLY BEEN TO TEST THEIR NEW WEAPONS.

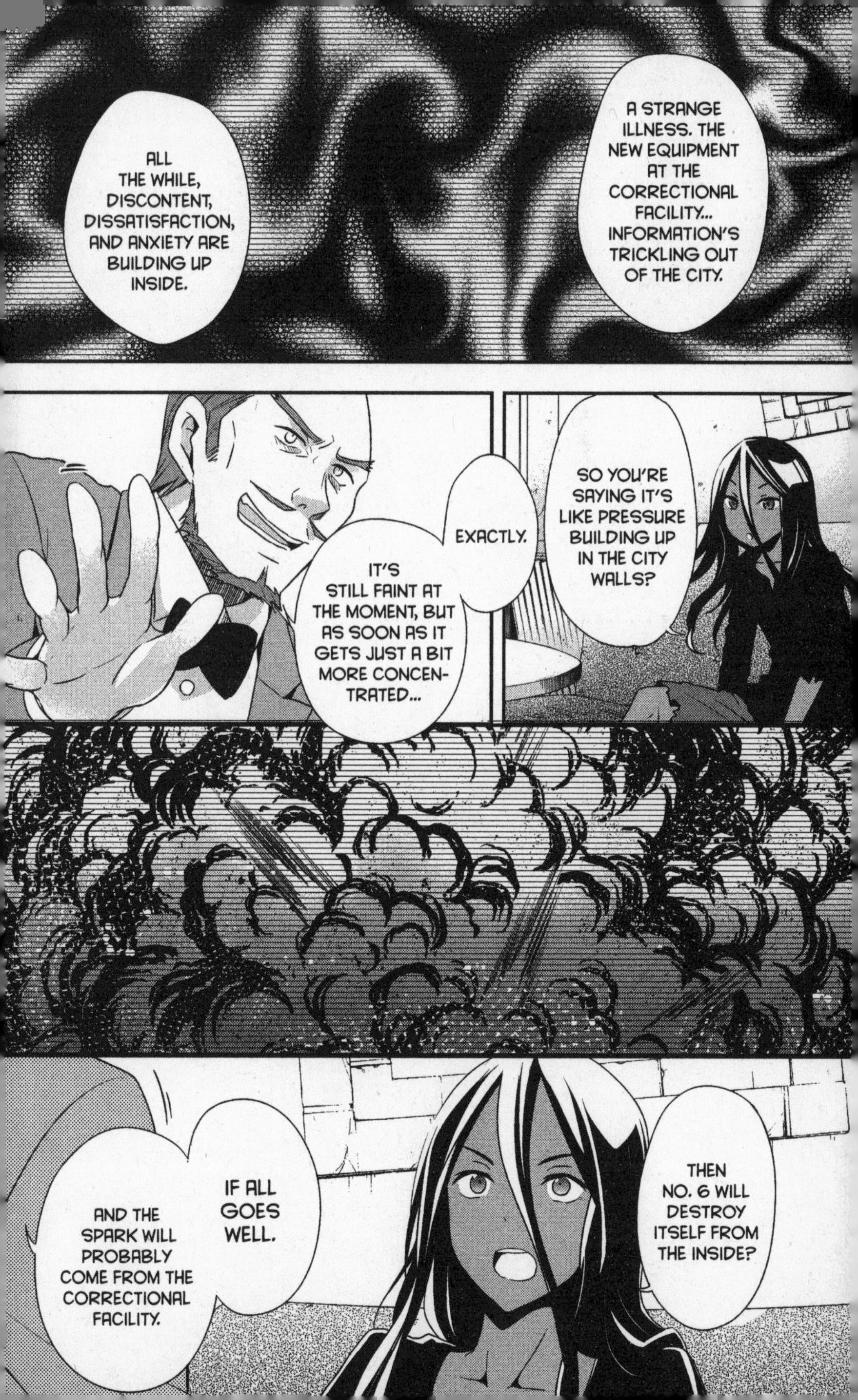
A STRANGE ILLNESS. THE NEW EQUIPMENT AT THE CORRECTIONAL FACILITY... INFORMATION'S TRICKLING OUT OF THE CITY.
ALL THE WHILE, DISCONTENT, DISSATISFACTION, AND ANXIETY ARE BUILDING UP INSIDE.
SO YOU'RE SAYING IT'S LIKE PRESSURE BUILDING UP IN THE CITY WALLS?
EXACTLY.
IT'S STILL FAINT AT THE MOMENT, BUT AS SOON AS IT GETS JUST A BIT MORE CONCEN-TRATED...
THEN NO. 6 WILL DESTROY ITSELF FROM THE INSIDE?
IF ALL GOES WELL.
AND THE SPARK WILL PROBABLY COME FROM THE CORRECTIONAL FACILITY.

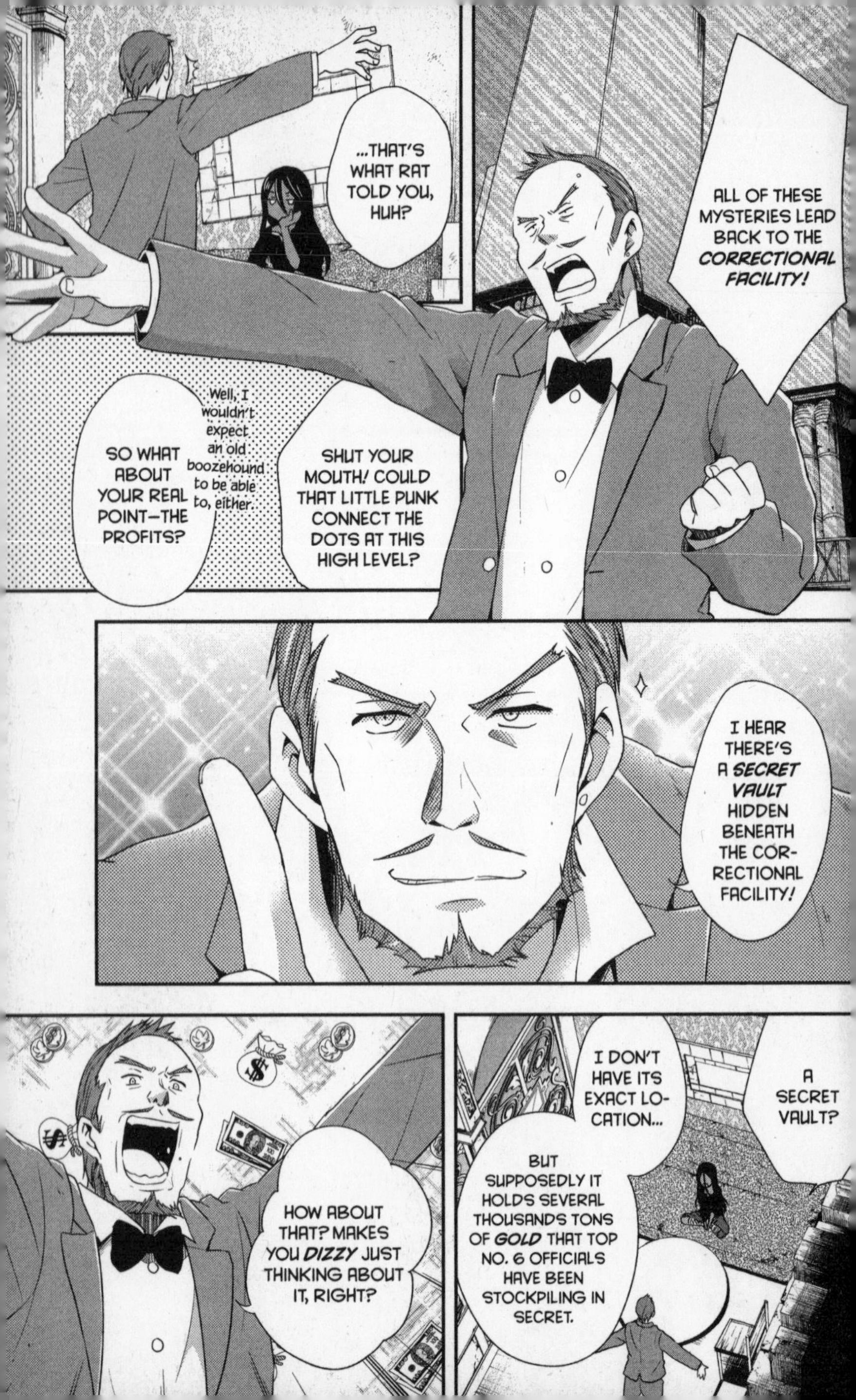

ALL OF THESE MYSTERIES LEAD BACK TO THE *CORRECTIONAL FACILITY!*
...THAT'S WHAT RAT TOLD YOU, HUH?
SHUT YOUR MOUTH! COULD THAT LITTLE PUNK CONNECT THE DOTS AT THIS HIGH LEVEL?
Well, I wouldn't expect an old boozehound to be able to, either.
SO WHAT ABOUT YOUR REAL POINT—THE PROFITS?
I HEAR THERE'S A *SECRET VAULT* HIDDEN BENEATH THE COR-RECTIONAL FACILITY!
A SECRET VAULT?
I DON'T HAVE ITS EXACT LO-CATION...
BUT SUPPOSEDLY IT HOLDS SEVERAL THOUSANDS TONS OF *GOLD* THAT TOP NO. 6 OFFICIALS HAVE BEEN STOCKPILING IN SECRET.
HOW ABOUT THAT? MAKES YOU *DIZZY* JUST THINKING ABOUT IT, RIGHT?

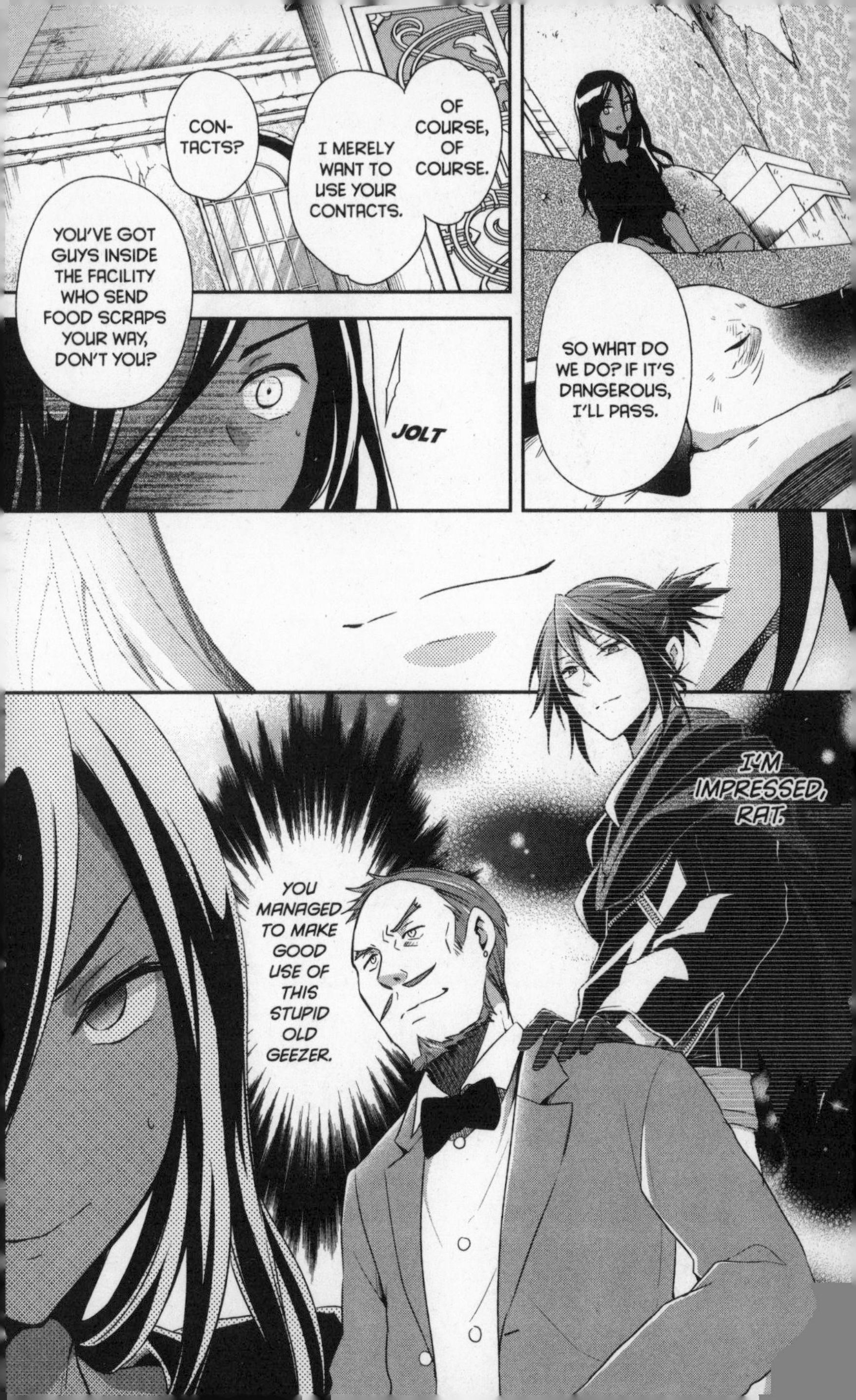
SO WHAT DO WE DO? IF IT'S DANGEROUS, I'LL PASS.
OF COURSE, OF COURSE.
I MERELY WANT TO USE YOUR CONTACTS.
CON-TACTS?
YOU'VE GOT GUYS INSIDE THE FACILITY WHO SEND FOOD SCRAPS YOUR WAY, DON'T YOU?
JOLT
I'M IMPRESSED, RAT.
YOU MANAGED TO MAKE GOOD USE OF THIS STUPID OLD GEEZER.

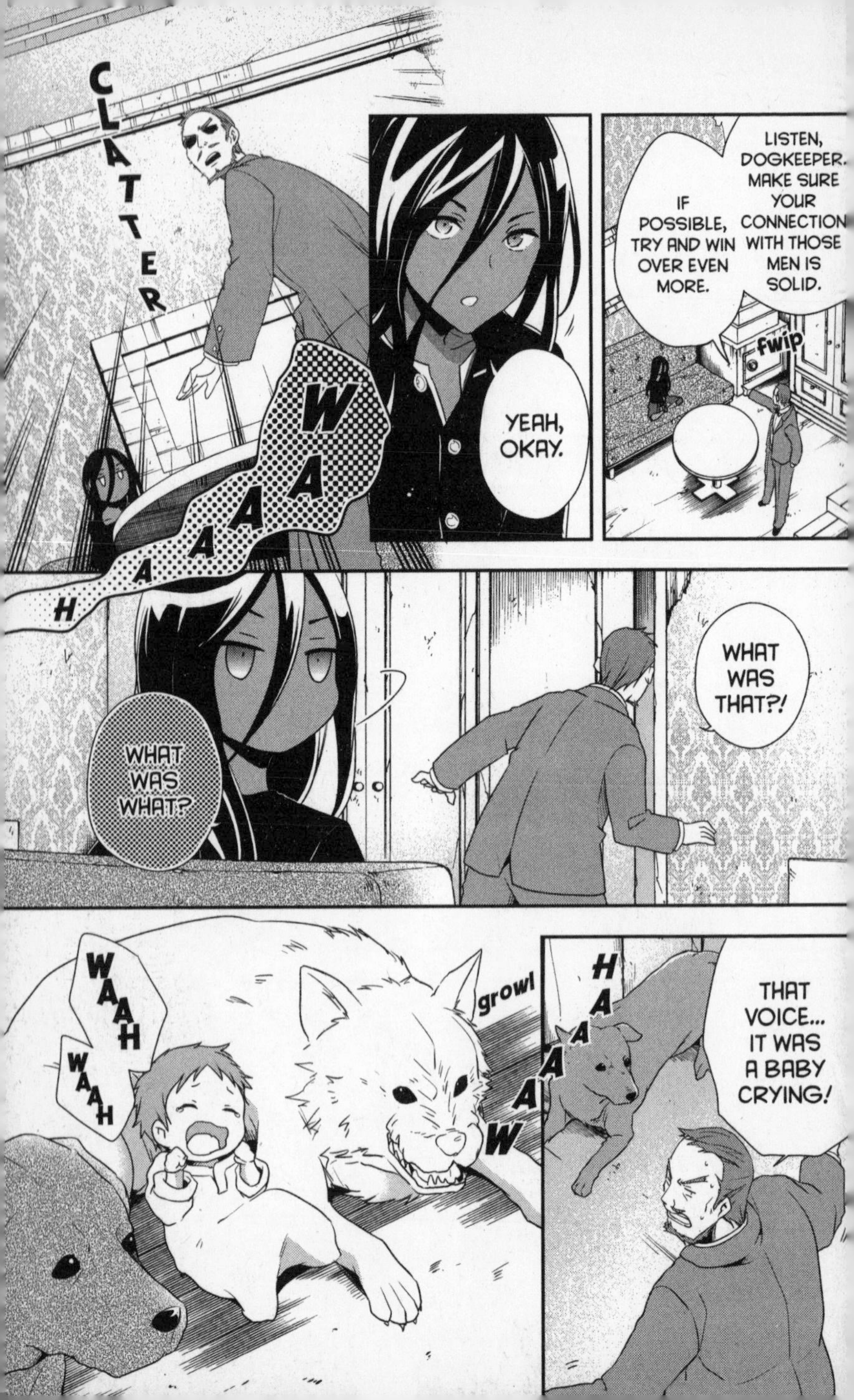
LISTEN, DOGKEEPER. MAKE SURE YOUR CONNECTION WITH THOSE MEN IS SOLID.
IF POSSIBLE, TRY AND WIN OVER EVEN MORE.
fwip
YEAH, OKAY.
CLATTER
WAAAAH
WHAT WAS THAT?!
WHAT WAS WHAT?
THAT VOICE... IT WAS A BABY CRYING!
WAAAAAH
growl
WAAAH
WAAAH

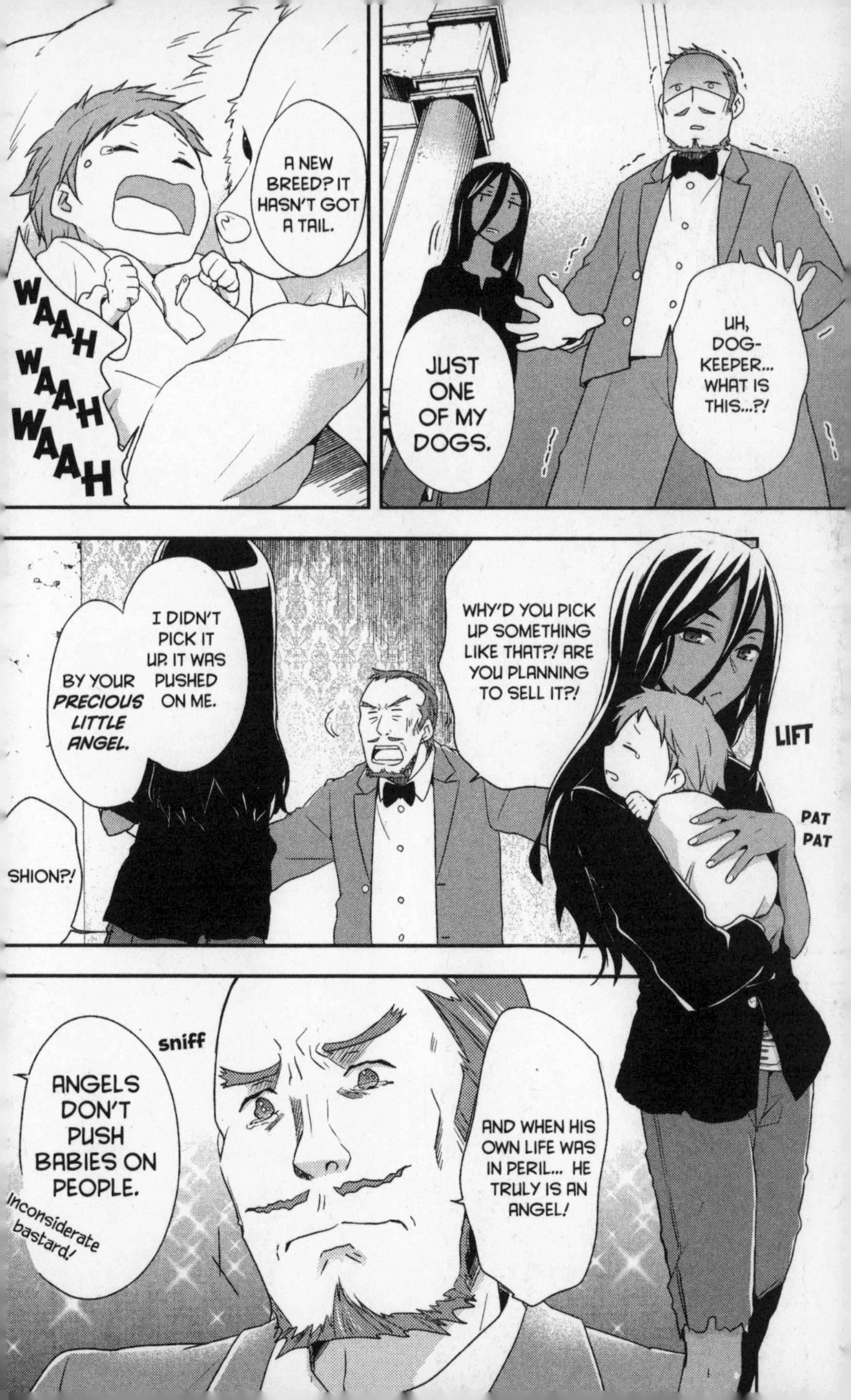
UH, DOG-KEEPER... WHAT IS THIS...?!
JUST ONE OF MY DOGS.
A NEW BREED? IT HASN'T GOT A TAIL.
WAAH WAAH WAAH
WHY'D YOU PICK UP SOMETHING LIKE THAT?! ARE YOU PLANNING TO SELL IT?!
LIFT
PAT PAT
I DIDN'T PICK IT UP. IT WAS PUSHED ON ME.
BY YOUR *PRECIOUS LITTLE ANGEL.*
SHION?!
AND WHEN HIS OWN LIFE WAS IN PERIL... HE TRULY IS AN ANGEL!
sniff
ANGELS DON'T PUSH BABIES ON PEOPLE.
Inconsiderate bastard!

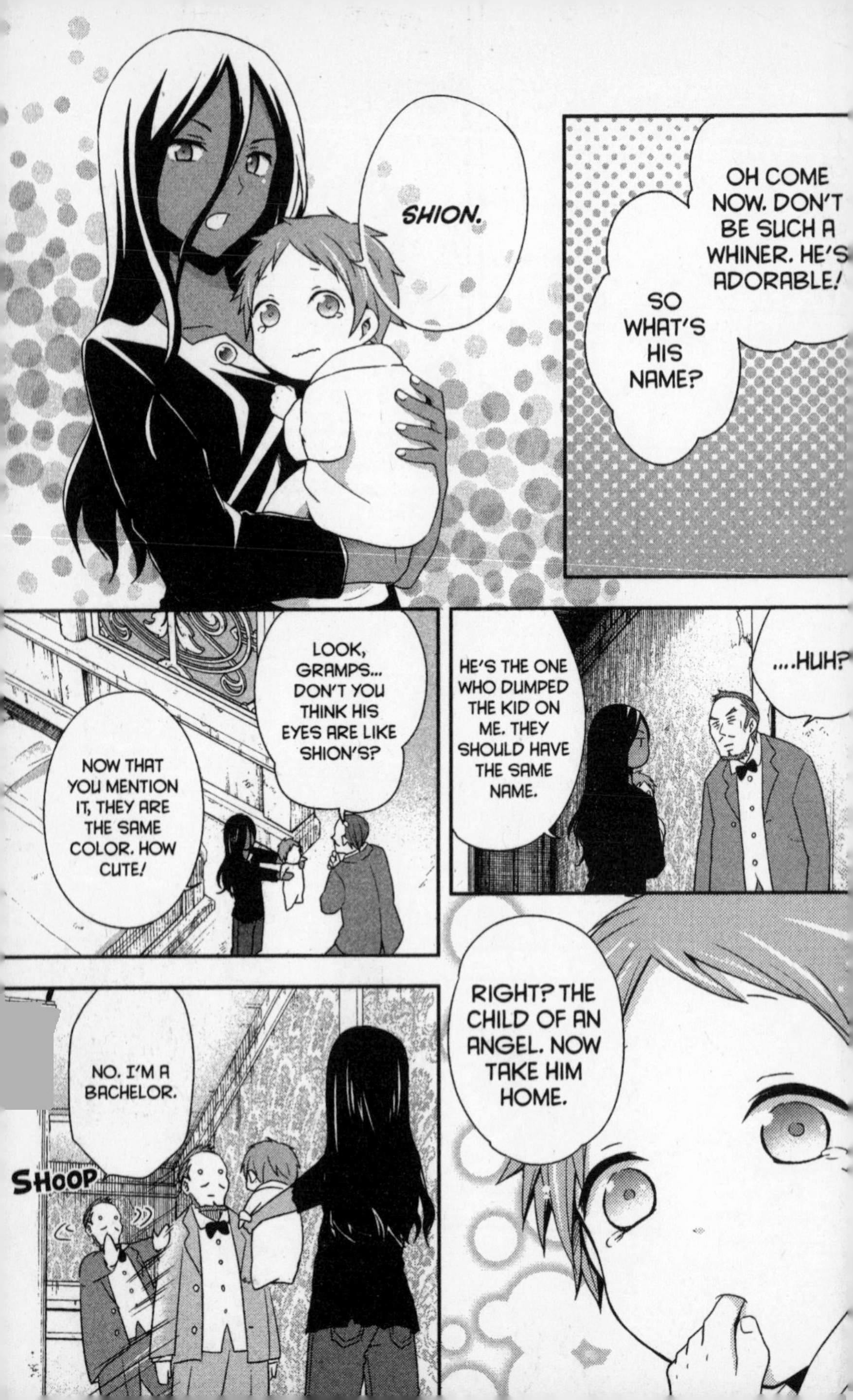
OH COME NOW. DON'T BE SUCH A WHINER. HE'S ADORABLE!
SO WHAT'S HIS NAME?
SHION.
....HUH?
HE'S THE ONE WHO DUMPED THE KID ON ME. THEY SHOULD HAVE THE SAME NAME.
LOOK, GRAMPS... DON'T YOU THINK HIS EYES ARE LIKE SHION'S?
NOW THAT YOU MENTION IT, THEY ARE THE SAME COLOR. HOW CUTE!
RIGHT? THE CHILD OF AN ANGEL. NOW TAKE HIM HOME.
NO. I'M A BACHELOR.
SHOOP

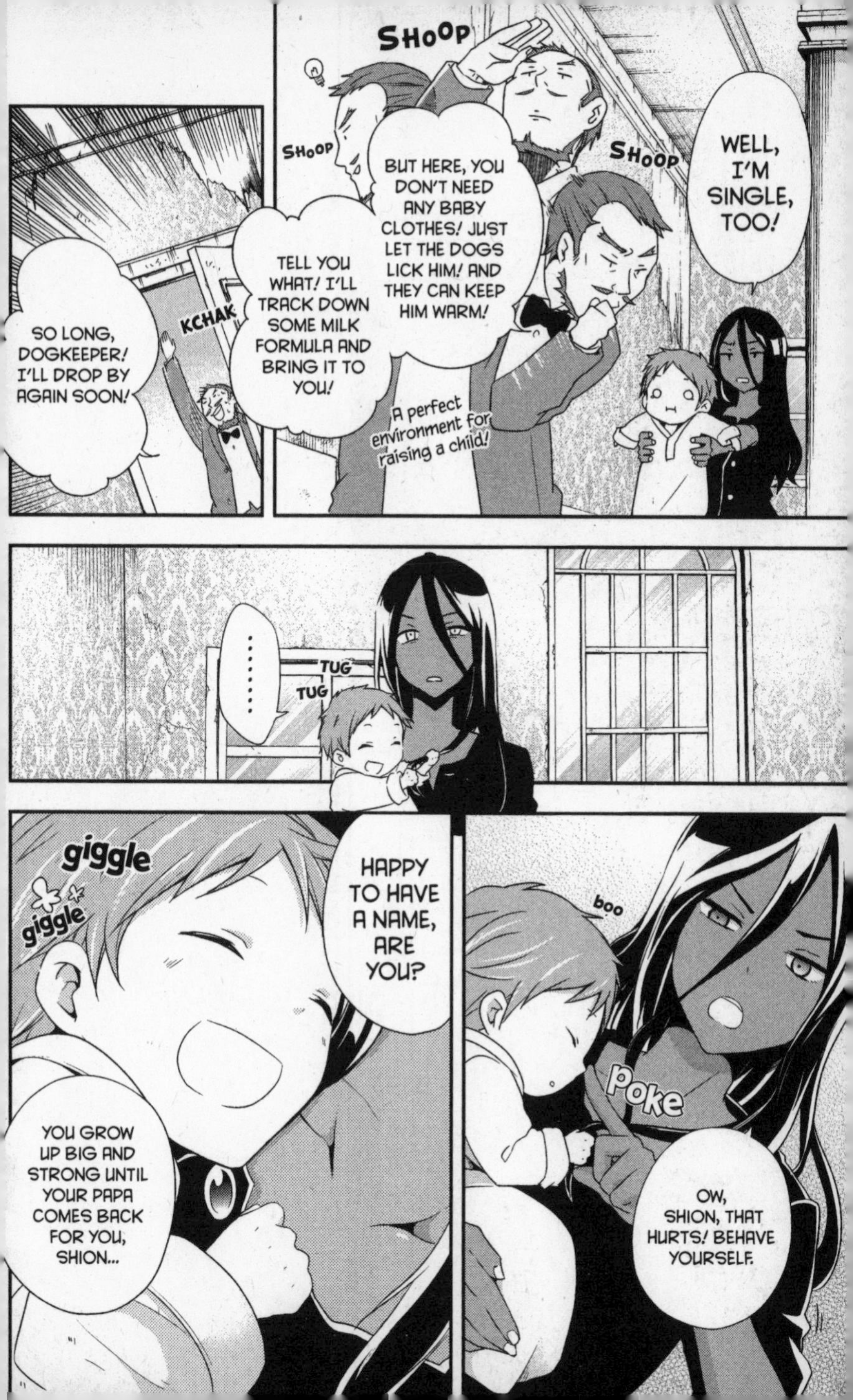
WELL, I'M SINGLE, TOO!
SHOOP
SHOOP
BUT HERE, YOU DON'T NEED ANY BABY CLOTHES! JUST LET THE DOGS LICK HIM! AND THEY CAN KEEP HIM WARM!
SHOOP
TELL YOU WHAT! I'LL TRACK DOWN SOME MILK FORMULA AND BRING IT TO YOU!
A perfect environment for raising a child!
KCHAK
SO LONG, DOGKEEPER! I'LL DROP BY AGAIN SOON!
TUG
TUG
......
boo
OW, SHION, THAT HURTS! BEHAVE YOURSELF.
Poke
HAPPY TO HAVE A NAME, ARE YOU?
giggle
giggle
YOU GROW UP BIG AND STRONG UNTIL YOUR PAPA COMES BACK FOR YOU, SHION...

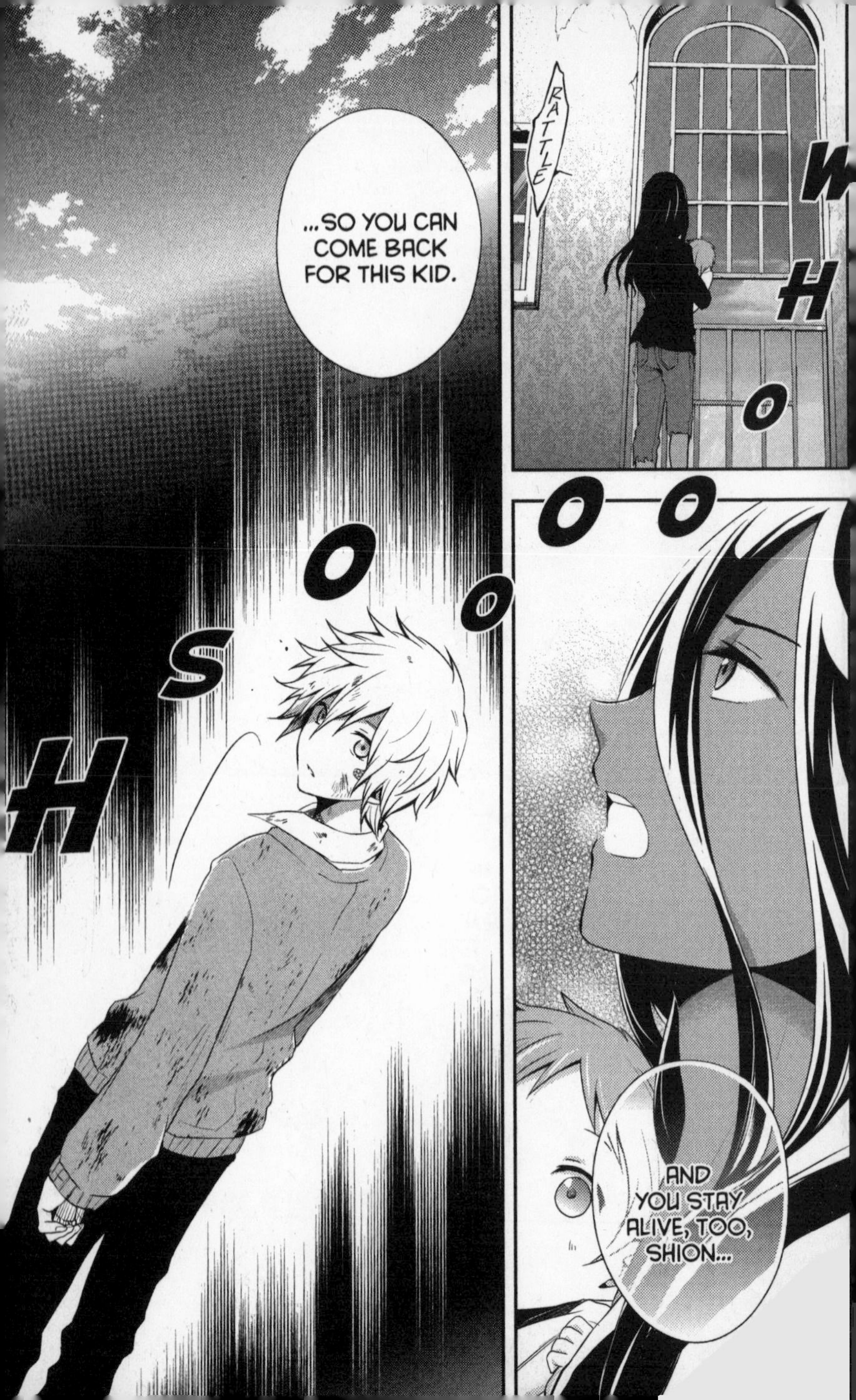
RATTLE
WHOOOOOOSH
...SO YOU CAN COME BACK FOR THIS KID.
AND YOU STAY ALIVE, TOO, SHION...

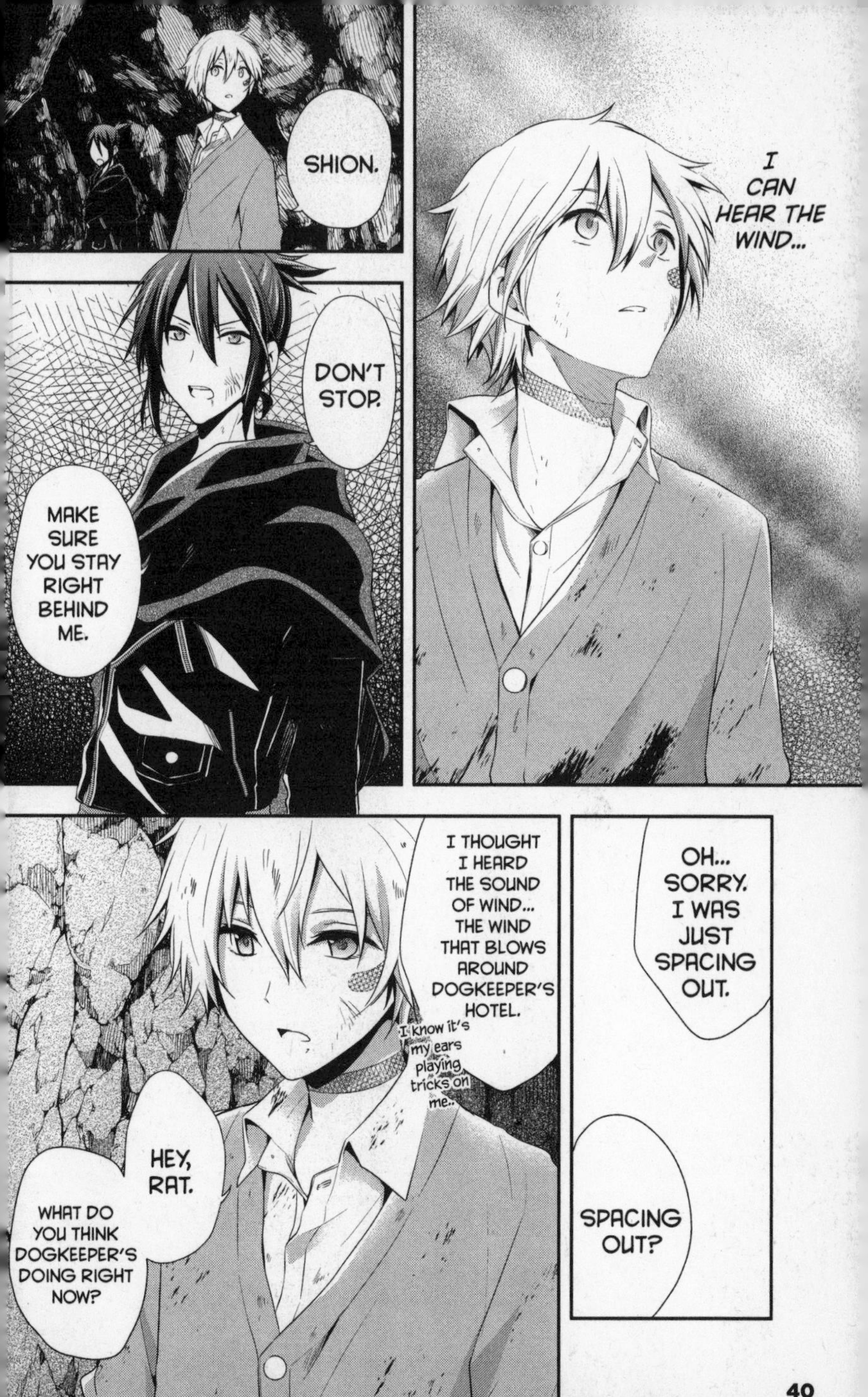
I CAN HEAR THE WIND...
SHION.
DON'T STOP.
MAKE SURE YOU STAY RIGHT BEHIND ME.
OH... SORRY. I WAS JUST SPACING OUT.
SPACING OUT?
I THOUGHT I HEARD THE SOUND OF WIND... THE WIND THAT BLOWS AROUND DOGKEEPER'S HOTEL.
I know it's my ears playing tricks on me..
HEY, RAT.
WHAT DO YOU THINK DOGKEEPER'S DOING RIGHT NOW?

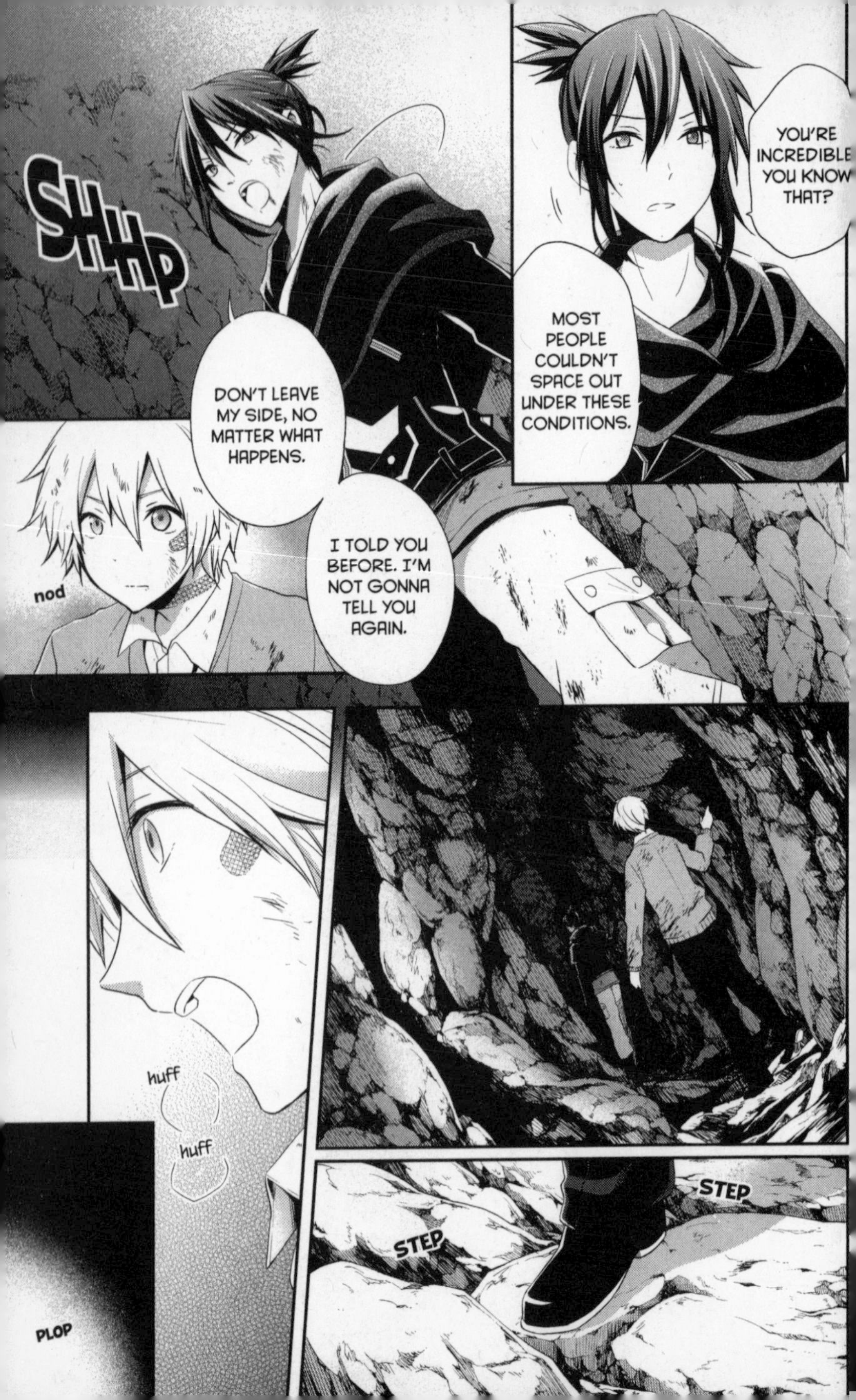
YOU'RE INCREDIBLE YOU KNOW THAT?
MOST PEOPLE COULDN'T SPACE OUT UNDER THESE CONDITIONS.
SHHP
DON'T LEAVE MY SIDE, NO MATTER WHAT HAPPENS.
I TOLD YOU BEFORE. I'M NOT GONNA TELL YOU AGAIN.
nod
STEP
STEP
huff
huff
PLOP

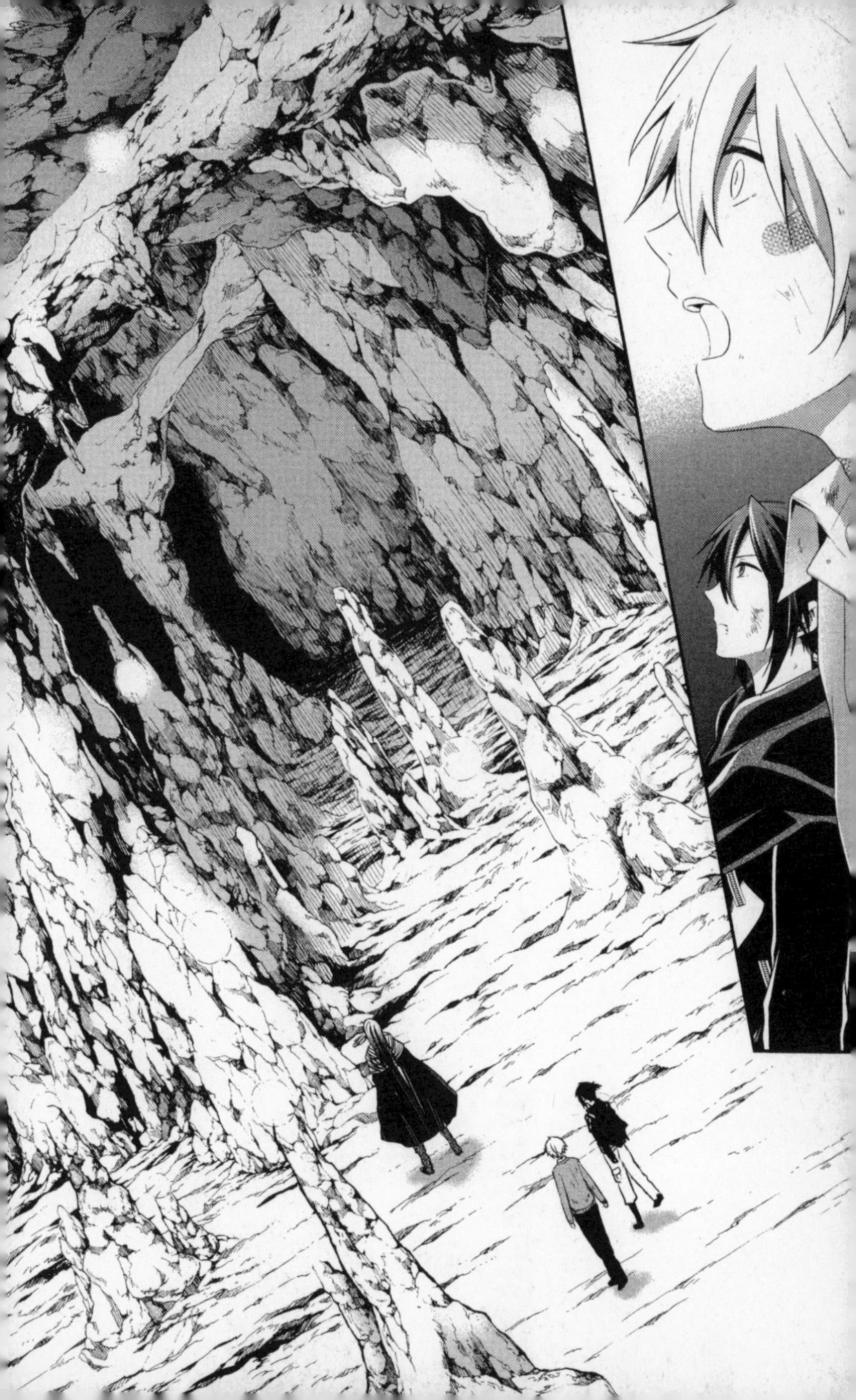

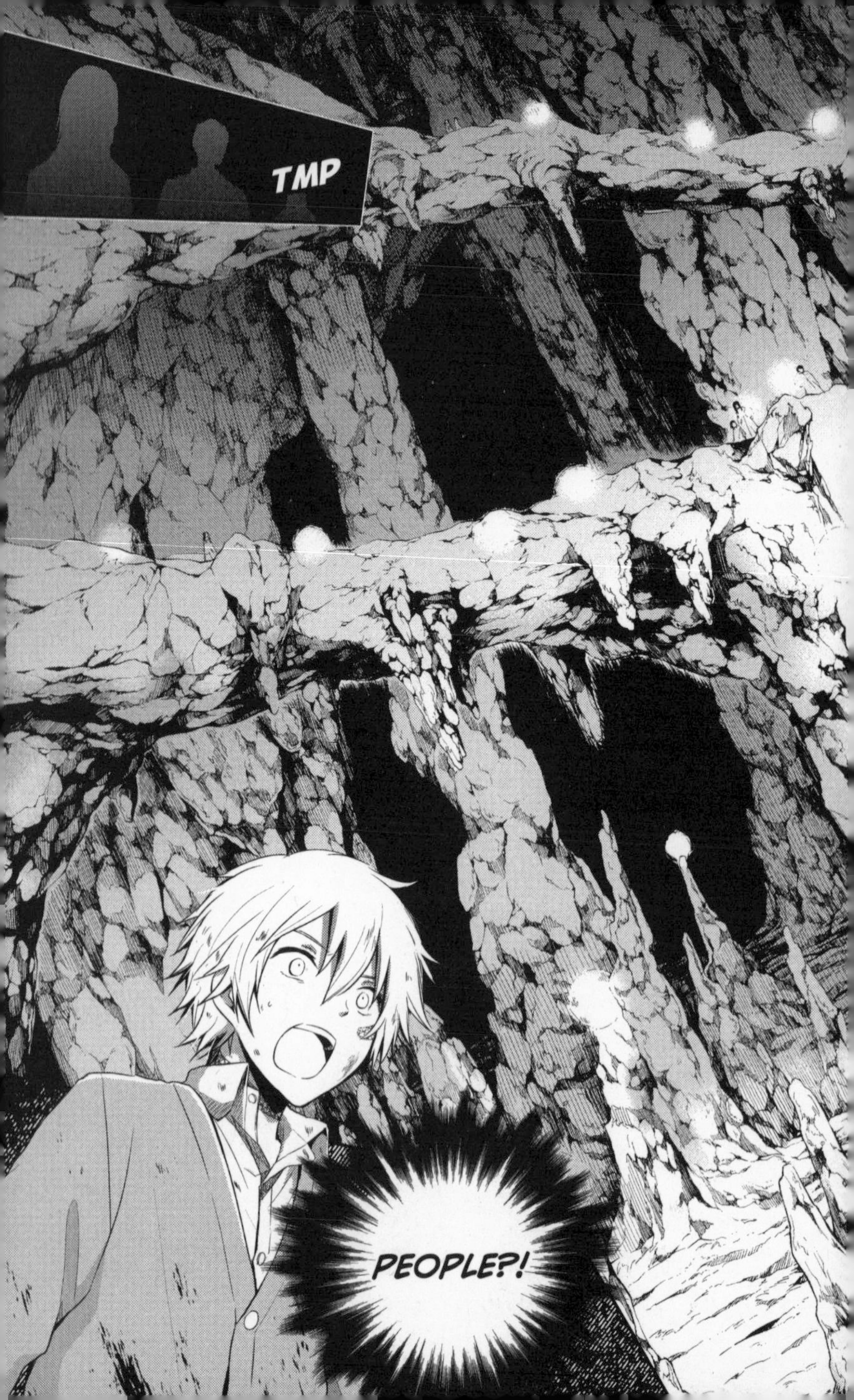
TMP
PEOPLE?!

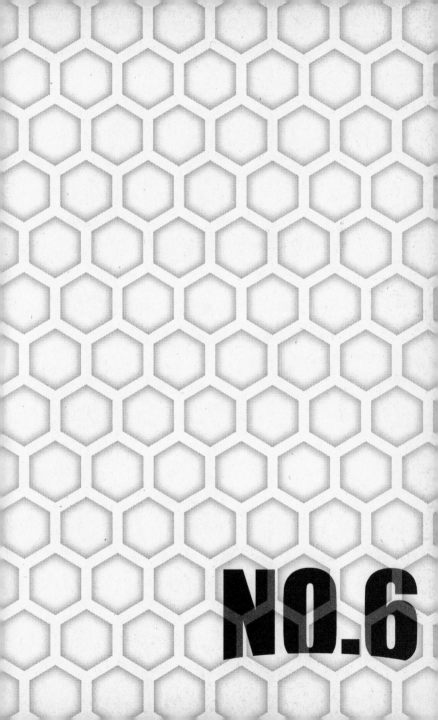

NO.6

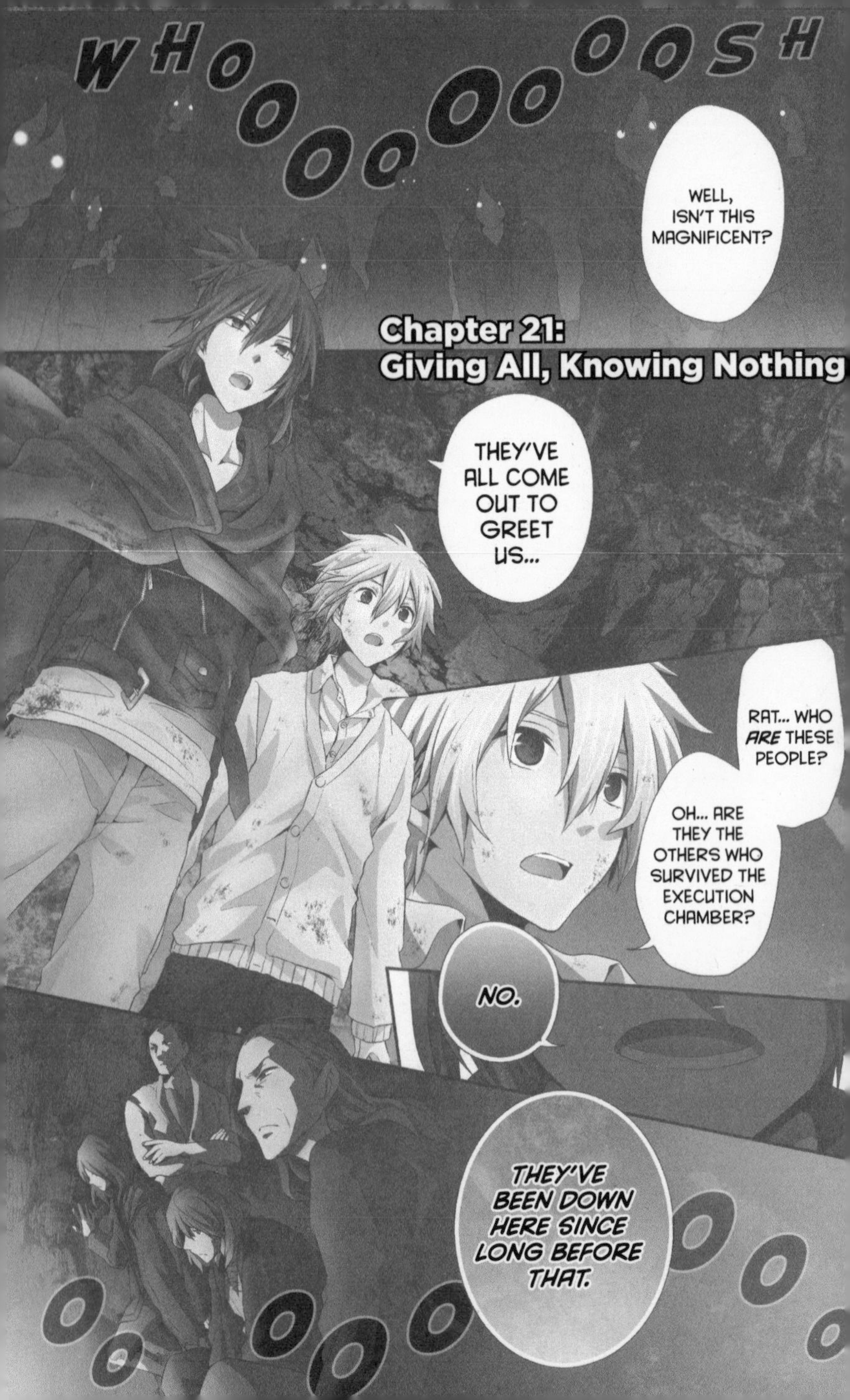
WHOOOOOOOOOOSH
WELL, ISN'T THIS MAGNIFICENT?
Chapter 21: Giving All, Knowing Nothing
THEY'VE ALL COME OUT TO GREET US...
RAT... WHO ARE THESE PEOPLE?
OH... ARE THEY THE OTHERS WHO SURVIVED THE EXECUTION CHAMBER?
NO.
THEY'VE BEEN DOWN HERE SINCE LONG BEFORE THAT.

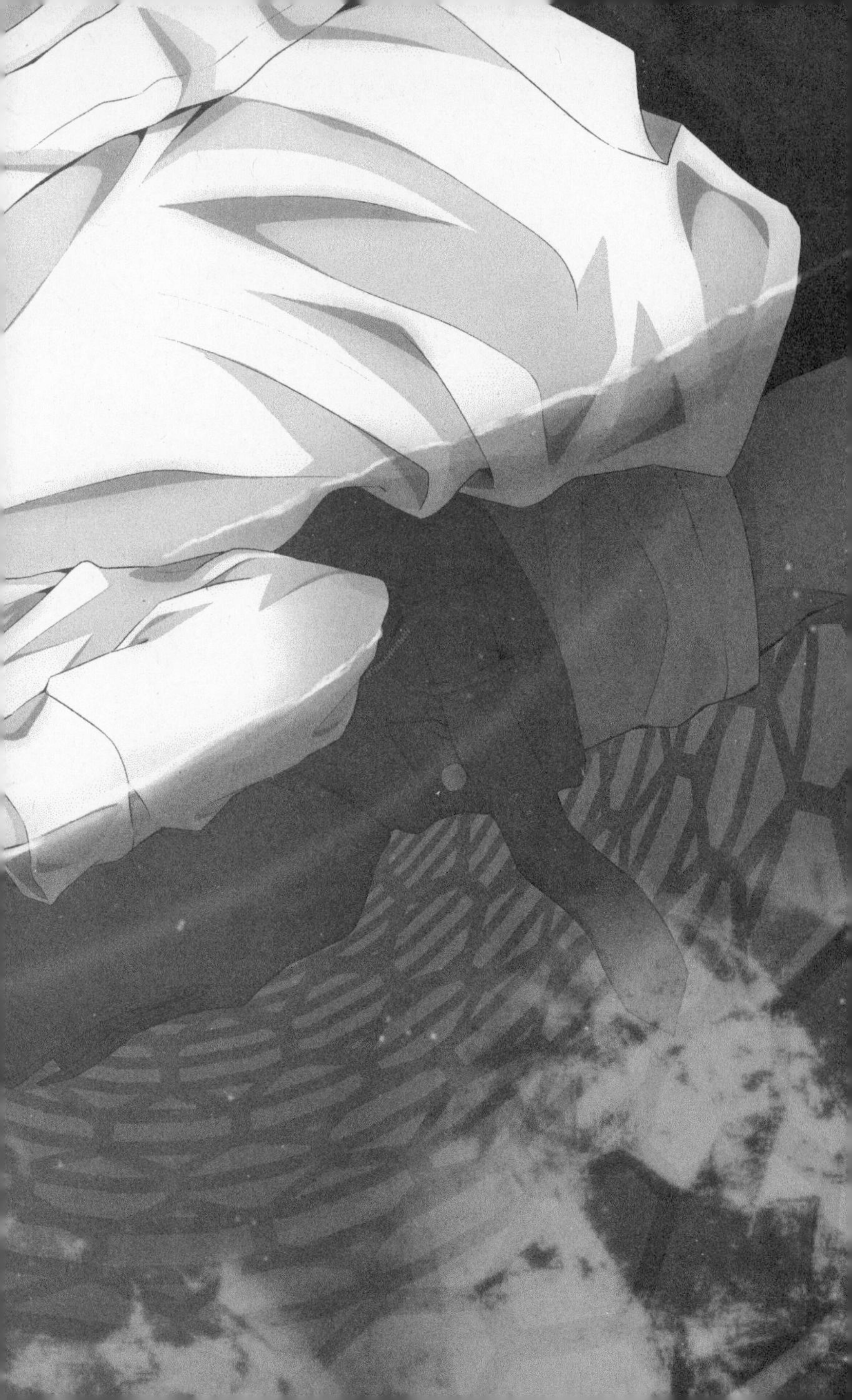

Chapter 21: Giving All, Knowing Nothing

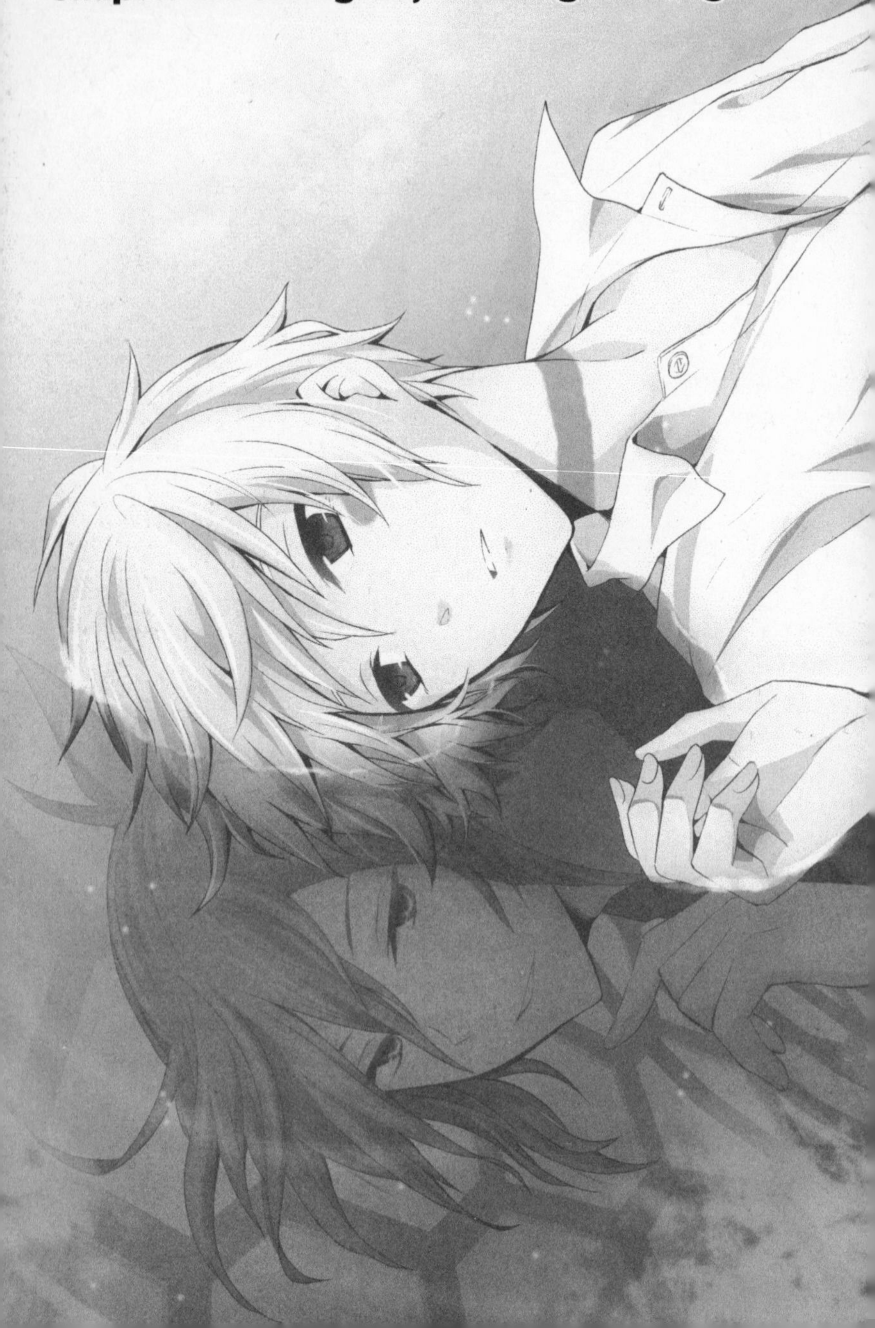

NO.6

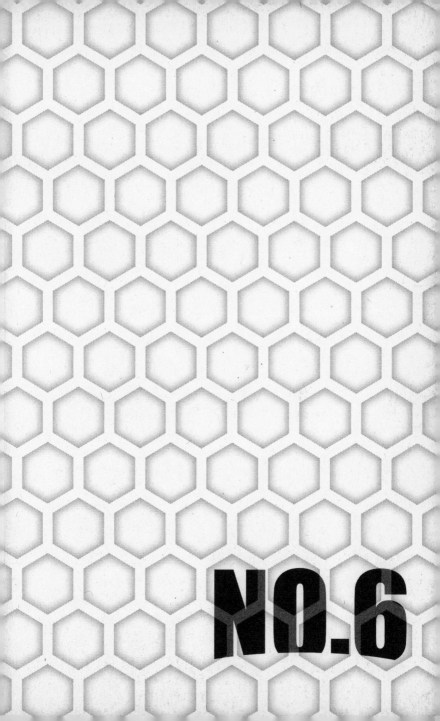

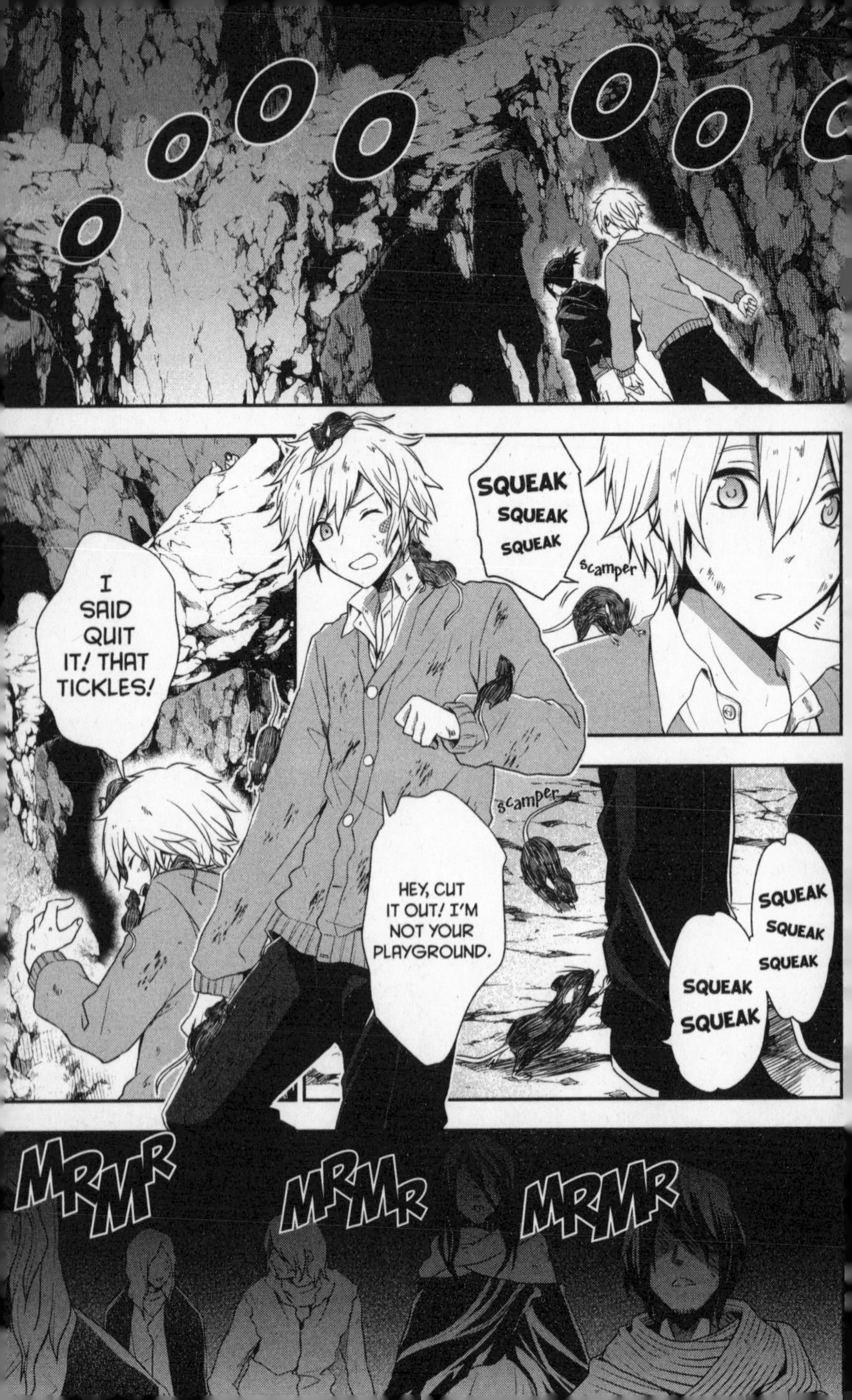
OOOOOOO
SQUEAK SQUEAK SQUEAK
scamper
scamper
SQUEAK SQUEAK SQUEAK
SQUEAK SQUEAK
I SAID QUIT IT! THAT TICKLES!
HEY, CUT IT OUT! I'M NOT YOUR PLAYGROUND.
MRMR
MRMR
MRMR

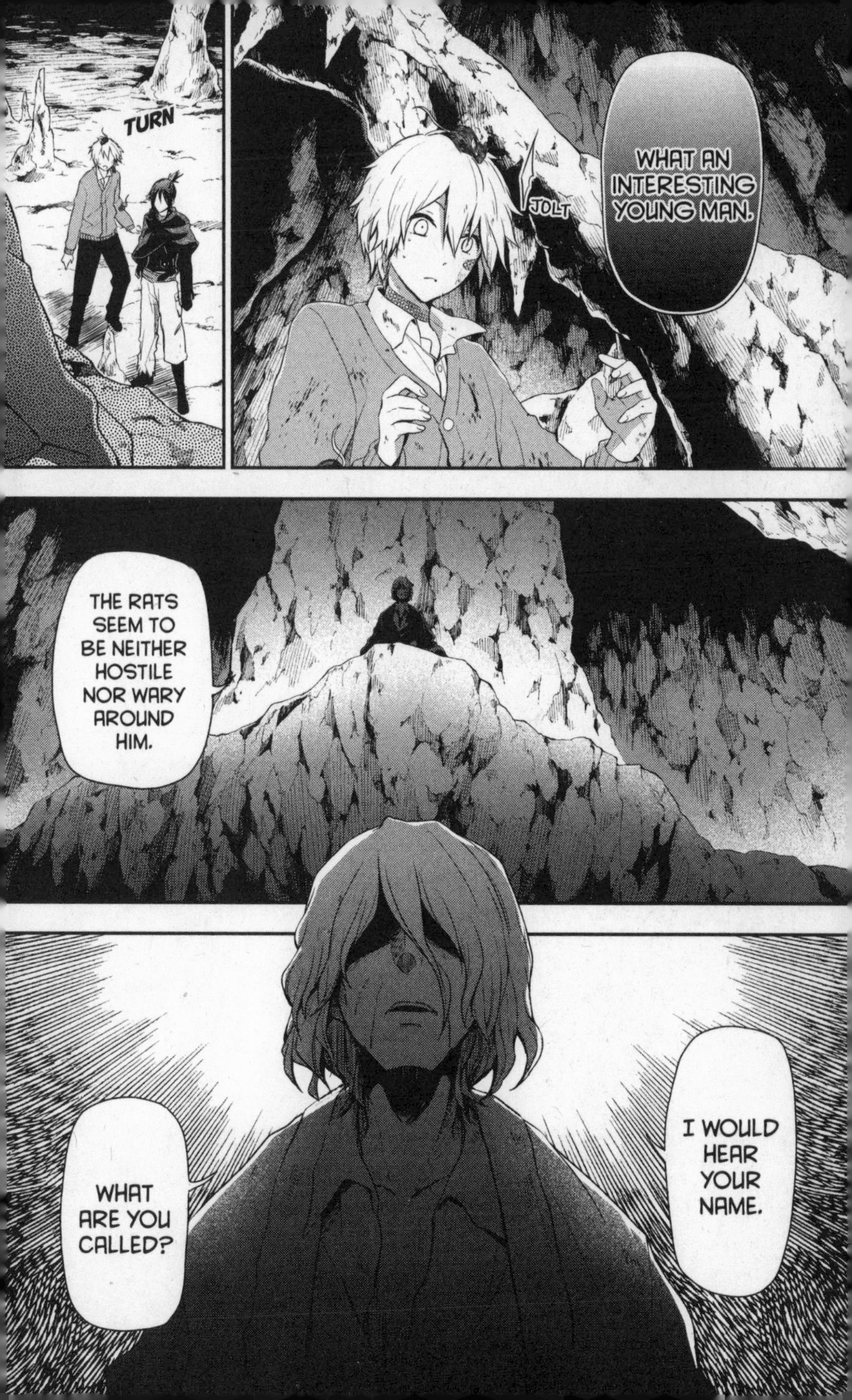
WHAT AN INTERESTING YOUNG MAN.
JOLT
TURN
THE RATS SEEM TO BE NEITHER HOSTILE NOR WARY AROUND HIM.
I WOULD HEAR YOUR NAME.
WHAT ARE YOU CALLED?

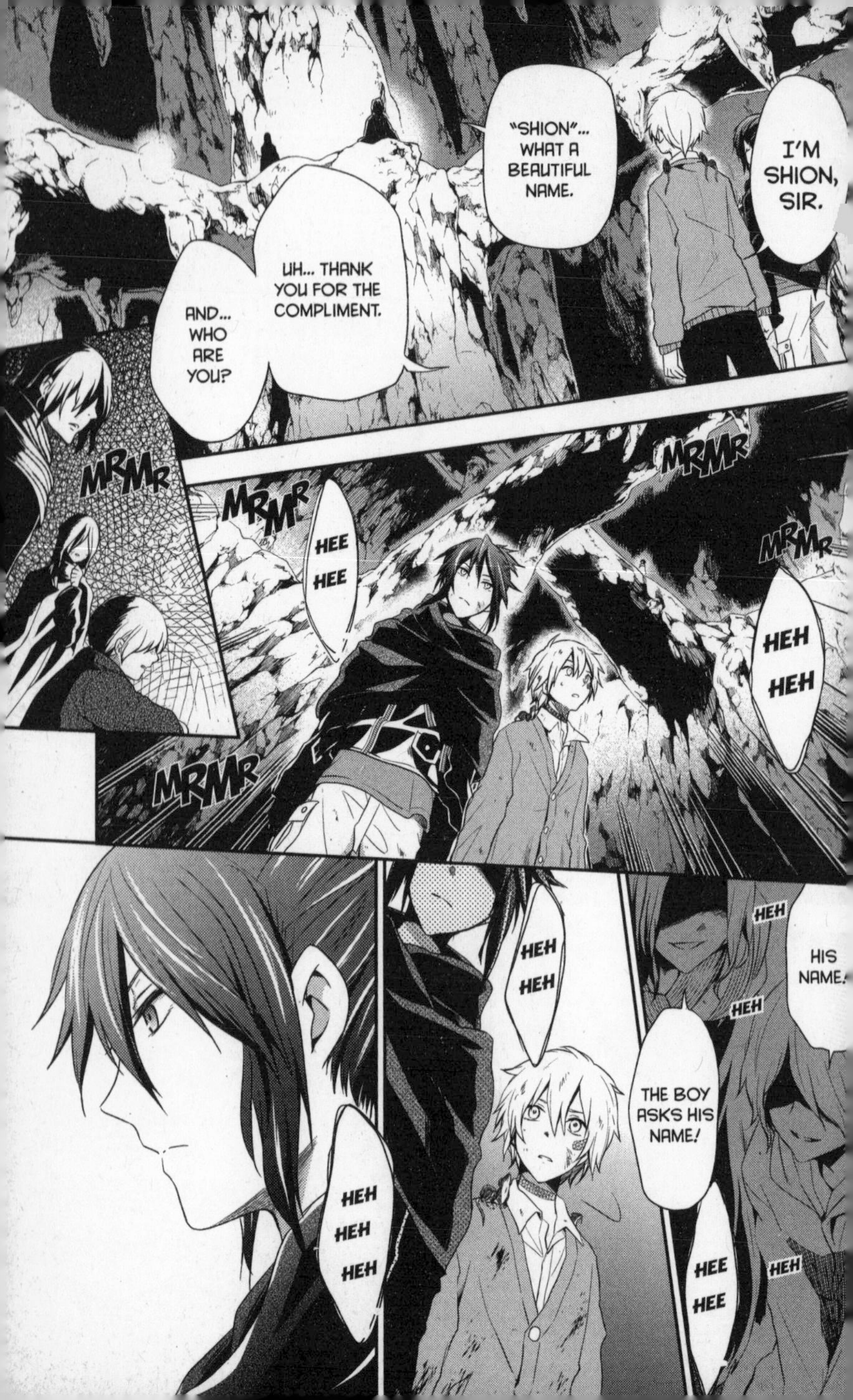
I'M SHION, SIR.
"SHION"... WHAT A BEAUTIFUL NAME.
UH... THANK YOU FOR THE COMPLIMENT.
AND... WHO ARE YOU?
MRMR
MRMR
HEH HEH
HEE HEE
MRMR
MRMR
MRMR
HEH
HIS NAME.
HEH
THE BOY ASKS HIS NAME!
HEH
HEE HEE
HEH HEH
HEH HEH HEH

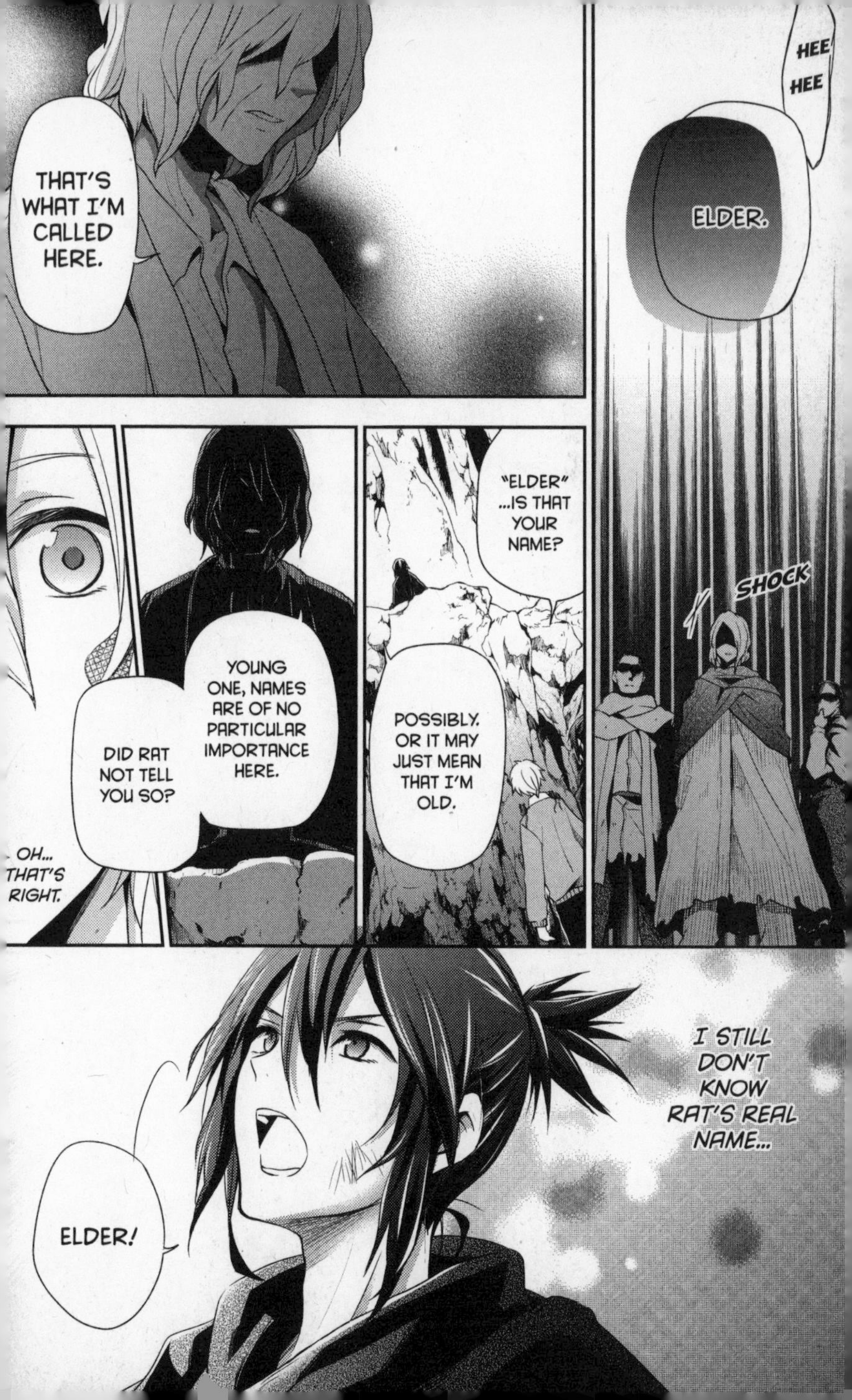
HEE HEE
ELDER.
SHOCK
THAT'S WHAT I'M CALLED HERE.
"ELDER" ...IS THAT YOUR NAME?
POSSIBLY. OR IT MAY JUST MEAN THAT I'M OLD.
YOUNG ONE, NAMES ARE OF NO PARTICULAR IMPORTANCE HERE.
DID RAT NOT TELL YOU SO?
OH... THAT'S RIGHT.
I STILL DON'T KNOW RAT'S REAL NAME...
ELDER!

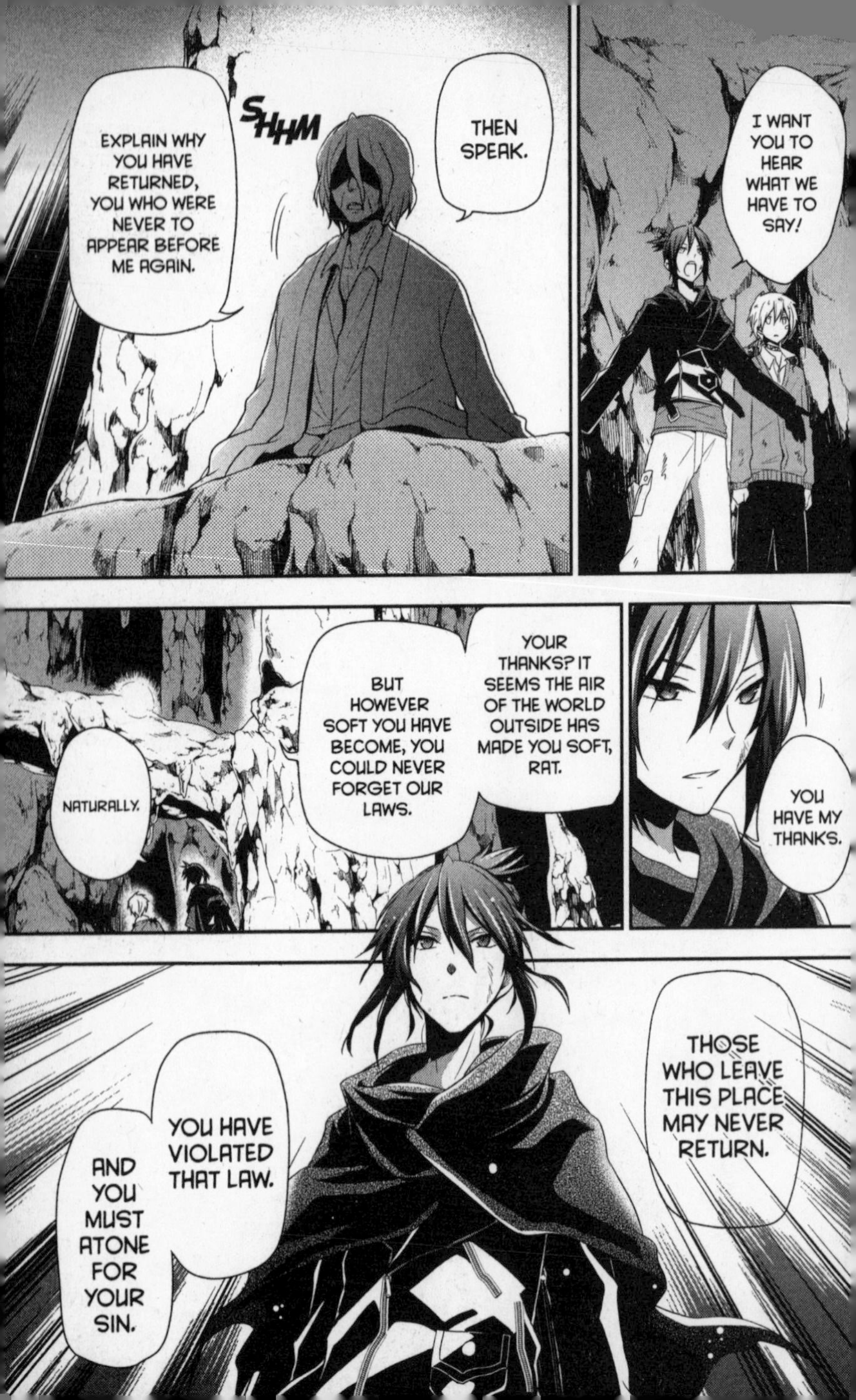
I WANT YOU TO HEAR WHAT WE HAVE TO SAY!
THEN SPEAK.
SHHM
EXPLAIN WHY YOU HAVE RETURNED, YOU WHO WERE NEVER TO APPEAR BEFORE ME AGAIN.
YOU HAVE MY THANKS.
YOUR THANKS? IT SEEMS THE AIR OF THE WORLD OUTSIDE HAS MADE YOU SOFT, RAT.
BUT HOWEVER SOFT YOU HAVE BECOME, YOU COULD NEVER FORGET OUR LAWS.
NATURALLY.
THOSE WHO LEAVE THIS PLACE MAY NEVER RETURN.
YOU HAVE VIOLATED THAT LAW.
AND YOU MUST ATONE FOR YOUR SIN.

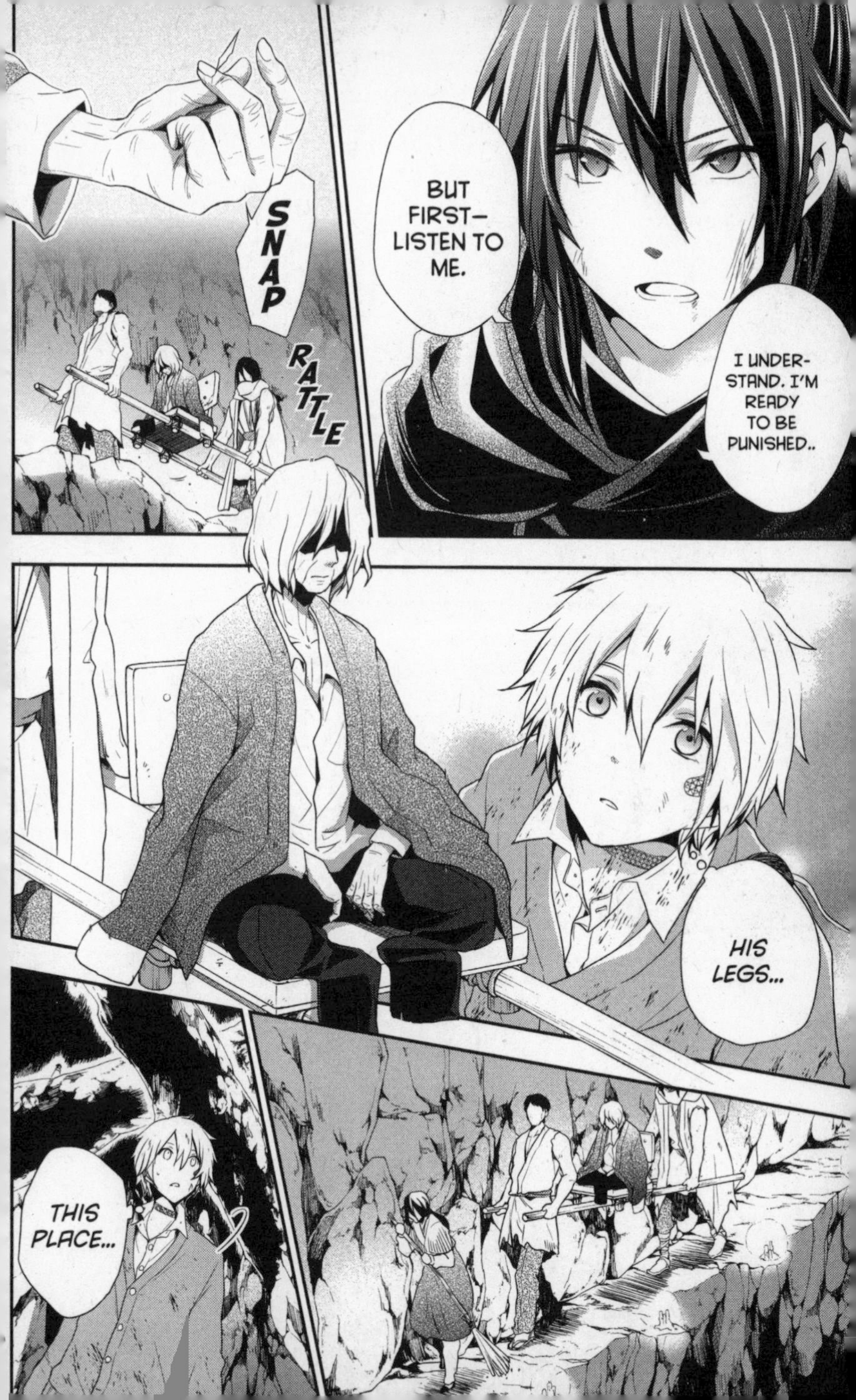
I UNDER-STAND. I'M READY TO BE PUNISHED..
BUT FIRST– LISTEN TO ME.
SNAP
RATTLE
HIS LEGS...
THIS PLACE...

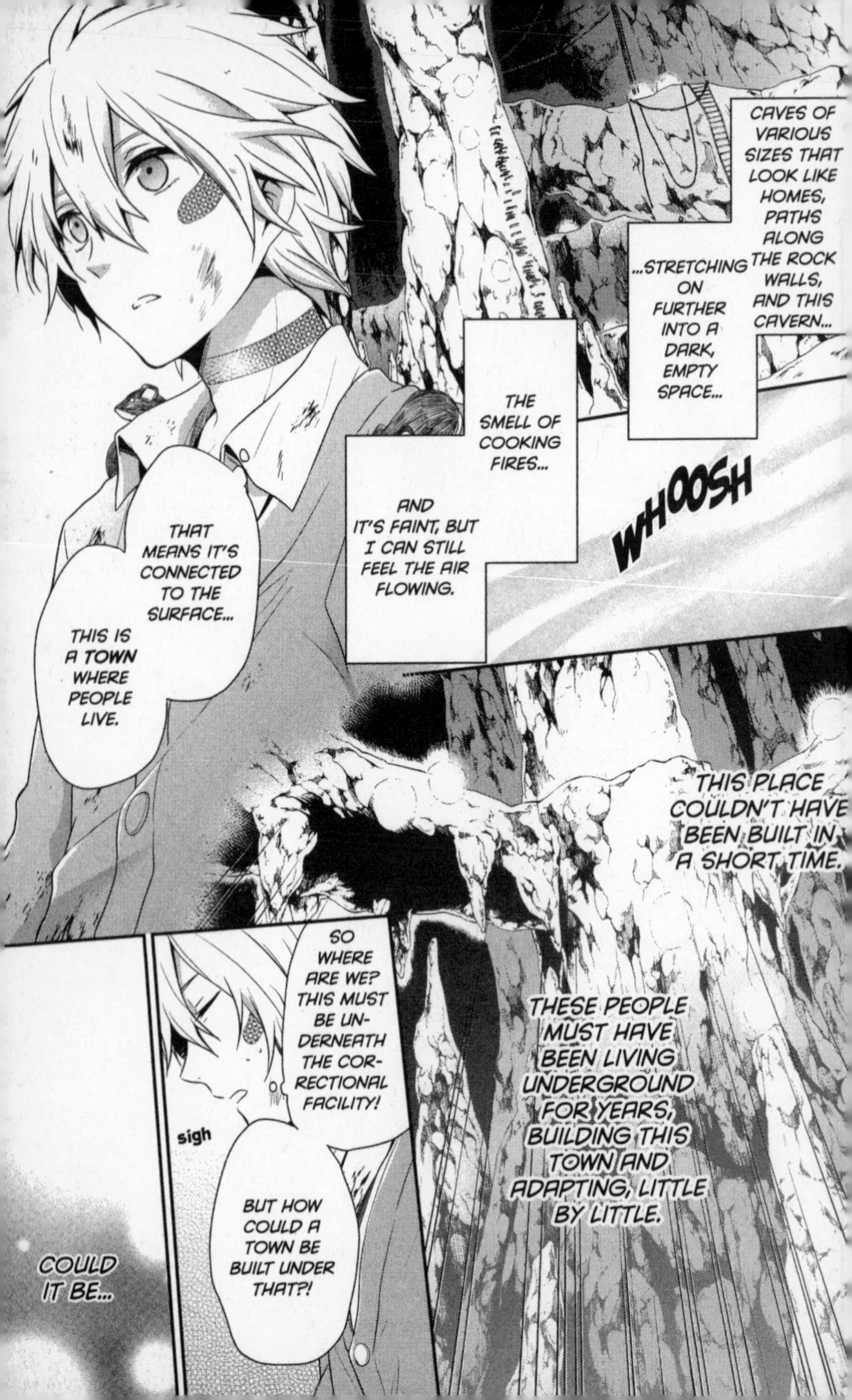
CAVES OF VARIOUS SIZES THAT LOOK LIKE HOMES, PATHS ALONG THE ROCK WALLS, AND THIS CAVERN...
...STRETCHING ON FURTHER INTO A DARK, EMPTY SPACE...
THE SMELL OF COOKING FIRES...
AND IT'S FAINT, BUT I CAN STILL FEEL THE AIR FLOWING.
WHOOSH
THAT MEANS IT'S CONNECTED TO THE SURFACE...
THIS IS A TOWN WHERE PEOPLE LIVE.
THIS PLACE COULDN'T HAVE BEEN BUILT IN A SHORT TIME.
THESE PEOPLE MUST HAVE BEEN LIVING UNDERGROUND FOR YEARS, BUILDING THIS TOWN AND ADAPTING, LITTLE BY LITTLE.
SO WHERE ARE WE? THIS MUST BE UNDERNEATH THE CORRECTIONAL FACILITY!
sigh
BUT HOW COULD A TOWN BE BUILT UNDER THAT?!
COULD IT BE...

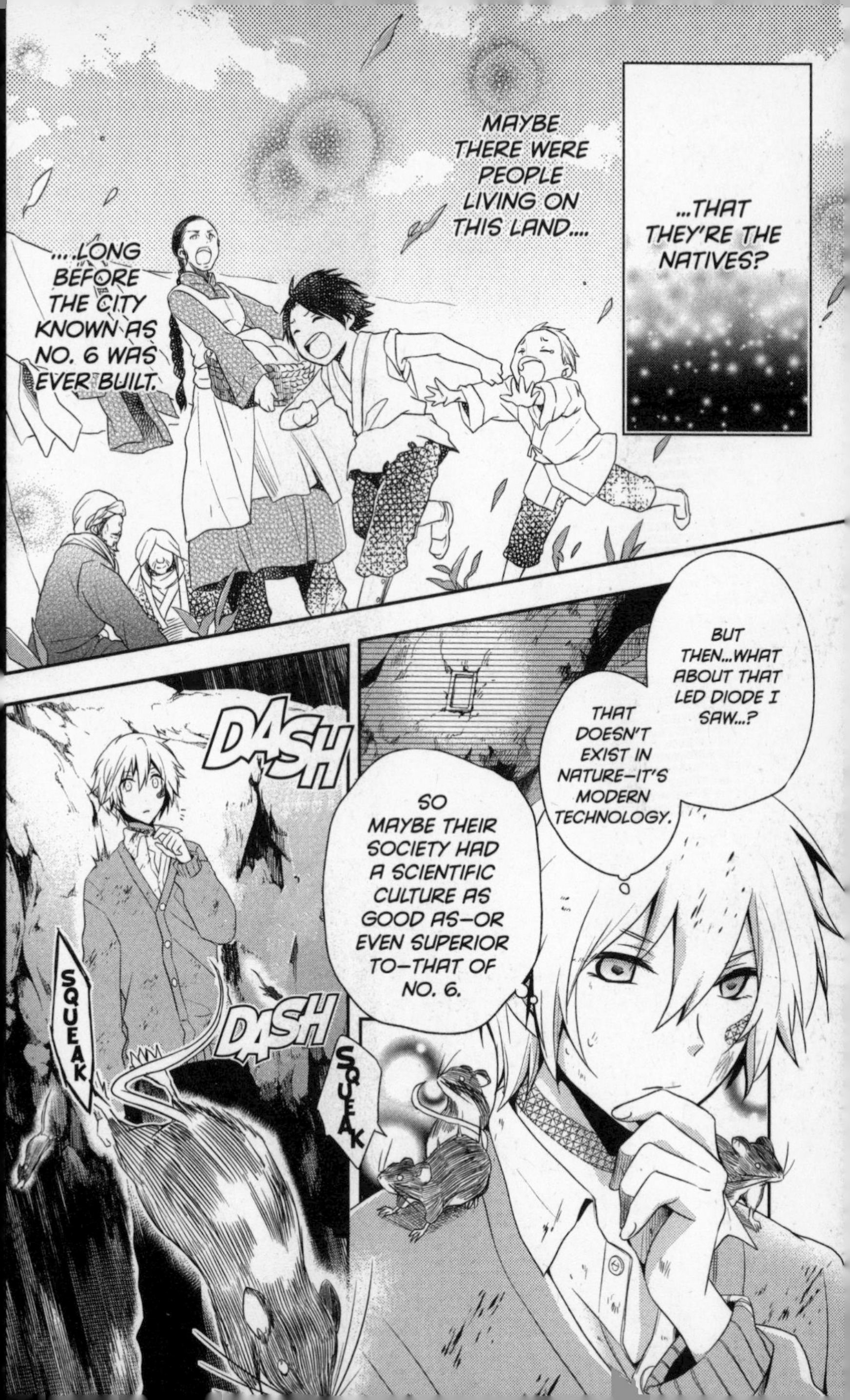

...THAT THEY'RE THE NATIVES?
MAYBE THERE WERE PEOPLE LIVING ON THIS LAND....
...LONG BEFORE THE CITY KNOWN AS NO. 6 WAS EVER BUILT.
BUT THEN...WHAT ABOUT THAT LED DIODE I SAW...?
THAT DOESN'T EXIST IN NATURE—IT'S MODERN TECHNOLOGY.
SO MAYBE THEIR SOCIETY HAD A SCIENTIFIC CULTURE AS GOOD AS—OR EVEN SUPERIOR TO—THAT OF NO. 6.
SQUEAK
DASH
SQUEAK
DASH

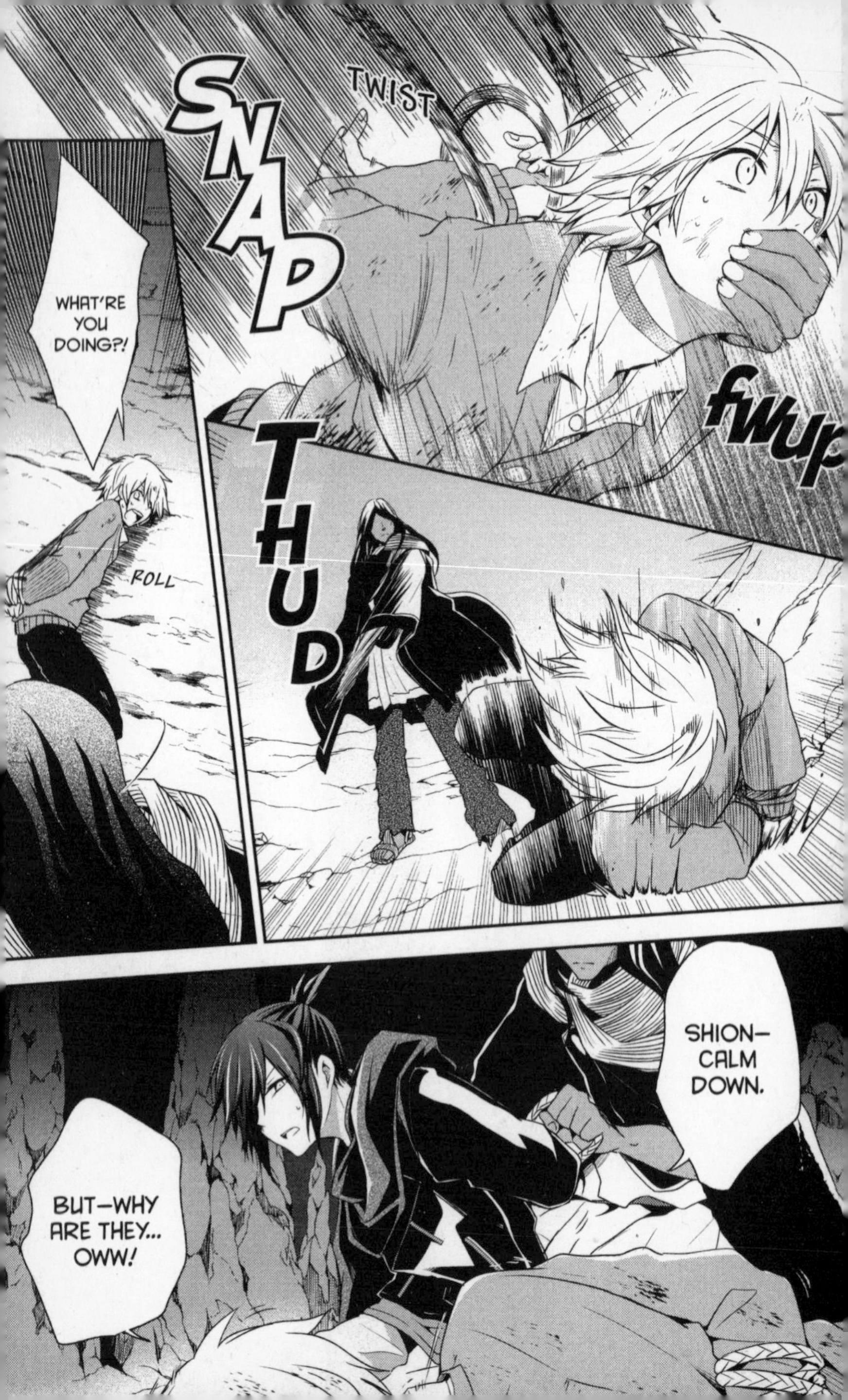
TWIST
SNAP
fwup
THUD
WHAT'RE YOU DOING?!
ROLL
SHION—CALM DOWN.
BUT—WHY ARE THEY... OWW!

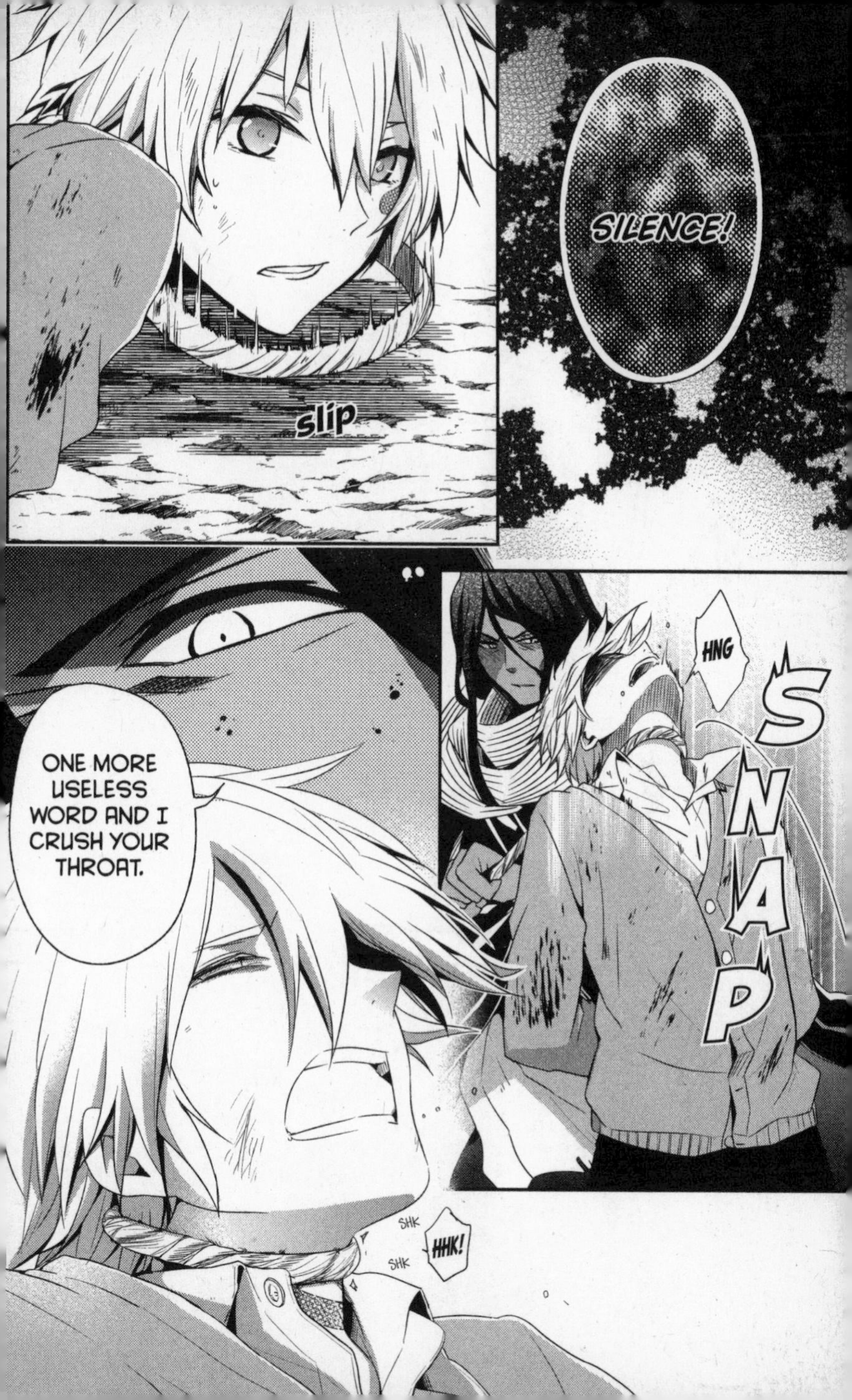
SILENCE!
slip
HNG
SNAP
ONE MORE USELESS WORD AND I CRUSH YOUR THROAT.
SHK
SHK
HHK!

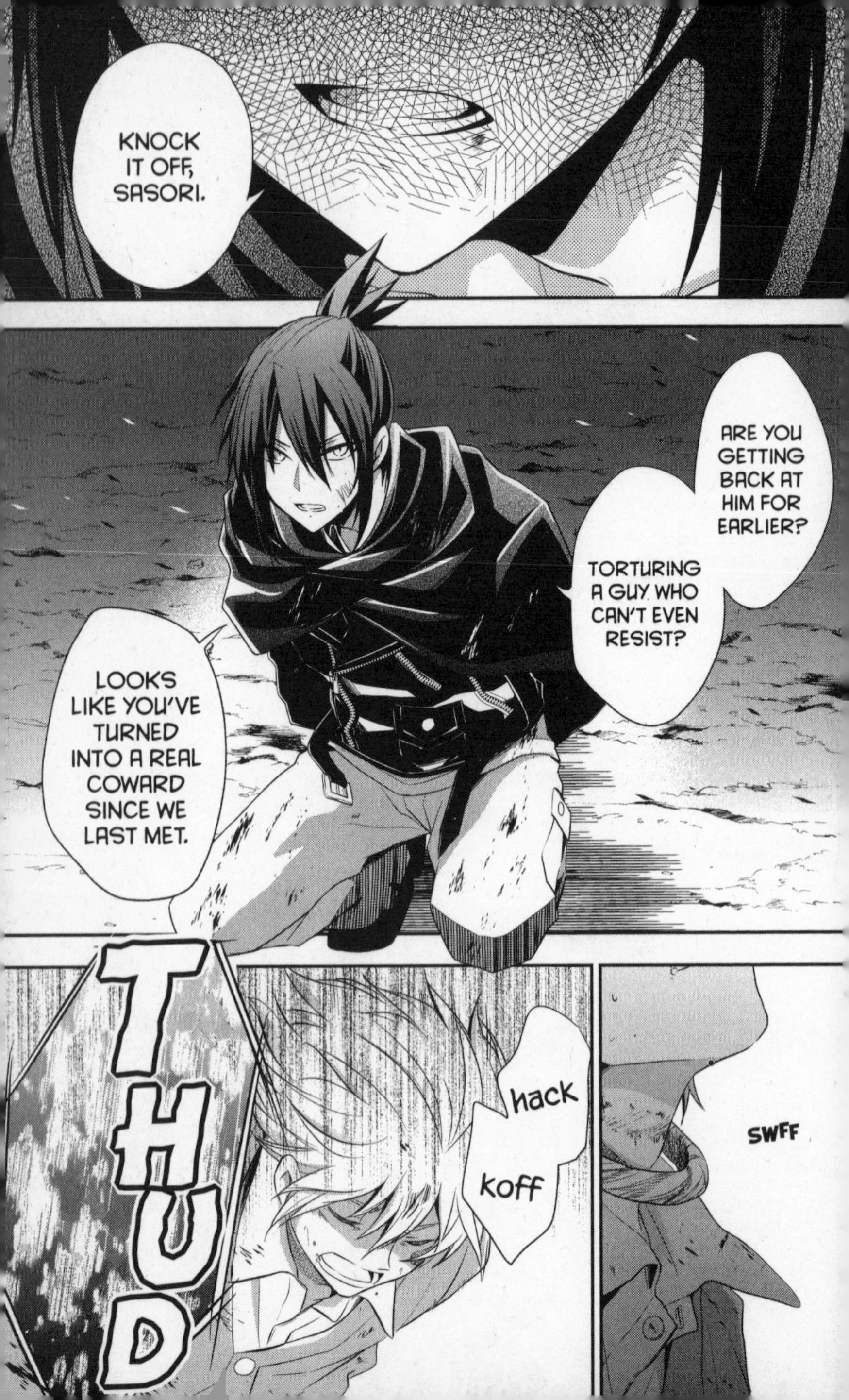
KNOCK IT OFF, SASORI.
ARE YOU GETTING BACK AT HIM FOR EARLIER?
TORTURING A GUY WHO CAN'T EVEN RESIST?
LOOKS LIKE YOU'VE TURNED INTO A REAL COWARD SINCE WE LAST MET.
SWFF
hack
koff
THUD

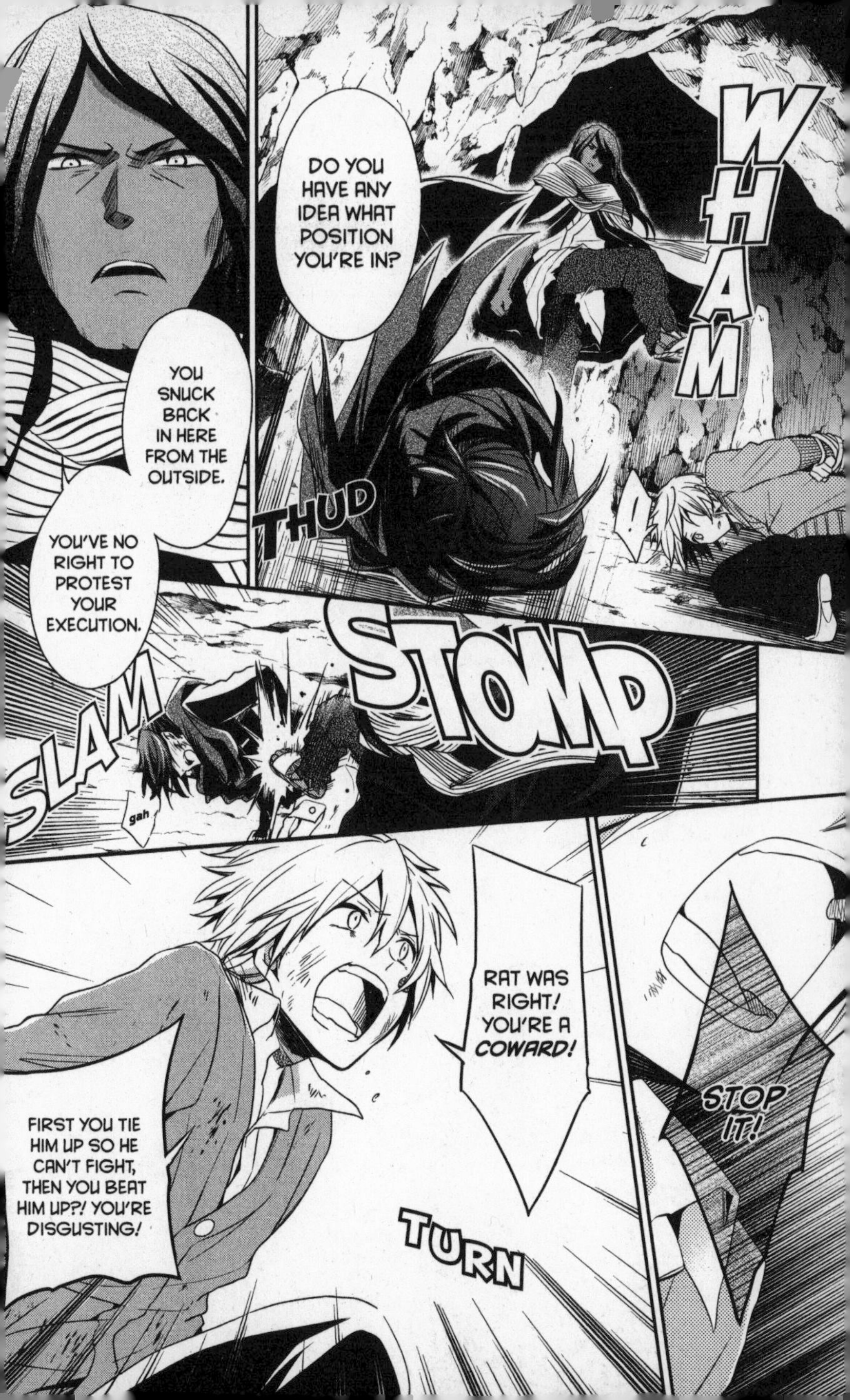
WHAM
DO YOU HAVE ANY IDEA WHAT POSITION YOU'RE IN?
THUD
!
YOU SNUCK BACK IN HERE FROM THE OUTSIDE.
YOU'VE NO RIGHT TO PROTEST YOUR EXECUTION.
STOMP
SLAM
gah
STOP IT!
RAT WAS RIGHT! YOU'RE A *COWARD!*
FIRST YOU TIE HIM UP SO HE CAN'T FIGHT, THEN YOU BEAT HIM UP?! YOU'RE DISGUSTING!
TURN

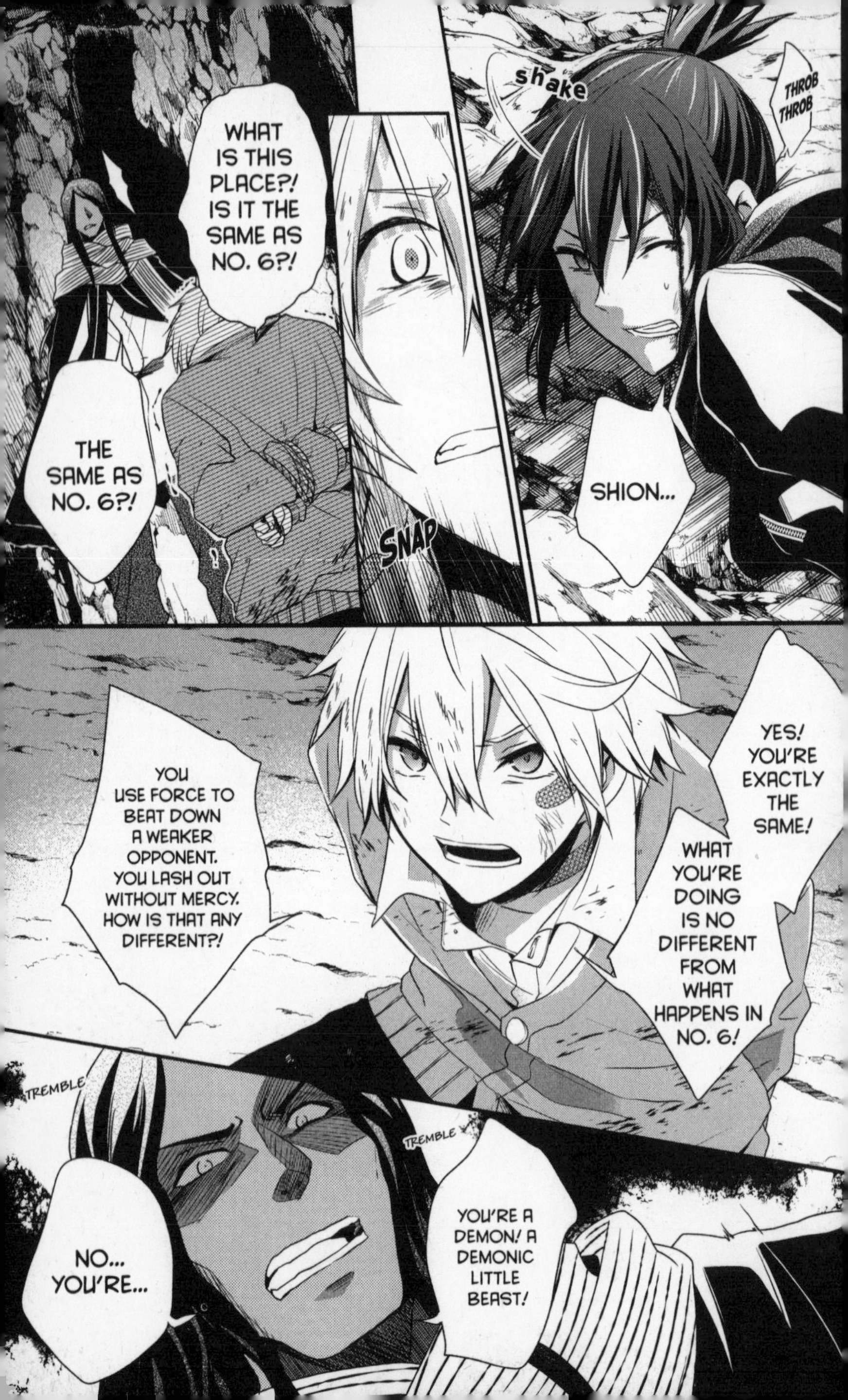
shake
THROB THROB
SHION...
SNAP
WHAT IS THIS PLACE?! IS IT THE SAME AS NO. 6?!
THE SAME AS NO. 6?!
YES! YOU'RE EXACTLY THE SAME!
WHAT YOU'RE DOING IS NO DIFFERENT FROM WHAT HAPPENS IN NO. 6!
YOU USE FORCE TO BEAT DOWN A WEAKER OPPONENT. YOU LASH OUT WITHOUT MERCY. HOW IS THAT ANY DIFFERENT?!
TREMBLE
TREMBLE
YOU'RE A DEMON! A DEMONIC LITTLE BEAST!
NO... YOU'RE...

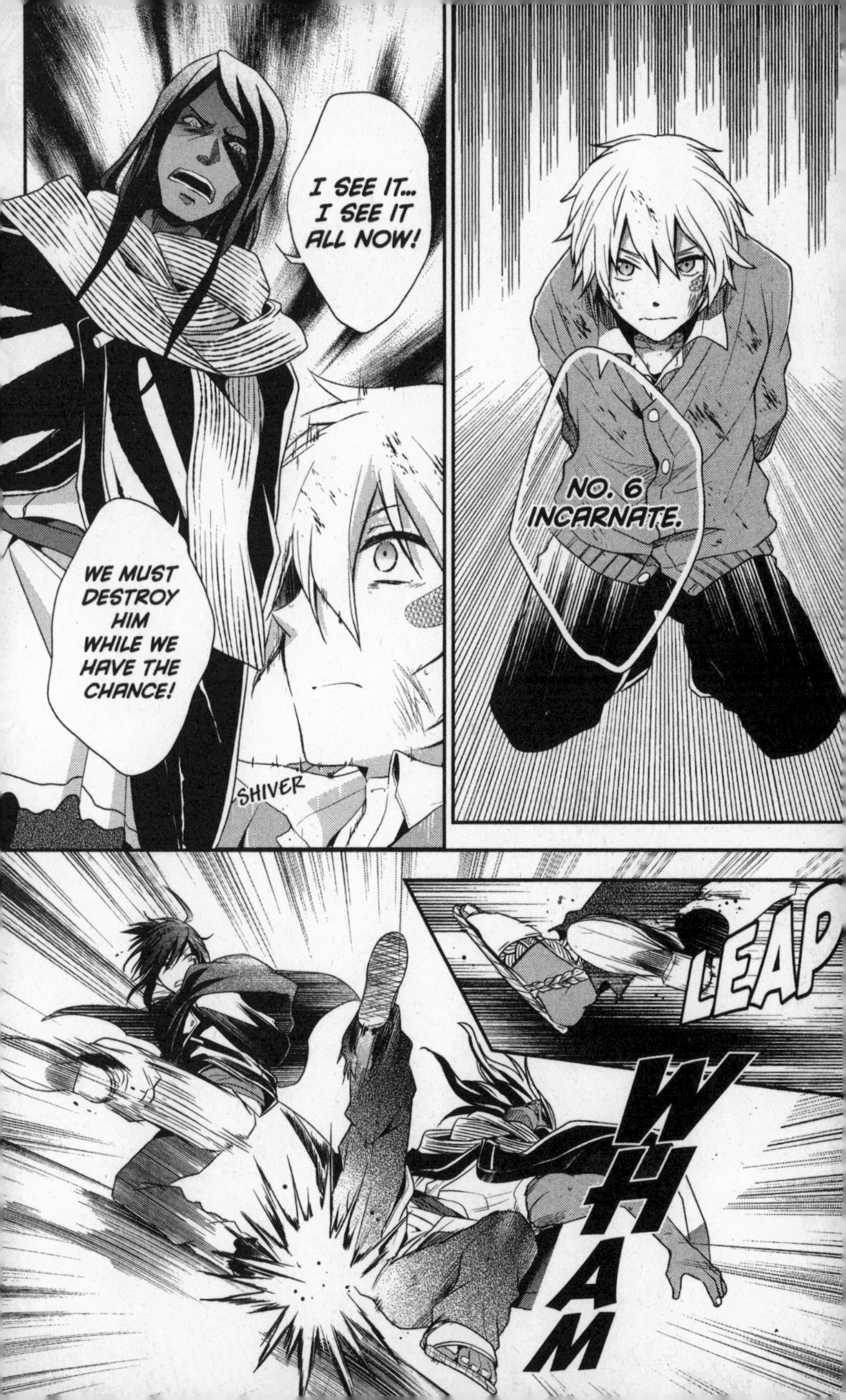
NO. 6 INCARNATE.
I SEE IT... I SEE IT ALL NOW!
WE MUST DESTROY HIM WHILE WE HAVE THE CHANCE!
SHIVER
LEAP
WHAM

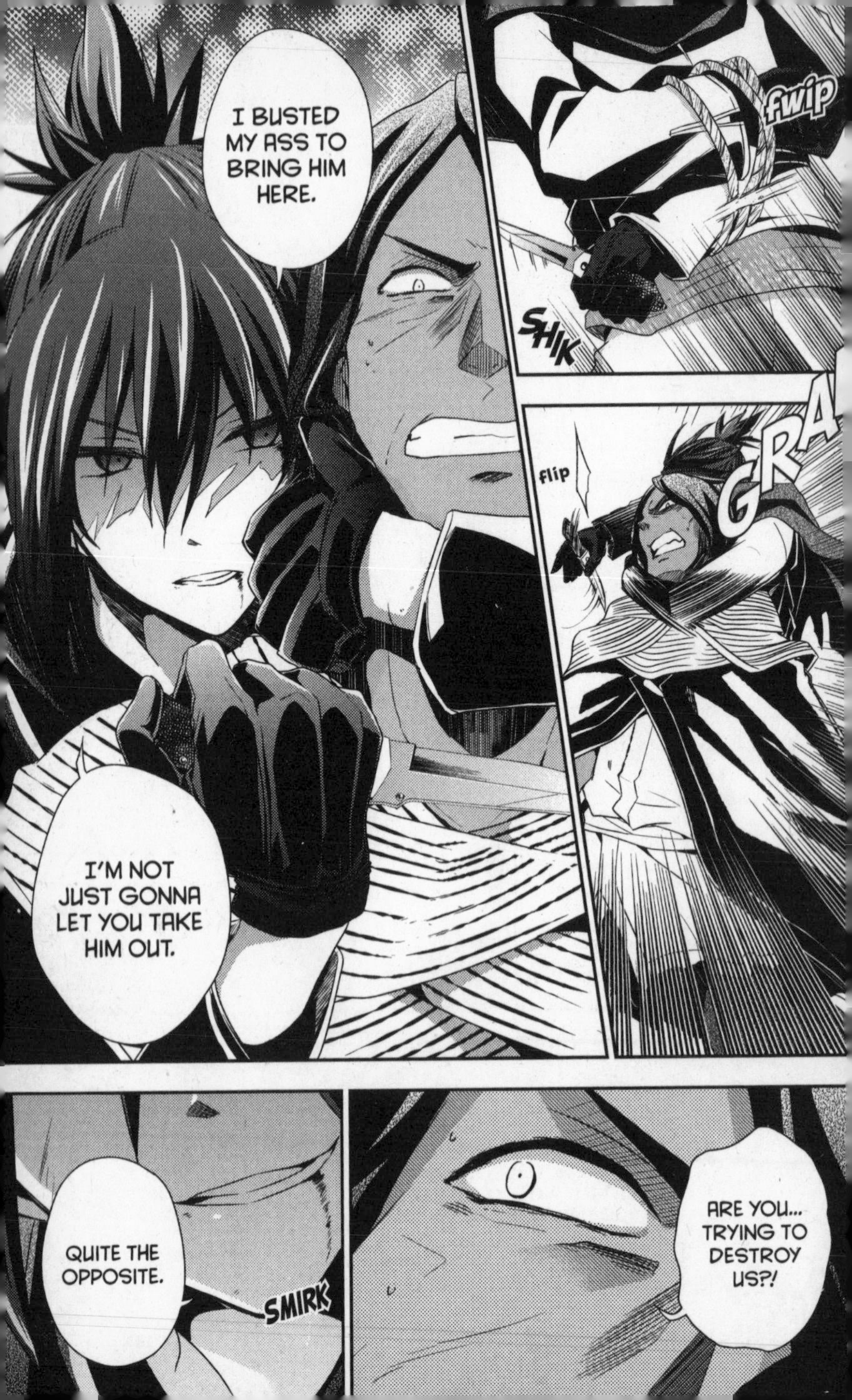
fwip
SHIK
flip
GRA
I BUSTED MY ASS TO BRING HIM HERE.
I'M NOT JUST GONNA LET YOU TAKE HIM OUT.
ARE YOU... TRYING TO DESTROY US?!
QUITE THE OPPOSITE.
SMIRK

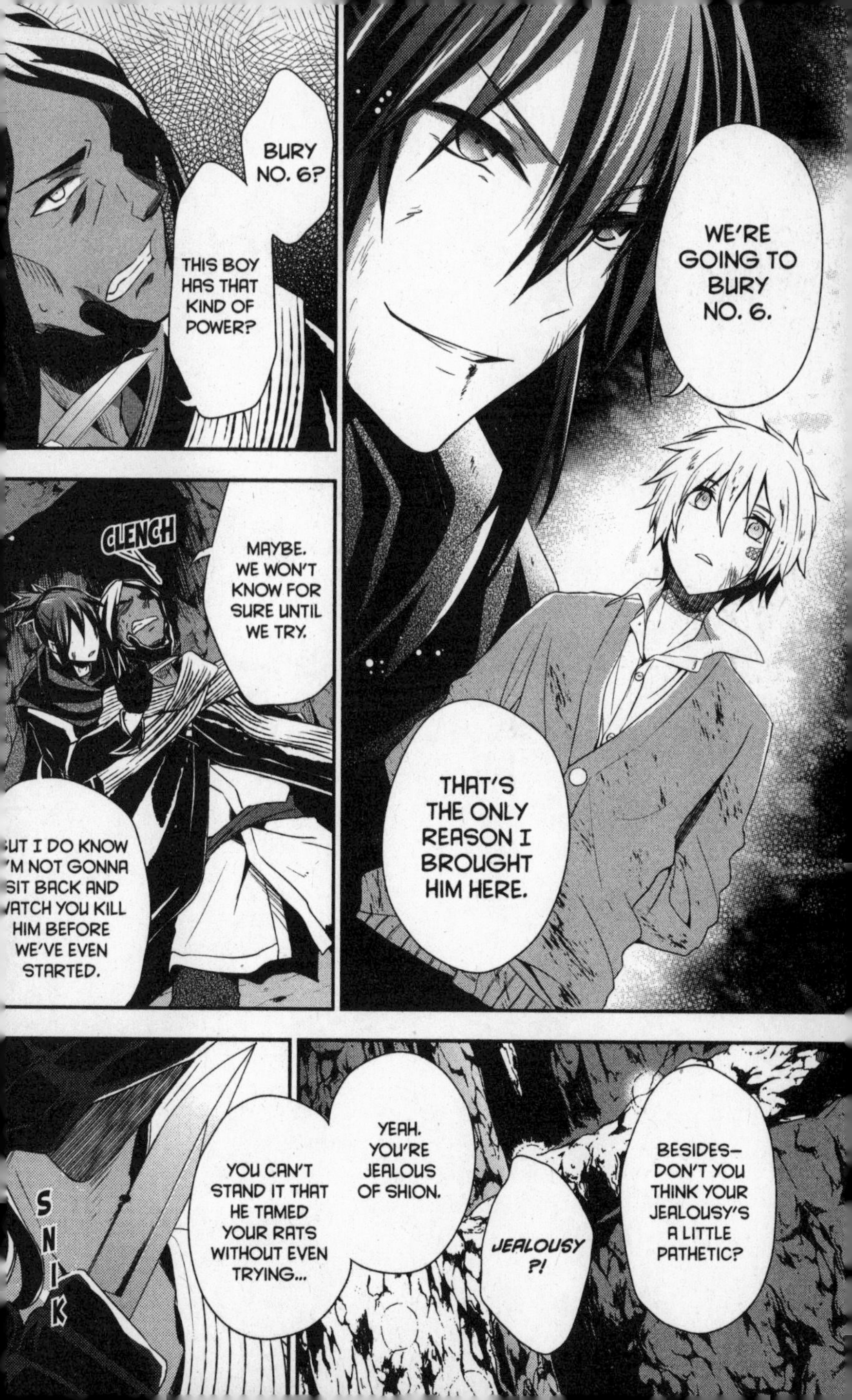
WE'RE GOING TO BURY NO. 6.
THAT'S THE ONLY REASON I BROUGHT HIM HERE.
BURY NO. 6?
THIS BOY HAS THAT KIND OF POWER?
CLENCH
MAYBE. WE WON'T KNOW FOR SURE UNTIL WE TRY.
UT I DO KNOW 'M NOT GONNA SIT BACK AND ATCH YOU KILL HIM BEFORE WE'VE EVEN STARTED.
BESIDES— DON'T YOU THINK YOUR JEALOUSY'S A LITTLE PATHETIC?
JEALOUSY?!
YEAH. YOU'RE JEALOUS OF SHION.
YOU CAN'T STAND IT THAT HE TAMED YOUR RATS WITHOUT EVEN TRYING...
SNIK

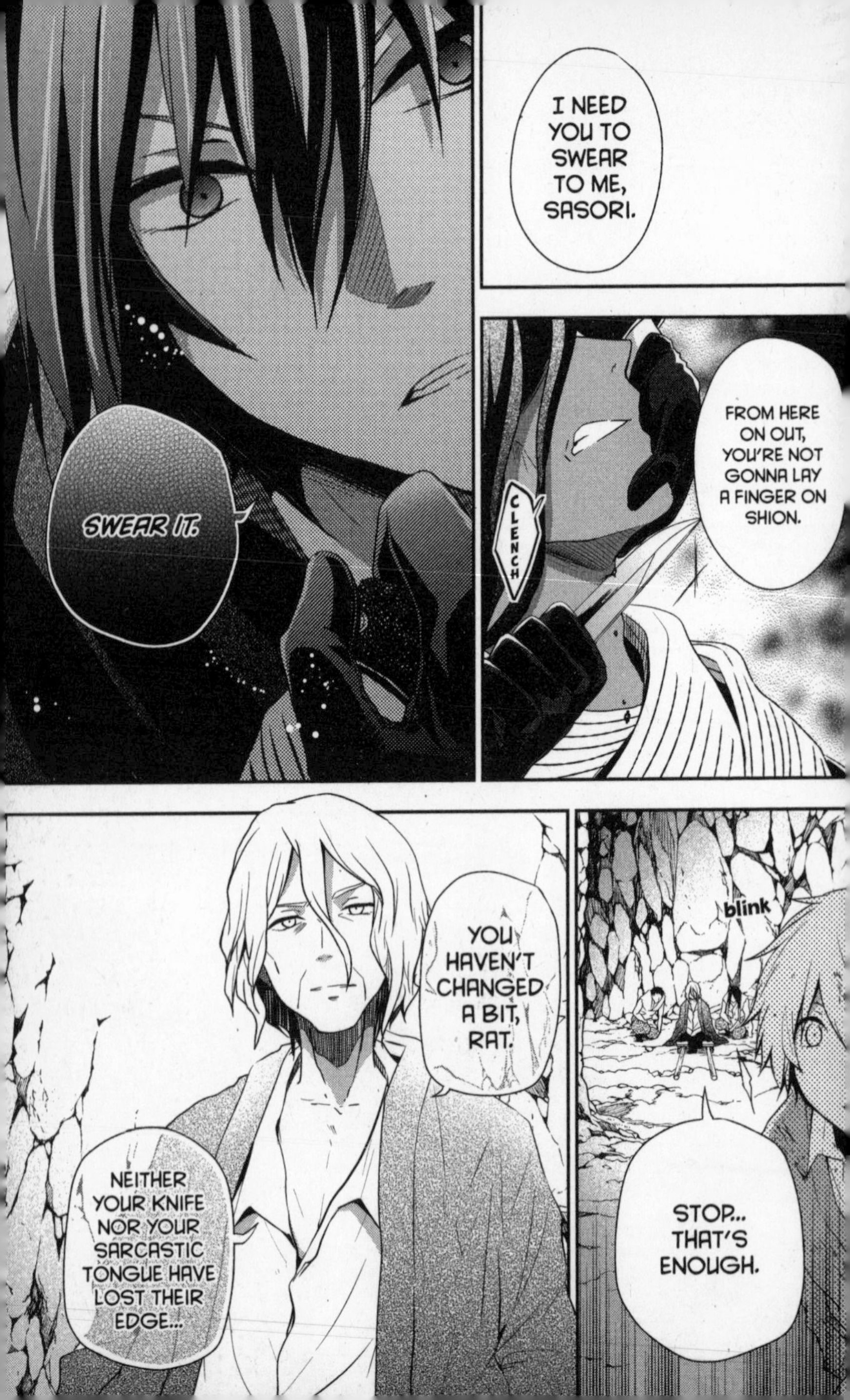
I NEED YOU TO SWEAR TO ME, SASORI.
FROM HERE ON OUT, YOU'RE NOT GONNA LAY A FINGER ON SHION.
CLENCH
SWEAR IT.
blink
STOP... THAT'S ENOUGH.
YOU HAVEN'T CHANGED A BIT, RAT.
NEITHER YOUR KNIFE NOR YOUR SARCASTIC TONGUE HAVE LOST THEIR EDGE...

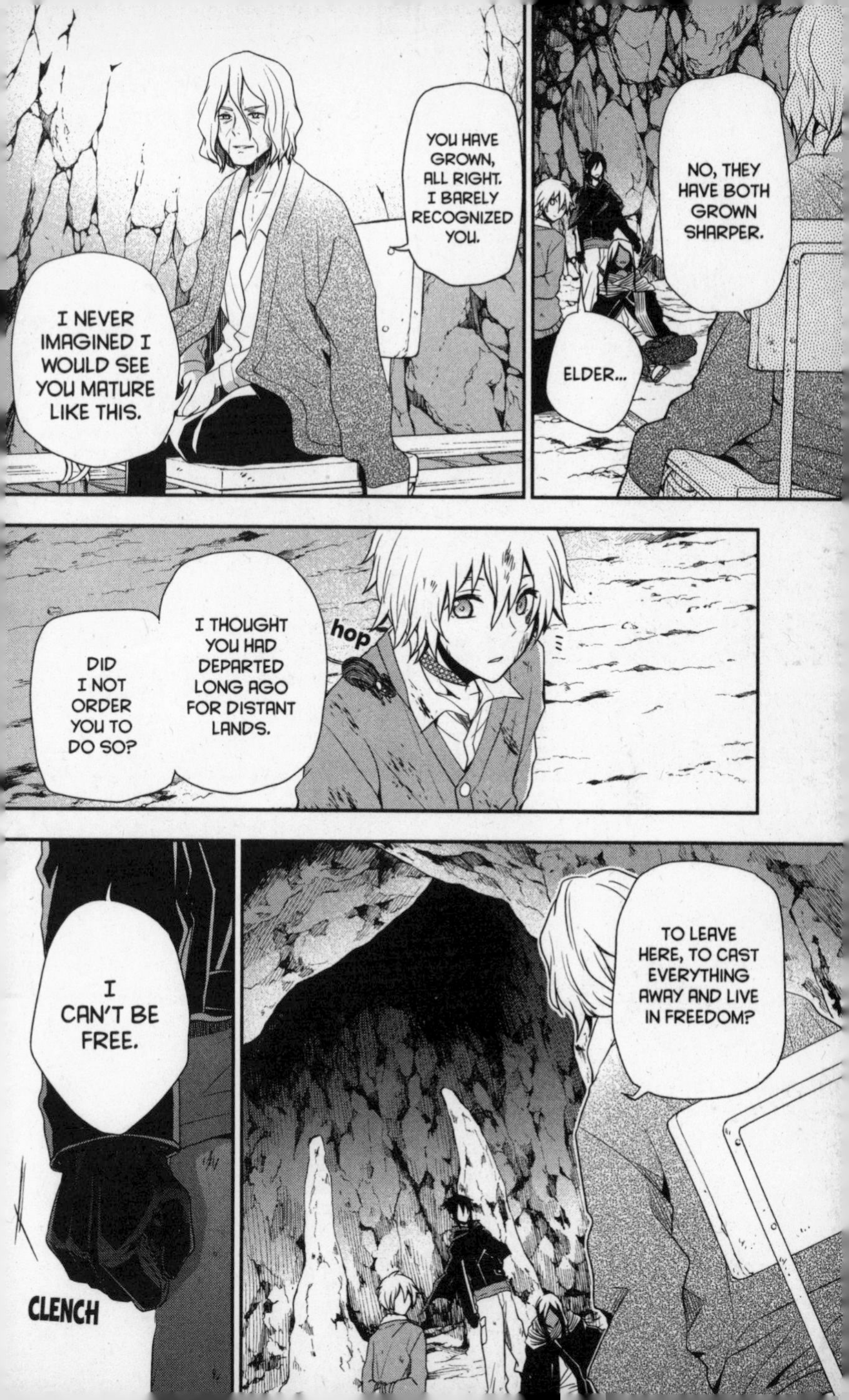
NO, THEY HAVE BOTH GROWN SHARPER.
ELDER...
YOU HAVE GROWN, ALL RIGHT. I BARELY RECOGNIZED YOU.
I NEVER IMAGINED I WOULD SEE YOU MATURE LIKE THIS.
hop
I THOUGHT YOU HAD DEPARTED LONG AGO FOR DISTANT LANDS.
DID I NOT ORDER YOU TO DO SO?
TO LEAVE HERE, TO CAST EVERYTHING AWAY AND LIVE IN FREEDOM?
I CAN'T BE FREE.
CLENCH

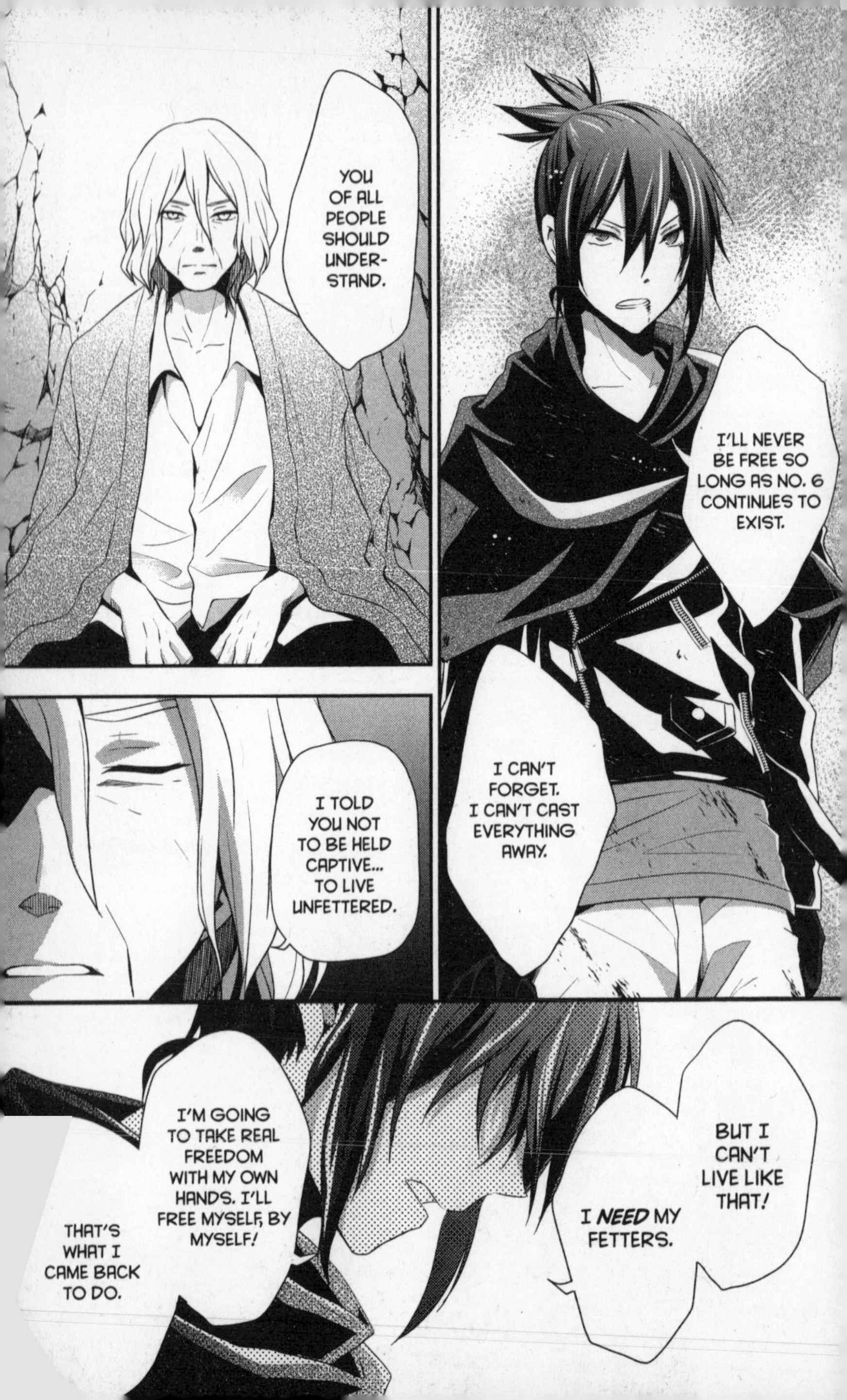
I'LL NEVER BE FREE SO LONG AS NO. 6 CONTINUES TO EXIST.
I CAN'T FORGET. I CAN'T CAST EVERYTHING AWAY.
YOU OF ALL PEOPLE SHOULD UNDER-STAND.
I TOLD YOU NOT TO BE HELD CAPTIVE... TO LIVE UNFETTERED.
BUT I CAN'T LIVE LIKE THAT!
I *NEED* MY FETTERS.
I'M GOING TO TAKE REAL FREEDOM WITH MY OWN HANDS. I'LL FREE MYSELF, BY MYSELF!
THAT'S WHAT I CAME BACK TO DO.

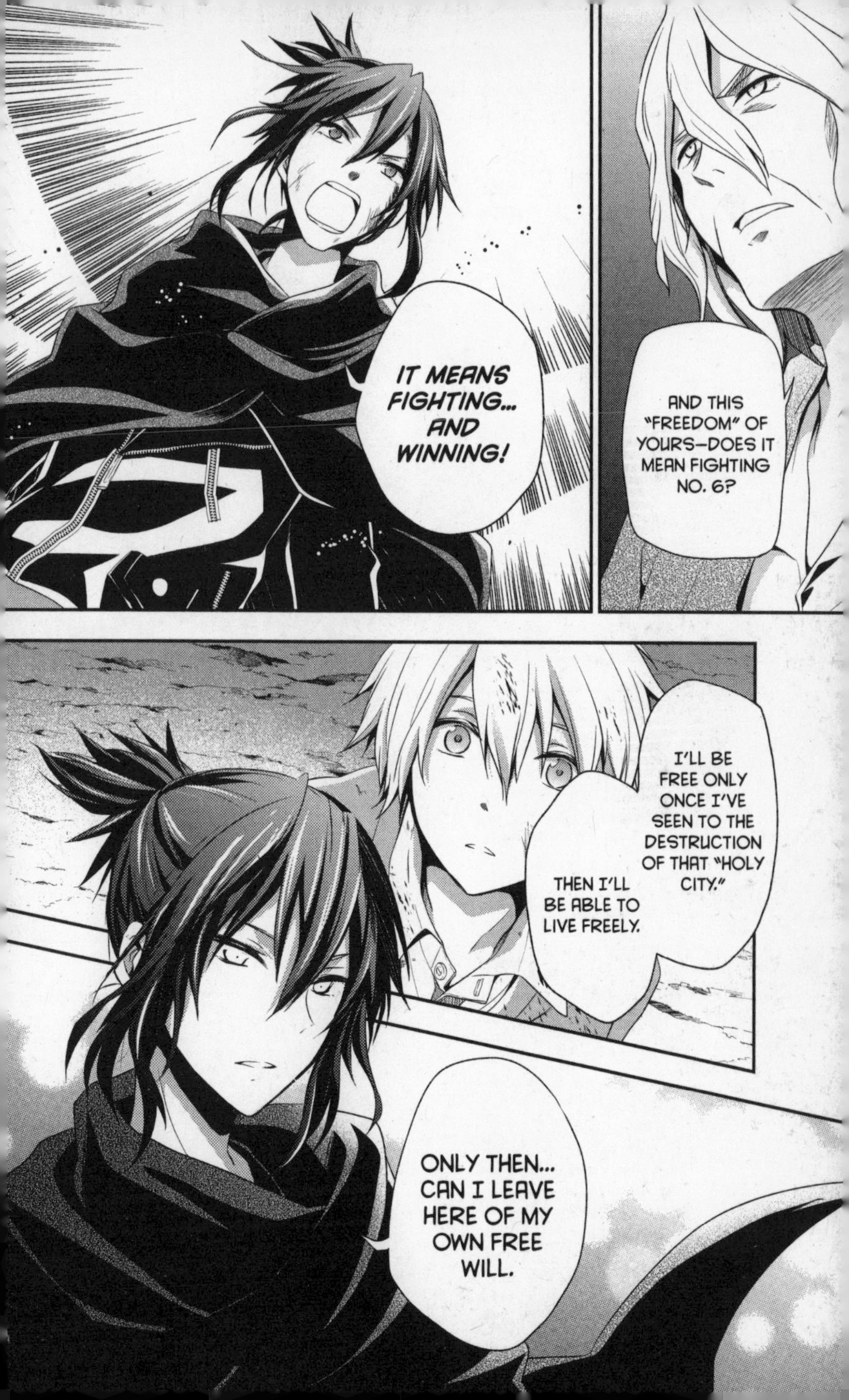
AND THIS "FREEDOM" OF YOURS—DOES IT MEAN FIGHTING NO. 6?
IT MEANS FIGHTING... AND WINNING!
I'LL BE FREE ONLY ONCE I'VE SEEN TO THE DESTRUCTION OF THAT "HOLY CITY."
THEN I'LL BE ABLE TO LIVE FREELY.
ONLY THEN... CAN I LEAVE HERE OF MY OWN FREE WILL.

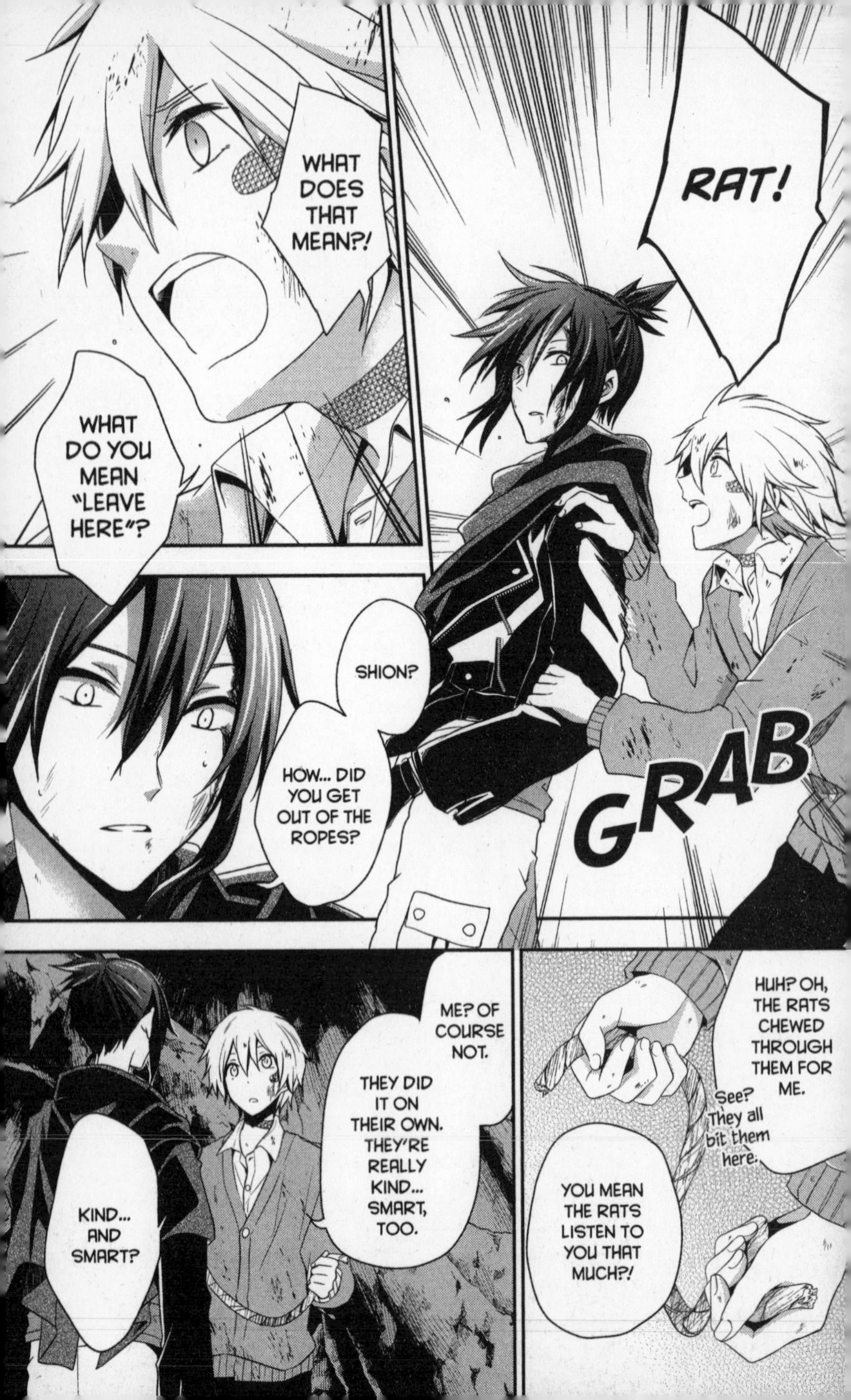
RAT!
GRAB
WHAT DOES THAT MEAN?!
WHAT DO YOU MEAN "LEAVE HERE"?
SHION?
HOW... DID YOU GET OUT OF THE ROPES?
HUH? OH, THE RATS CHEWED THROUGH THEM FOR ME.
See? They all bit them here.
YOU MEAN THE RATS LISTEN TO YOU THAT MUCH?!
ME? OF COURSE NOT.
THEY DID IT ON THEIR OWN. THEY'RE REALLY KIND... SMART, TOO.
KIND... AND SMART?

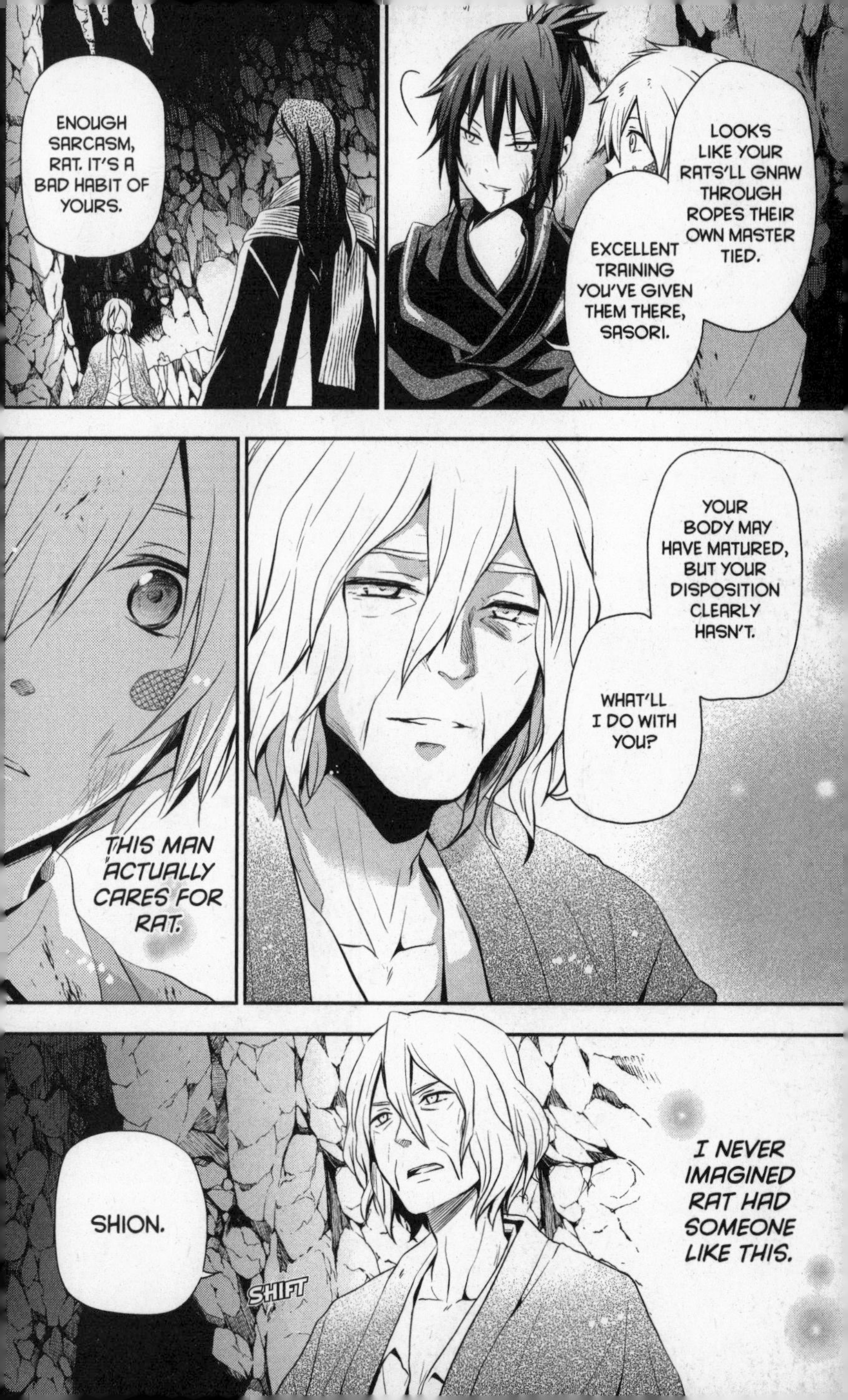
LOOKS LIKE YOUR RATS'LL GNAW THROUGH ROPES THEIR OWN MASTER TIED.
EXCELLENT TRAINING YOU'VE GIVEN THEM THERE, SASORI.
ENOUGH SARCASM, RAT. IT'S A BAD HABIT OF YOURS.
YOUR BODY MAY HAVE MATURED, BUT YOUR DISPOSITION CLEARLY HASN'T.
WHAT'LL I DO WITH YOU?
THIS MAN ACTUALLY CARES FOR RAT.
I NEVER IMAGINED RAT HAD SOMEONE LIKE THIS.
SHIFT
SHION.

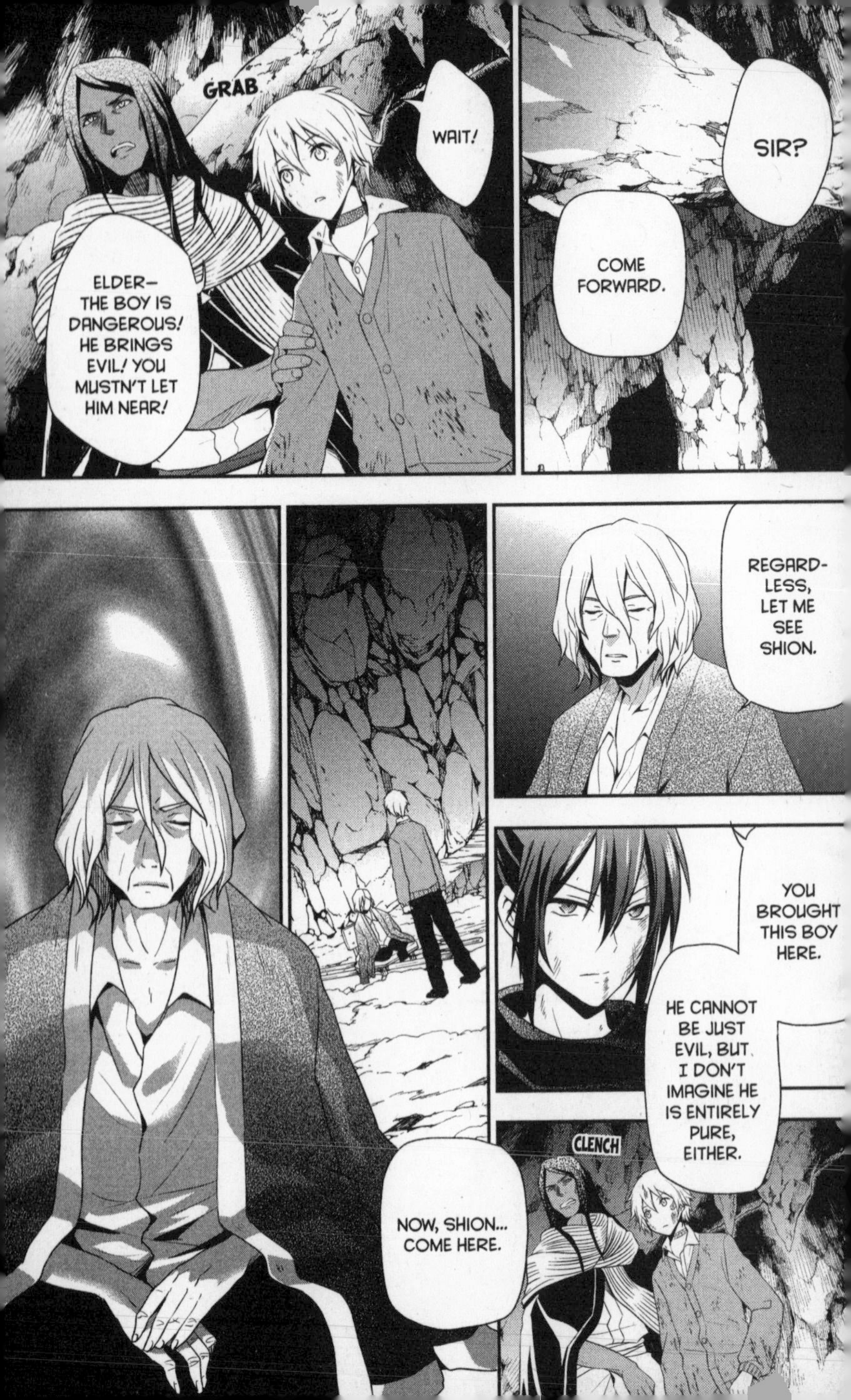
SIR?
COME FORWARD.
WAIT!
GRAB
ELDER— THE BOY IS DANGEROUS! HE BRINGS EVIL! YOU MUSTN'T LET HIM NEAR!
REGARDLESS, LET ME SEE SHION.
YOU BROUGHT THIS BOY HERE.
HE CANNOT BE JUST EVIL, BUT I DON'T IMAGINE HE IS ENTIRELY PURE, EITHER.
CLENCH
NOW, SHION... COME HERE.

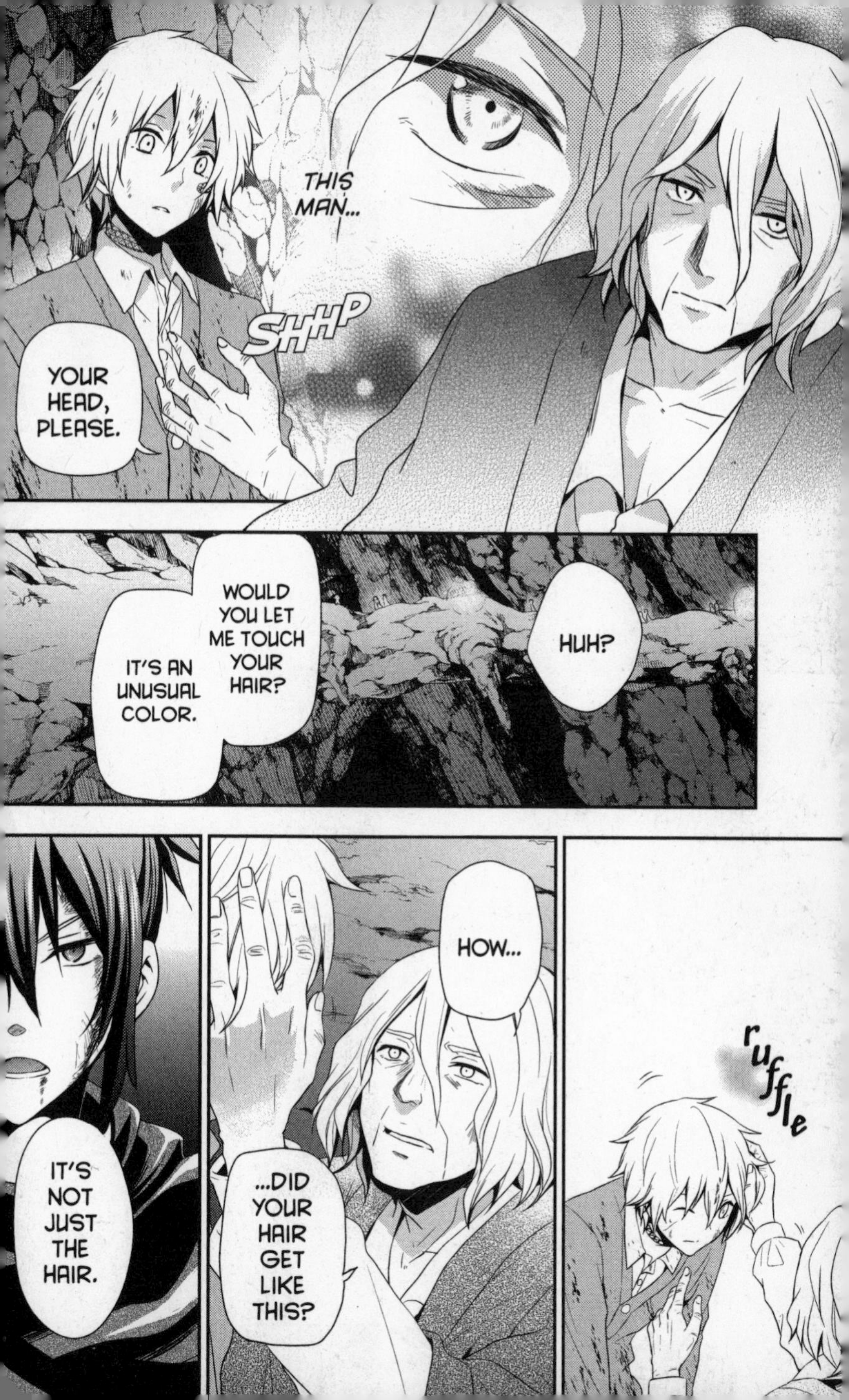
THIS MAN...
SHHP
YOUR HEAD, PLEASE.
HUH?
WOULD YOU LET ME TOUCH YOUR HAIR?
IT'S AN UNUSUAL COLOR.
ruffle
HOW...
...DID YOUR HAIR GET LIKE THIS?
IT'S NOT JUST THE HAIR.

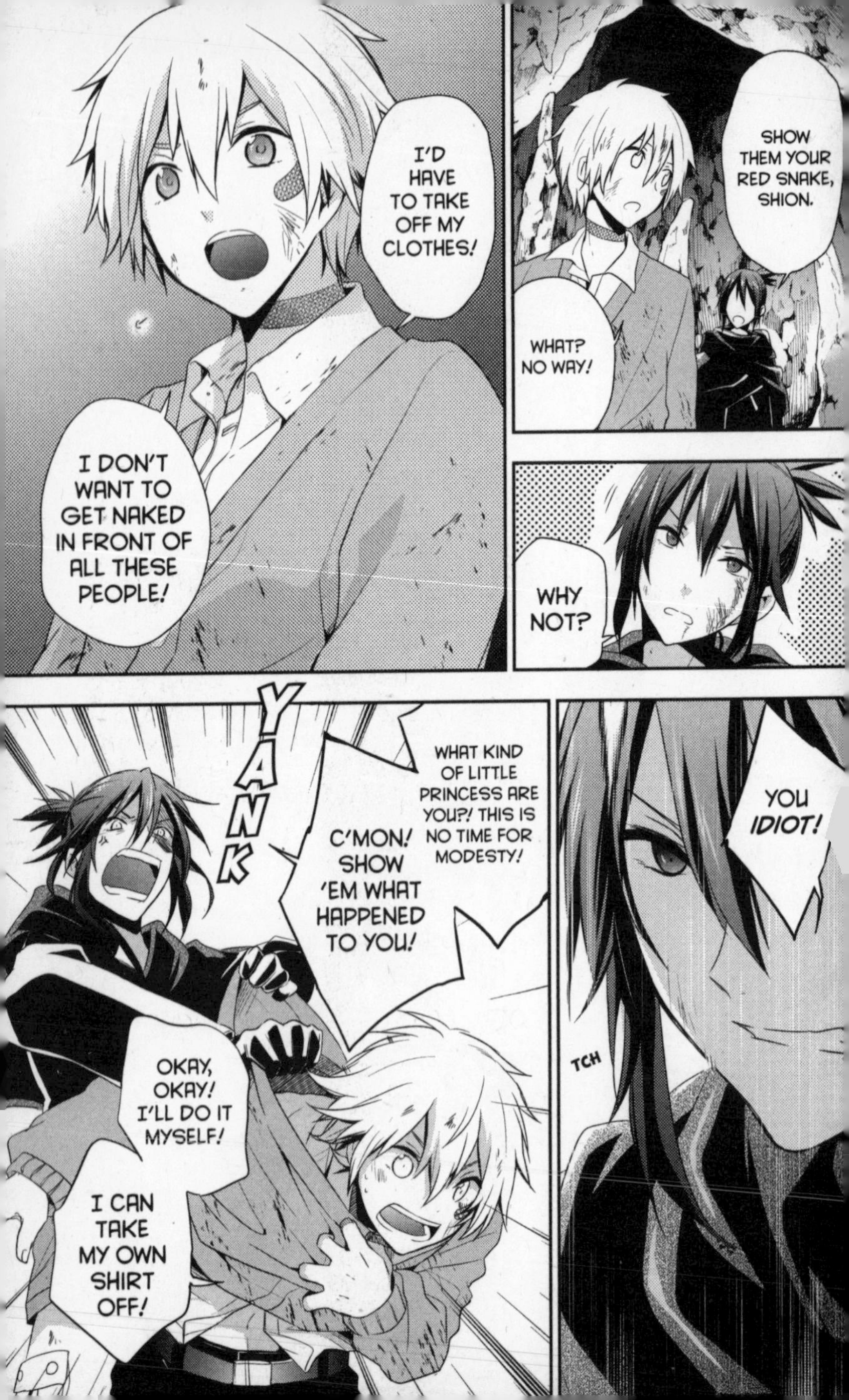
SHOW THEM YOUR RED SNAKE, SHION.
WHAT? NO WAY!
WHY NOT?
I'D HAVE TO TAKE OFF MY CLOTHES!
I DON'T WANT TO GET NAKED IN FRONT OF ALL THESE PEOPLE!
YOU IDIOT!
TCH
YANK
WHAT KIND OF LITTLE PRINCESS ARE YOU?! THIS IS NO TIME FOR MODESTY!
C'MON! SHOW 'EM WHAT HAPPENED TO YOU!
OKAY, OKAY! I'LL DO IT MYSELF!
I CAN TAKE MY OWN SHIRT OFF!

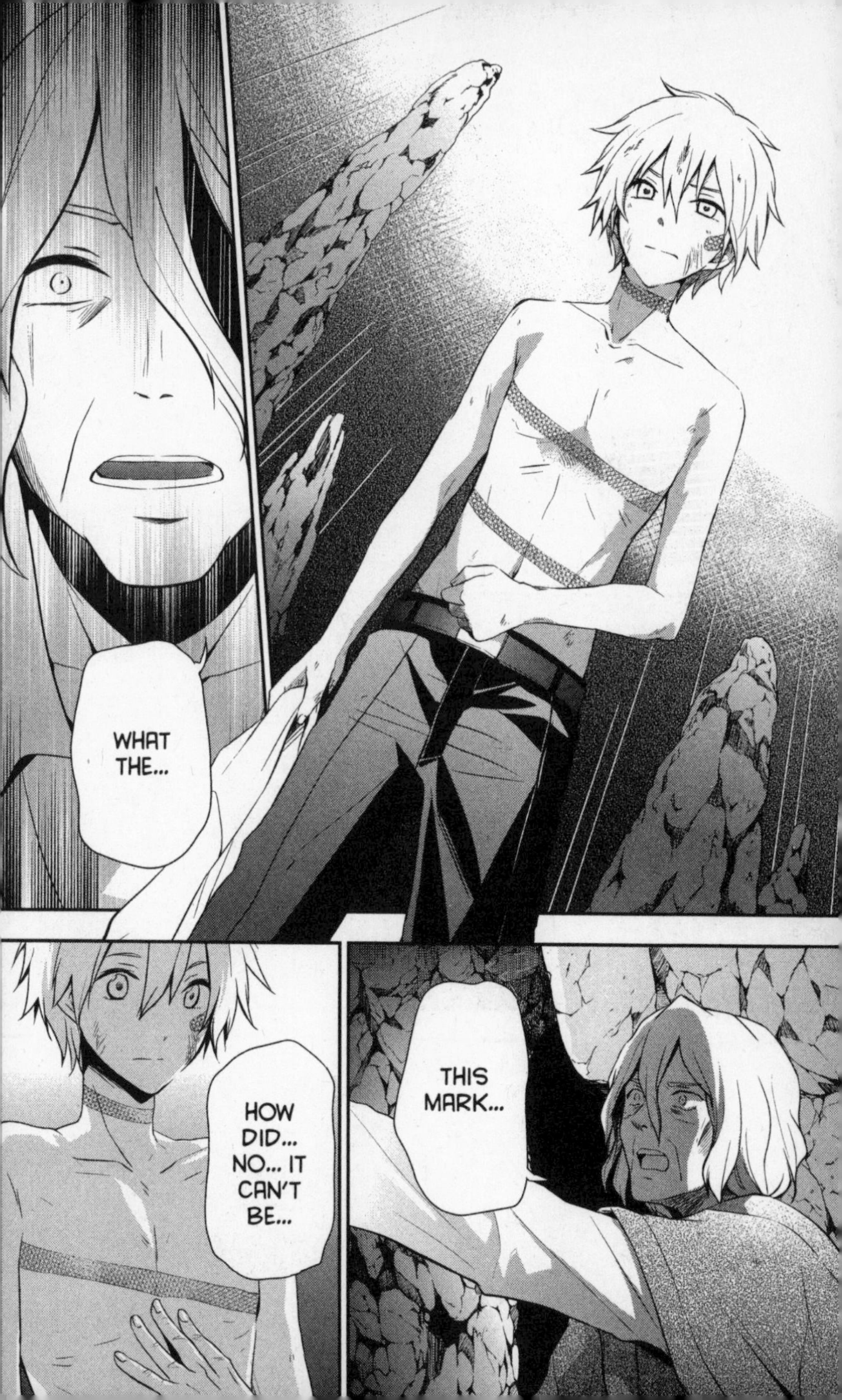
WHAT THE...
THIS MARK...
HOW DID... NO... IT CAN'T BE...

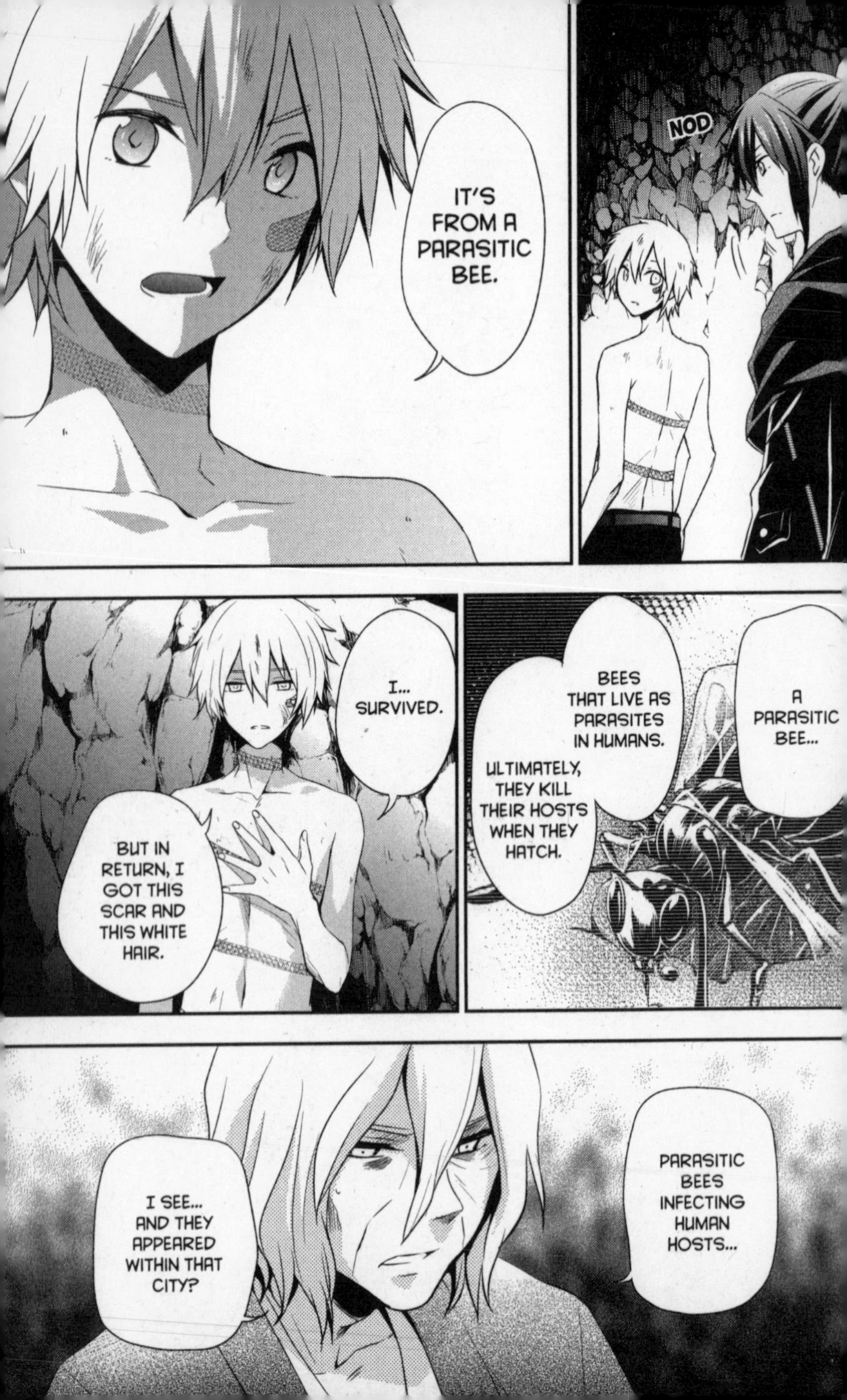
NOD
IT'S FROM A PARASITIC BEE.
A PARASITIC BEE...
BEES THAT LIVE AS PARASITES IN HUMANS.
ULTIMATELY, THEY KILL THEIR HOSTS WHEN THEY HATCH.
I... SURVIVED.
BUT IN RETURN, I GOT THIS SCAR AND THIS WHITE HAIR.
PARASITIC BEES INFECTING HUMAN HOSTS...
I SEE... AND THEY APPEARED WITHIN THAT CITY?

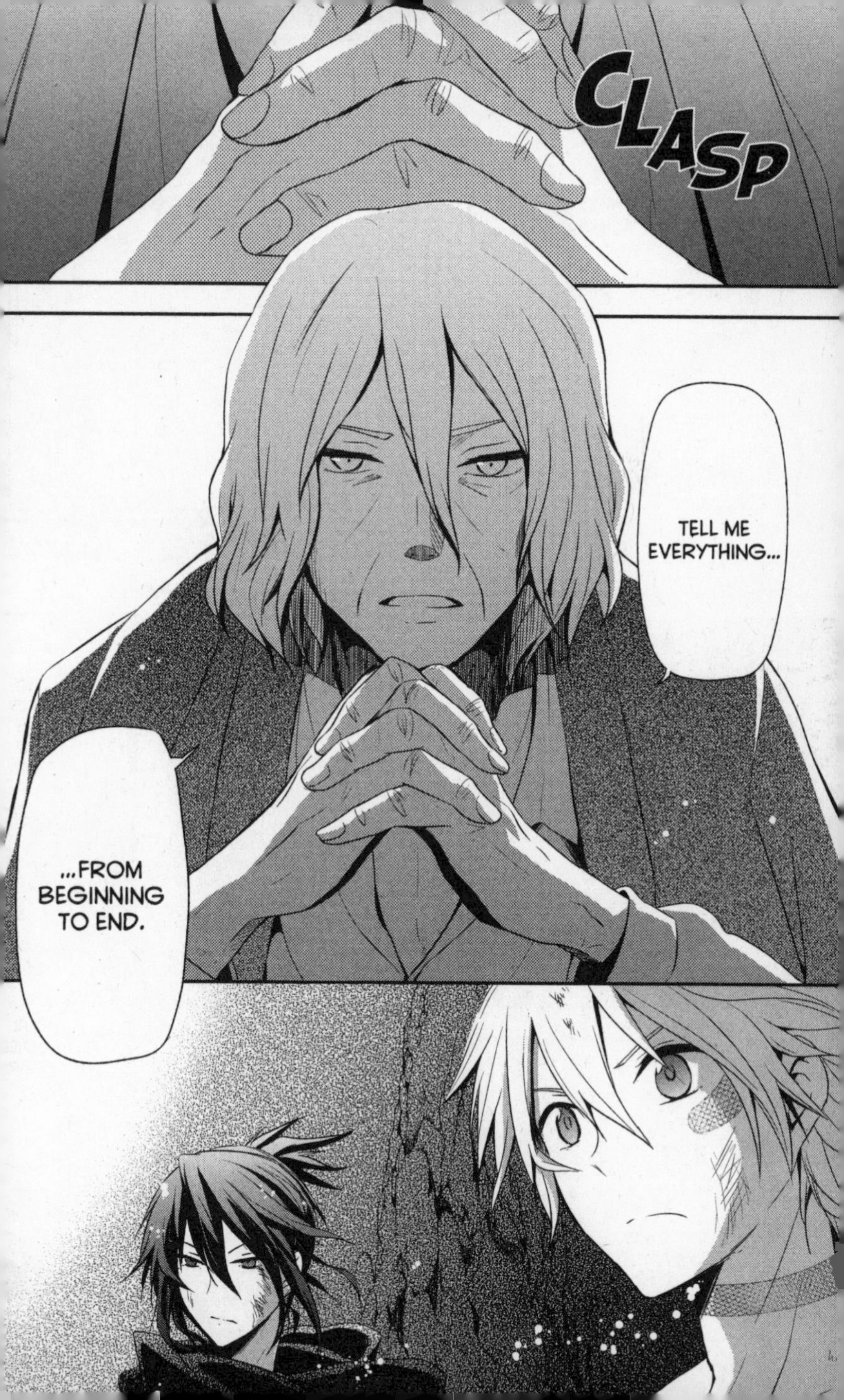
CLASP
TELL ME EVERYTHING...
...FROM BEGINNING TO END.

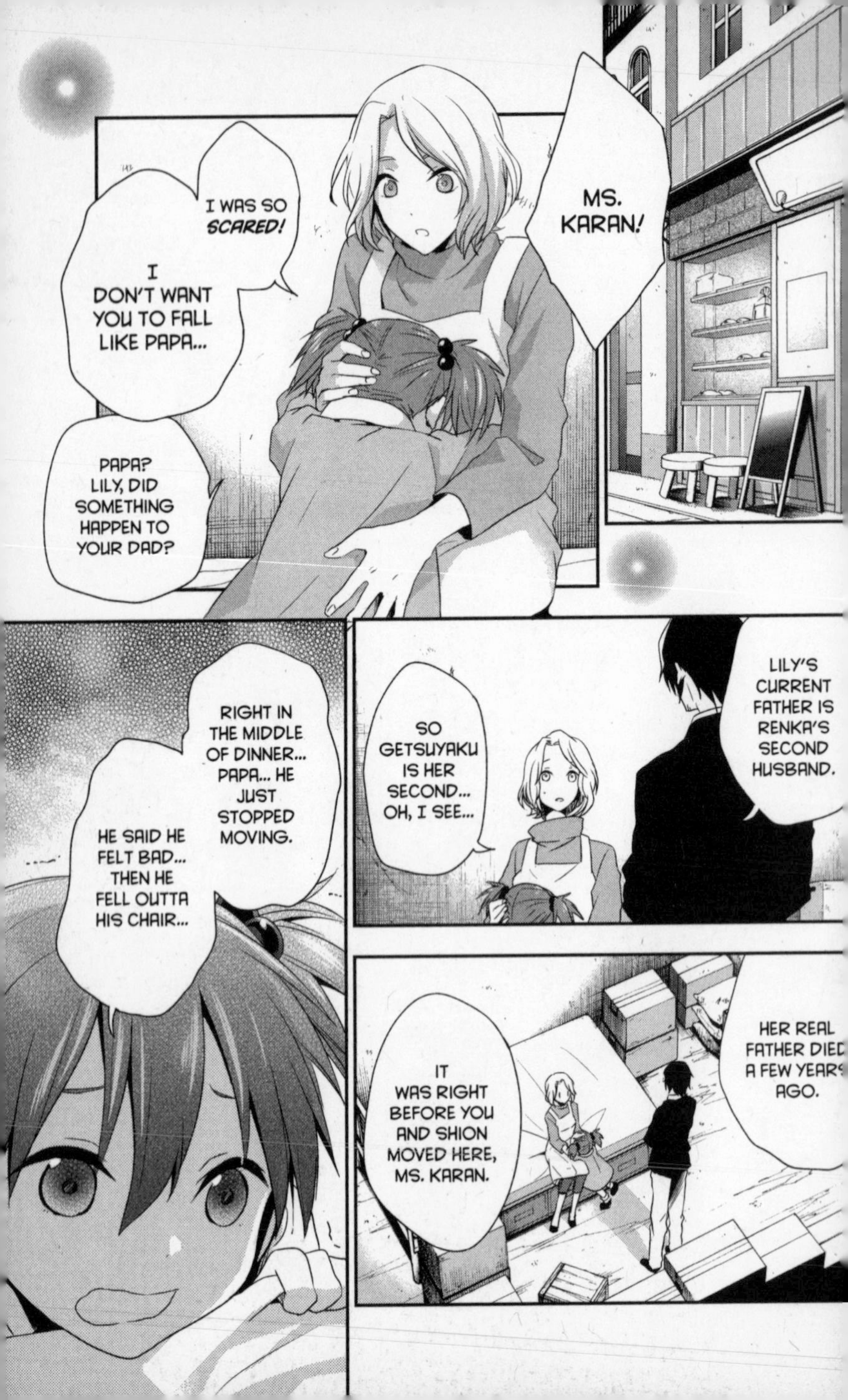
MS. KARAN!
I WAS SO *SCARED!*
I DON'T WANT YOU TO FALL LIKE PAPA...
PAPA? LILY, DID SOMETHING HAPPEN TO YOUR DAD?
LILY'S CURRENT FATHER IS RENKA'S SECOND HUSBAND.
SO GETSUYAKU IS HER SECOND... OH, I SEE...
HER REAL FATHER DIED A FEW YEARS AGO.
IT WAS RIGHT BEFORE YOU AND SHION MOVED HERE, MS. KARAN.
RIGHT IN THE MIDDLE OF DINNER... PAPA... HE JUST STOPPED MOVING.
HE SAID HE FELT BAD... THEN HE FELL OUTTA HIS CHAIR...

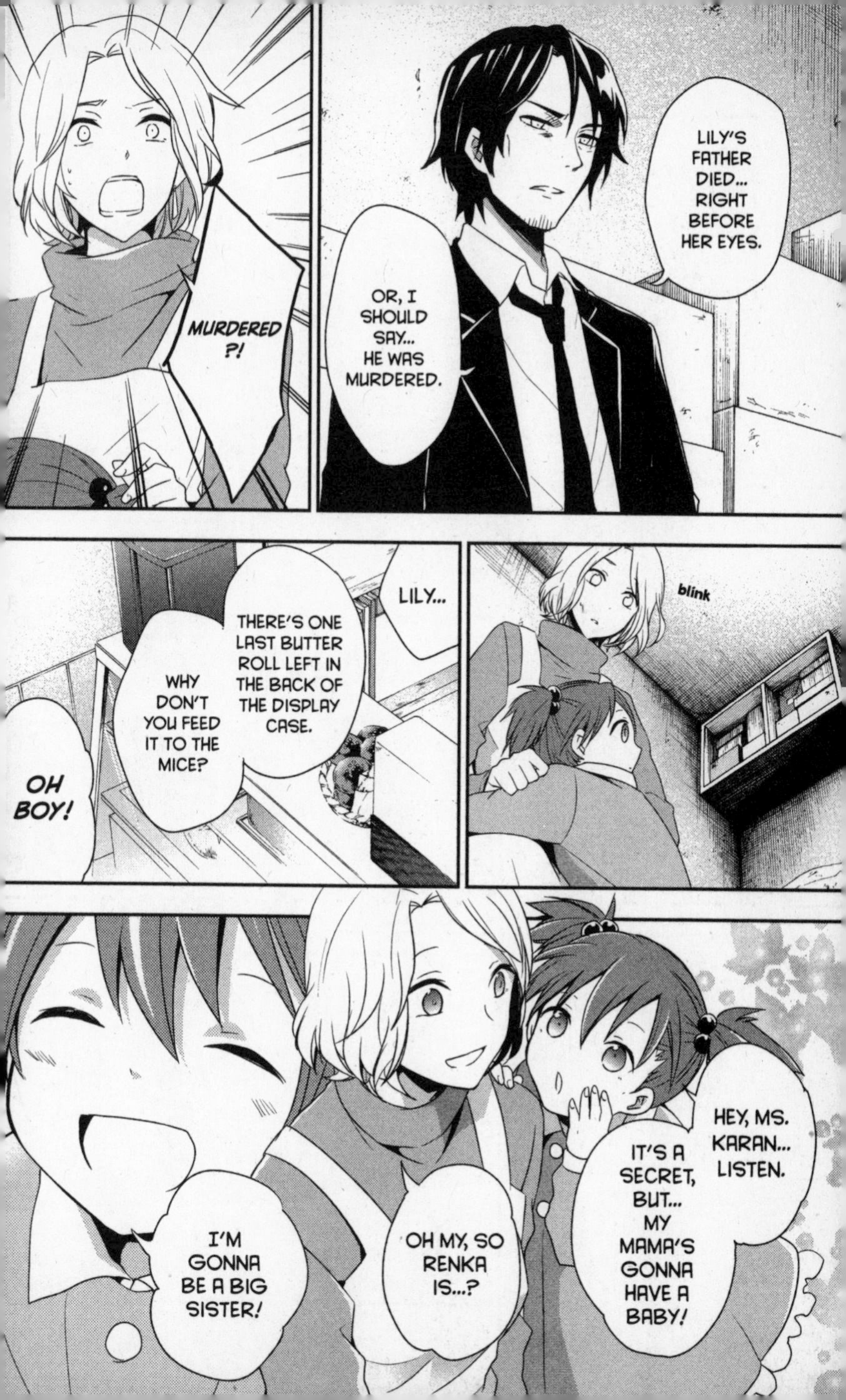
LILY'S FATHER DIED... RIGHT BEFORE HER EYES.
OR, I SHOULD SAY... HE WAS MURDERED.
MURDERED?!
blink
LILY...
THERE'S ONE LAST BUTTER ROLL LEFT IN THE BACK OF THE DISPLAY CASE.
WHY DON'T YOU FEED IT TO THE MICE?
OH BOY!
HEY, MS. KARAN... LISTEN.
IT'S A SECRET, BUT... MY MAMA'S GONNA HAVE A BABY!
OH MY, SO RENKA IS...?
I'M GONNA BE A BIG SISTER!

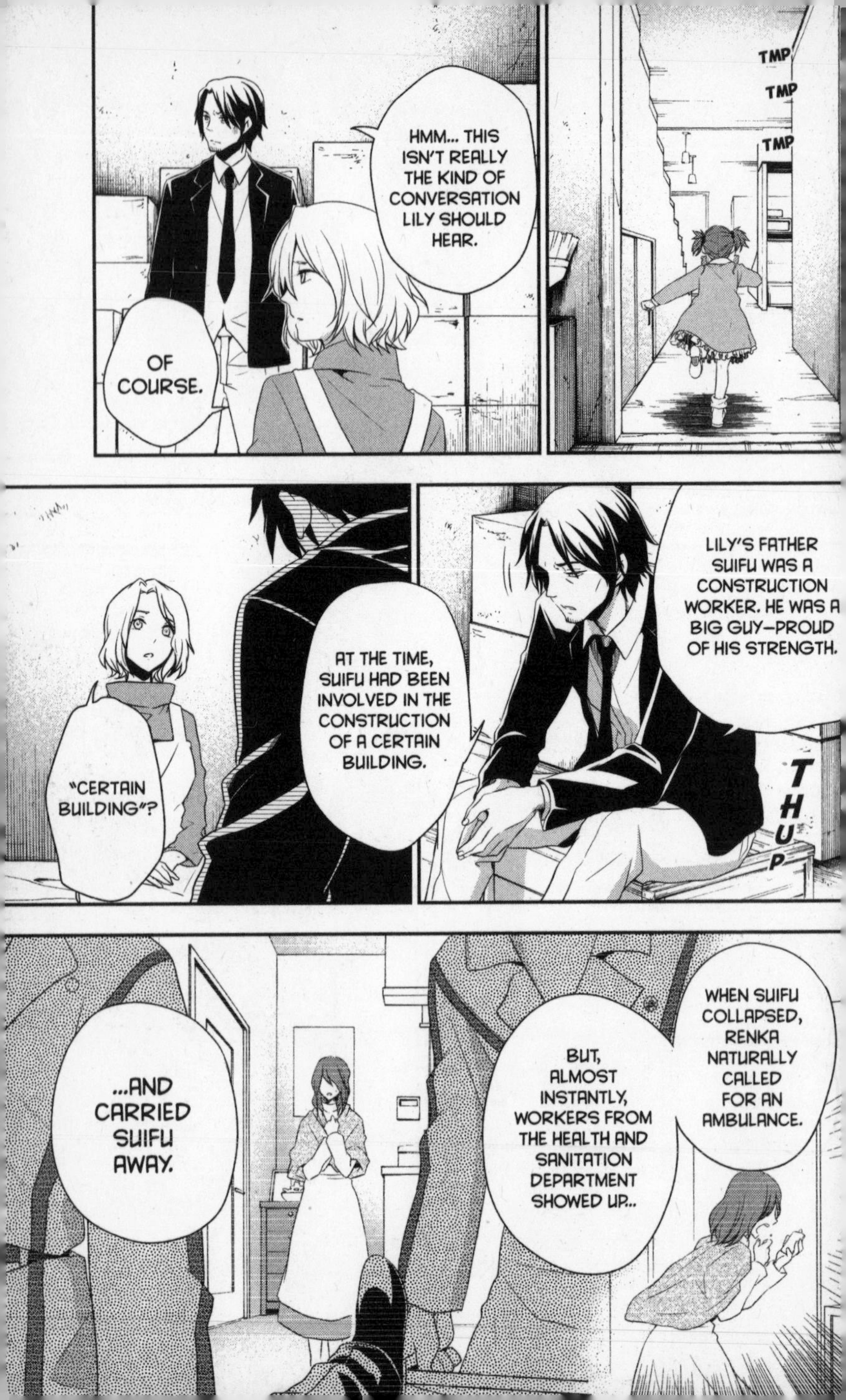
TMP
TMP
TMP
HMM... THIS ISN'T REALLY THE KIND OF CONVERSATION LILY SHOULD HEAR.
OF COURSE.
LILY'S FATHER SUIFU WAS A CONSTRUCTION WORKER. HE WAS A BIG GUY—PROUD OF HIS STRENGTH.
THUP
AT THE TIME, SUIFU HAD BEEN INVOLVED IN THE CONSTRUCTION OF A CERTAIN BUILDING.
"CERTAIN BUILDING"?
WHEN SUIFU COLLAPSED, RENKA NATURALLY CALLED FOR AN AMBULANCE.
BUT, ALMOST INSTANTLY, WORKERS FROM THE HEALTH AND SANITATION DEPARTMENT SHOWED UP...
...AND CARRIED SUIFU AWAY.

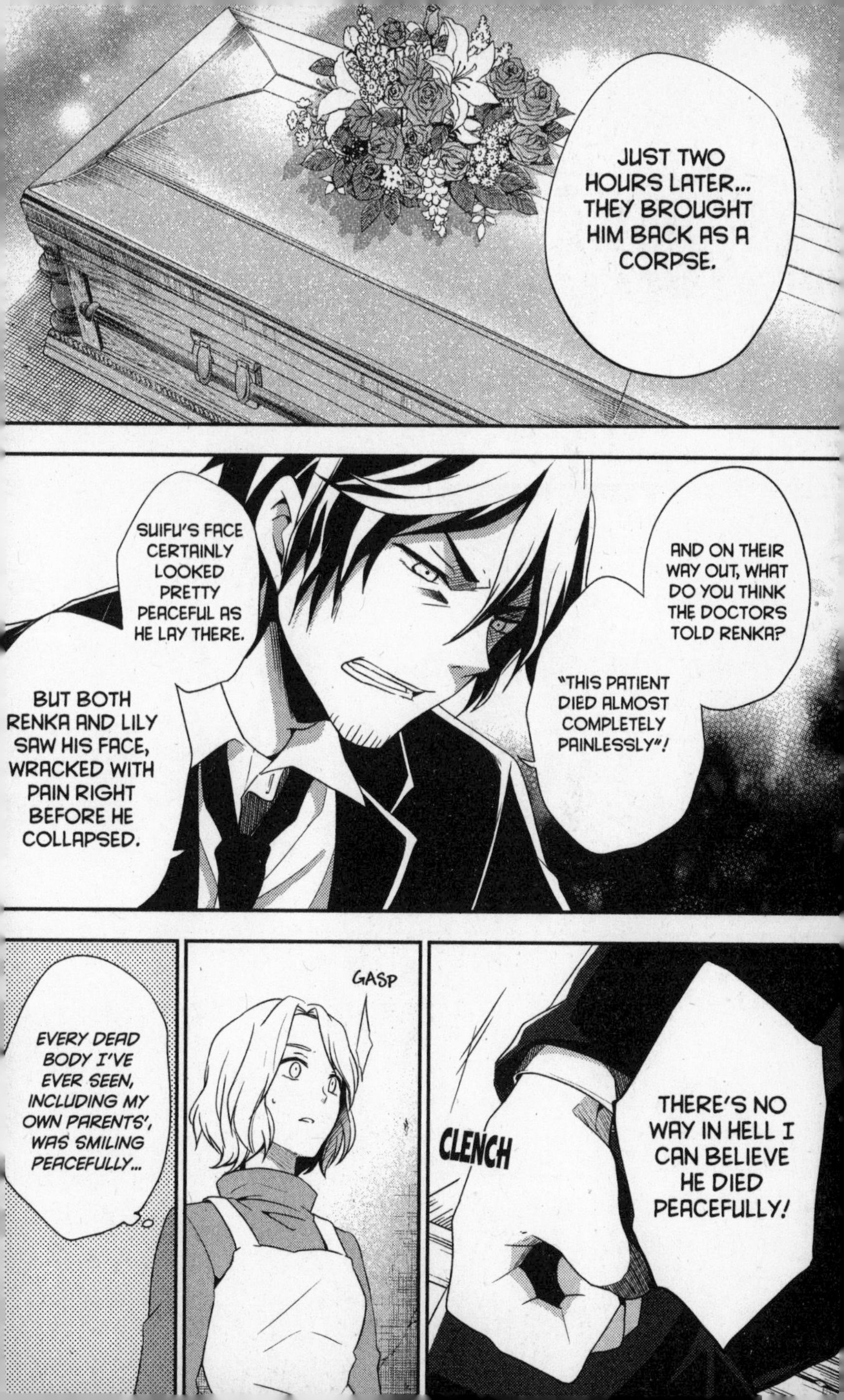
JUST TWO HOURS LATER... THEY BROUGHT HIM BACK AS A CORPSE.
AND ON THEIR WAY OUT, WHAT DO YOU THINK THE DOCTORS TOLD RENKA?
"THIS PATIENT DIED ALMOST COMPLETELY PAINLESSLY"!
SUIFU'S FACE CERTAINLY LOOKED PRETTY PEACEFUL AS HE LAY THERE.
BUT BOTH RENKA AND LILY SAW HIS FACE, WRACKED WITH PAIN RIGHT BEFORE HE COLLAPSED.
THERE'S NO WAY IN HELL I CAN BELIEVE HE DIED PEACEFULLY!
CLENCH
GASP
EVERY DEAD BODY I'VE EVER SEEN, INCLUDING MY OWN PARENTS', WAS SMILING PEACEFULLY...

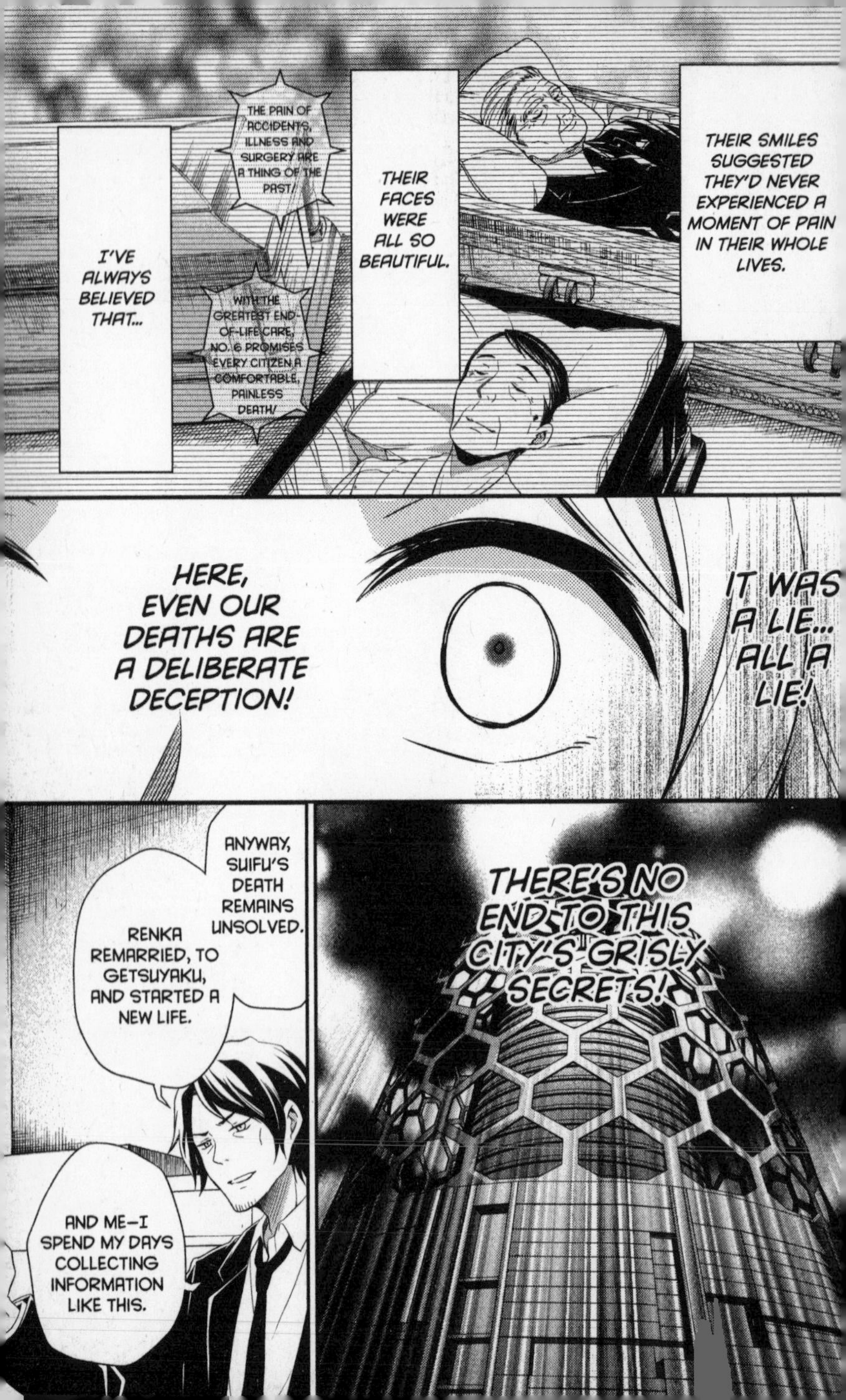
THEIR SMILES SUGGESTED THEY'D NEVER EXPERIENCED A MOMENT OF PAIN IN THEIR WHOLE LIVES.
THEIR FACES WERE ALL SO BEAUTIFUL.
THE PAIN OF ACCIDENTS, ILLNESS AND SURGERY ARE A THING OF THE PAST!
I'VE ALWAYS BELIEVED THAT...
WITH THE GREATEST END-OF-LIFE CARE, NO. 6 PROMISES EVERY CITIZEN A COMFORTABLE, PAINLESS DEATH!
IT WAS A LIE... ALL A LIE!
HERE, EVEN OUR DEATHS ARE A DELIBERATE DECEPTION!
THERE'S NO END TO THIS CITY'S GRISLY SECRETS!
ANYWAY, SUIFU'S DEATH REMAINS UNSOLVED.
RENKA REMARRIED, TO GETSUYAKU, AND STARTED A NEW LIFE.
AND ME—I SPEND MY DAYS COLLECTING INFORMATION LIKE THIS.

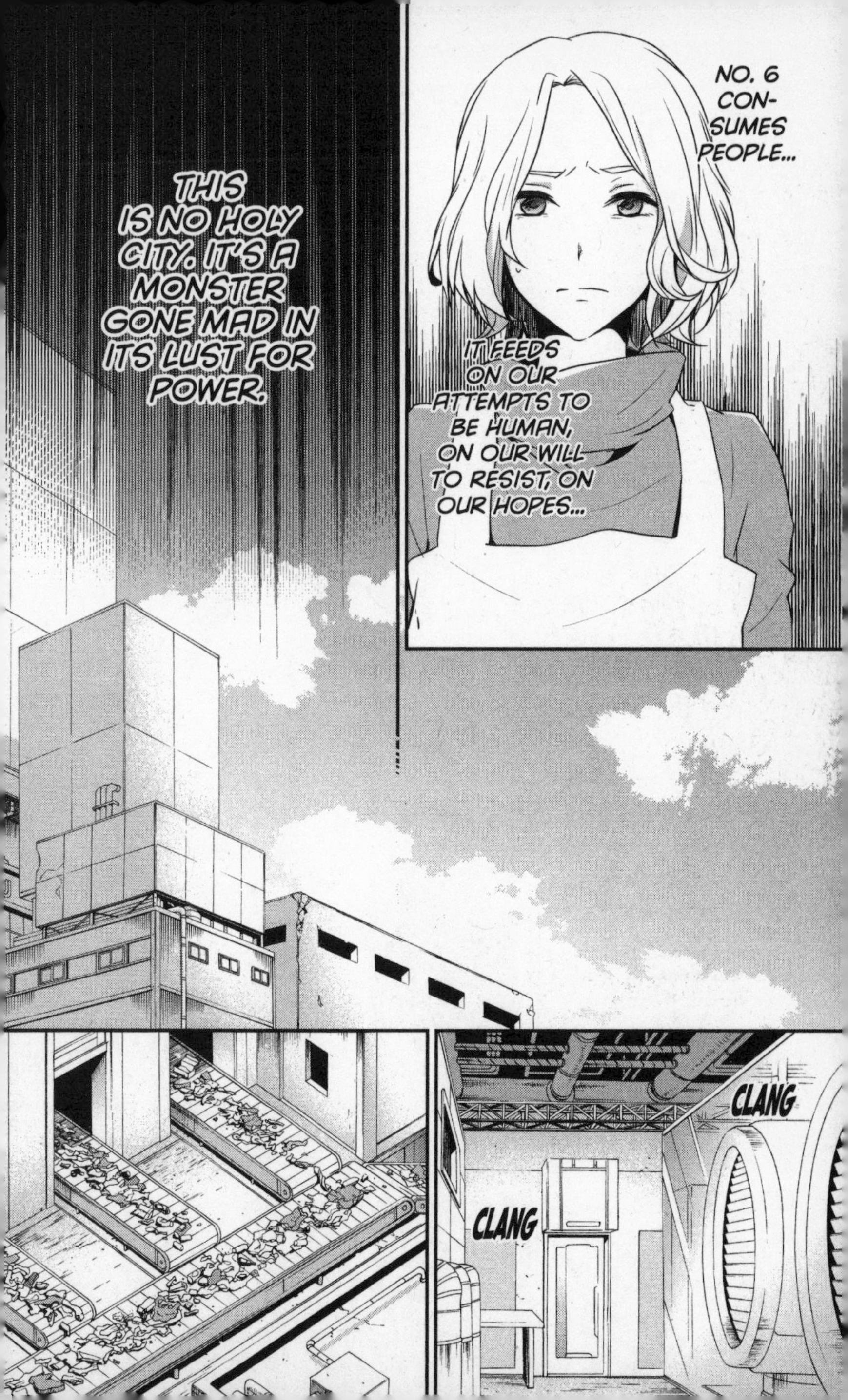
NO. 6 CON-SUMES PEOPLE...
IT FEEDS ON OUR ATTEMPTS TO BE HUMAN, ON OUR WILL TO RESIST, ON OUR HOPES...
THIS IS NO HOLY CITY. IT'S A MONSTER GONE MAD IN ITS LUST FOR POWER.
CLANG
CLANG

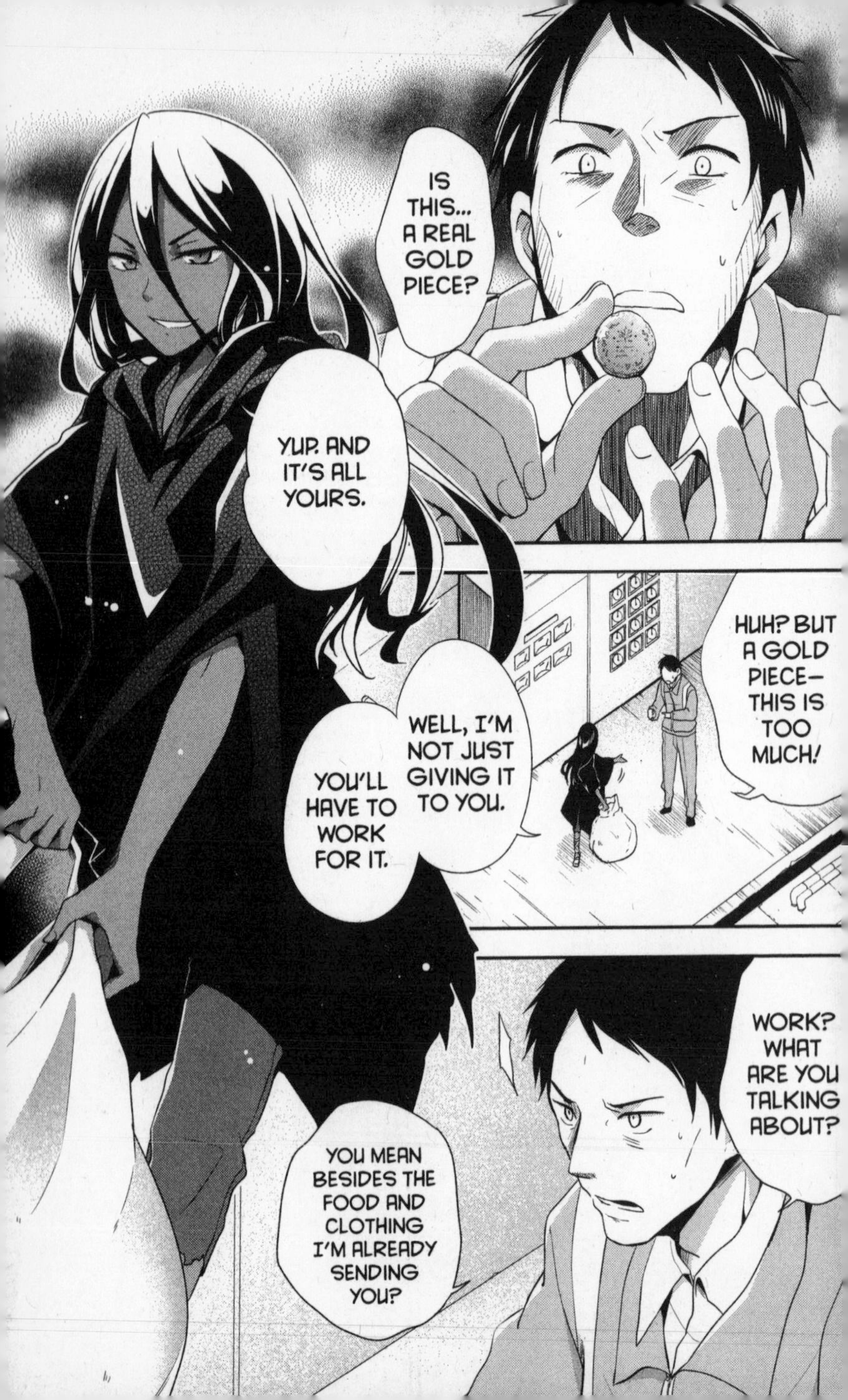
IS THIS... A REAL GOLD PIECE?
YUP. AND IT'S ALL YOURS.
HUH? BUT A GOLD PIECE— THIS IS TOO MUCH!
WELL, I'M NOT JUST GIVING IT TO YOU.
YOU'LL HAVE TO WORK FOR IT.
WORK? WHAT ARE YOU TALKING ABOUT?
YOU MEAN BESIDES THE FOOD AND CLOTHING I'M ALREADY SENDING YOU?

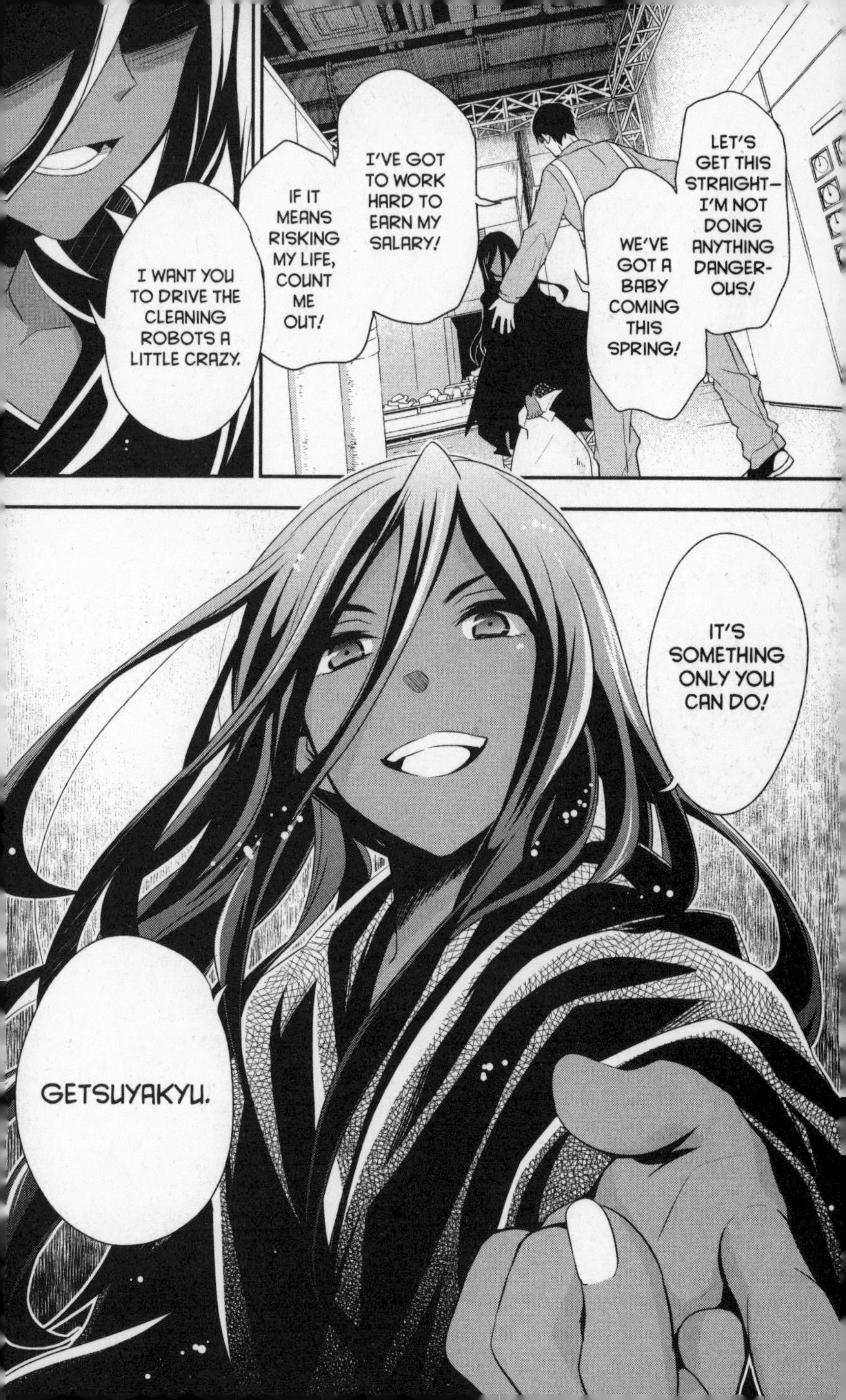
LET'S GET THIS STRAIGHT— I'M NOT DOING ANYTHING DANGER-OUS!
WE'VE GOT A BABY COMING THIS SPRING!
I'VE GOT TO WORK HARD TO EARN MY SALARY!
IF IT MEANS RISKING MY LIFE, COUNT ME OUT!
I WANT YOU TO DRIVE THE CLEANING ROBOTS A LITTLE CRAZY.
IT'S SOMETHING ONLY YOU CAN DO!
GETSUYAKYU.

Chapter 22: That Reason Is...

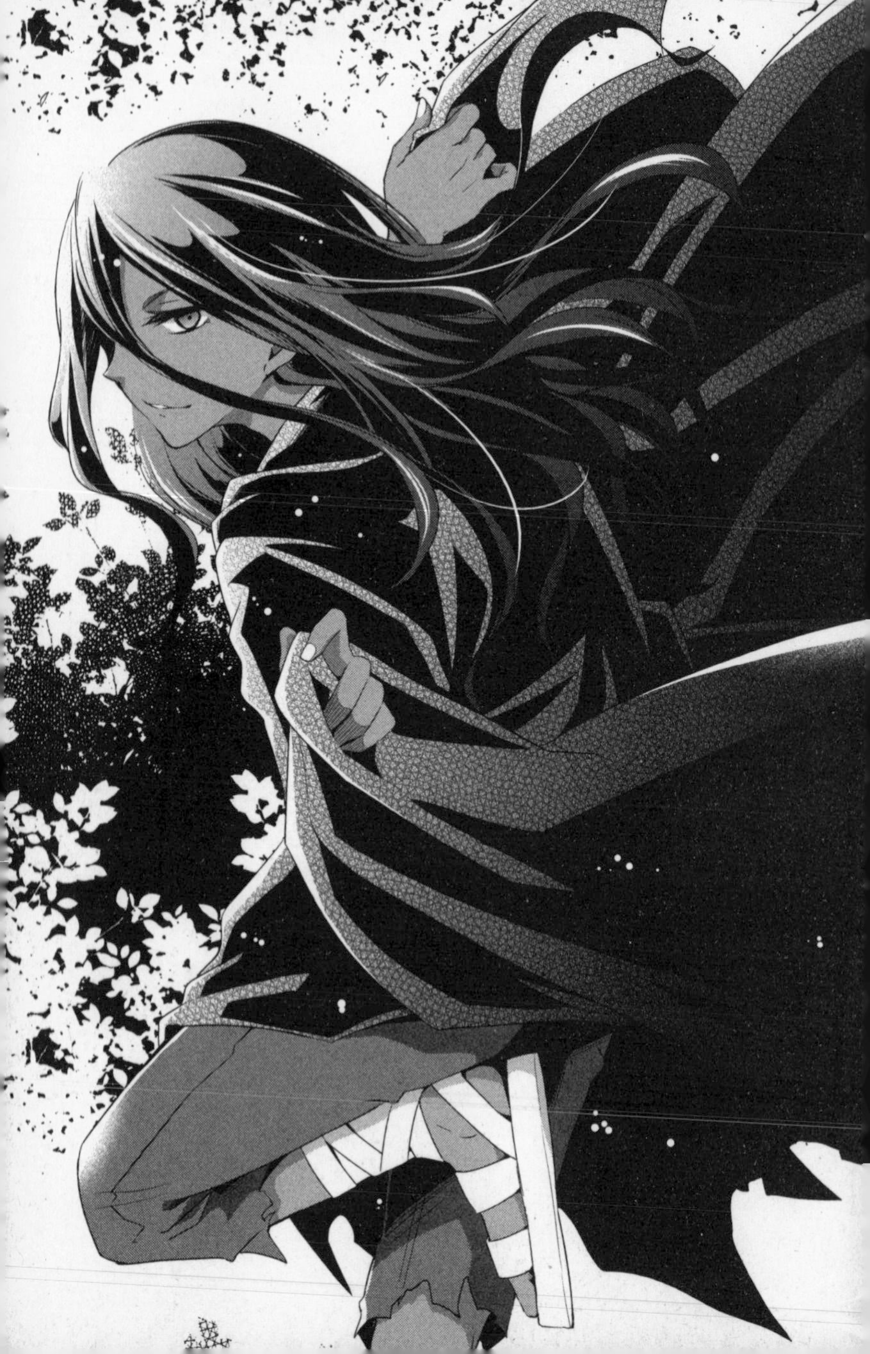

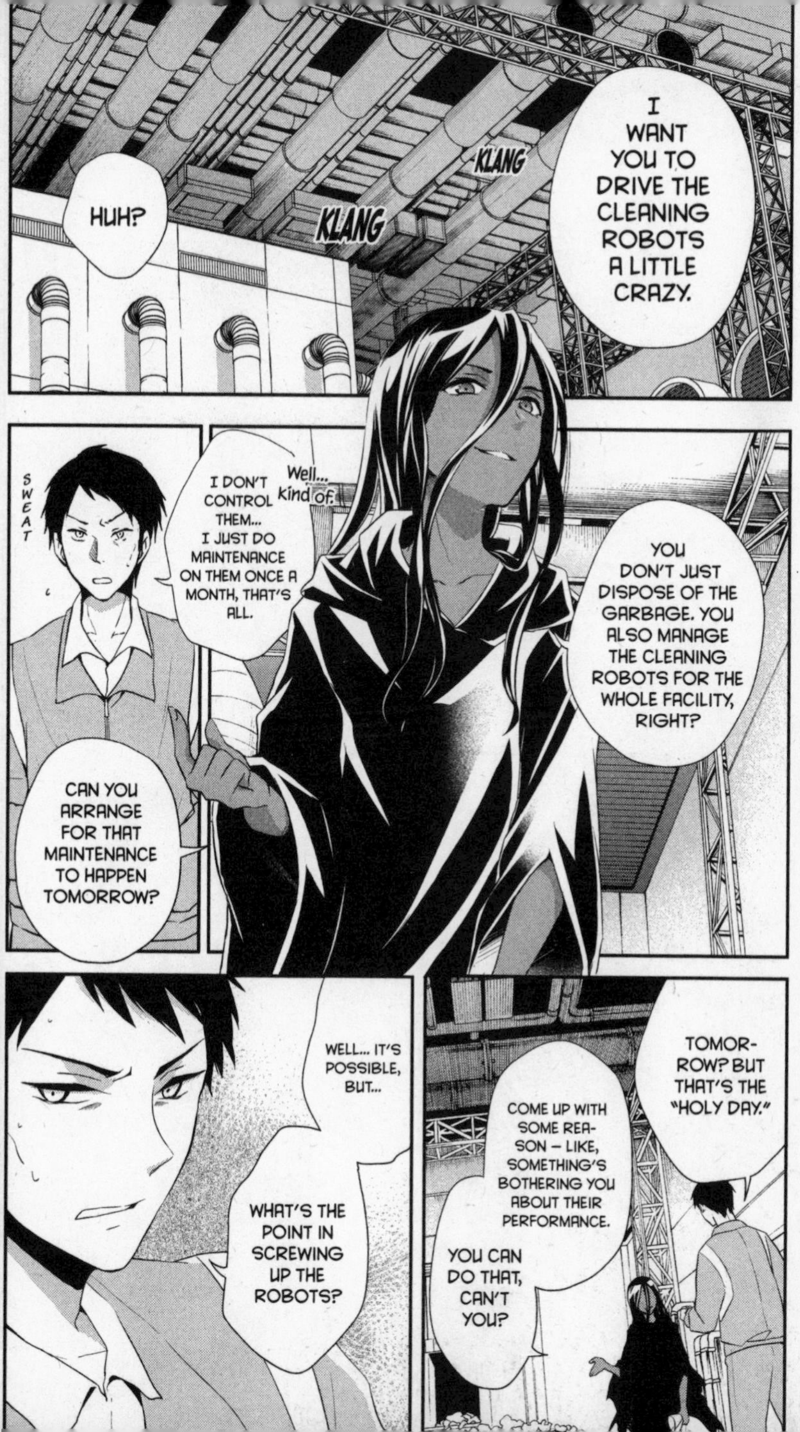
I WANT YOU TO DRIVE THE CLEANING ROBOTS A LITTLE CRAZY.
KLANG
KLANG
HUH?
YOU DON'T JUST DISPOSE OF THE GARBAGE. YOU ALSO MANAGE THE CLEANING ROBOTS FOR THE WHOLE FACILITY, RIGHT?
Well... kind of.
I DON'T CONTROL THEM... I JUST DO MAINTENANCE ON THEM ONCE A MONTH, THAT'S ALL.
SWEAT
CAN YOU ARRANGE FOR THAT MAINTENANCE TO HAPPEN TOMORROW?
TOMOR-ROW? BUT THAT'S THE "HOLY DAY."
COME UP WITH SOME REA-SON – LIKE, SOMETHING'S BOTHERING YOU ABOUT THEIR PERFORMANCE.
YOU CAN DO THAT, CAN'T YOU?
WELL... IT'S POSSIBLE, BUT...
WHAT'S THE POINT IN SCREWING UP THE ROBOTS?

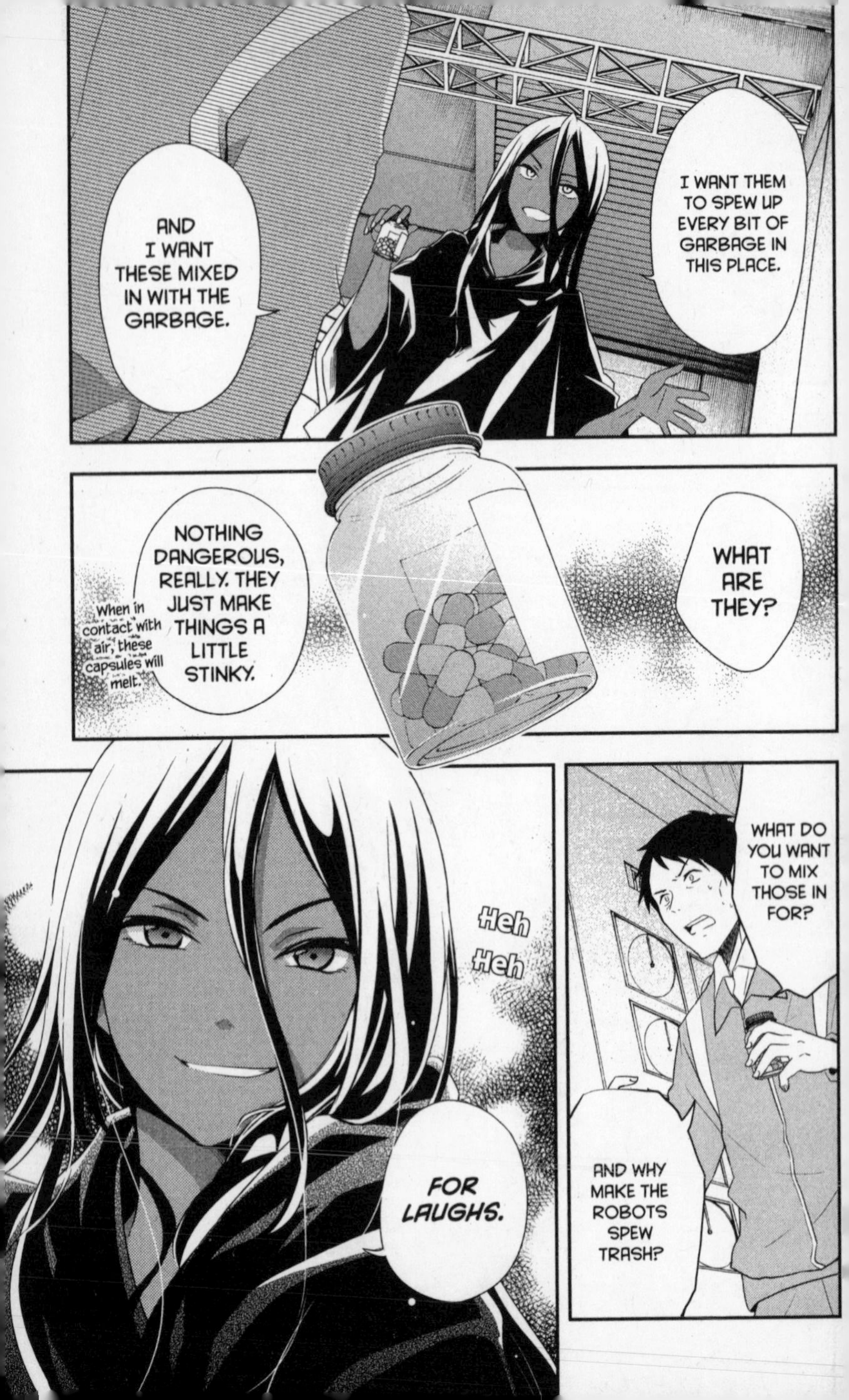
I WANT THEM TO SPEW UP EVERY BIT OF GARBAGE IN THIS PLACE.
AND I WANT THESE MIXED IN WITH THE GARBAGE.
WHAT ARE THEY?
NOTHING DANGEROUS, REALLY. THEY JUST MAKE THINGS A LITTLE STINKY.
When in contact with air, these capsules will melt.
WHAT DO YOU WANT TO MIX THOSE IN FOR?
AND WHY MAKE THE ROBOTS SPEW TRASH?
Heh
Heh
FOR LAUGHS.

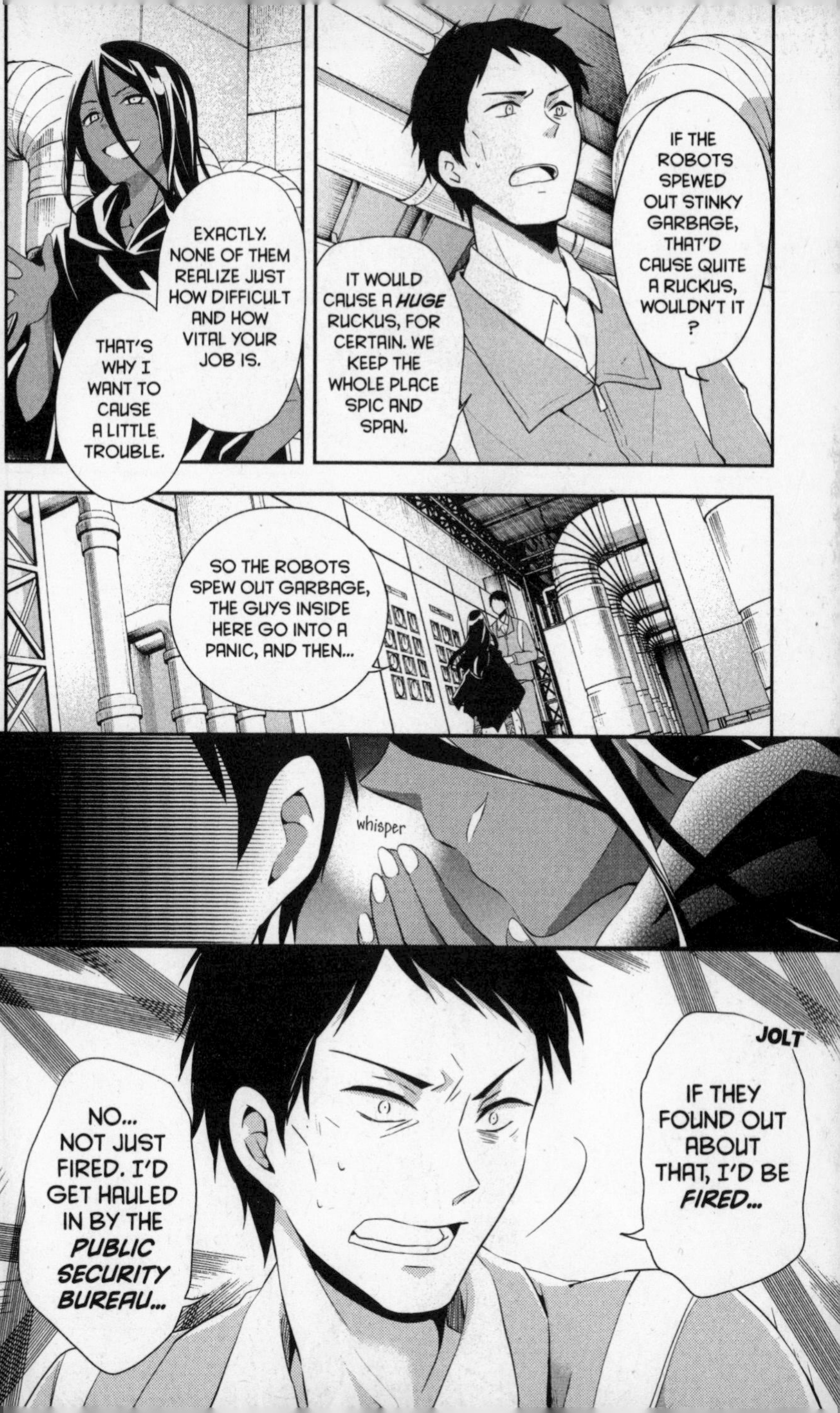
IF THE ROBOTS SPEWED OUT STINKY GARBAGE, THAT'D CAUSE QUITE A RUCKUS, WOULDN'T IT?
IT WOULD CAUSE A *HUGE* RUCKUS, FOR CERTAIN. WE KEEP THE WHOLE PLACE SPIC AND SPAN.
EXACTLY. NONE OF THEM REALIZE JUST HOW DIFFICULT AND HOW VITAL YOUR JOB IS.
THAT'S WHY I WANT TO CAUSE A LITTLE TROUBLE.
SO THE ROBOTS SPEW OUT GARBAGE, THE GUYS INSIDE HERE GO INTO A PANIC, AND THEN...
whisper
JOLT
IF THEY FOUND OUT ABOUT THAT, I'D BE *FIRED...*
NO... NOT JUST FIRED. I'D GET HAULED IN BY THE *PUBLIC SECURITY BUREAU...*

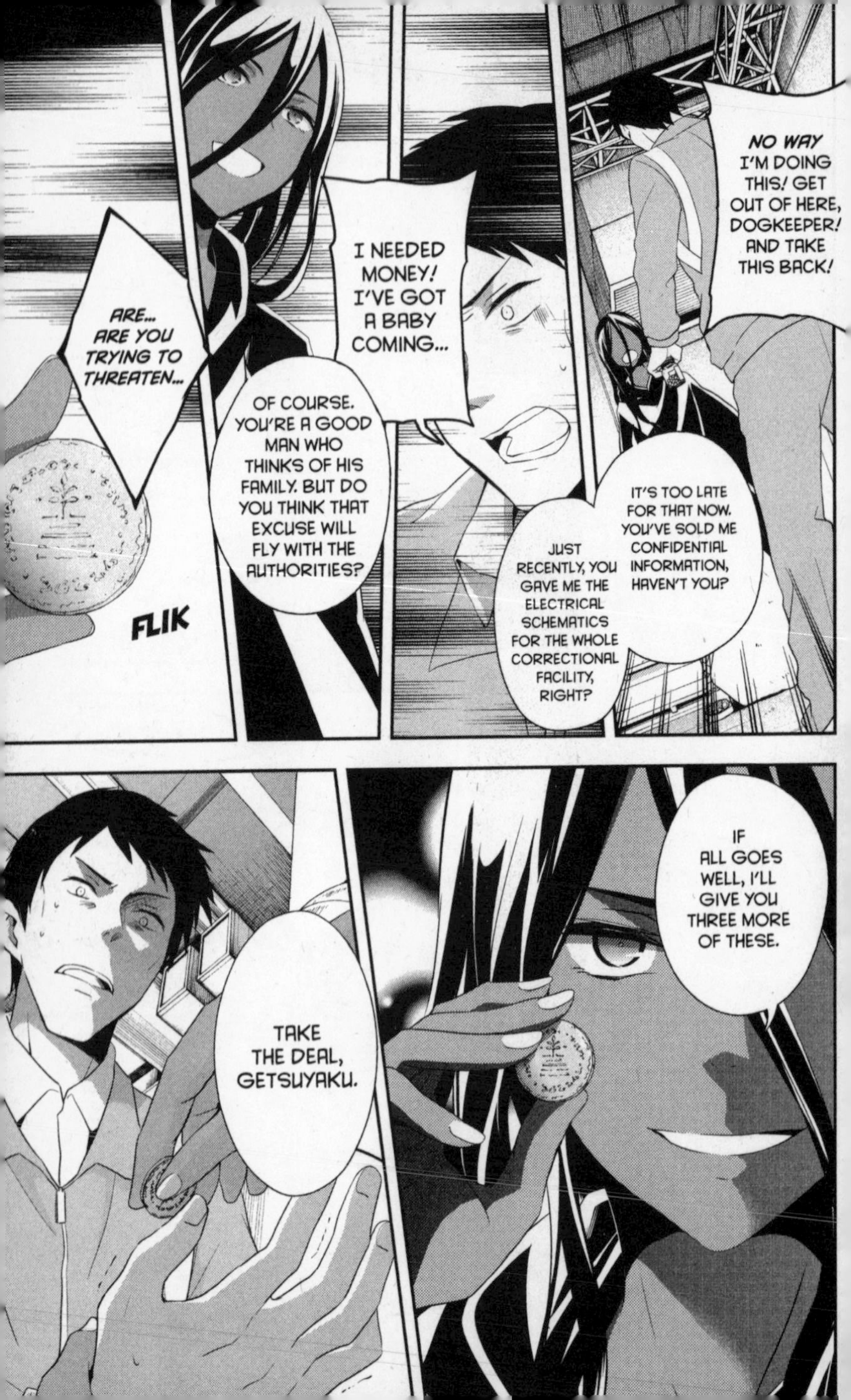
NO WAY I'M DOING THIS! GET OUT OF HERE, DOGKEEPER! AND TAKE THIS BACK!
I NEEDED MONEY! I'VE GOT A BABY COMING...
OF COURSE. YOU'RE A GOOD MAN WHO THINKS OF HIS FAMILY. BUT DO YOU THINK THAT EXCUSE WILL FLY WITH THE AUTHORITIES?
IT'S TOO LATE FOR THAT NOW. YOU'VE SOLD ME CONFIDENTIAL INFORMATION, HAVEN'T YOU?
JUST RECENTLY, YOU GAVE ME THE ELECTRICAL SCHEMATICS FOR THE WHOLE CORRECTIONAL FACILITY, RIGHT?
ARE... ARE YOU TRYING TO THREATEN...
FLIK
IF ALL GOES WELL, I'LL GIVE YOU THREE MORE OF THESE.
TAKE THE DEAL, GETSUYAKU.

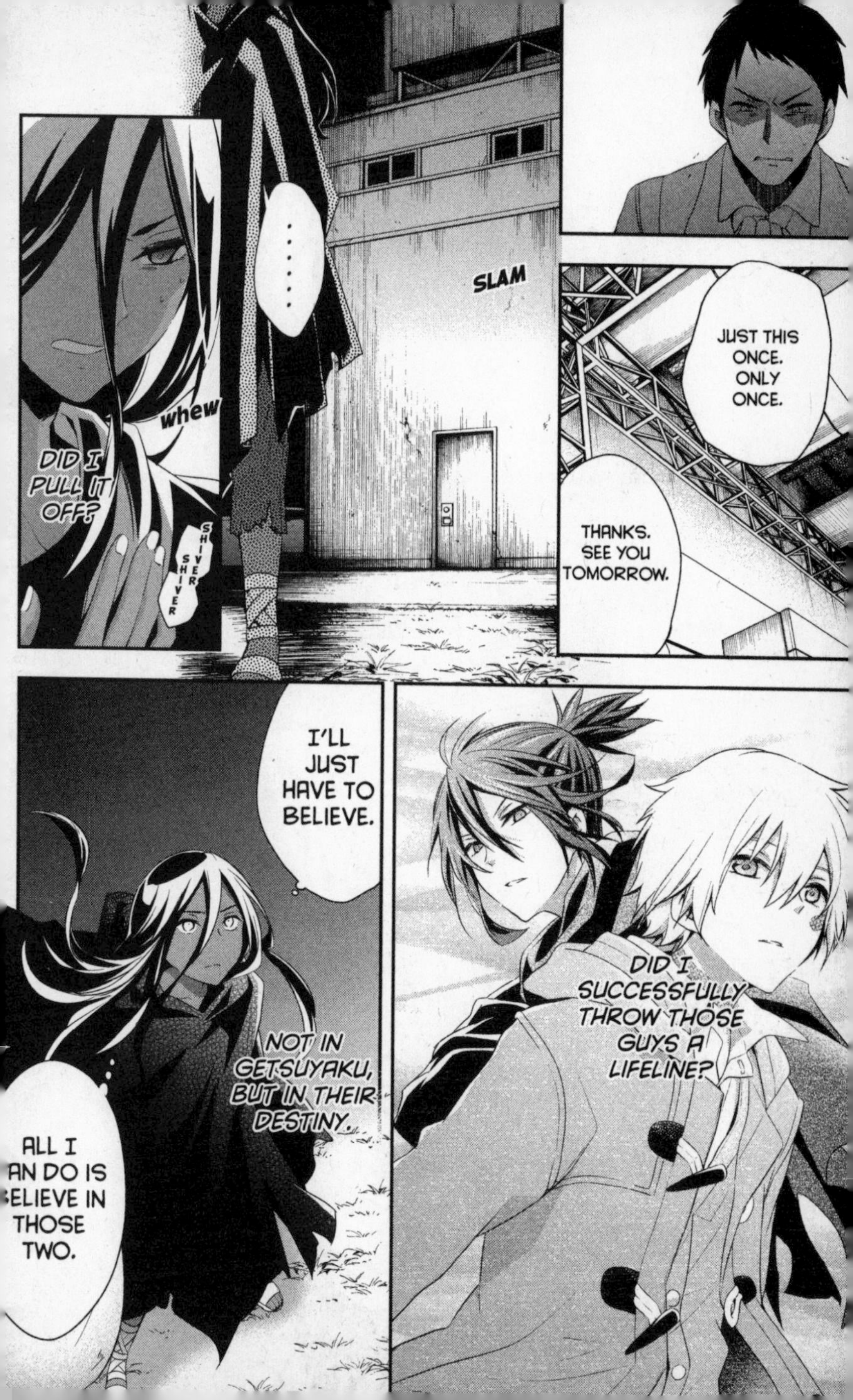
JUST THIS ONCE. ONLY ONCE.
THANKS. SEE YOU TOMORROW.
SLAM
......
whew
DID I PULL IT OFF?
SHIVER SHIVER
DID I SUCCESSFULLY THROW THOSE GUYS A LIFELINE?
I'LL JUST HAVE TO BELIEVE.
NOT IN GETSUYAKU, BUT IN THEIR DESTINY.
ALL I AN DO IS ELIEVE IN THOSE TWO.

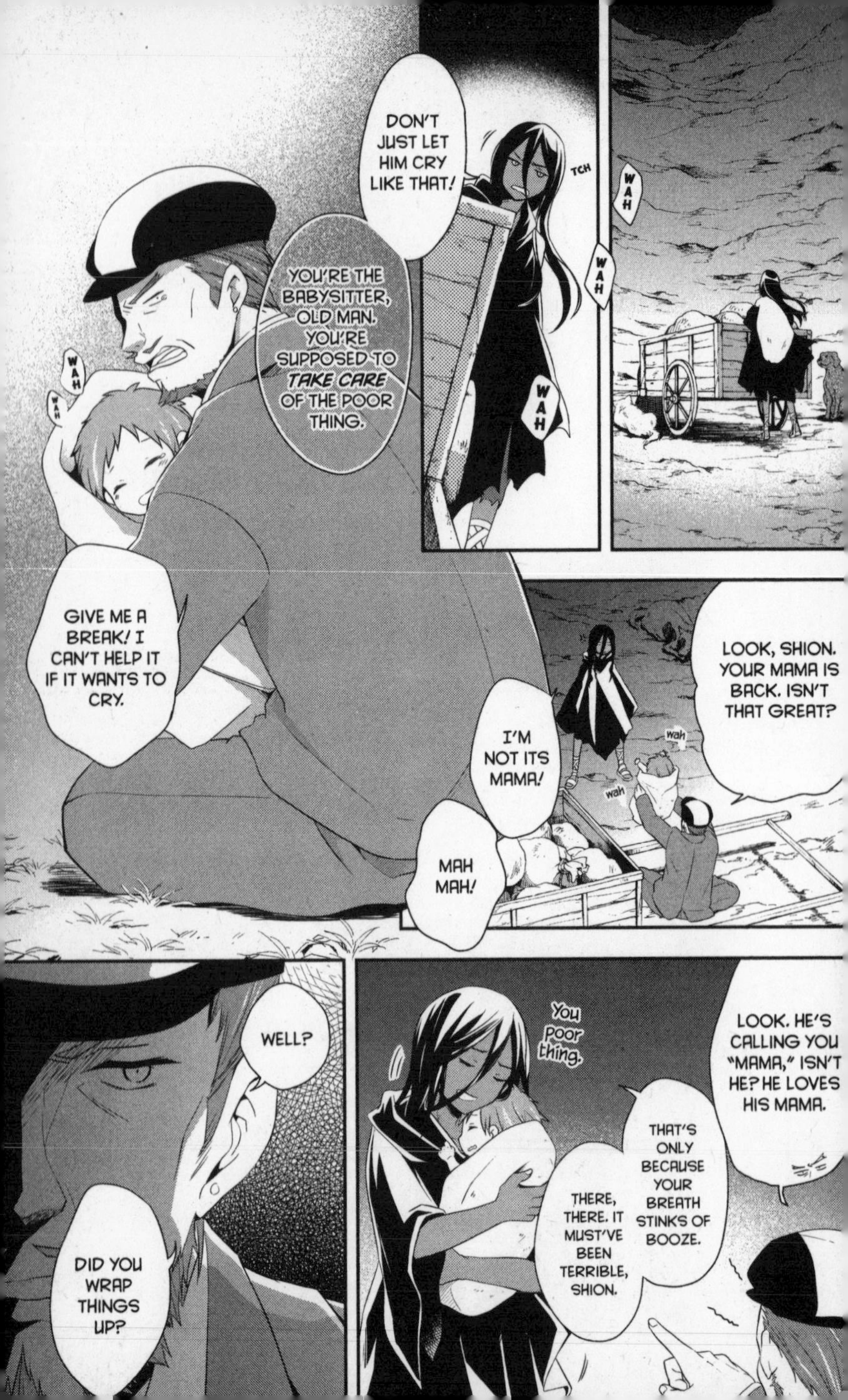
WAH
WAH
DON'T JUST LET HIM CRY LIKE THAT!
TCH
WAH
LOOK, SHION. YOUR MAMA IS BACK. ISN'T THAT GREAT?
wah
wah
I'M NOT ITS MAMA!
MAH MAH!
YOU'RE THE BABYSITTER, OLD MAN. YOU'RE SUPPOSED TO *TAKE CARE* OF THE POOR THING.
WAH
WAH
GIVE ME A BREAK! I CAN'T HELP IT IF IT WANTS TO CRY.
LOOK. HE'S CALLING YOU "MAMA," ISN'T HE? HE LOVES HIS MAMA.
THAT'S ONLY BECAUSE YOUR BREATH STINKS OF BOOZE.
You poor thing.
THERE, THERE. IT MUST'VE BEEN TERRIBLE, SHION.
WELL?
DID YOU WRAP THINGS UP?

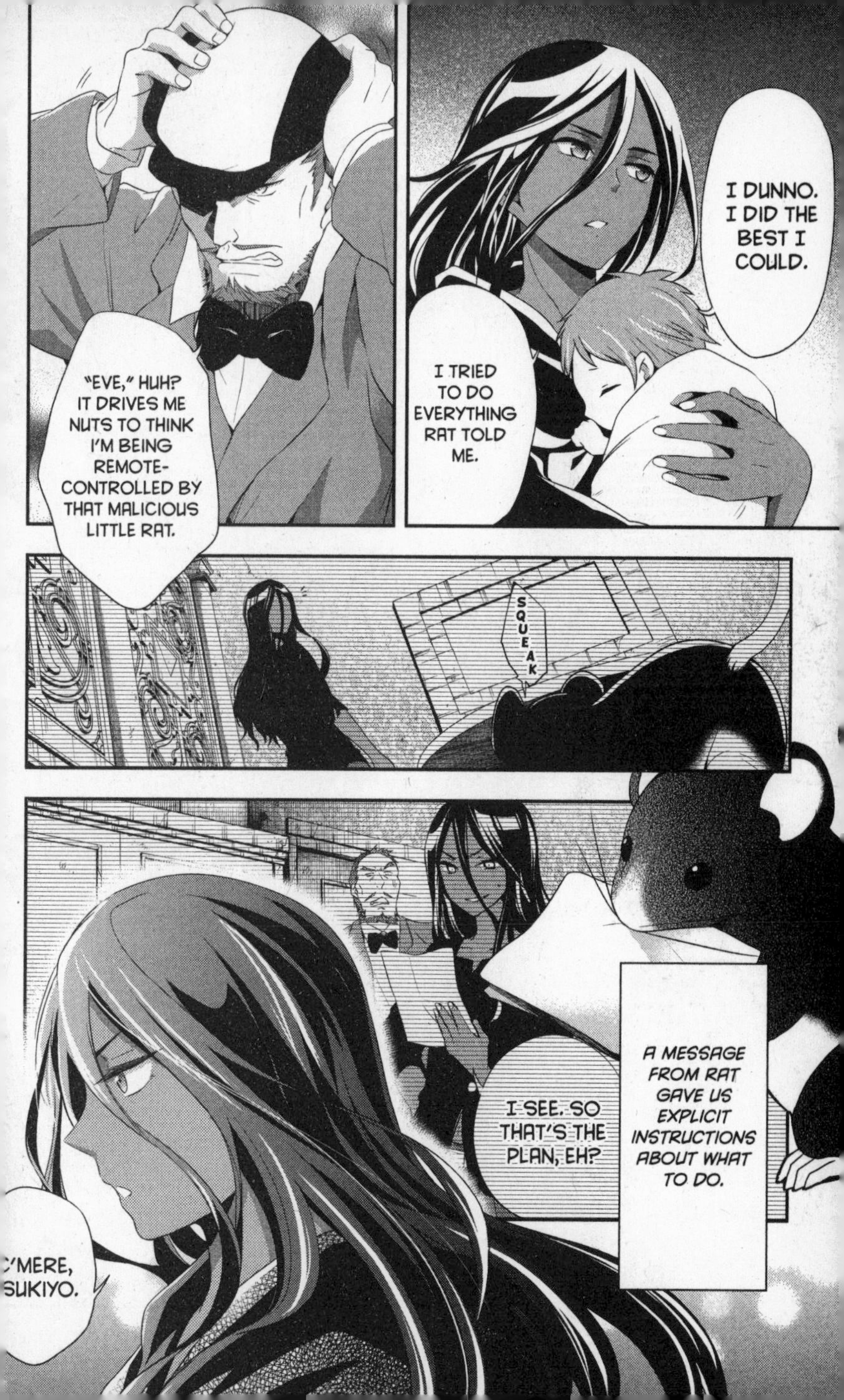
I DUNNO. I DID THE BEST I COULD.
I TRIED TO DO EVERYTHING RAT TOLD ME.
"EVE," HUH? IT DRIVES ME NUTS TO THINK I'M BEING REMOTE-CONTROLLED BY THAT MALICIOUS LITTLE RAT.
SQUEAK
A MESSAGE FROM RAT GAVE US EXPLICIT INSTRUCTIONS ABOUT WHAT TO DO.
I SEE. SO THAT'S THE PLAN, EH?
C'MERE, SUKIYO.

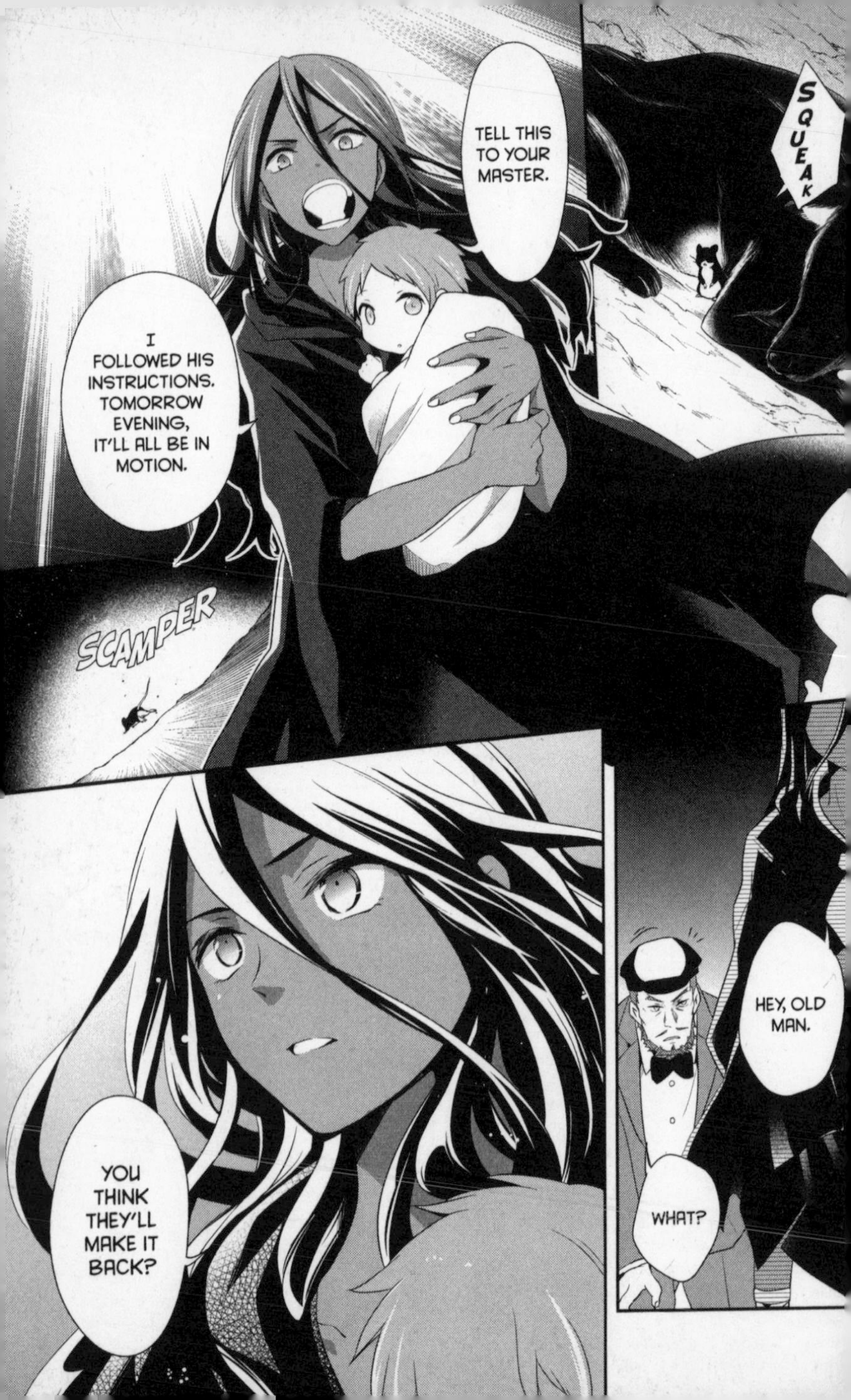
SQUEAK
TELL THIS TO YOUR MASTER.
I FOLLOWED HIS INSTRUCTIONS. TOMORROW EVENING, IT'LL ALL BE IN MOTION.
SCAMPER
HEY, OLD MAN.
WHAT?
YOU THINK THEY'LL MAKE IT BACK?

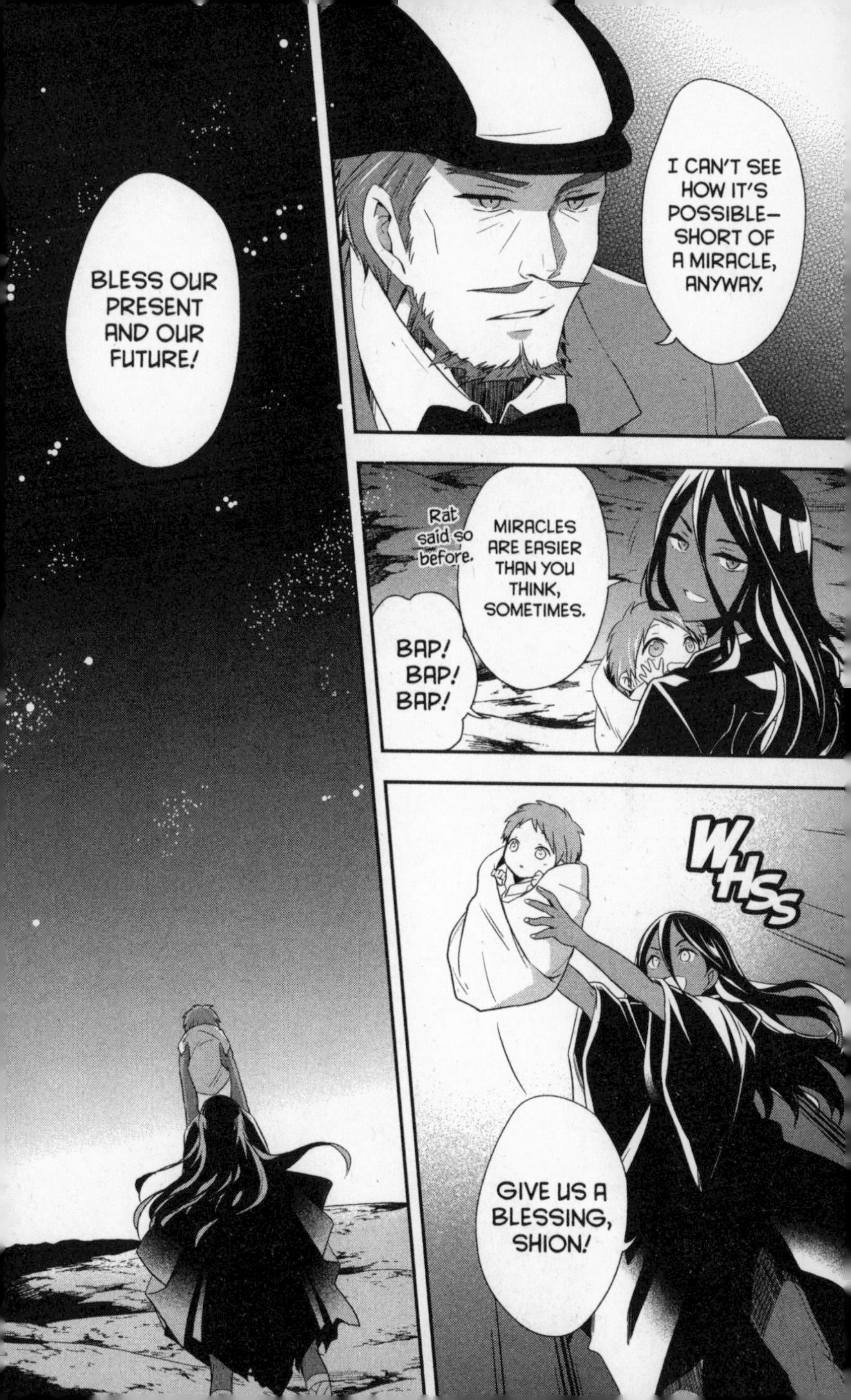
I CAN'T SEE HOW IT'S POSSIBLE—SHORT OF A MIRACLE, ANYWAY.
MIRACLES ARE EASIER THAN YOU THINK, SOMETIMES.
Rat said so before.
BAP! BAP! BAP!
WHSS
GIVE US A BLESSING, SHION!
BLESS OUR PRESENT AND OUR FUTURE!

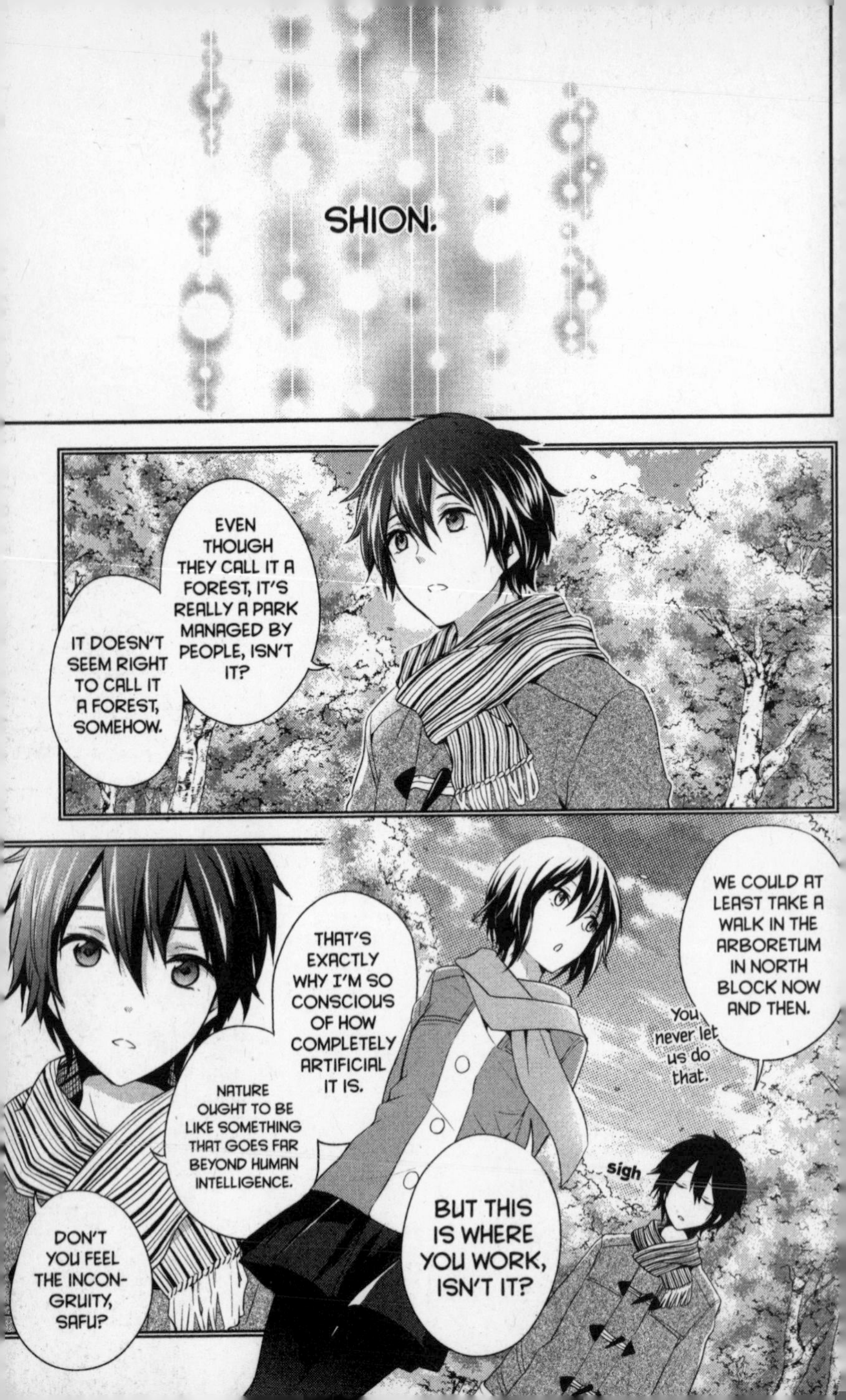
SHION.
EVEN THOUGH THEY CALL IT A FOREST, IT'S REALLY A PARK MANAGED BY PEOPLE, ISN'T IT?
IT DOESN'T SEEM RIGHT TO CALL IT A FOREST, SOMEHOW.
WE COULD AT LEAST TAKE A WALK IN THE ARBORETUM IN NORTH BLOCK NOW AND THEN.
You never let us do that.
Sigh
BUT THIS IS WHERE YOU WORK, ISN'T IT?
THAT'S EXACTLY WHY I'M SO CONSCIOUS OF HOW COMPLETELY ARTIFICIAL IT IS.
NATURE OUGHT TO BE LIKE SOMETHING THAT GOES FAR BEYOND HUMAN INTELLIGENCE.
DON'T YOU FEEL THE INCON-GRUITY, SAFU?

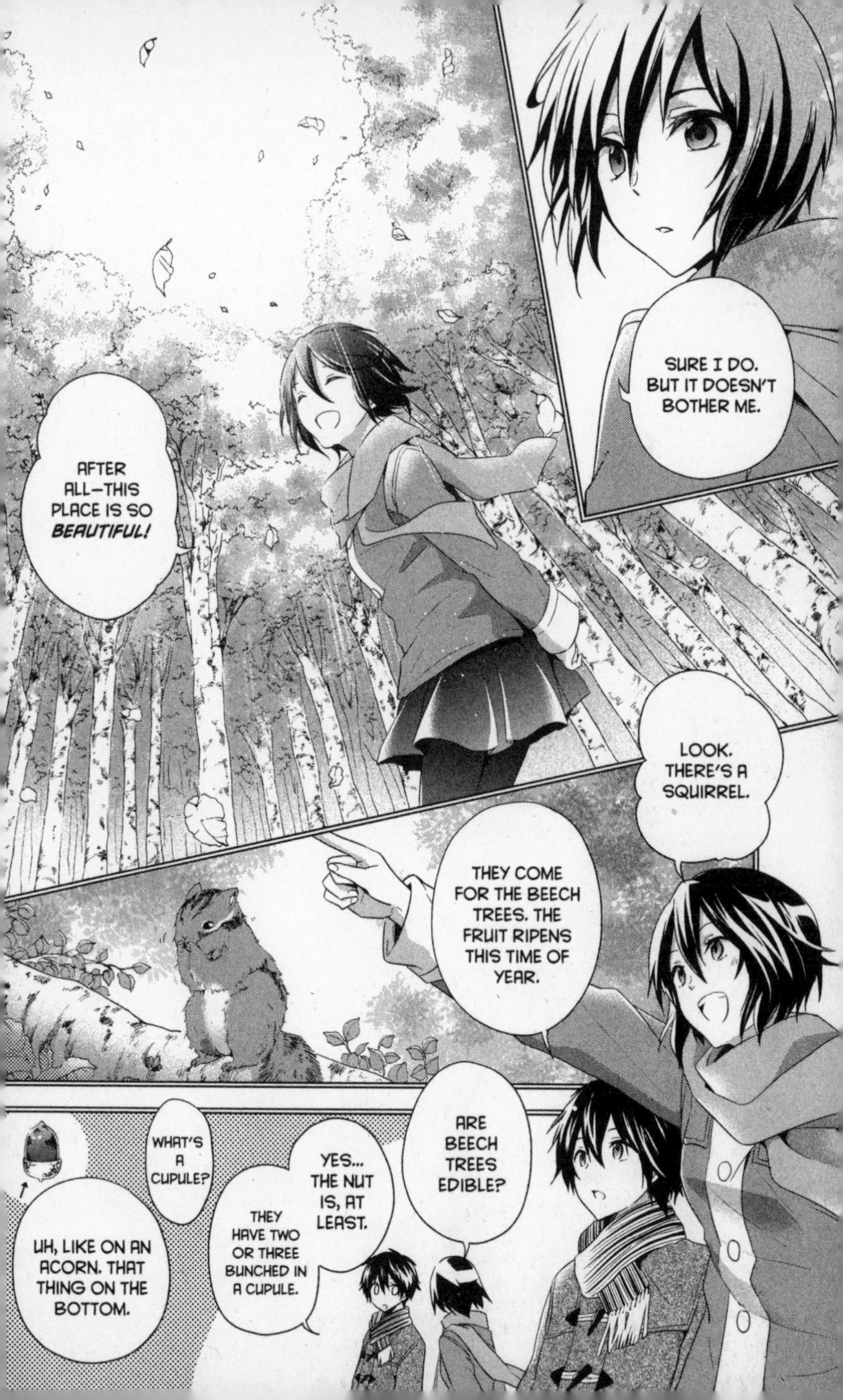
SURE I DO. BUT IT DOESN'T BOTHER ME.
AFTER ALL—THIS PLACE IS SO *BEAUTIFUL!*
LOOK. THERE'S A SQUIRREL.
THEY COME FOR THE BEECH TREES. THE FRUIT RIPENS THIS TIME OF YEAR.
ARE BEECH TREES EDIBLE?
YES... THE NUT IS, AT LEAST.
THEY HAVE TWO OR THREE BUNCHED IN A CUPULE.
WHAT'S A CUPULE?
UH, LIKE ON AN ACORN. THAT THING ON THE BOTTOM.

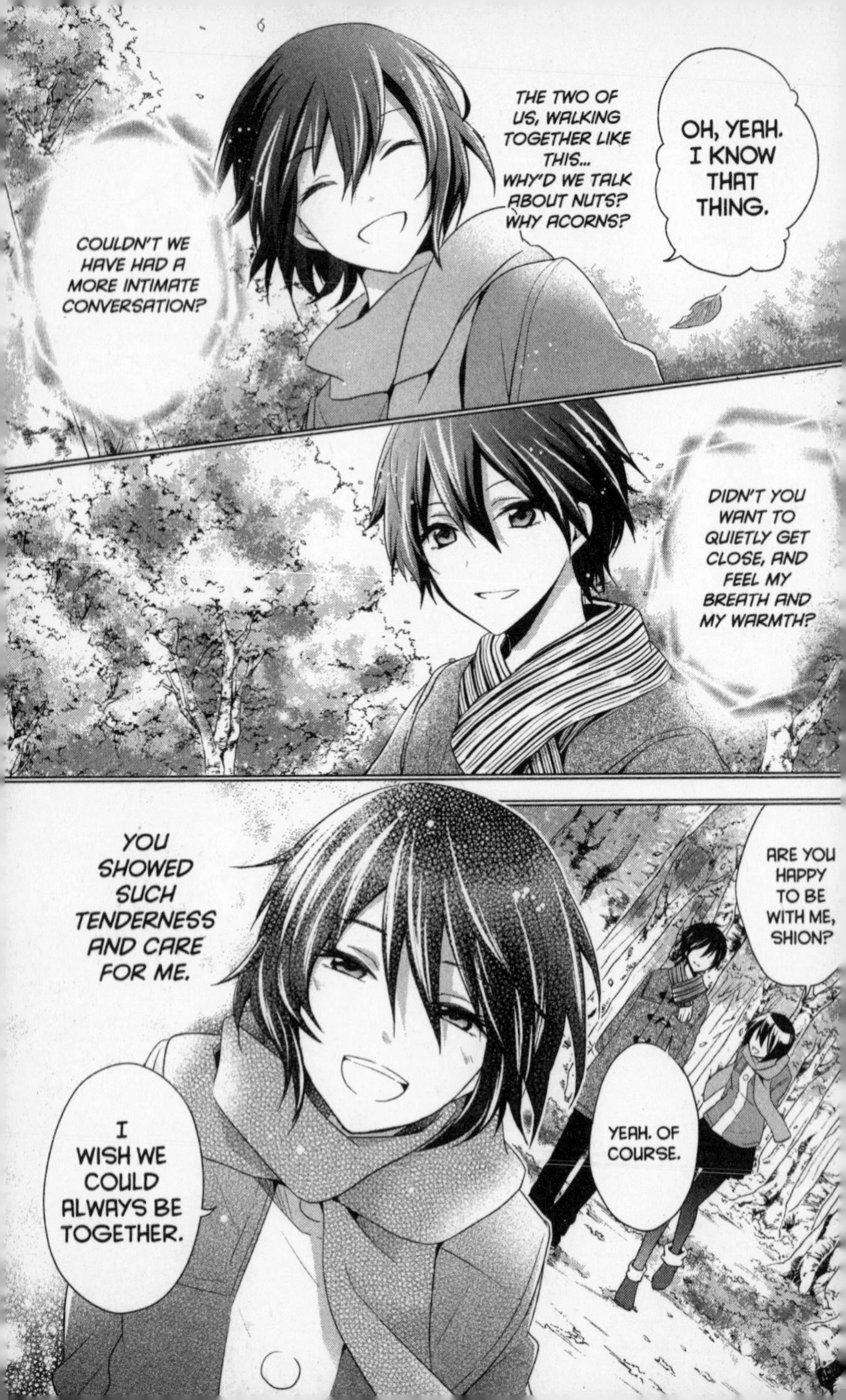
OH, YEAH. I KNOW THAT THING.
THE TWO OF US, WALKING TOGETHER LIKE THIS... WHY'D WE TALK ABOUT NUTS? WHY ACORNS?
COULDN'T WE HAVE HAD A MORE INTIMATE CONVERSATION?
DIDN'T YOU WANT TO QUIETLY GET CLOSE, AND FEEL MY BREATH AND MY WARMTH?
ARE YOU HAPPY TO BE WITH ME, SHION?
YOU SHOWED SUCH TENDERNESS AND CARE FOR ME.
YEAH. OF COURSE.
I WISH WE COULD ALWAYS BE TOGETHER.

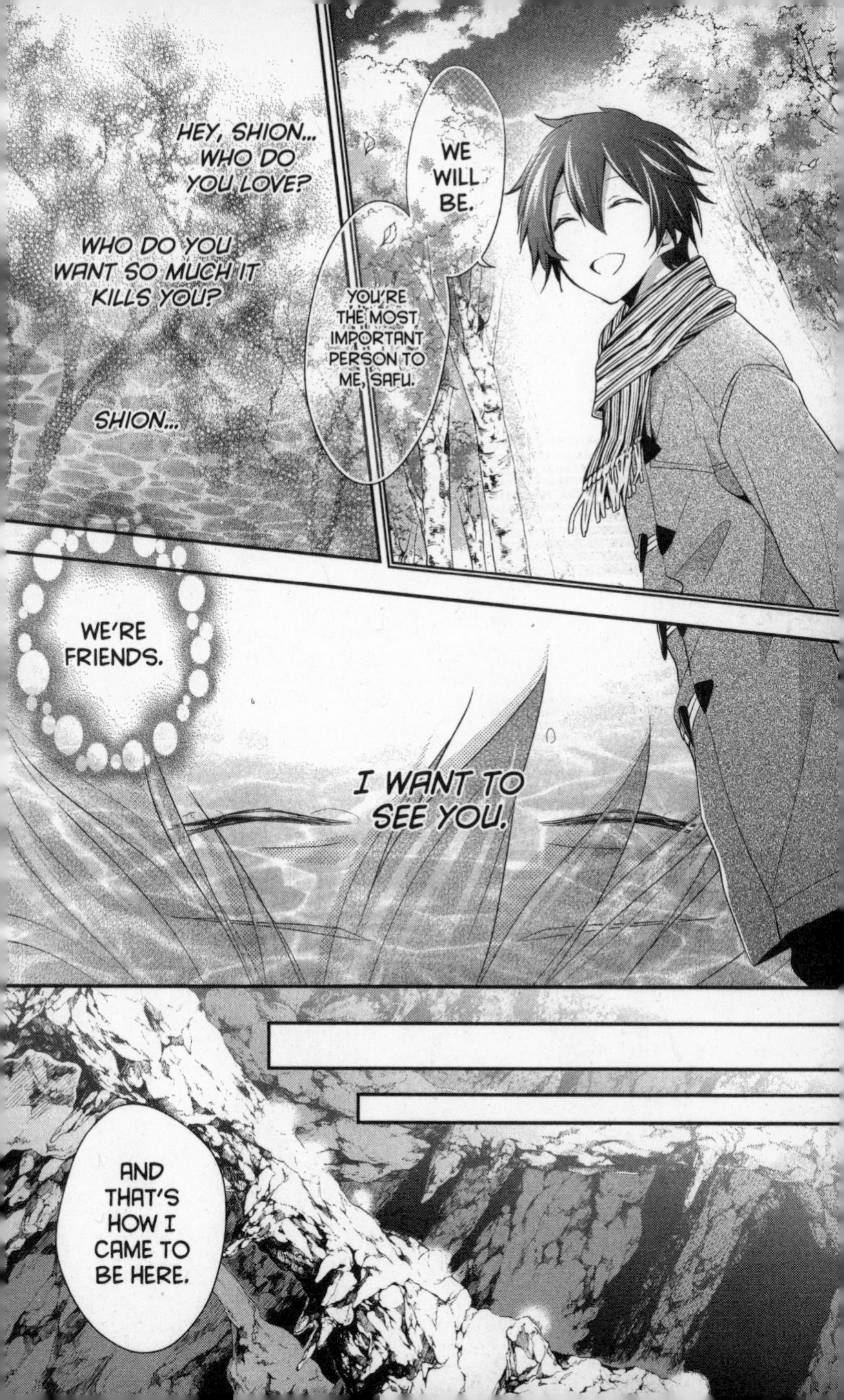
WE WILL BE.
YOU'RE THE MOST IMPORTANT PERSON TO ME, SAFU.
HEY, SHION... WHO DO YOU LOVE?
WHO DO YOU WANT SO MUCH IT KILLS YOU?
SHION...
WE'RE FRIENDS.
I WANT TO SEE YOU.
AND THAT'S HOW I CAME TO BE HERE.

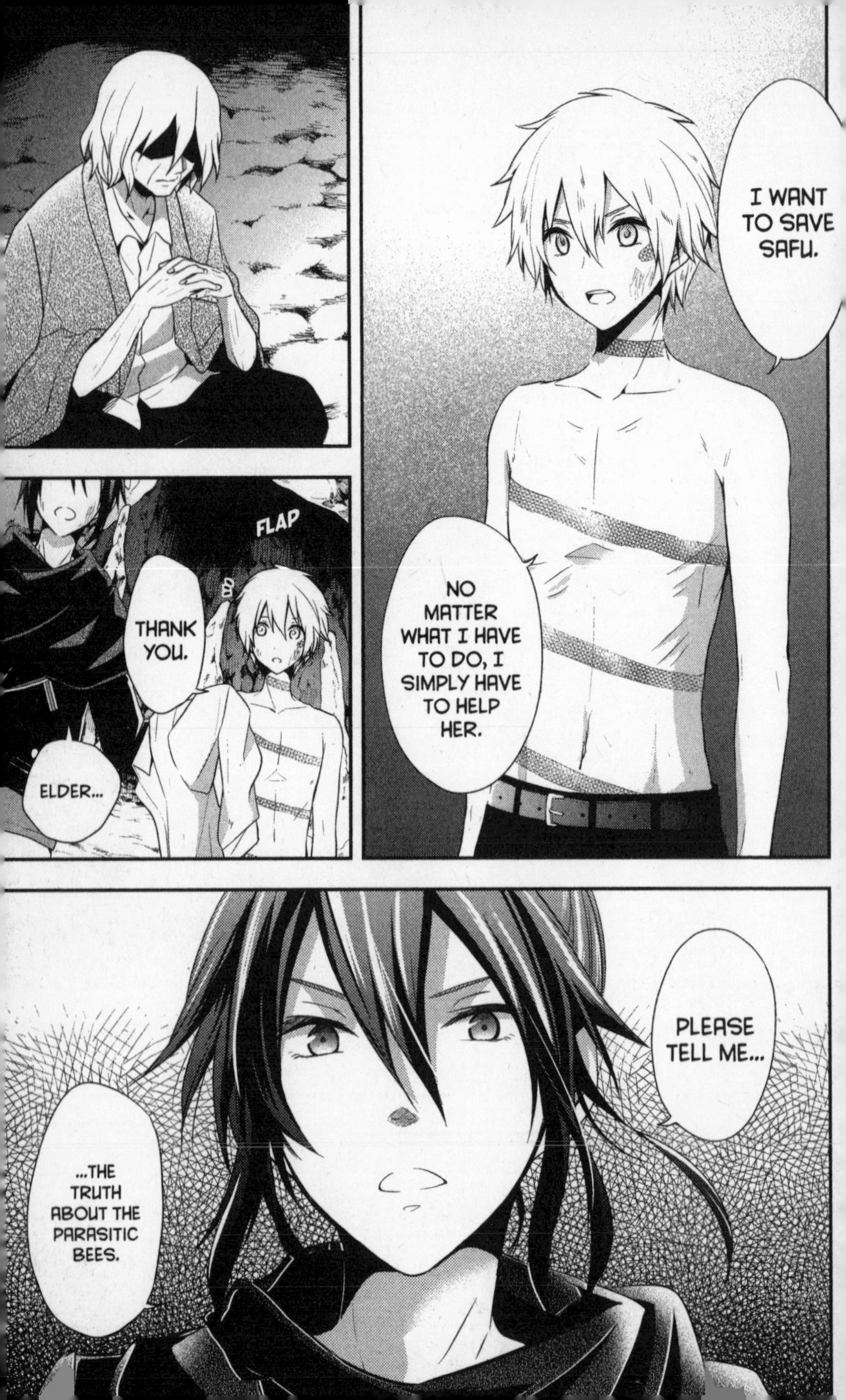
I WANT TO SAVE SAFU.
NO MATTER WHAT I HAVE TO DO, I SIMPLY HAVE TO HELP HER.
FLAP
THANK YOU.
ELDER...
PLEASE TELL ME...
...THE TRUTH ABOUT THE PARASITIC BEES.

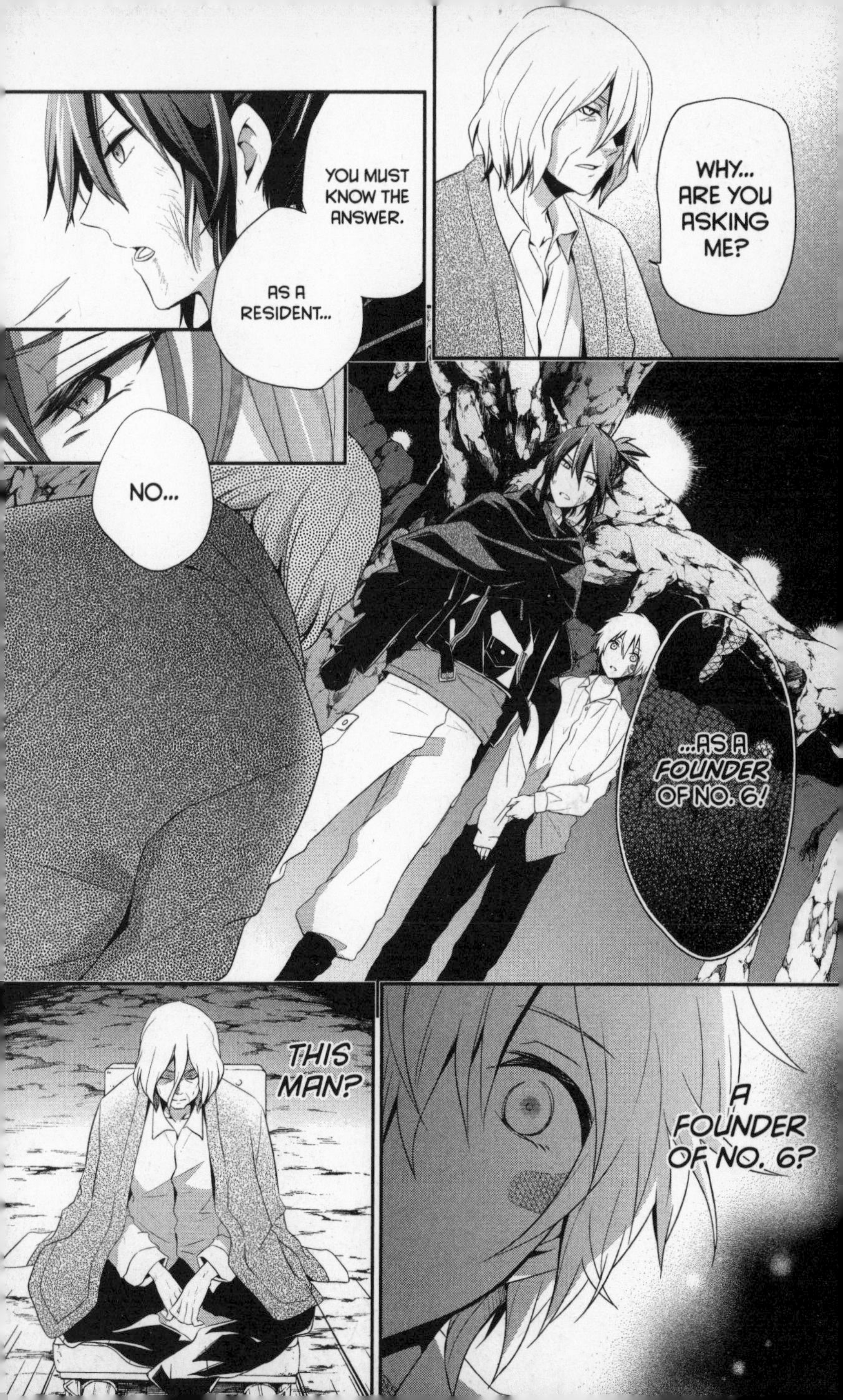
WHY... ARE YOU ASKING ME?
YOU MUST KNOW THE ANSWER.
AS A RESIDENT...
NO...
...AS A FOUNDER OF NO. 6!
A FOUNDER OF NO. 6?
THIS MAN?

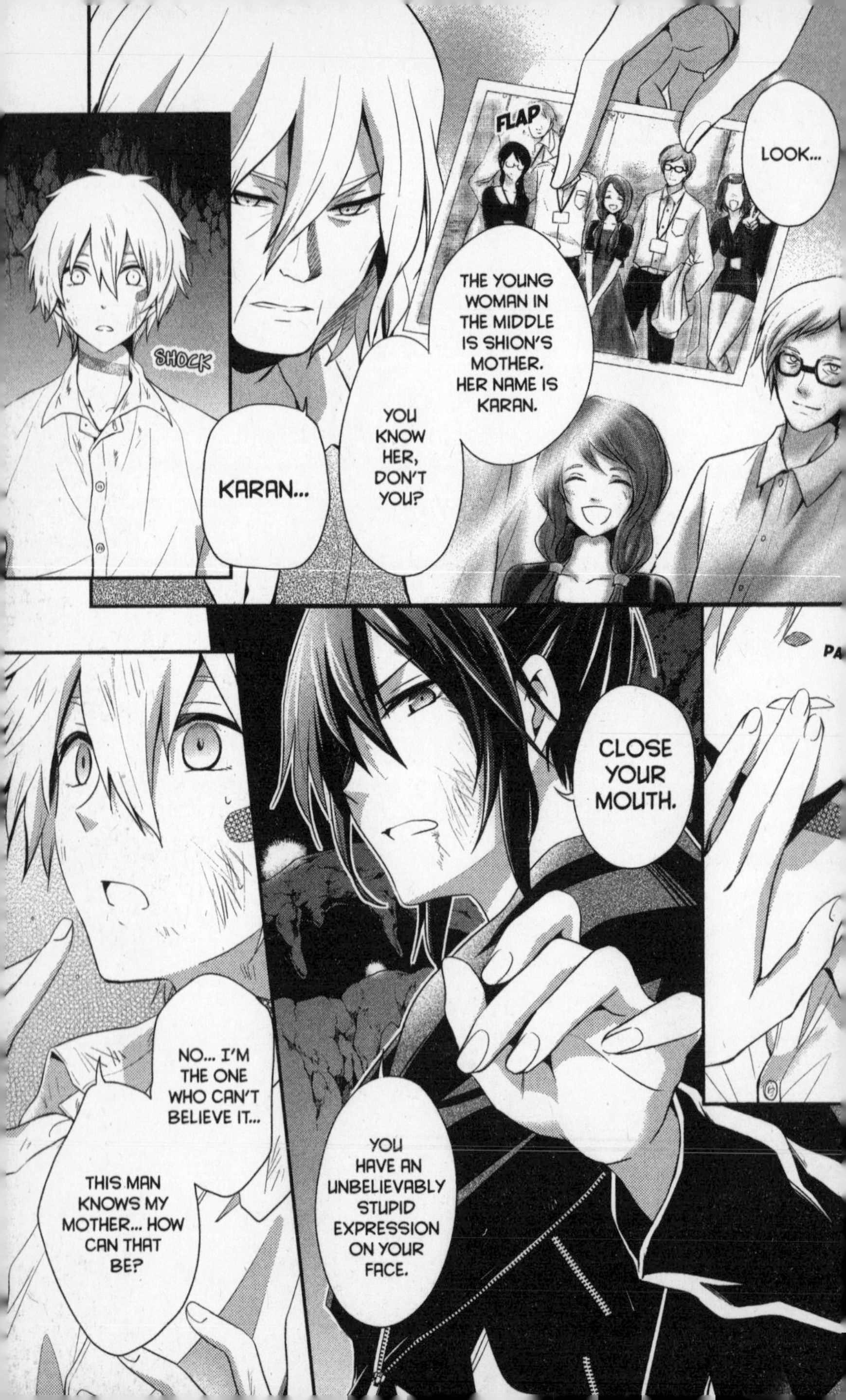
LOOK...
FLAP
THE YOUNG WOMAN IN THE MIDDLE IS SHION'S MOTHER. HER NAME IS KARAN.
YOU KNOW HER, DON'T YOU?
KARAN...
SHOCK
CLOSE YOUR MOUTH.
YOU HAVE AN UNBELIEVABLY STUPID EXPRESSION ON YOUR FACE.
NO... I'M THE ONE WHO CAN'T BELIEVE IT...
THIS MAN KNOWS MY MOTHER... HOW CAN THAT BE?

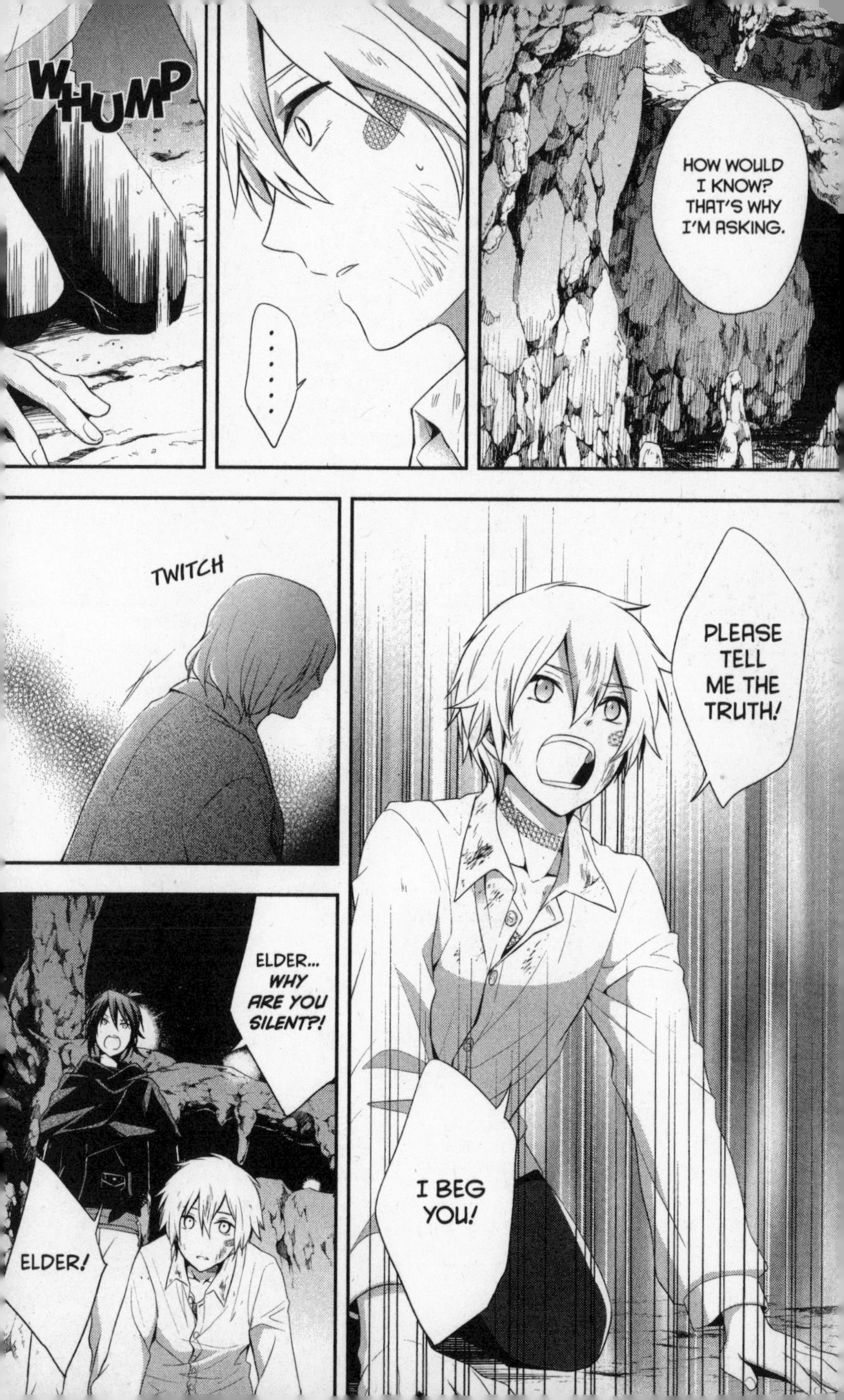
HOW WOULD I KNOW? THAT'S WHY I'M ASKING.
....
WHUMP
PLEASE TELL ME THE TRUTH!
I BEG YOU!
TWITCH
ELDER... WHY ARE YOU SILENT?!
ELDER!

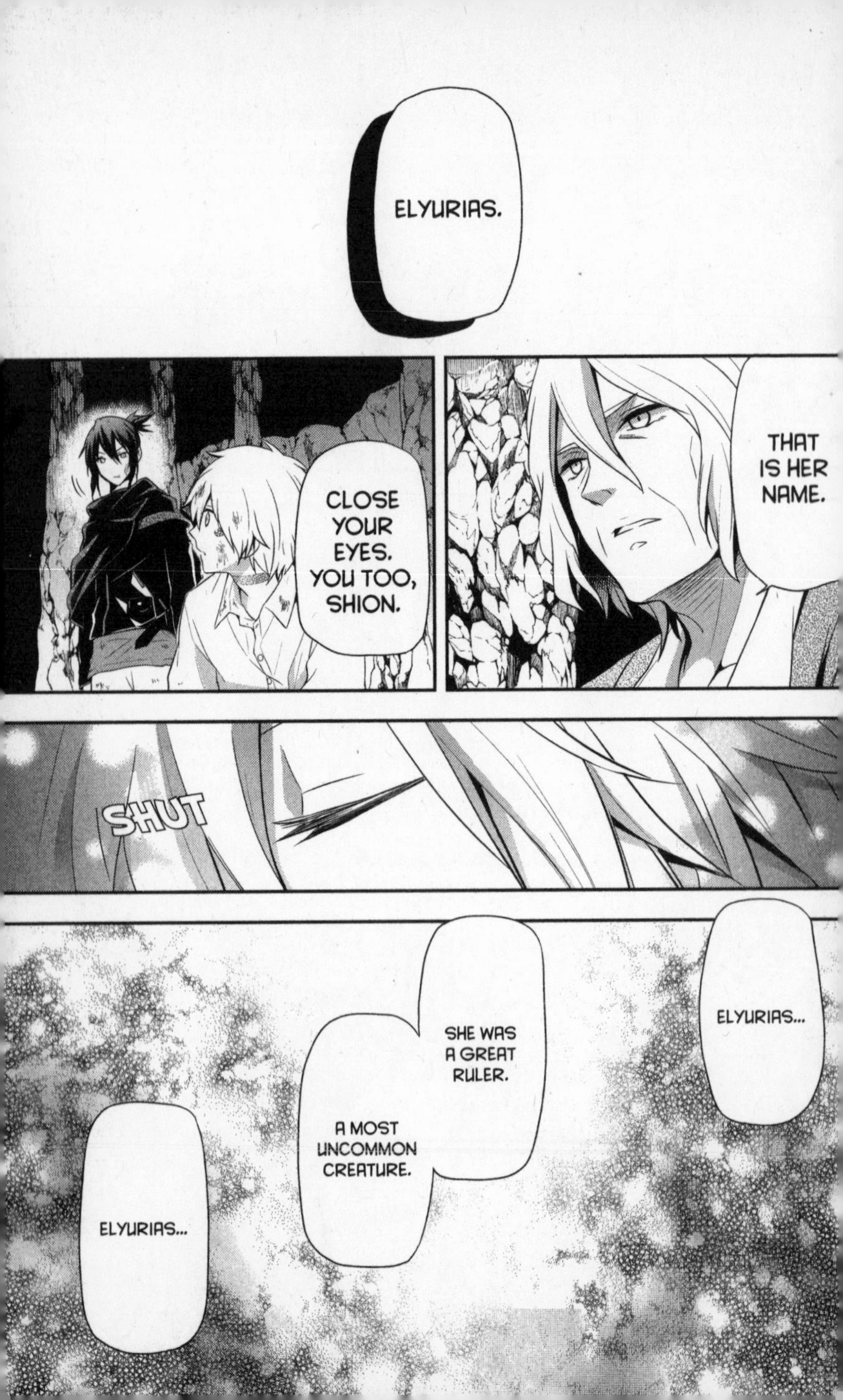
ELYURIAS.
THAT IS HER NAME.
CLOSE YOUR EYES. YOU TOO, SHION.
SHUT
ELYURIAS...
SHE WAS A GREAT RULER.
A MOST UNCOMMON CREATURE.
ELYURIAS...

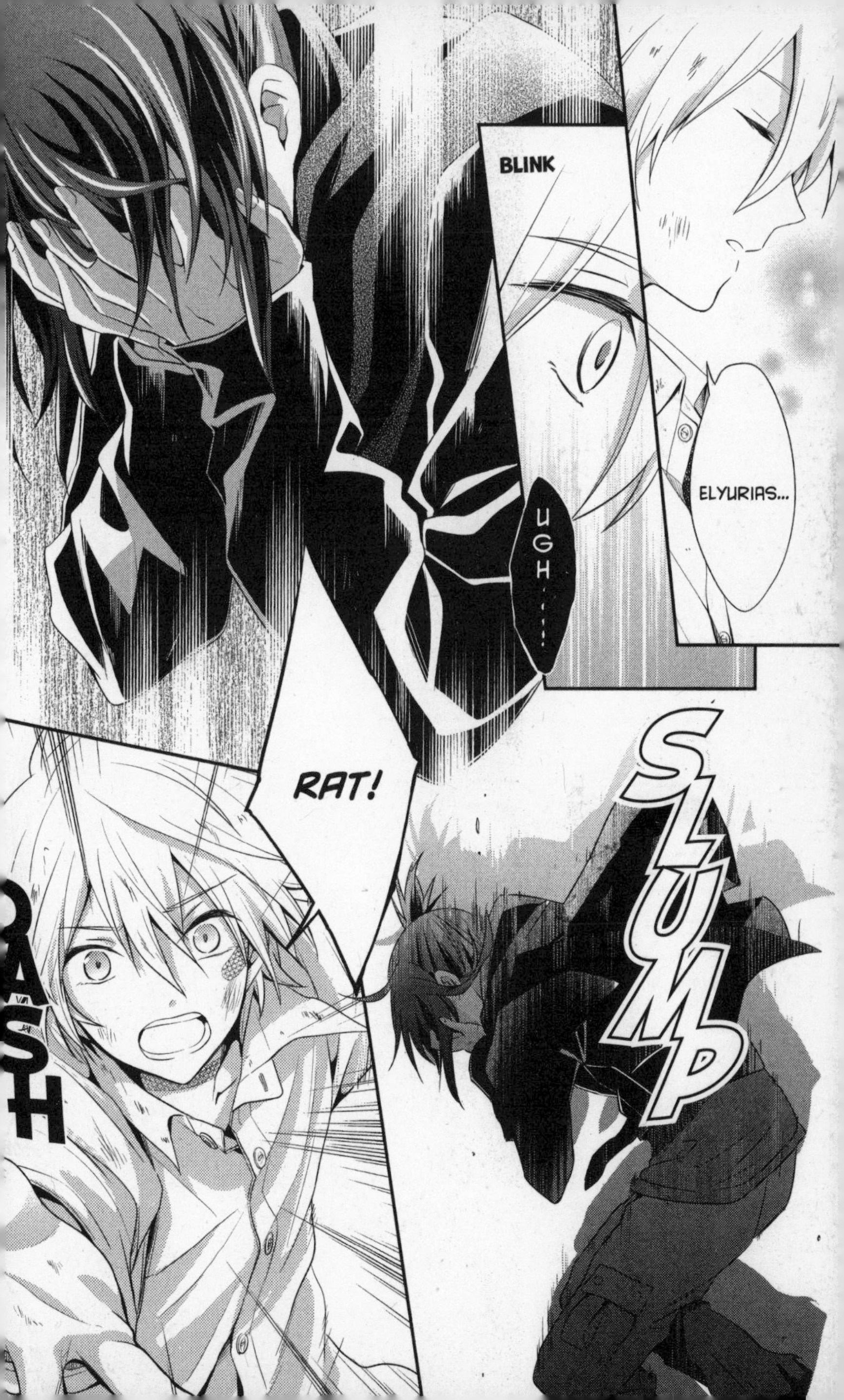
ELYURIAS...
BLINK
UGH......
SLUMP
RAT!
DASH

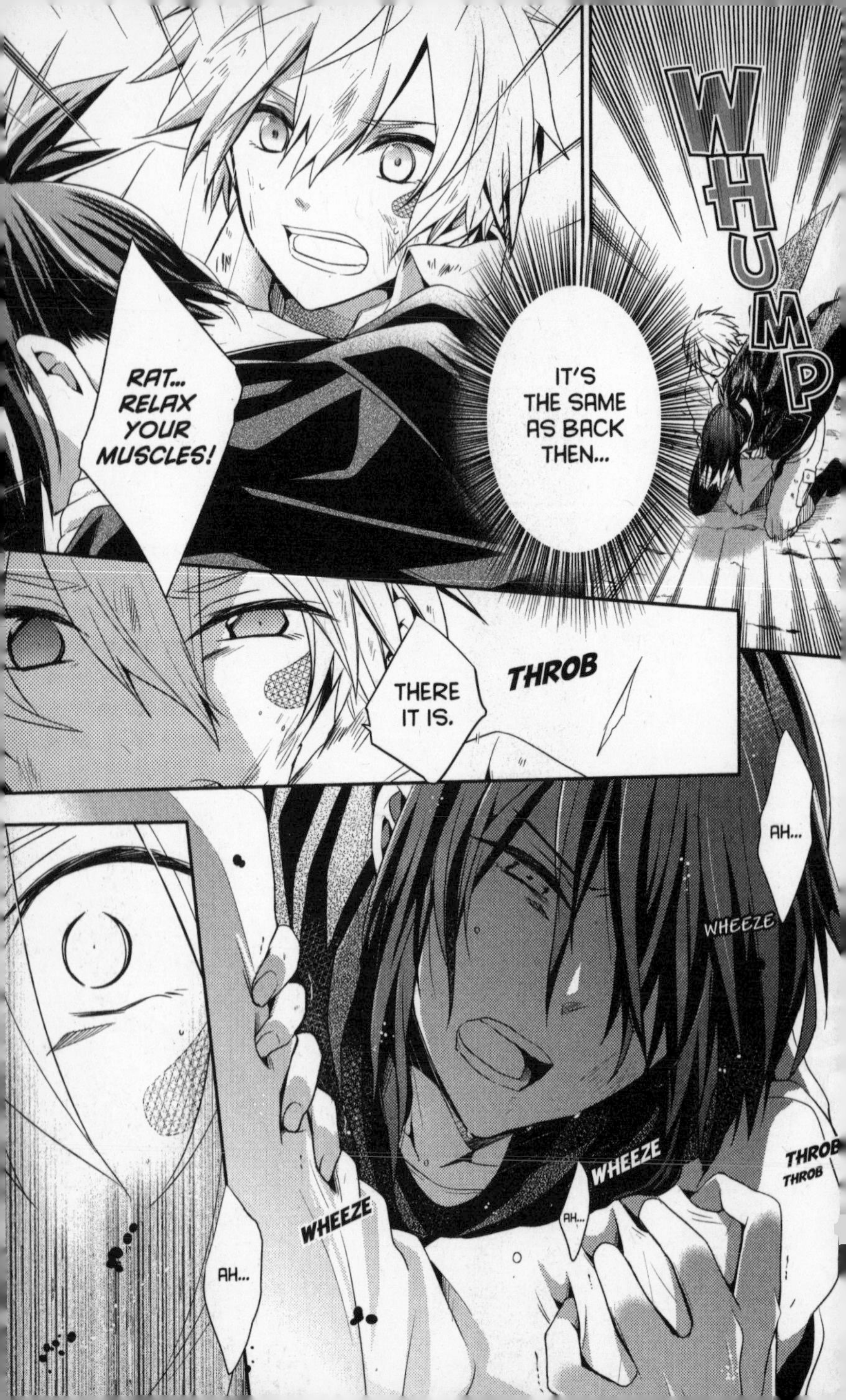
WHUMP
IT'S THE SAME AS BACK THEN...
RAT... RELAX YOUR MUSCLES!
THROB
THERE IT IS.
AH...
WHEEZE
THROB
THROB
WHEEZE
AH...
WHEEZE
AH...

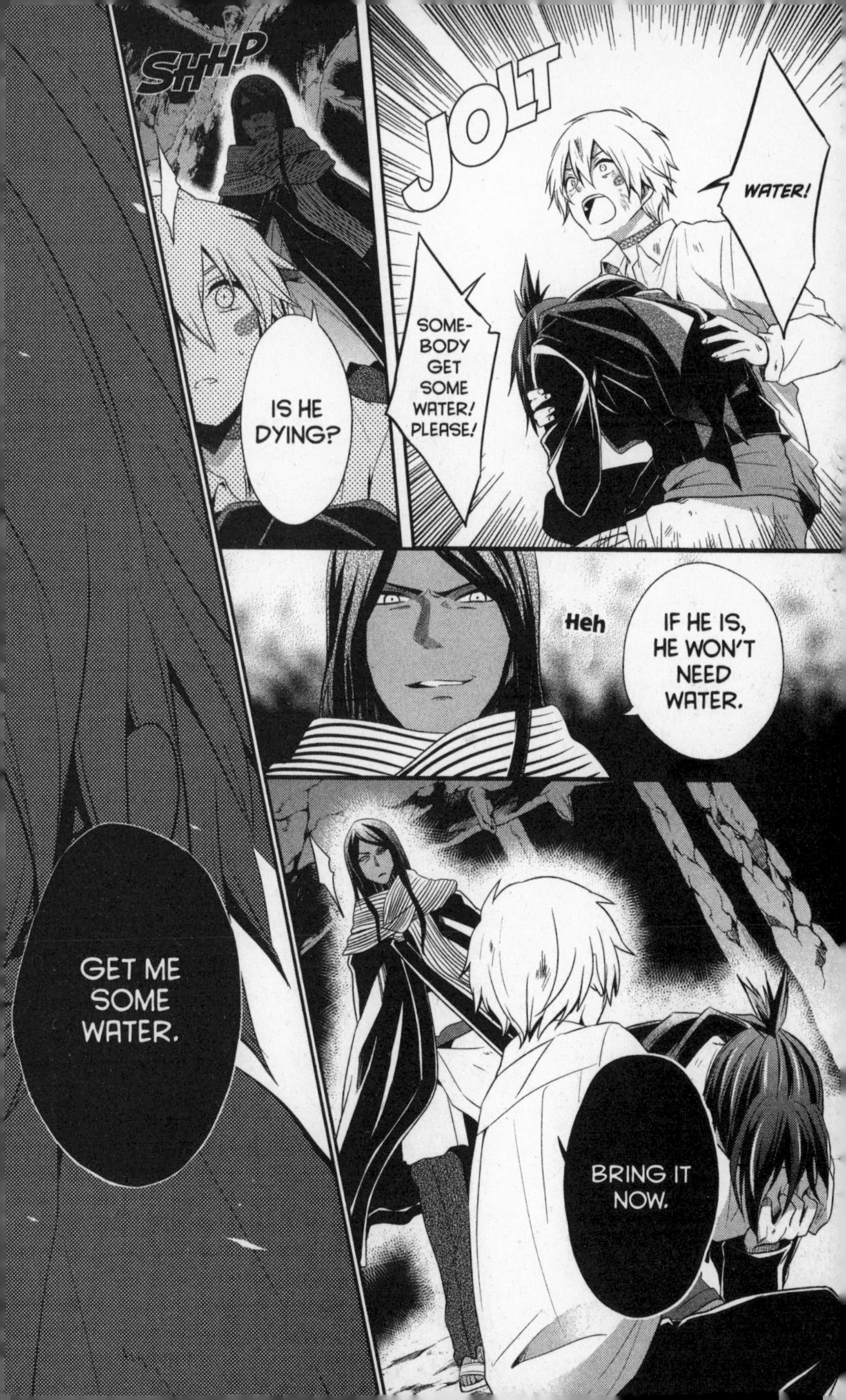
JOLT
WATER!
SOME-BODY GET SOME WATER! PLEASE!
SHHP
IS HE DYING?
Heh
IF HE IS, HE WON'T NEED WATER.
GET ME SOME WATER.
BRING IT NOW.

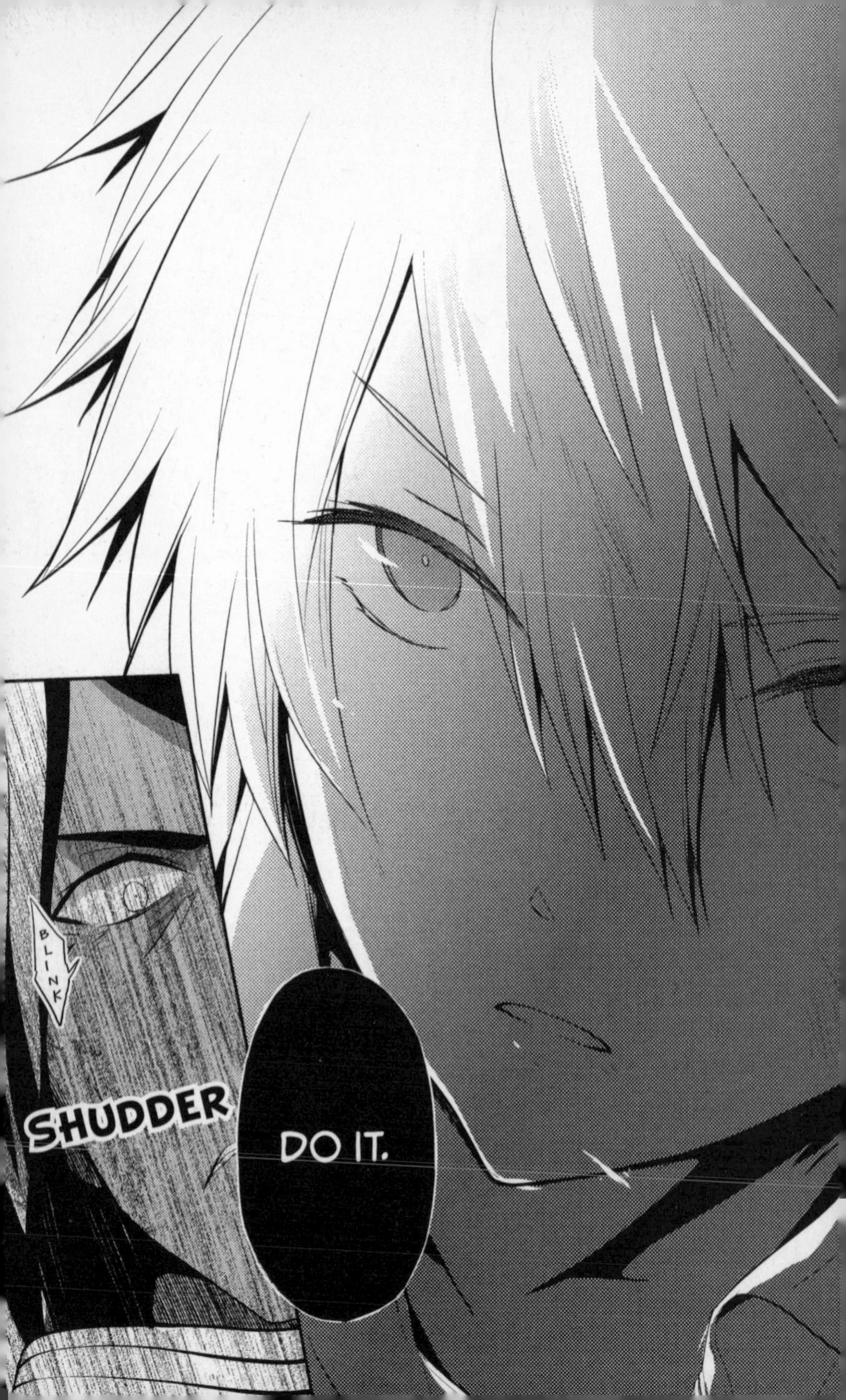
DO IT.
BLINK
SHUDDER

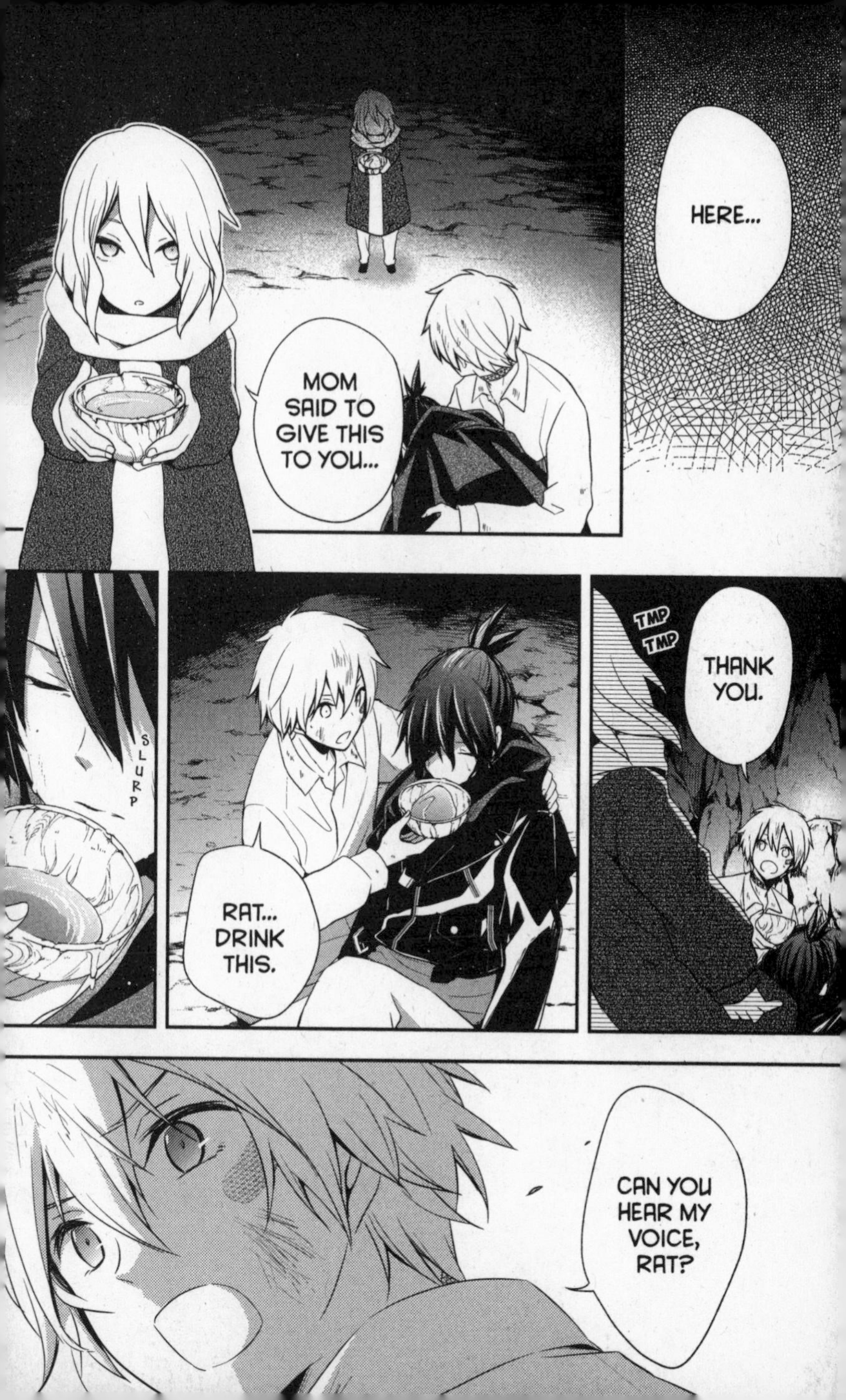
HERE...
MOM SAID TO GIVE THIS TO YOU...
TMP TMP
THANK YOU.
RAT... DRINK THIS.
SLURP
CAN YOU HEAR MY VOICE, RAT?

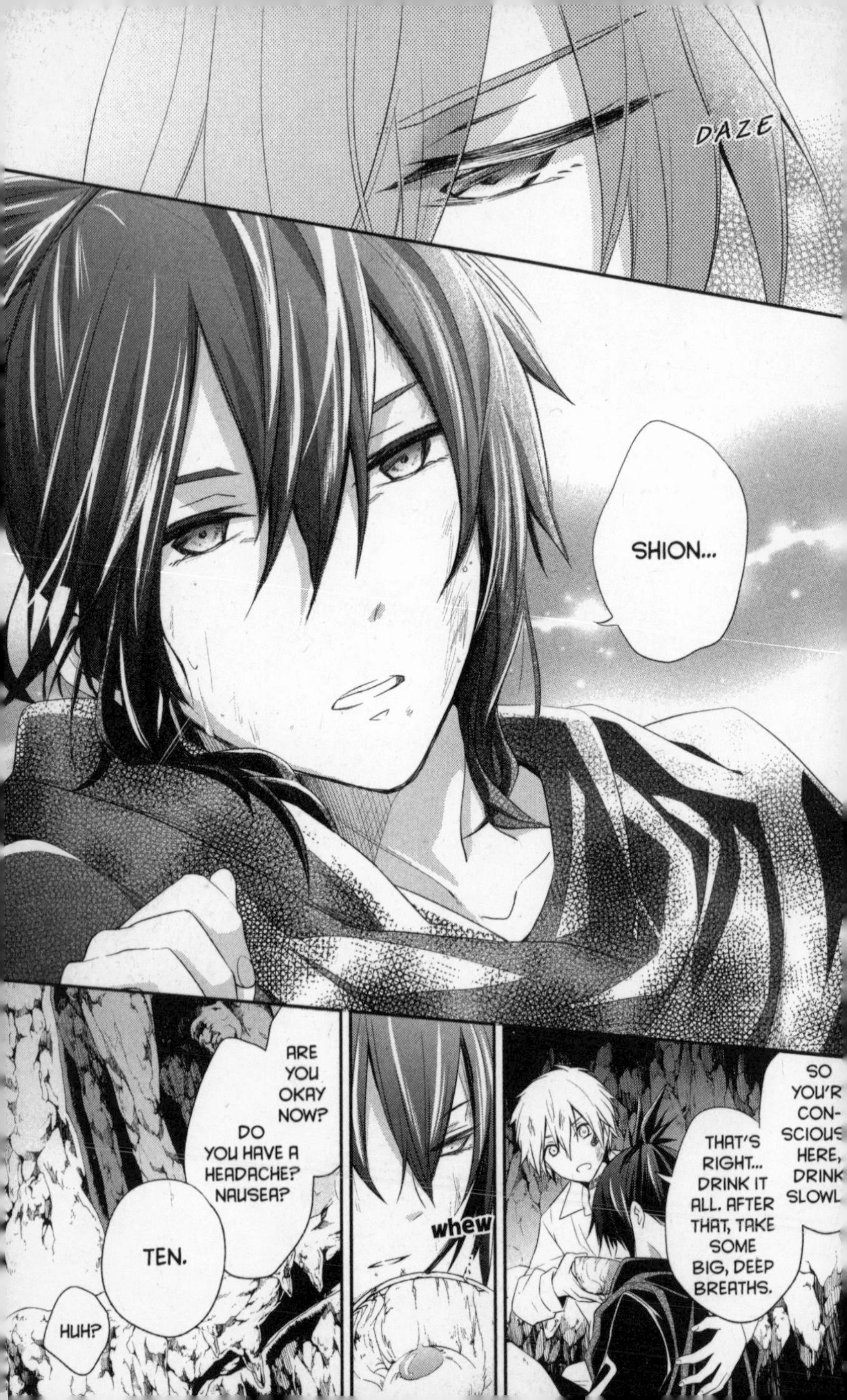
DAZE
SHION...
SO YOU'R CON-SCIOUS HERE, DRINK SLOWL
THAT'S RIGHT... DRINK IT ALL. AFTER THAT, TAKE SOME BIG, DEEP BREATHS.
whew
ARE YOU OKAY NOW?
DO YOU HAVE A HEADACHE? NAUSEA?
TEN.
HUH?

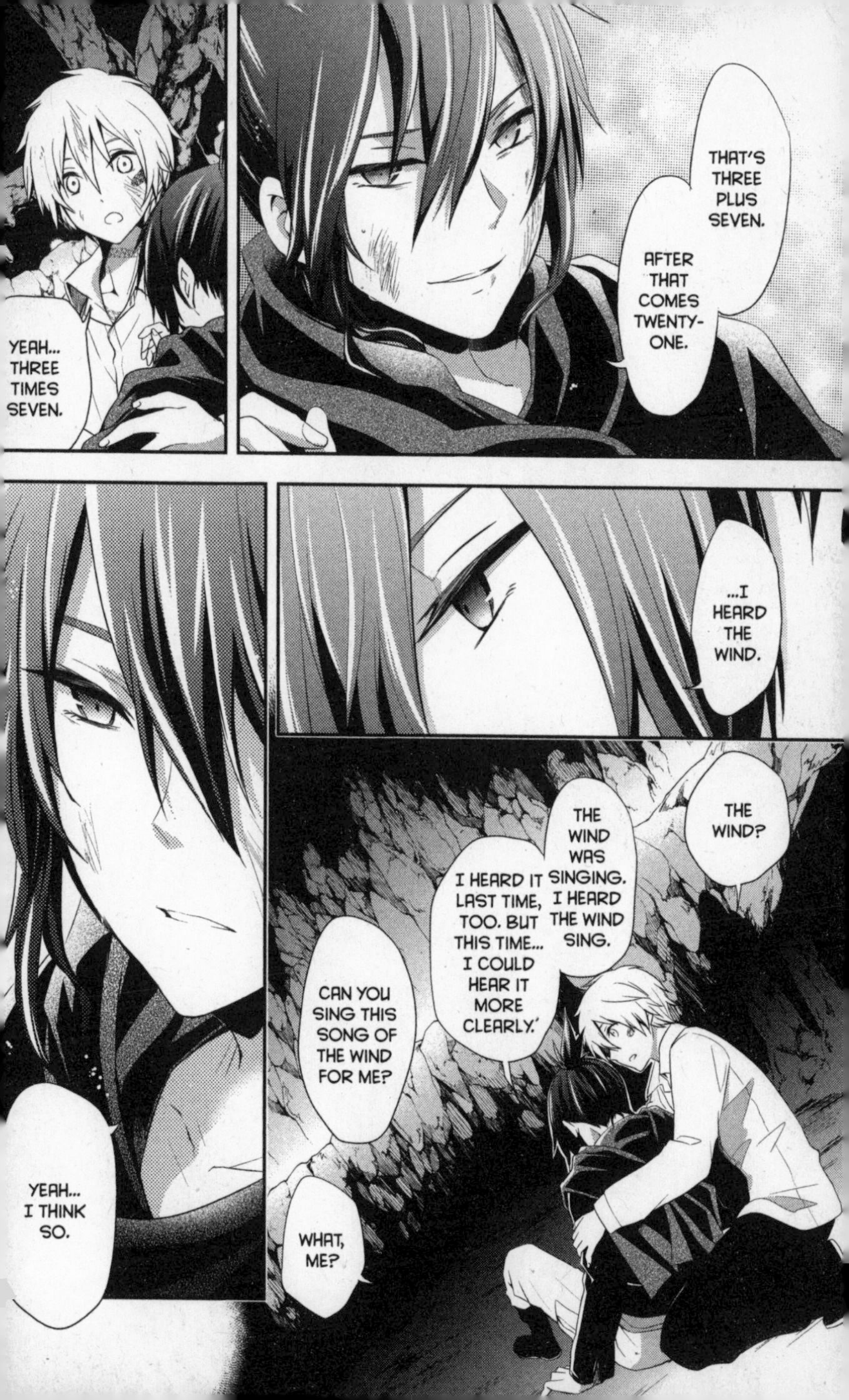
THAT'S THREE PLUS SEVEN.
AFTER THAT COMES TWENTY-ONE.
YEAH... THREE TIMES SEVEN.
...I HEARD THE WIND.
THE WIND?
THE WIND WAS SINGING. I HEARD THE WIND SING.
I HEARD IT LAST TIME, TOO. BUT THIS TIME... I COULD HEAR IT MORE CLEARLY.
CAN YOU SING THIS SONG OF THE WIND FOR ME?
WHAT, ME?
YEAH... I THINK SO.

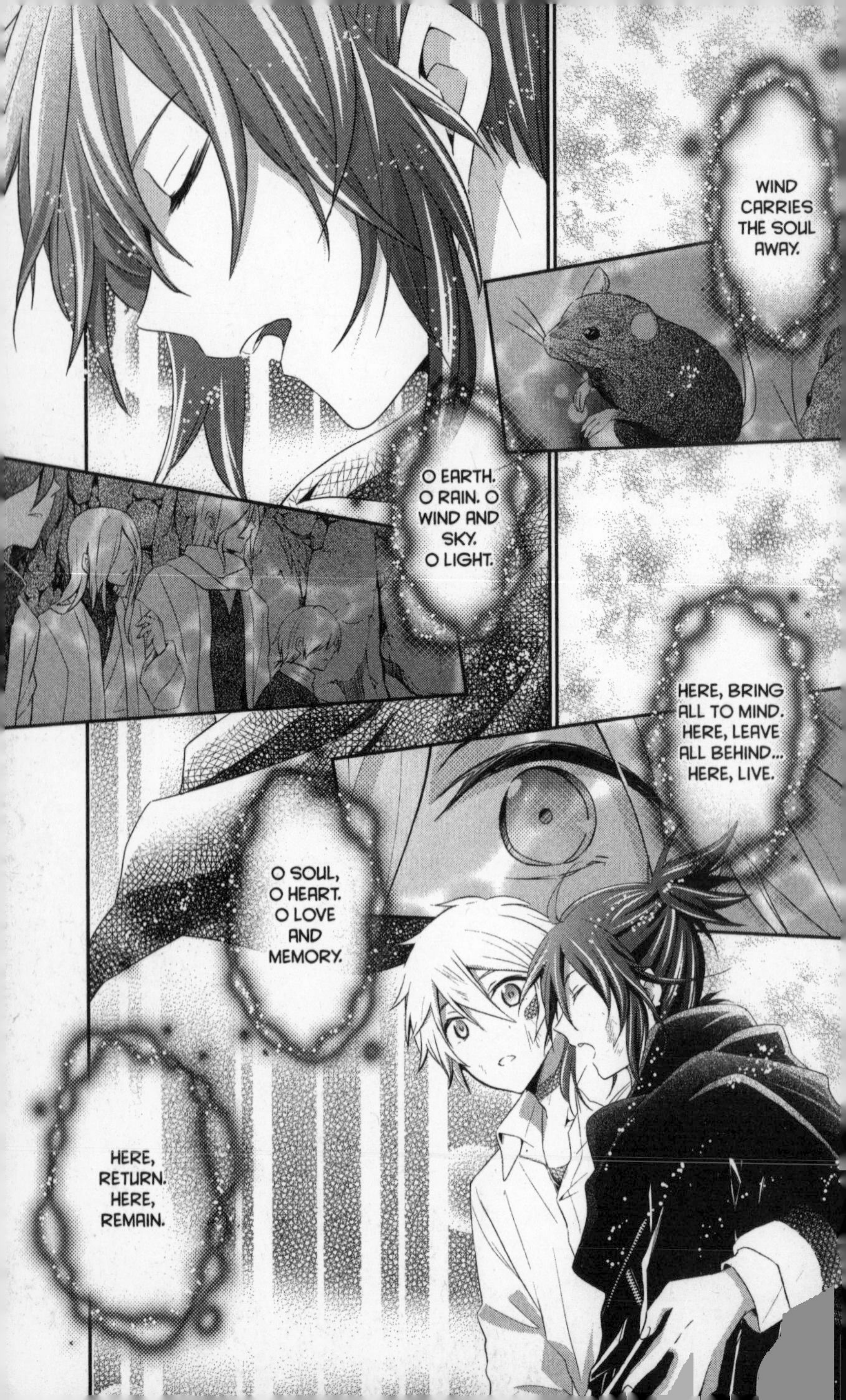
WIND CARRIES THE SOUL AWAY.
O EARTH. O RAIN. O WIND AND SKY. O LIGHT.
HERE, BRING ALL TO MIND. HERE, LEAVE ALL BEHIND... HERE, LIVE.
O SOUL, O HEART. O LOVE AND MEMORY.
HERE, RETURN. HERE, REMAIN.

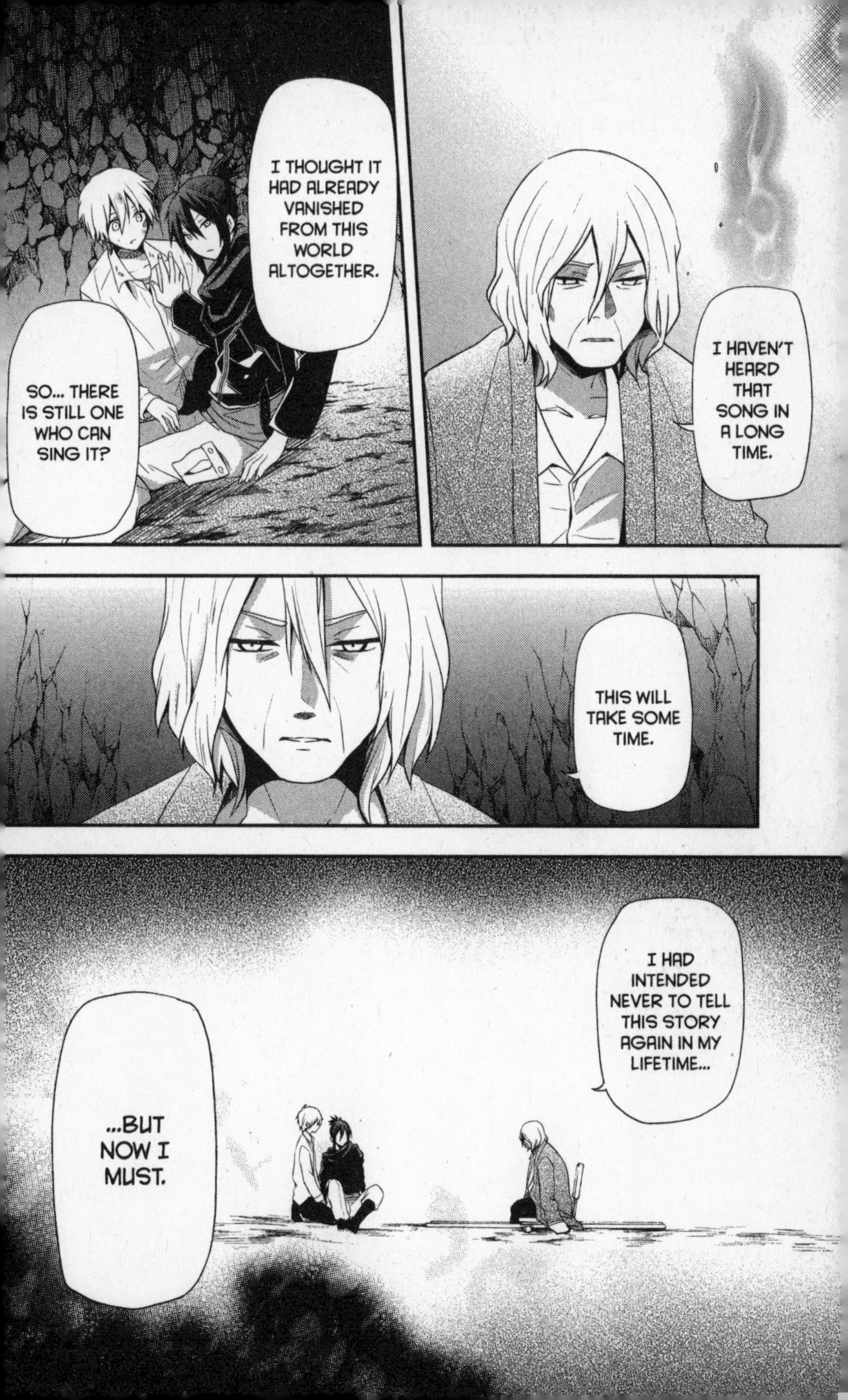
I HAVEN'T HEARD THAT SONG IN A LONG TIME.
I THOUGHT IT HAD ALREADY VANISHED FROM THIS WORLD ALTOGETHER.
SO... THERE IS STILL ONE WHO CAN SING IT?
THIS WILL TAKE SOME TIME.
I HAD INTENDED NEVER TO TELL THIS STORY AGAIN IN MY LIFETIME...
...BUT NOW I MUST.

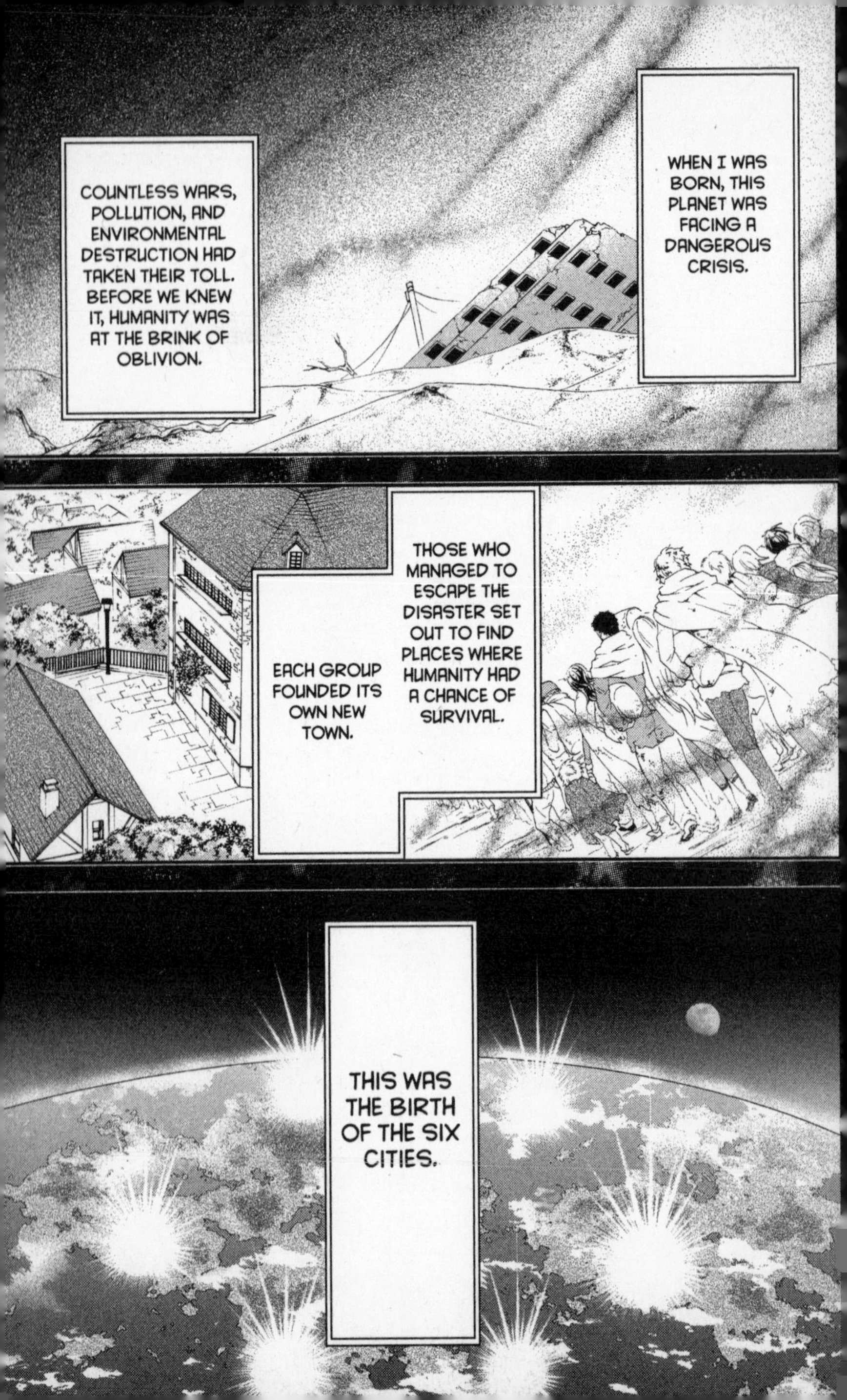
WHEN I WAS BORN, THIS PLANET WAS FACING A DANGEROUS CRISIS.
COUNTLESS WARS, POLLUTION, AND ENVIRONMENTAL DESTRUCTION HAD TAKEN THEIR TOLL. BEFORE WE KNEW IT, HUMANITY WAS AT THE BRINK OF OBLIVION.
THOSE WHO MANAGED TO ESCAPE THE DISASTER SET OUT TO FIND PLACES WHERE HUMANITY HAD A CHANCE OF SURVIVAL.
EACH GROUP FOUNDED ITS OWN NEW TOWN.
THIS WAS THE BIRTH OF THE SIX CITIES.

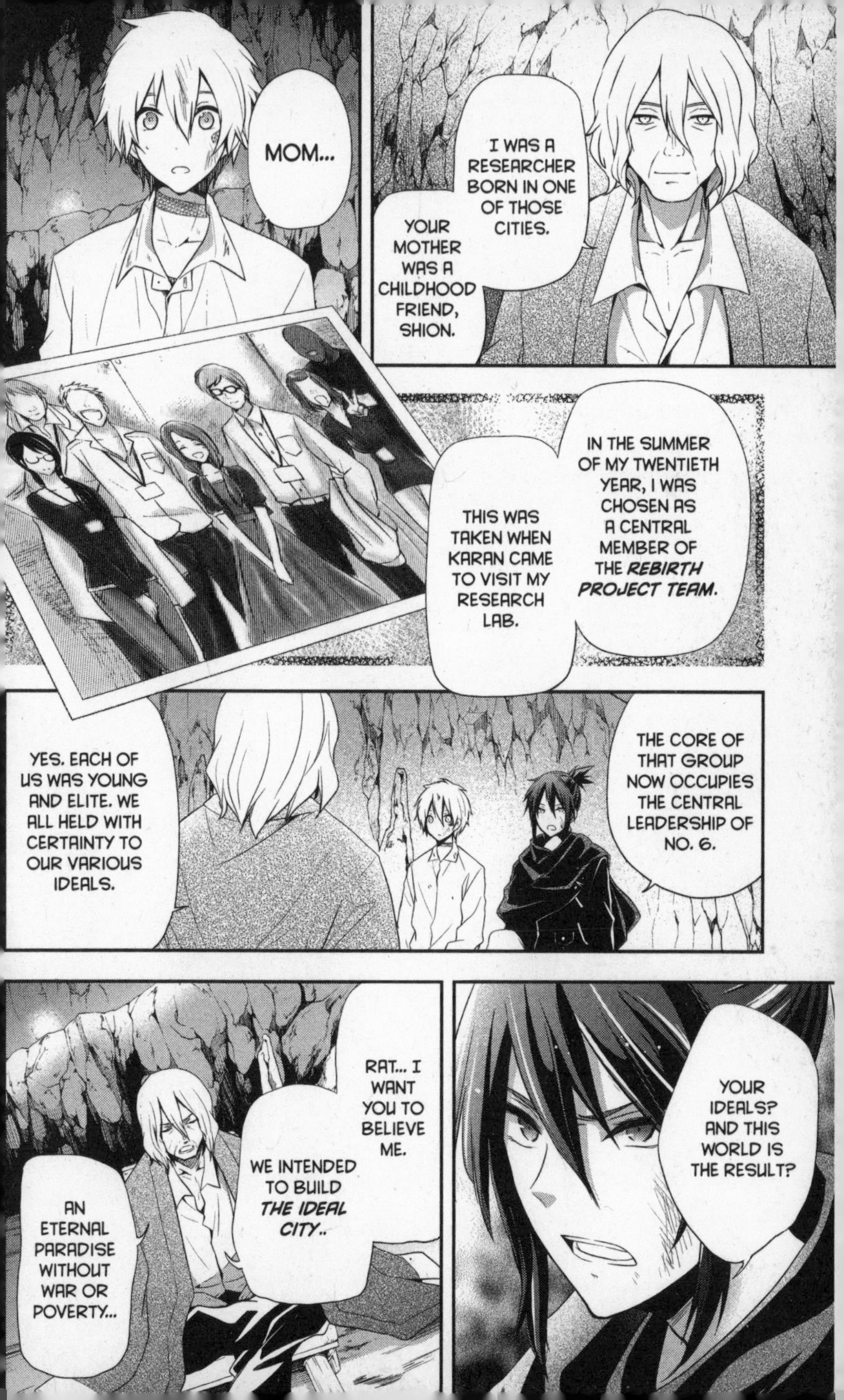
I WAS A RESEARCHER BORN IN ONE OF THOSE CITIES.
YOUR MOTHER WAS A CHILDHOOD FRIEND, SHION.
MOM...
IN THE SUMMER OF MY TWENTIETH YEAR, I WAS CHOSEN AS A CENTRAL MEMBER OF THE *REBIRTH PROJECT TEAM*.
THIS WAS TAKEN WHEN KARAN CAME TO VISIT MY RESEARCH LAB.
THE CORE OF THAT GROUP NOW OCCUPIES THE CENTRAL LEADERSHIP OF NO. 6.
YES. EACH OF US WAS YOUNG AND ELITE. WE ALL HELD WITH CERTAINTY TO OUR VARIOUS IDEALS.
YOUR IDEALS? AND THIS WORLD IS THE RESULT?
RAT... I WANT YOU TO BELIEVE ME.
WE INTENDED TO BUILD *THE IDEAL CITY*..
AN ETERNAL PARADISE WITHOUT WAR OR POVERTY...

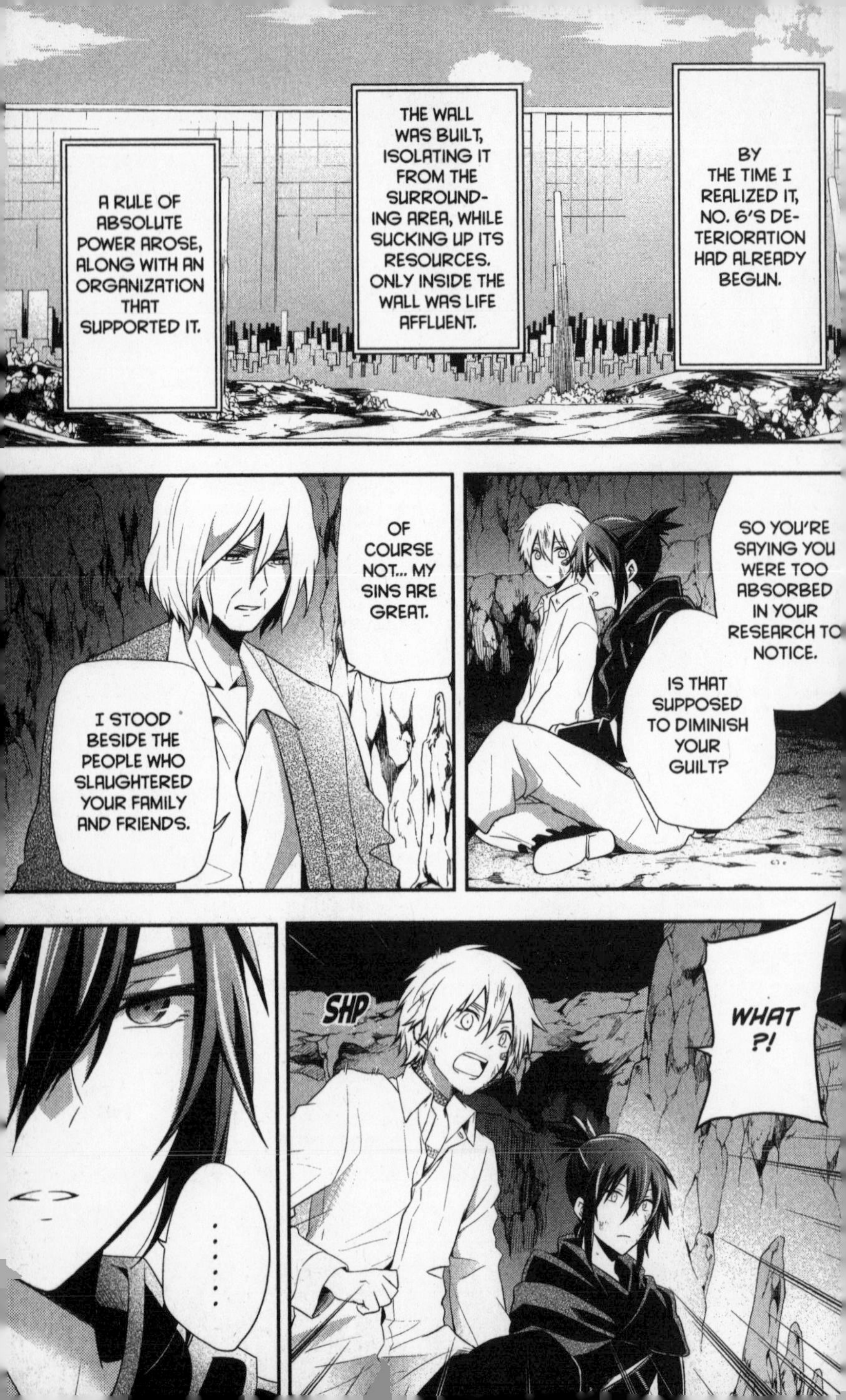
BY THE TIME I REALIZED IT, NO. 6'S DETERIORATION HAD ALREADY BEGUN.
THE WALL WAS BUILT, ISOLATING IT FROM THE SURROUNDING AREA, WHILE SUCKING UP ITS RESOURCES. ONLY INSIDE THE WALL WAS LIFE AFFLUENT.
A RULE OF ABSOLUTE POWER AROSE, ALONG WITH AN ORGANIZATION THAT SUPPORTED IT.
SO YOU'RE SAYING YOU WERE TOO ABSORBED IN YOUR RESEARCH TO NOTICE.
IS THAT SUPPOSED TO DIMINISH YOUR GUILT?
OF COURSE NOT... MY SINS ARE GREAT.
I STOOD BESIDE THE PEOPLE WHO SLAUGHTERED YOUR FAMILY AND FRIENDS.
WHAT ?!
SHP
......

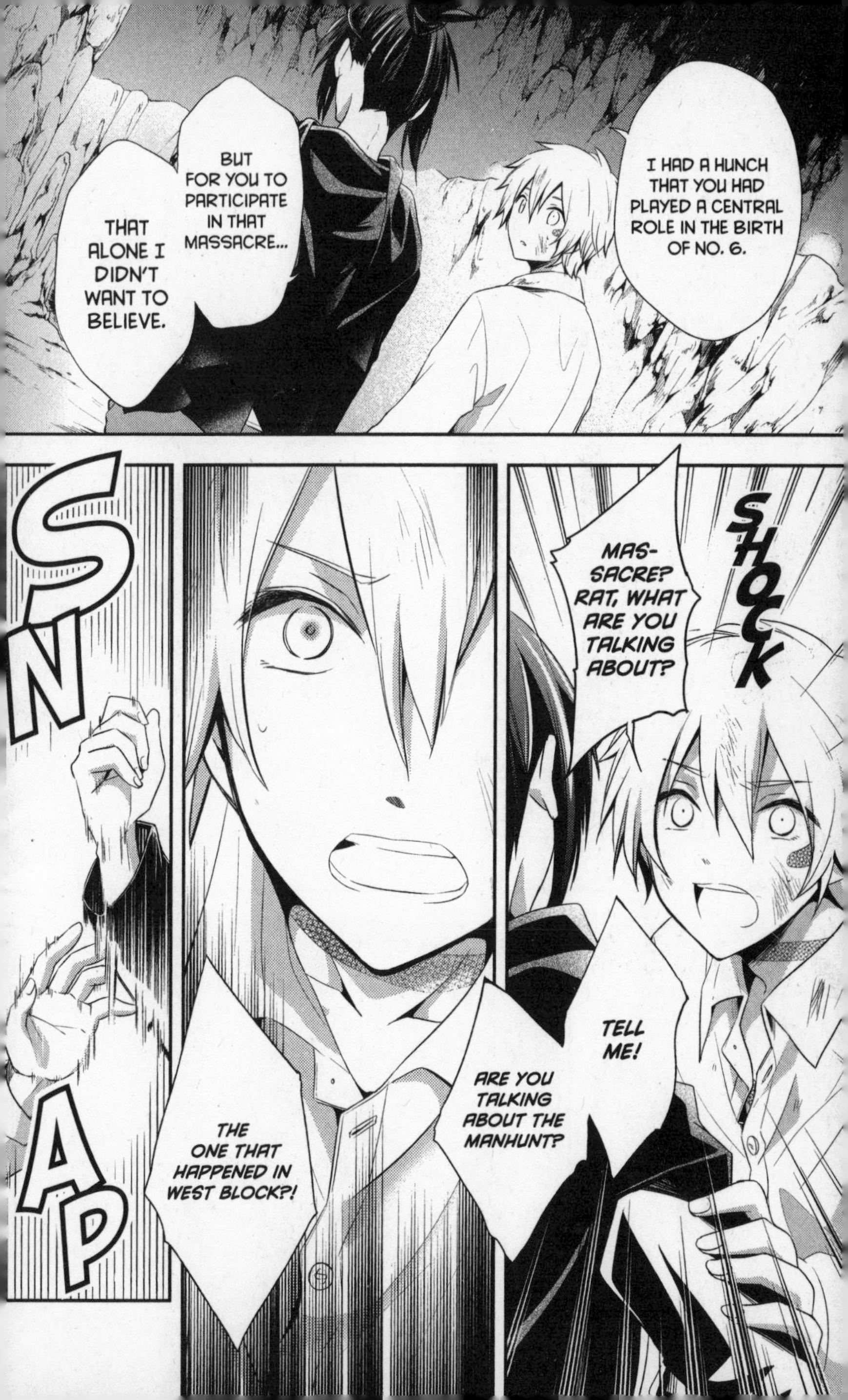
I HAD A HUNCH THAT YOU HAD PLAYED A CENTRAL ROLE IN THE BIRTH OF NO. 6.
BUT FOR YOU TO PARTICIPATE IN THAT MASSACRE...
THAT ALONE I DIDN'T WANT TO BELIEVE.
SHOCK
MAS-SACRE? RAT, WHAT ARE YOU TALKING ABOUT?
TELL ME!
ARE YOU TALKING ABOUT THE MANHUNT?
THE ONE THAT HAPPENED IN WEST BLOCK?!
SNAP

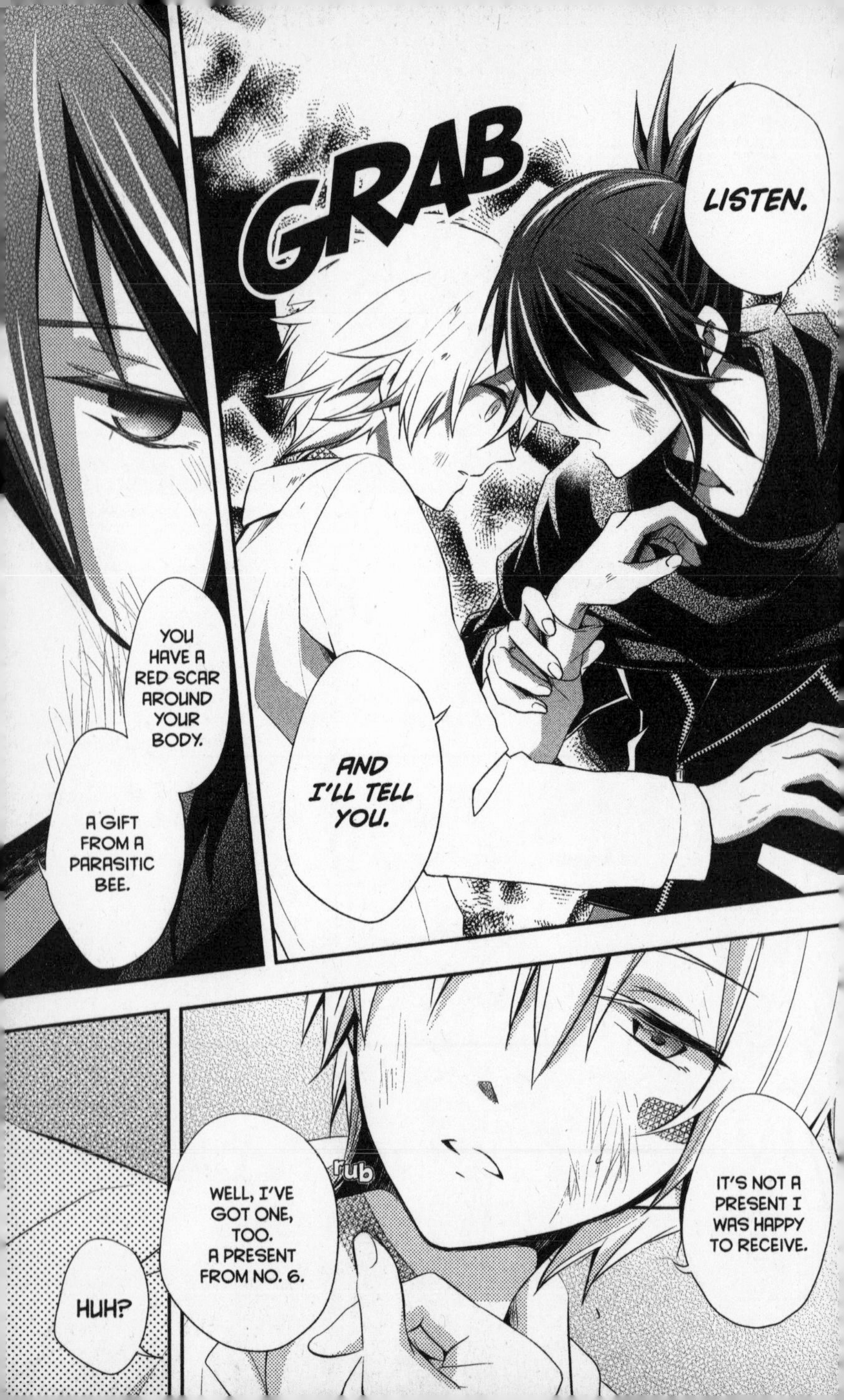
GRAB
LISTEN.
AND I'LL TELL YOU.
YOU HAVE A RED SCAR AROUND YOUR BODY.
A GIFT FROM A PARASITIC BEE.
IT'S NOT A PRESENT I WAS HAPPY TO RECEIVE.
rub
WELL, I'VE GOT ONE, TOO. A PRESENT FROM NO. 6.
HUH?

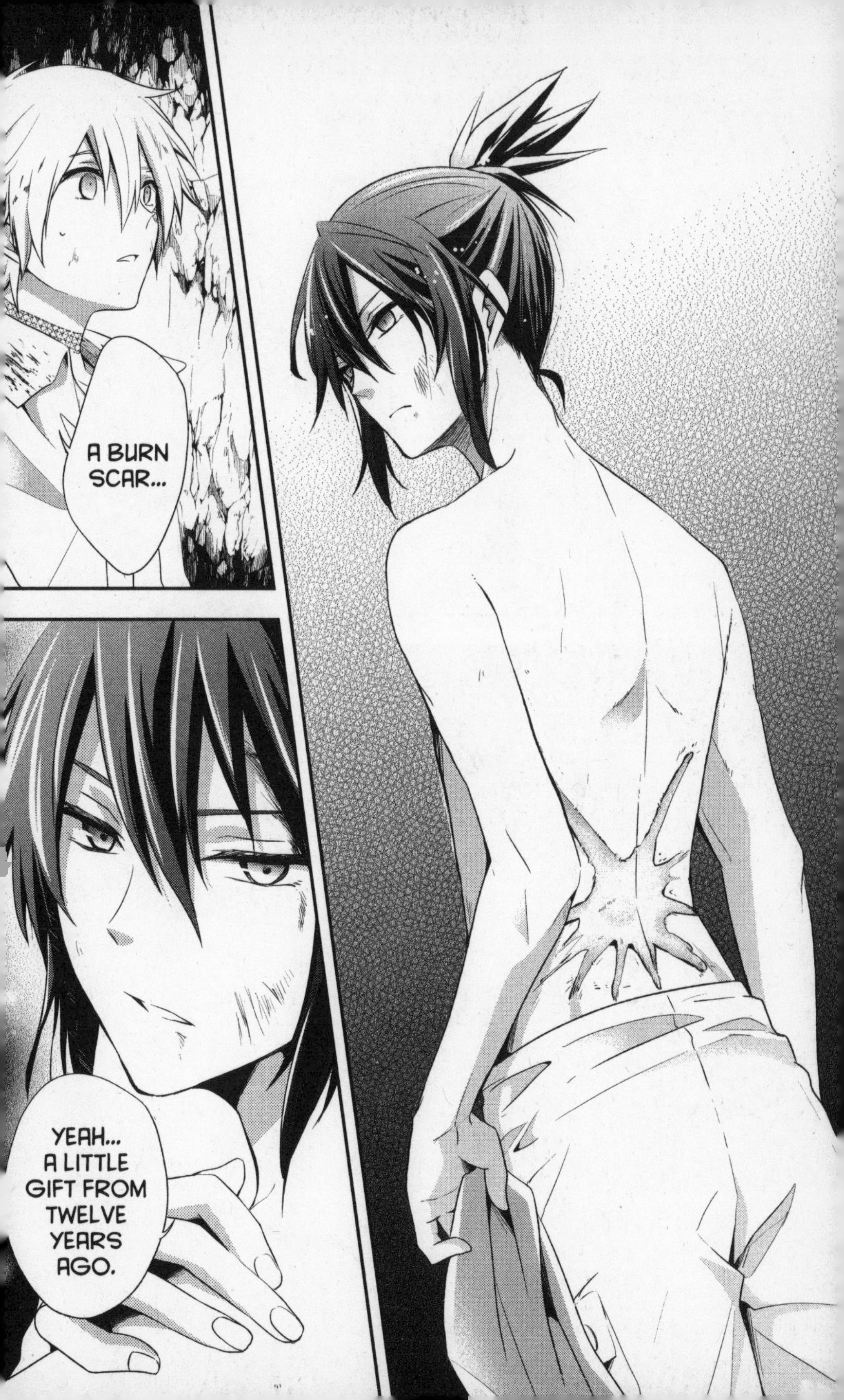
A BURN SCAR...
YEAH... A LITTLE GIFT FROM TWELVE YEARS AGO.

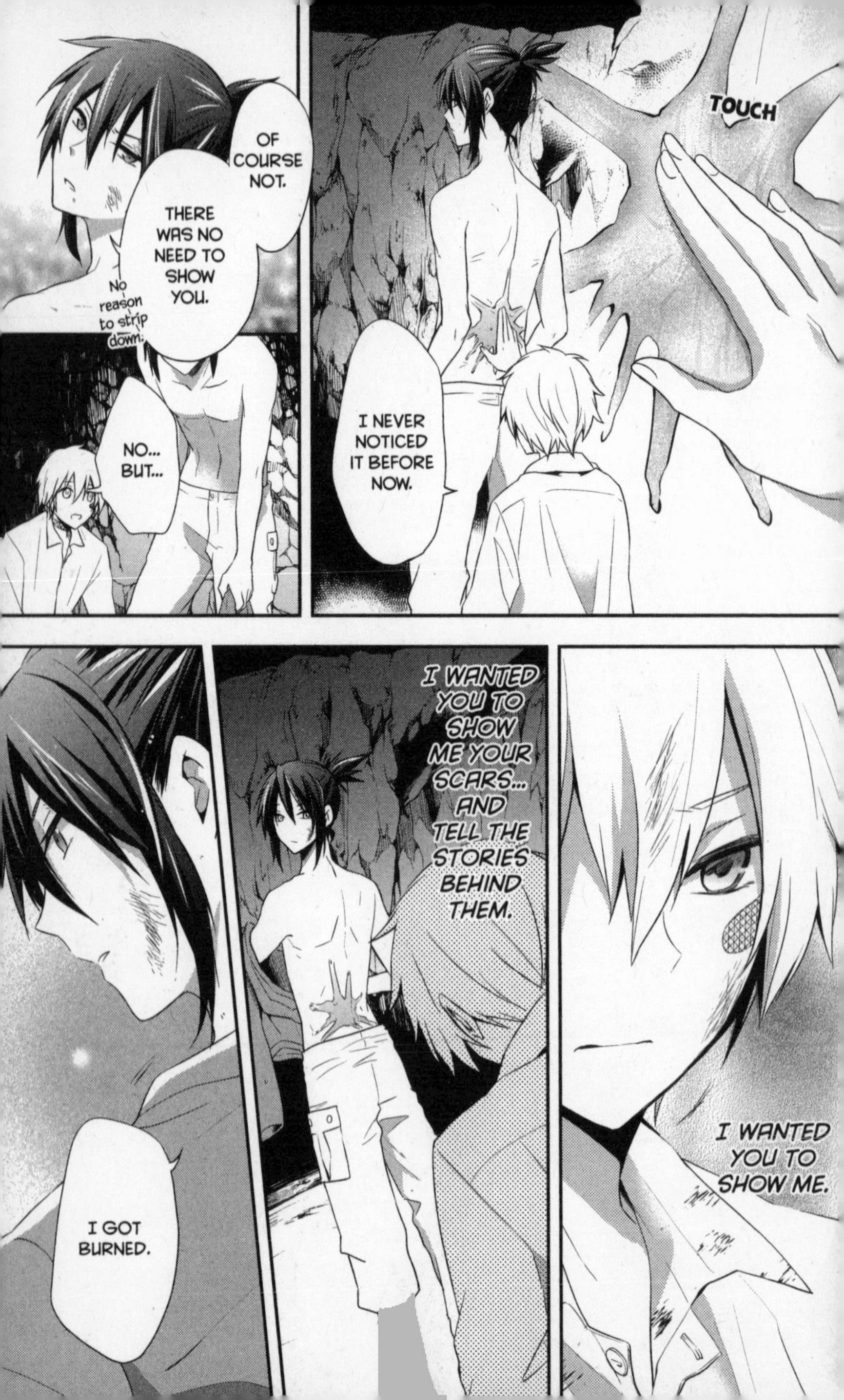
TOUCH
I NEVER NOTICED IT BEFORE NOW.
OF COURSE NOT.
THERE WAS NO NEED TO SHOW YOU.
No reason to strip down.
NO... BUT...
I WANTED YOU TO SHOW ME.
I WANTED YOU TO SHOW ME YOUR SCARS... AND TELL THE STORIES BEHIND THEM.
I GOT BURNED.

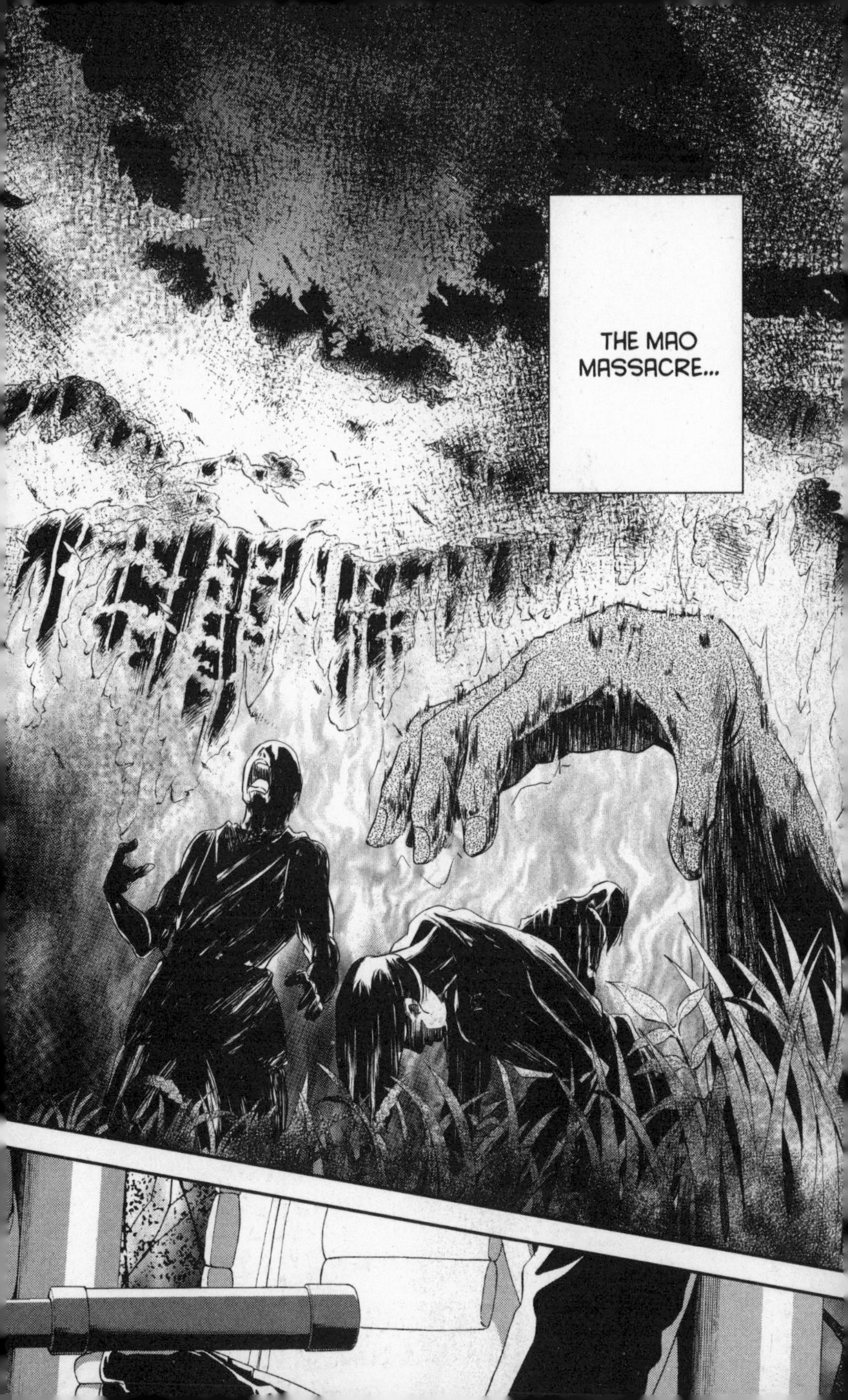
THE MAO MASSACRE...

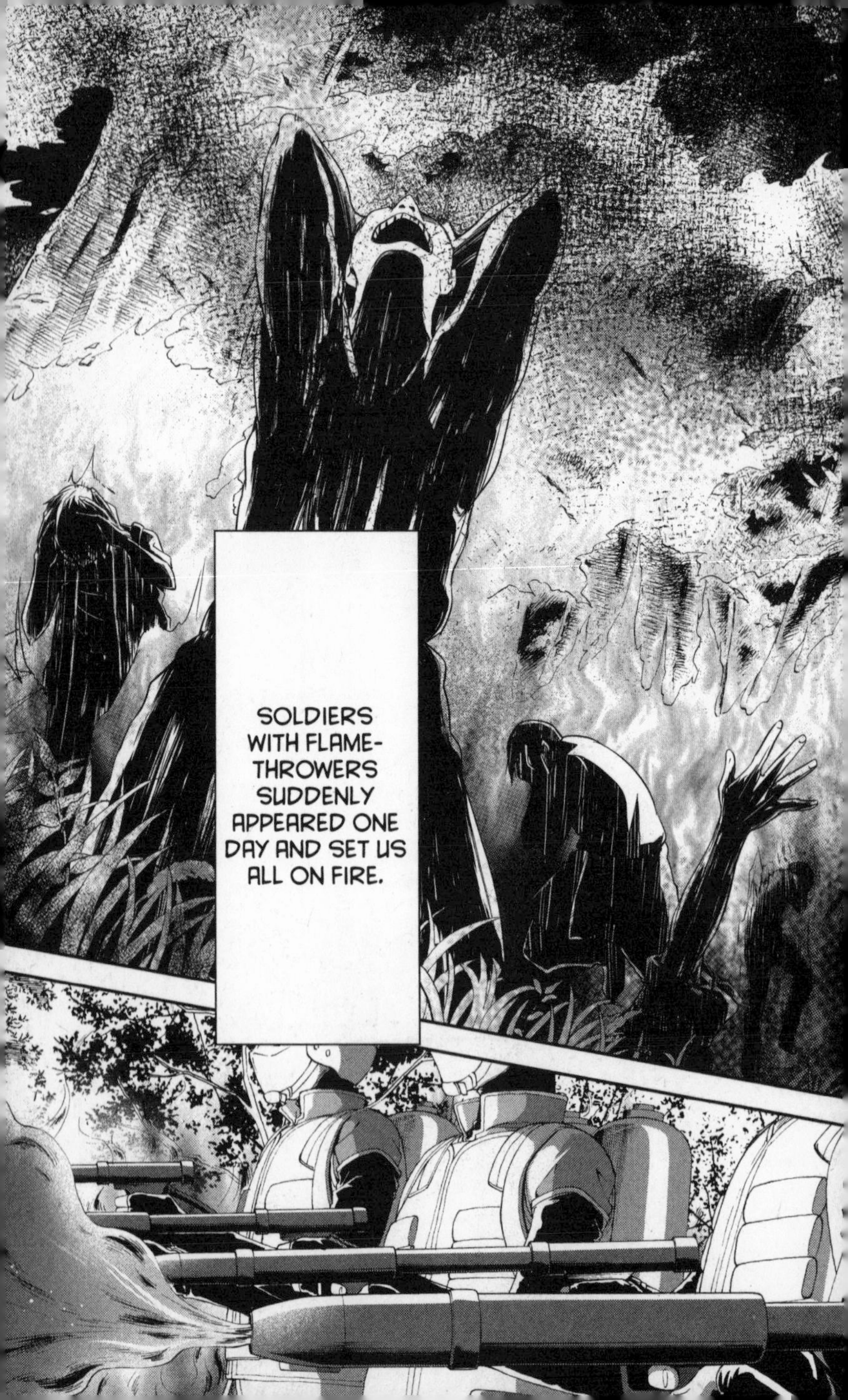
SOLDIERS WITH FLAME-THROWERS SUDDENLY APPEARED ONE DAY AND SET US ALL ON FIRE.

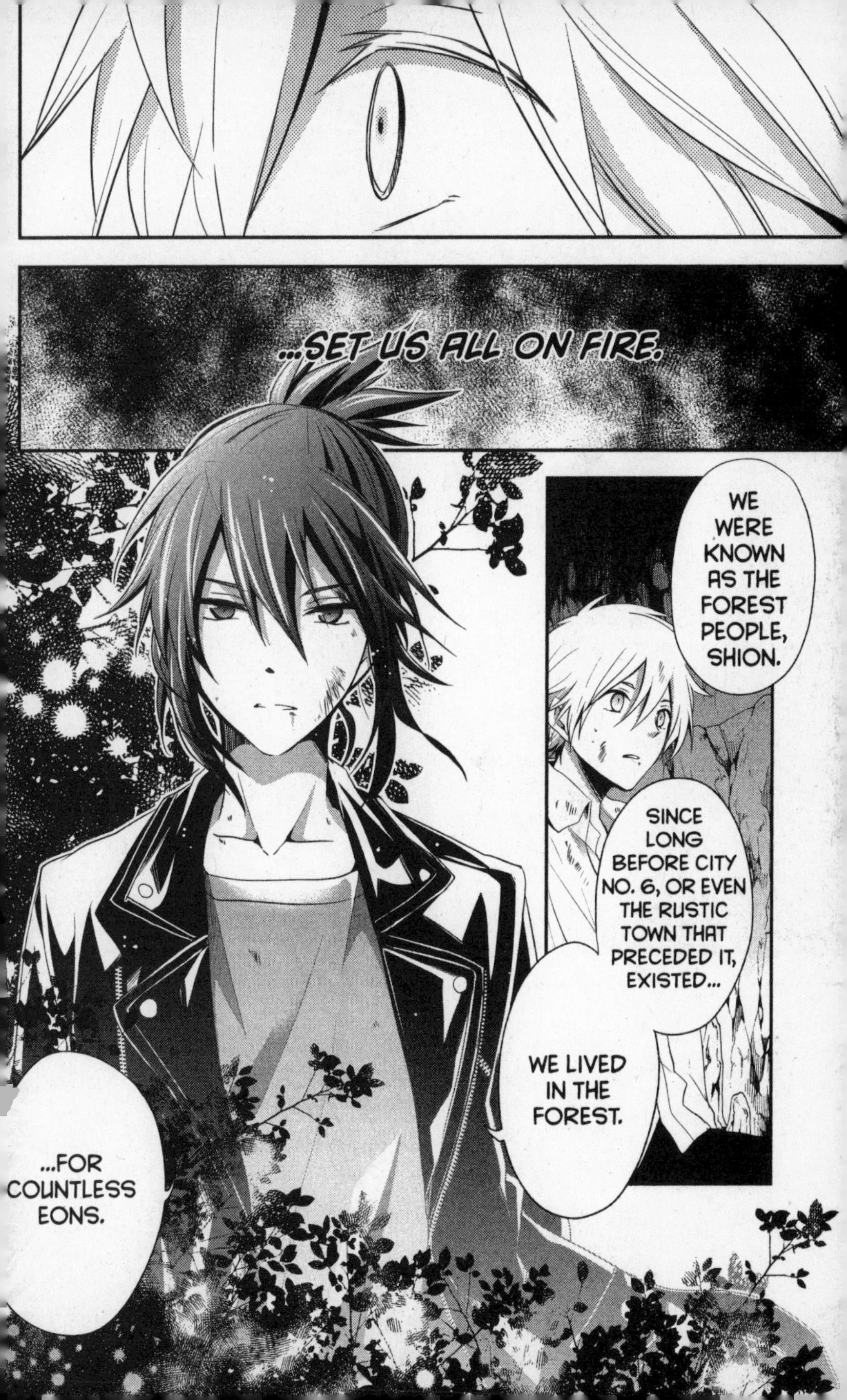
...SET US ALL ON FIRE.
WE WERE KNOWN AS THE FOREST PEOPLE, SHION.
SINCE LONG BEFORE CITY NO. 6, OR EVEN THE RUSTIC TOWN THAT PRECEDED IT, EXISTED...
WE LIVED IN THE FOREST.
...FOR COUNTLESS EONS.

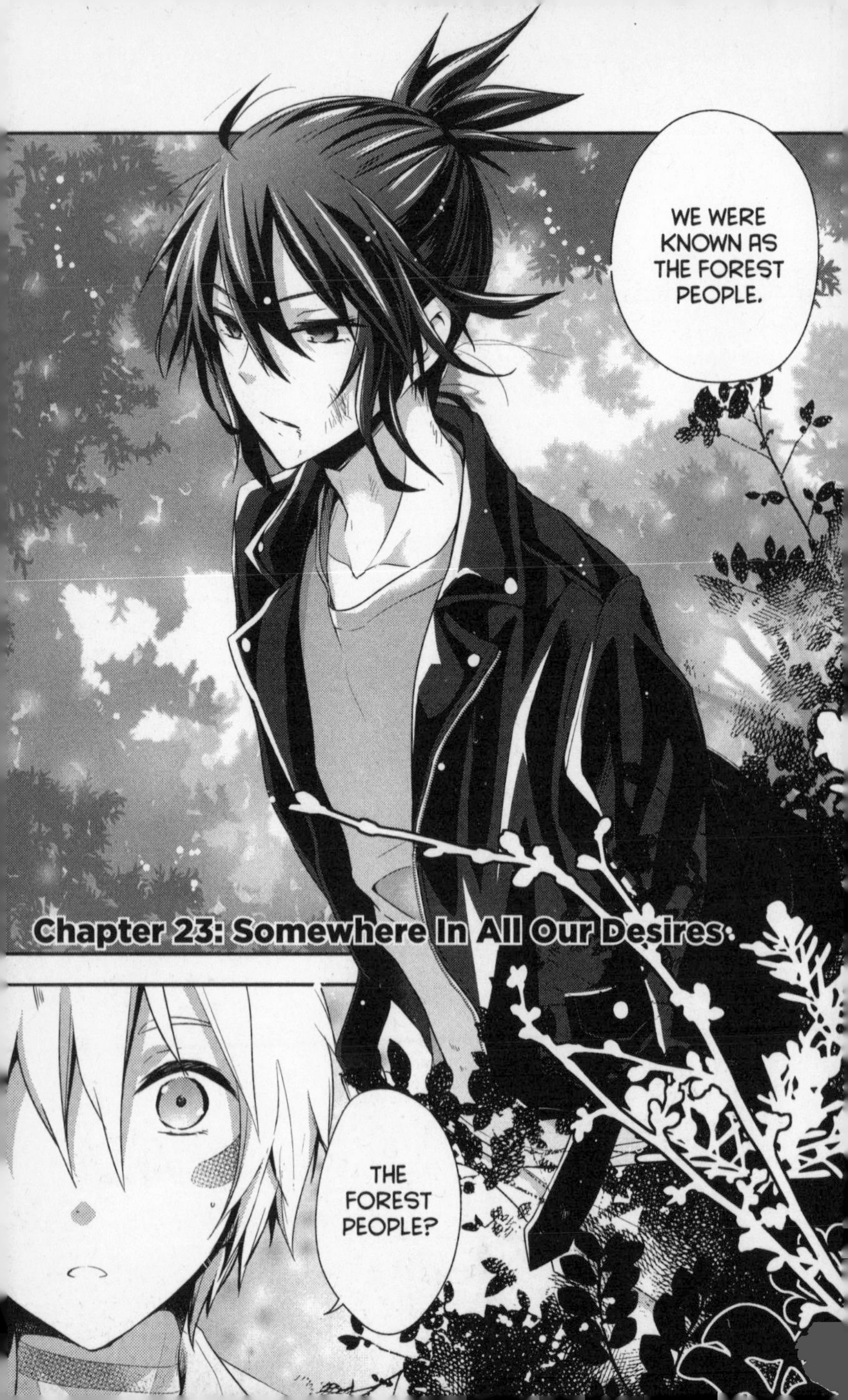
WE WERE KNOWN AS THE FOREST PEOPLE.
Chapter 23: Somewhere In All Our Desires
THE FOREST PEOPLE?

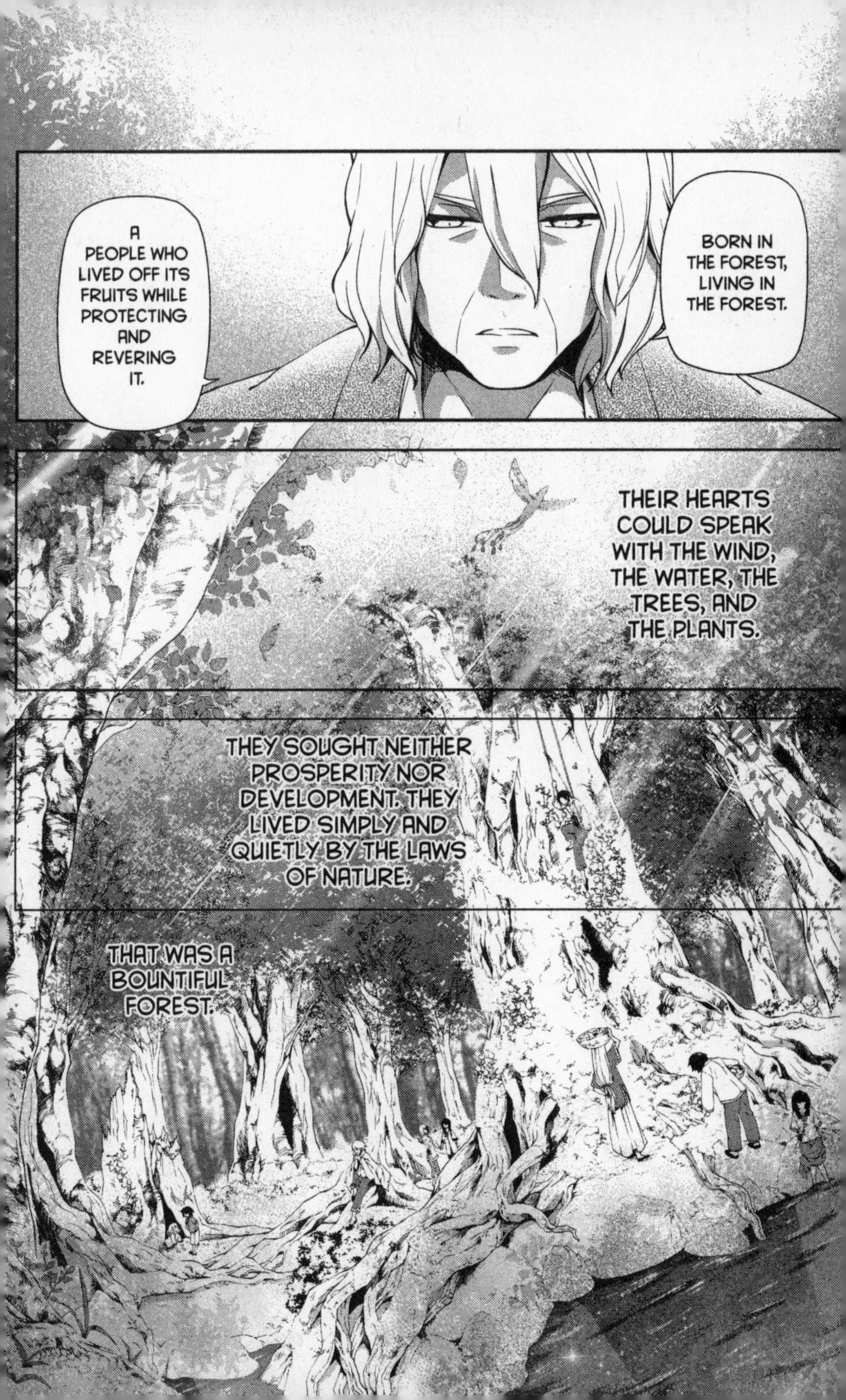
BORN IN THE FOREST, LIVING IN THE FOREST.
A PEOPLE WHO LIVED OFF ITS FRUITS WHILE PROTECTING AND REVERING IT.
THEIR HEARTS COULD SPEAK WITH THE WIND, THE WATER, THE TREES, AND THE PLANTS.
THEY SOUGHT NEITHER PROSPERITY NOR DEVELOPMENT. THEY LIVED SIMPLY AND QUIETLY BY THE LAWS OF NATURE.
THAT WAS A BOUNTIFUL FOREST.

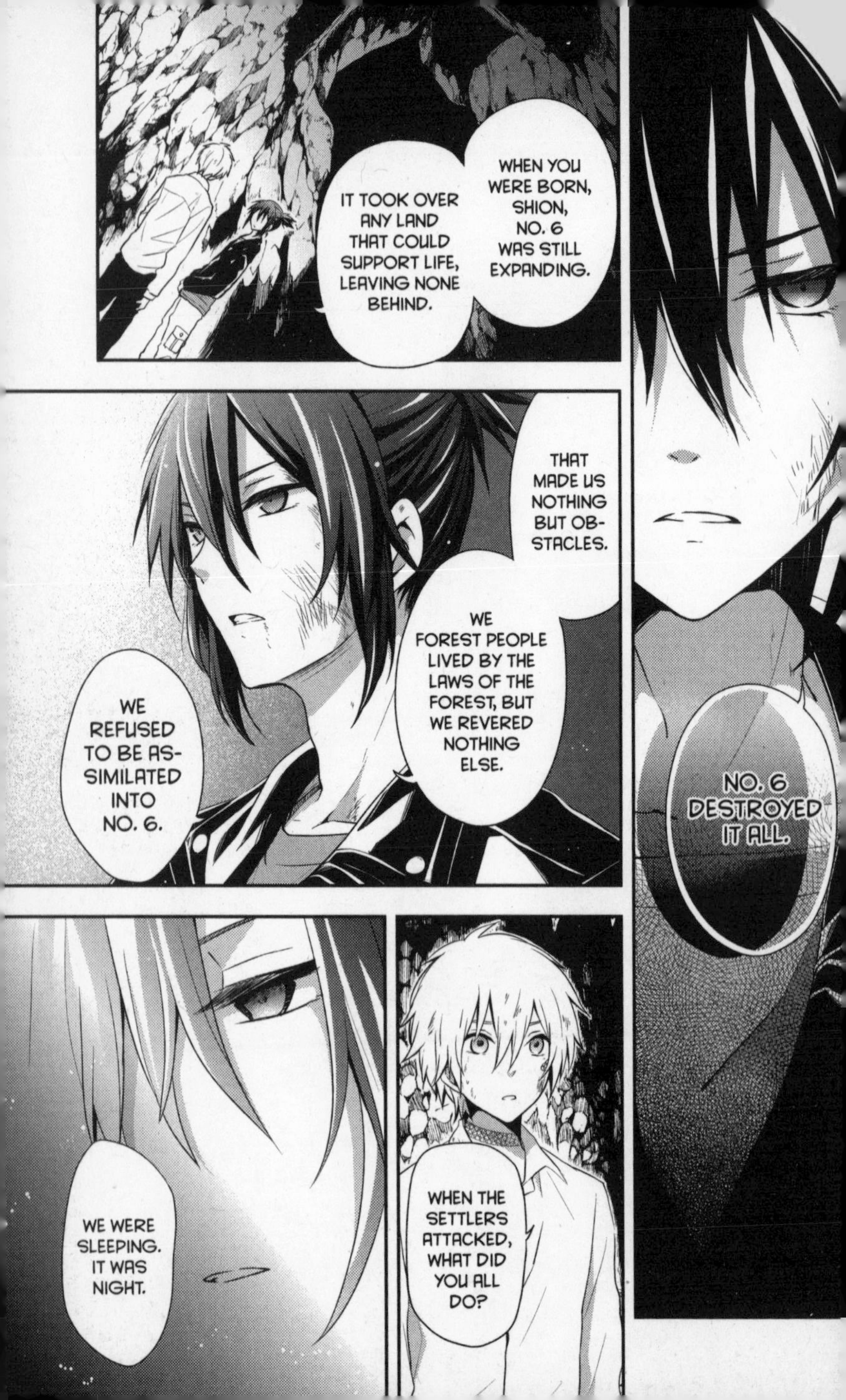
NO. 6 DESTROYED IT ALL.
WHEN YOU WERE BORN, SHION, NO. 6 WAS STILL EXPANDING.
IT TOOK OVER ANY LAND THAT COULD SUPPORT LIFE, LEAVING NONE BEHIND.
THAT MADE US NOTHING BUT OB-STACLES.
WE FOREST PEOPLE LIVED BY THE LAWS OF THE FOREST, BUT WE REVERED NOTHING ELSE.
WE REFUSED TO BE AS-SIMILATED INTO NO. 6.
WHEN THE SETTLERS ATTACKED, WHAT DID YOU ALL DO?
WE WERE SLEEPING. IT WAS NIGHT.

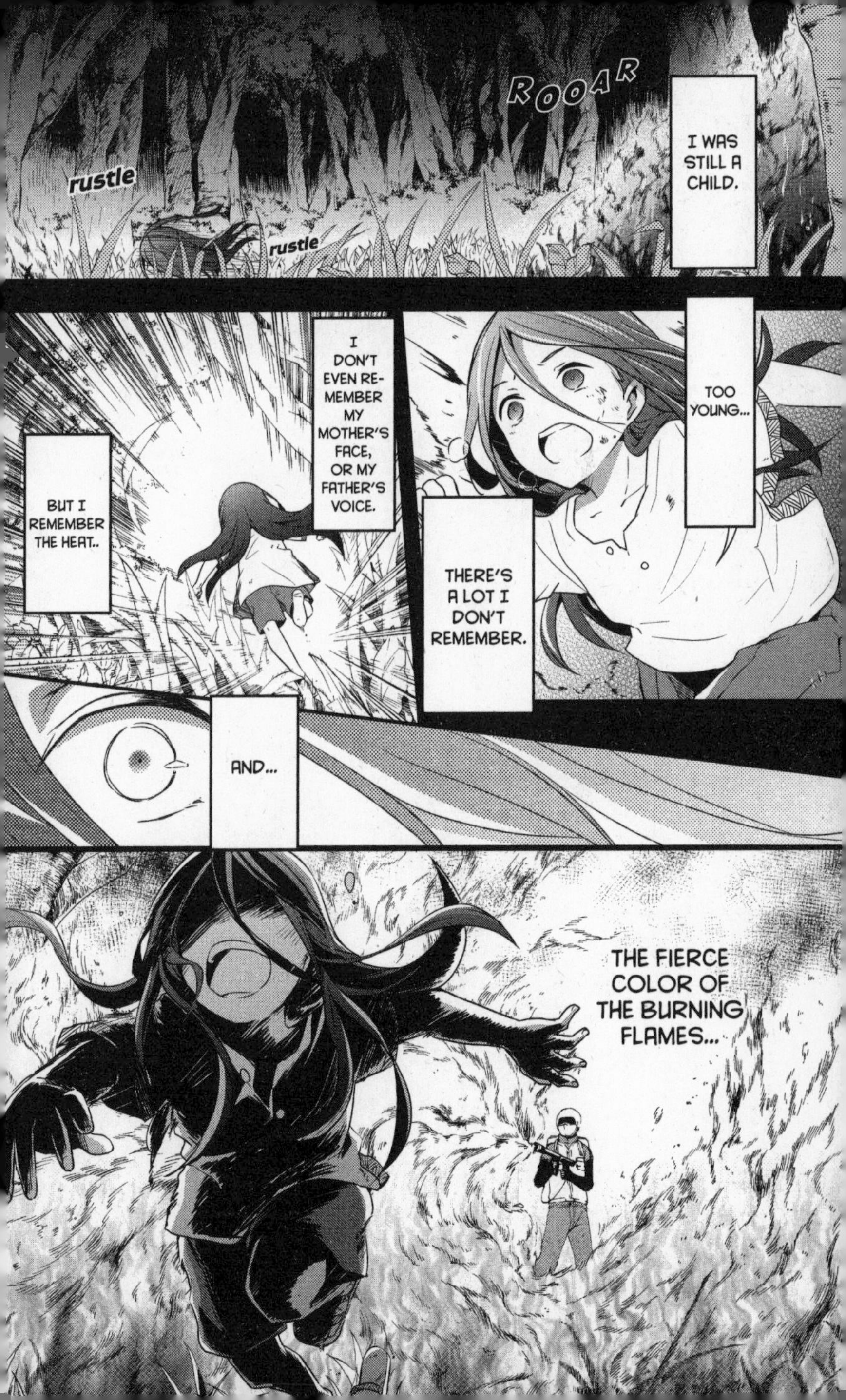
I WAS STILL A CHILD.
ROOAR
rustle
rustle
TOO YOUNG...
THERE'S A LOT I DON'T REMEMBER.
I DON'T EVEN RE-MEMBER MY MOTHER'S FACE, OR MY FATHER'S VOICE.
BUT I REMEMBER THE HEAT..
AND...
THE FIERCE COLOR OF THE BURNING FLAMES...

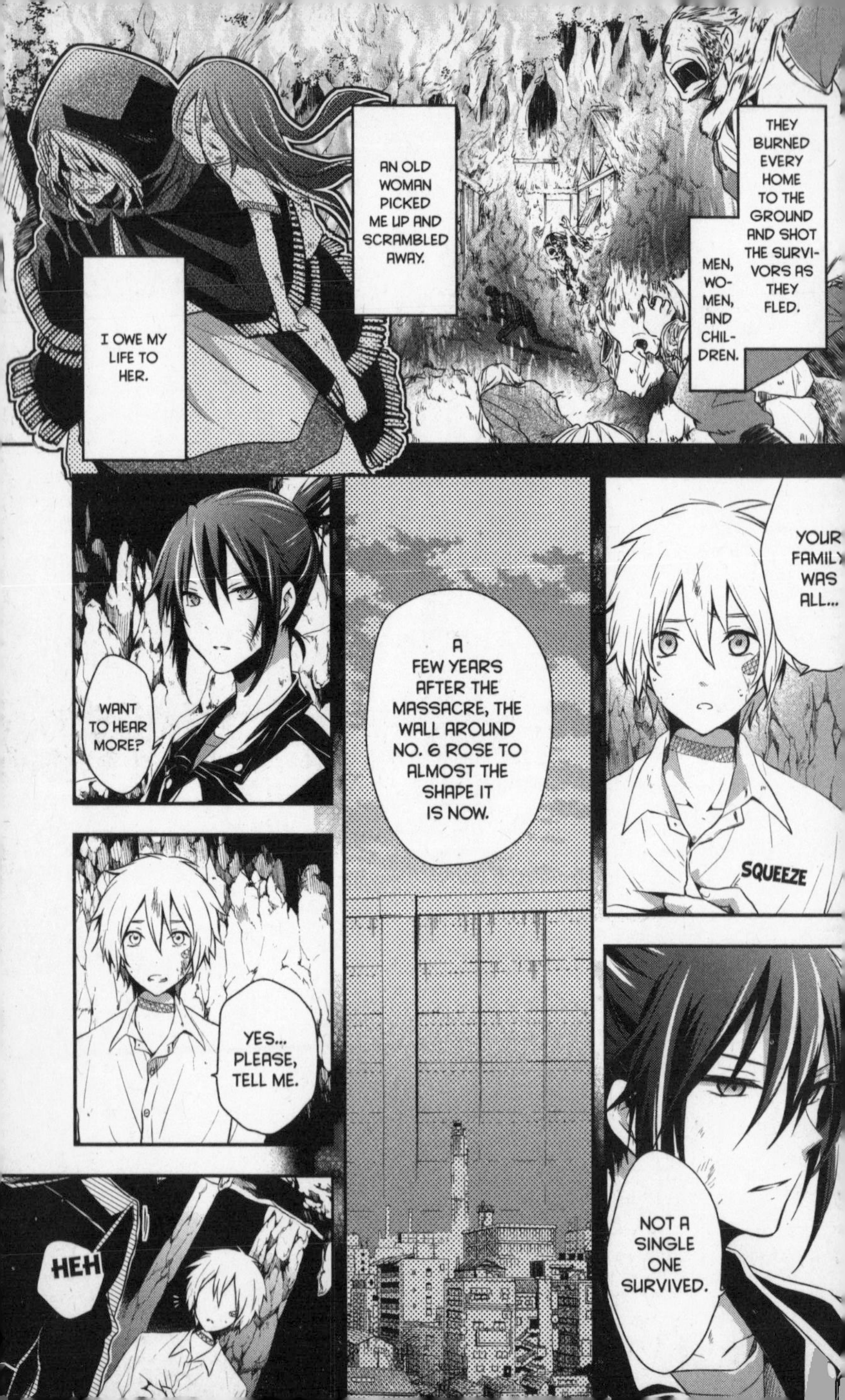
THEY BURNED EVERY HOME TO THE GROUND AND SHOT THE SURVIVORS AS THEY FLED.
MEN, WOMEN, AND CHILDREN.
AN OLD WOMAN PICKED ME UP AND SCRAMBLED AWAY.
I OWE MY LIFE TO HER.
YOUR FAMILY WAS ALL...
SQUEEZE
NOT A SINGLE ONE SURVIVED.
A FEW YEARS AFTER THE MASSACRE, THE WALL AROUND NO. 6 ROSE TO ALMOST THE SHAPE IT IS NOW.
WANT TO HEAR MORE?
YES... PLEASE, TELL ME.
HEH

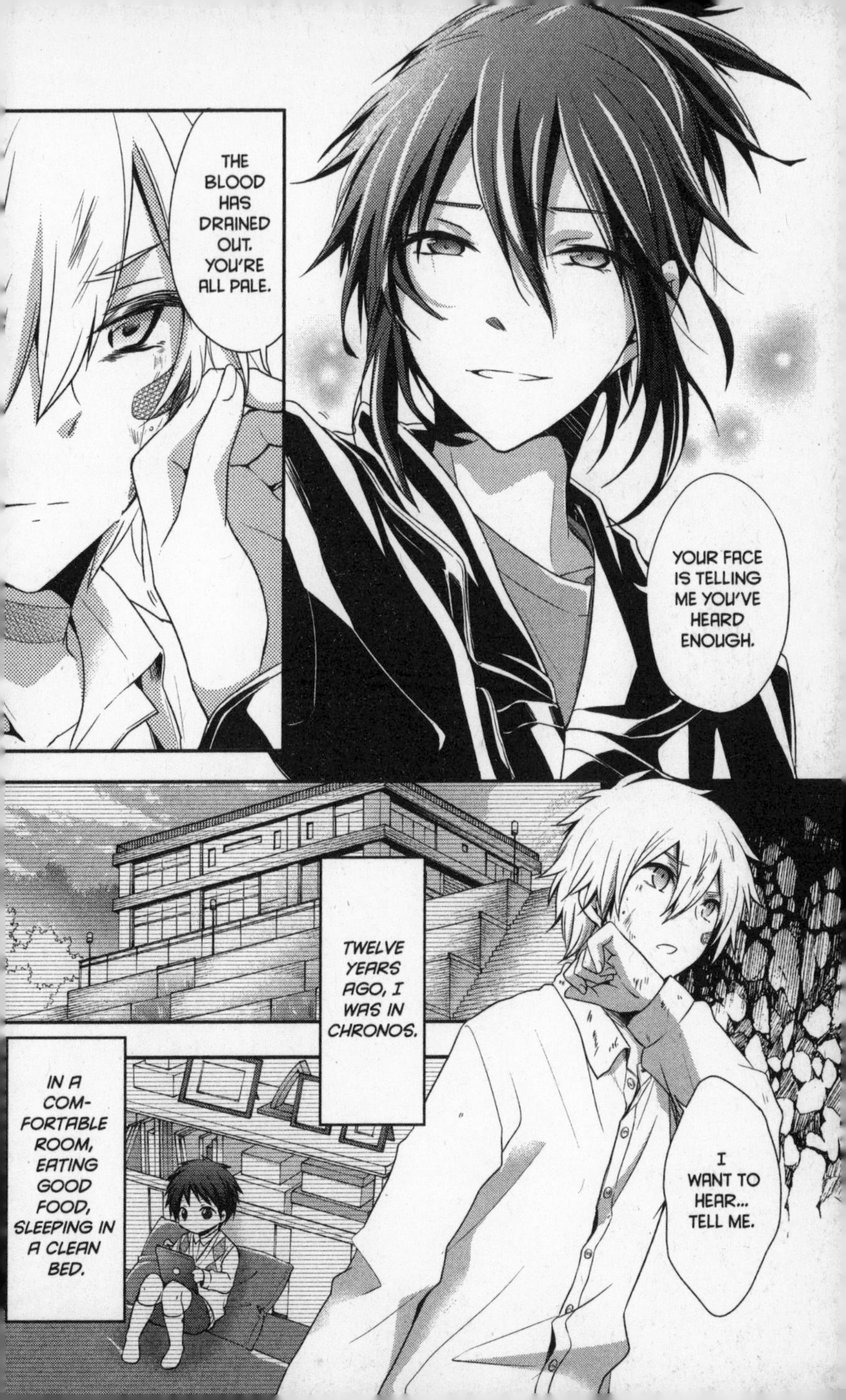
YOUR FACE IS TELLING ME YOU'VE HEARD ENOUGH.
THE BLOOD HAS DRAINED OUT. YOU'RE ALL PALE.
I WANT TO HEAR... TELL ME.
TWELVE YEARS AGO, I WAS IN CHRONOS.
IN A COM-FORTABLE ROOM, EATING GOOD FOOD, SLEEPING IN A CLEAN BED.

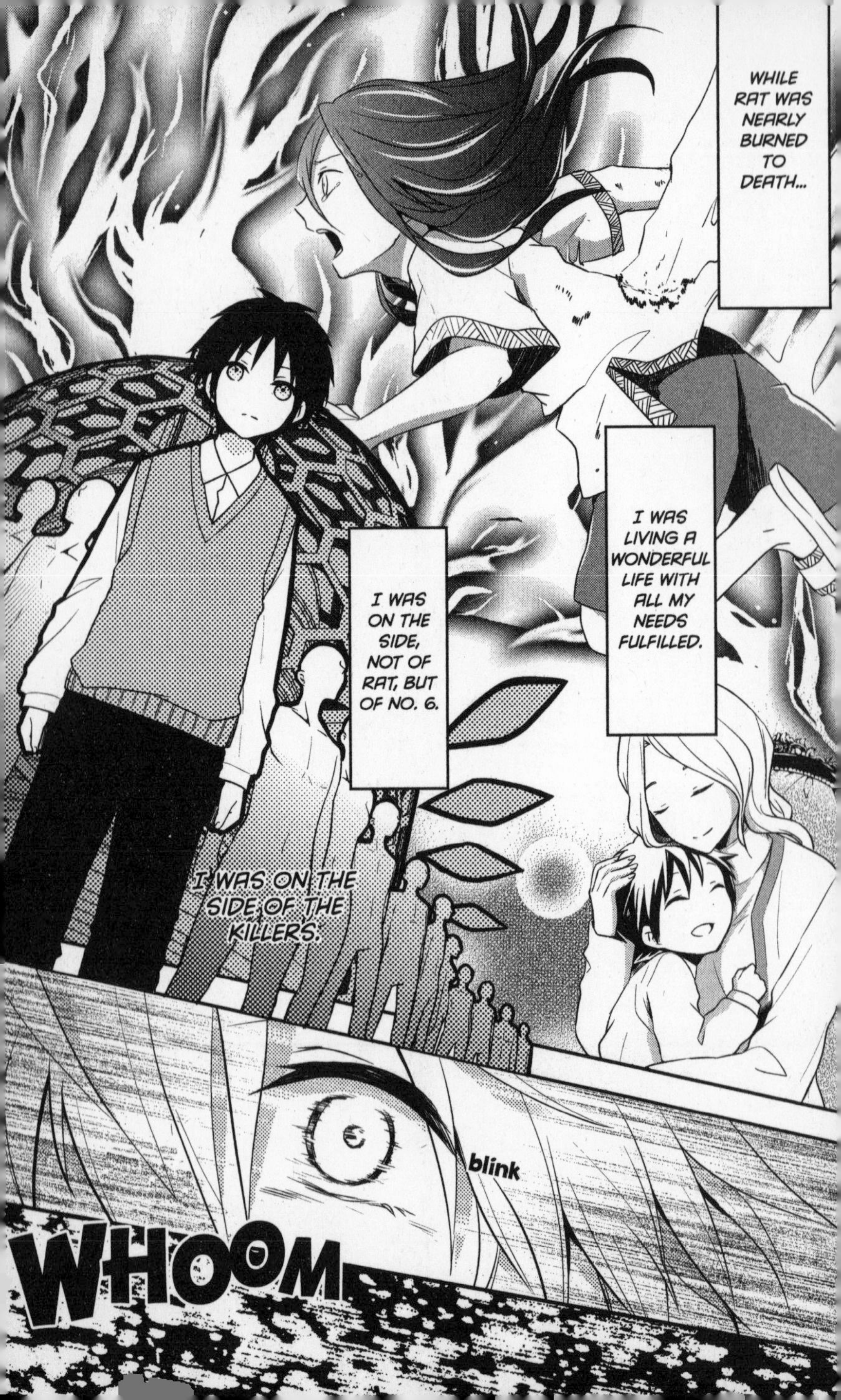
WHILE RAT WAS NEARLY BURNED TO DEATH...
I WAS LIVING A WONDERFUL LIFE WITH ALL MY NEEDS FULFILLED.
I WAS ON THE SIDE, NOT OF RAT, BUT OF NO. 6.
I WAS ON THE SIDE OF THE KILLERS.
blink
WHOOM

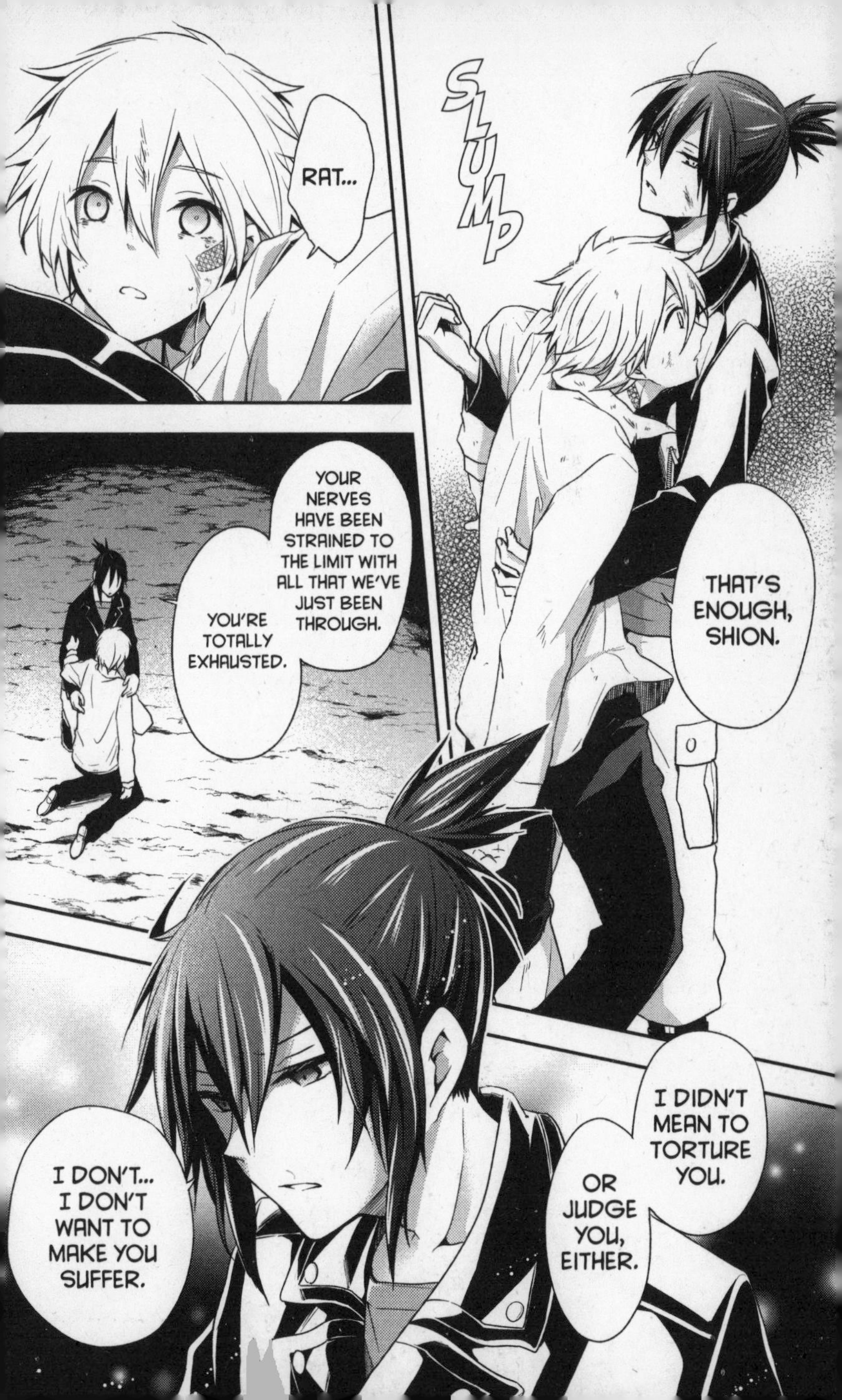
SLUMP
THAT'S ENOUGH, SHION.
RAT...
YOUR NERVES HAVE BEEN STRAINED TO THE LIMIT WITH ALL THAT WE'VE JUST BEEN THROUGH.
YOU'RE TOTALLY EXHAUSTED.
I DIDN'T MEAN TO TORTURE YOU.
OR JUDGE YOU, EITHER.
I DON'T... I DON'T WANT TO MAKE YOU SUFFER.

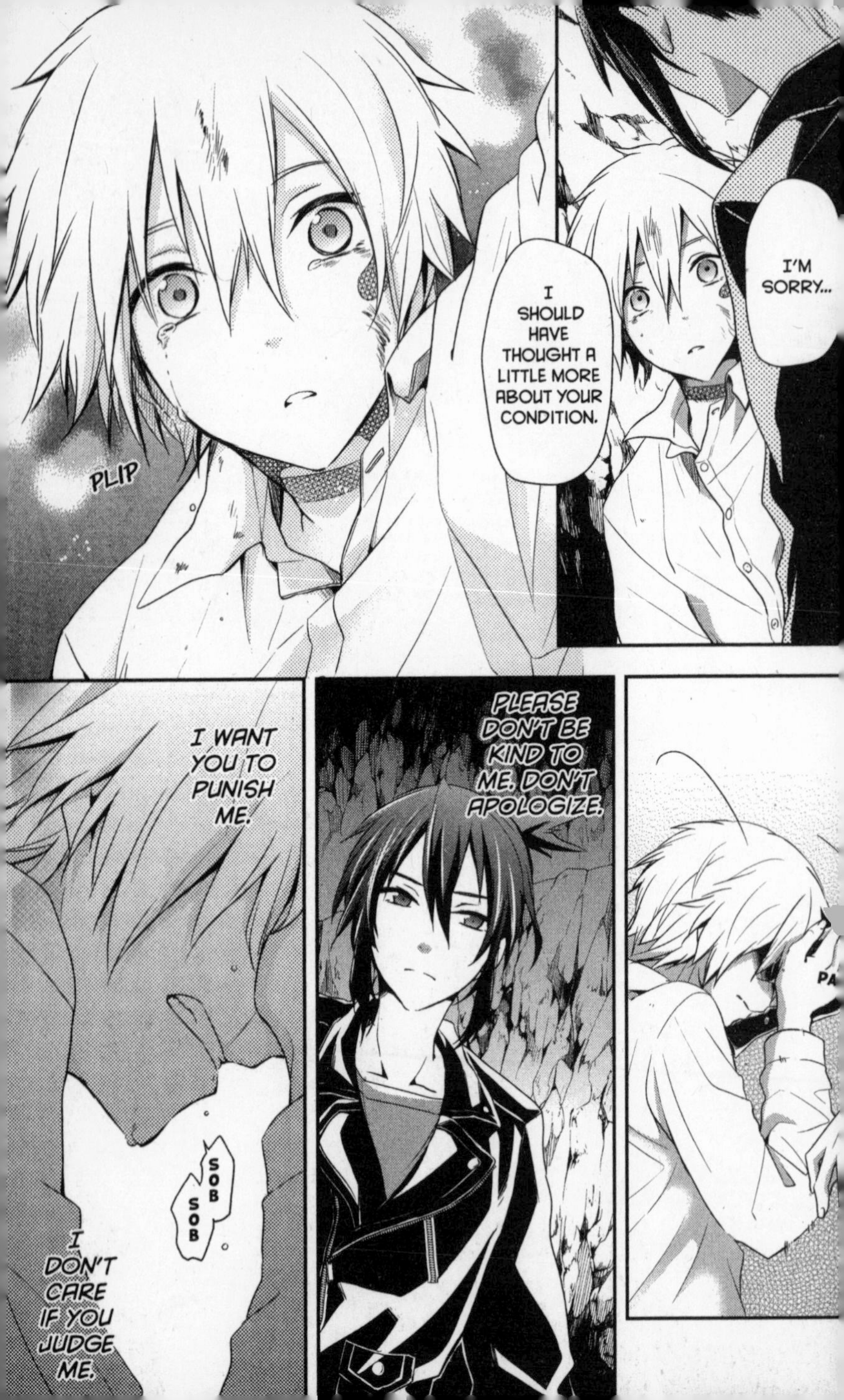
I'M SORRY...
I SHOULD HAVE THOUGHT A LITTLE MORE ABOUT YOUR CONDITION.
PLIP
PLEASE DON'T BE KIND TO ME. DON'T APOLOGIZE.
I WANT YOU TO PUNISH ME.
SOB SOB
I DON'T CARE IF YOU JUDGE ME.

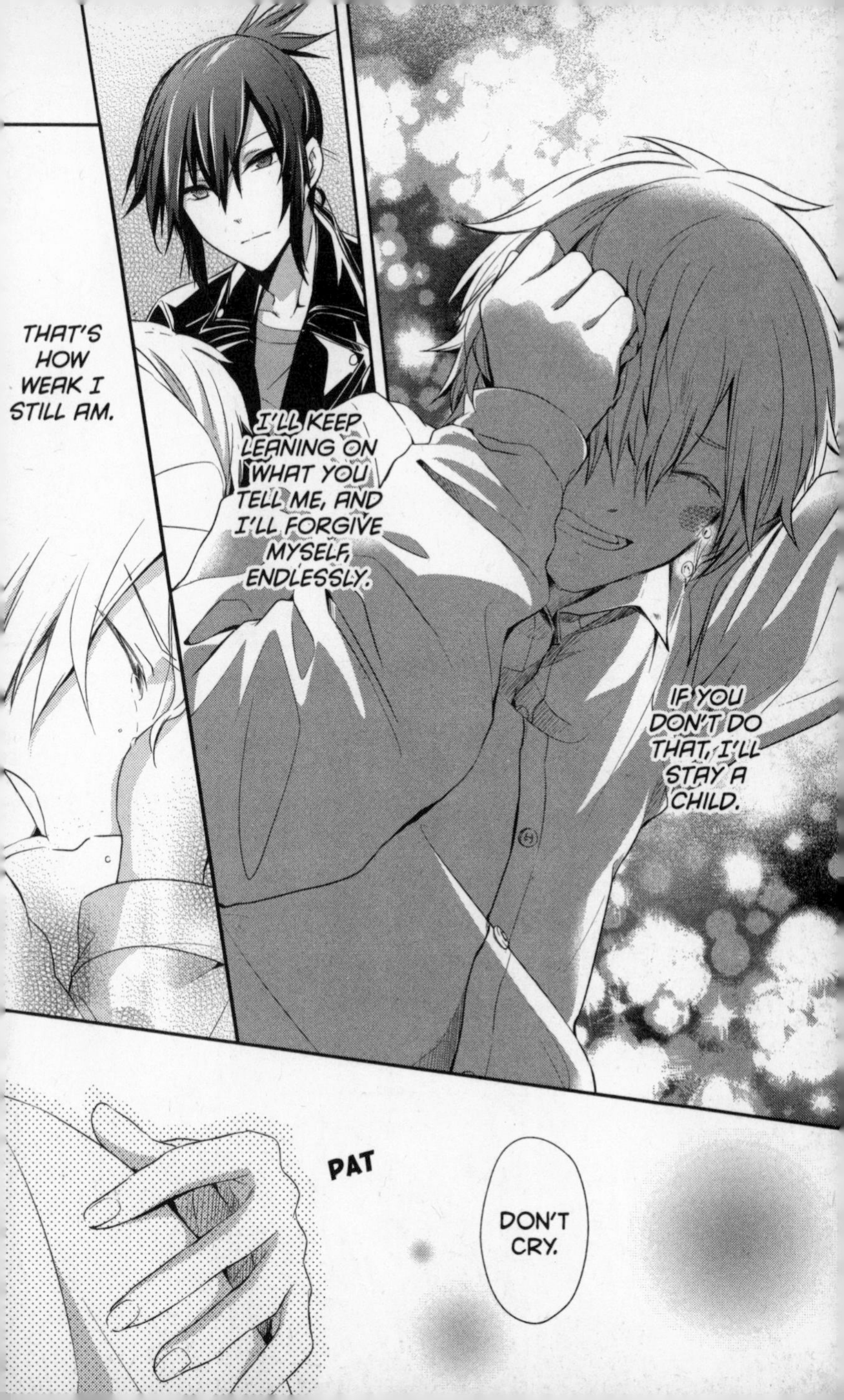
I'LL KEEP LEANING ON WHAT YOU TELL ME, AND I'LL FORGIVE MYSELF, ENDLESSLY.
IF YOU DON'T DO THAT, I'LL STAY A CHILD.
THAT'S HOW WEAK I STILL AM.
PAT
DON'T CRY.

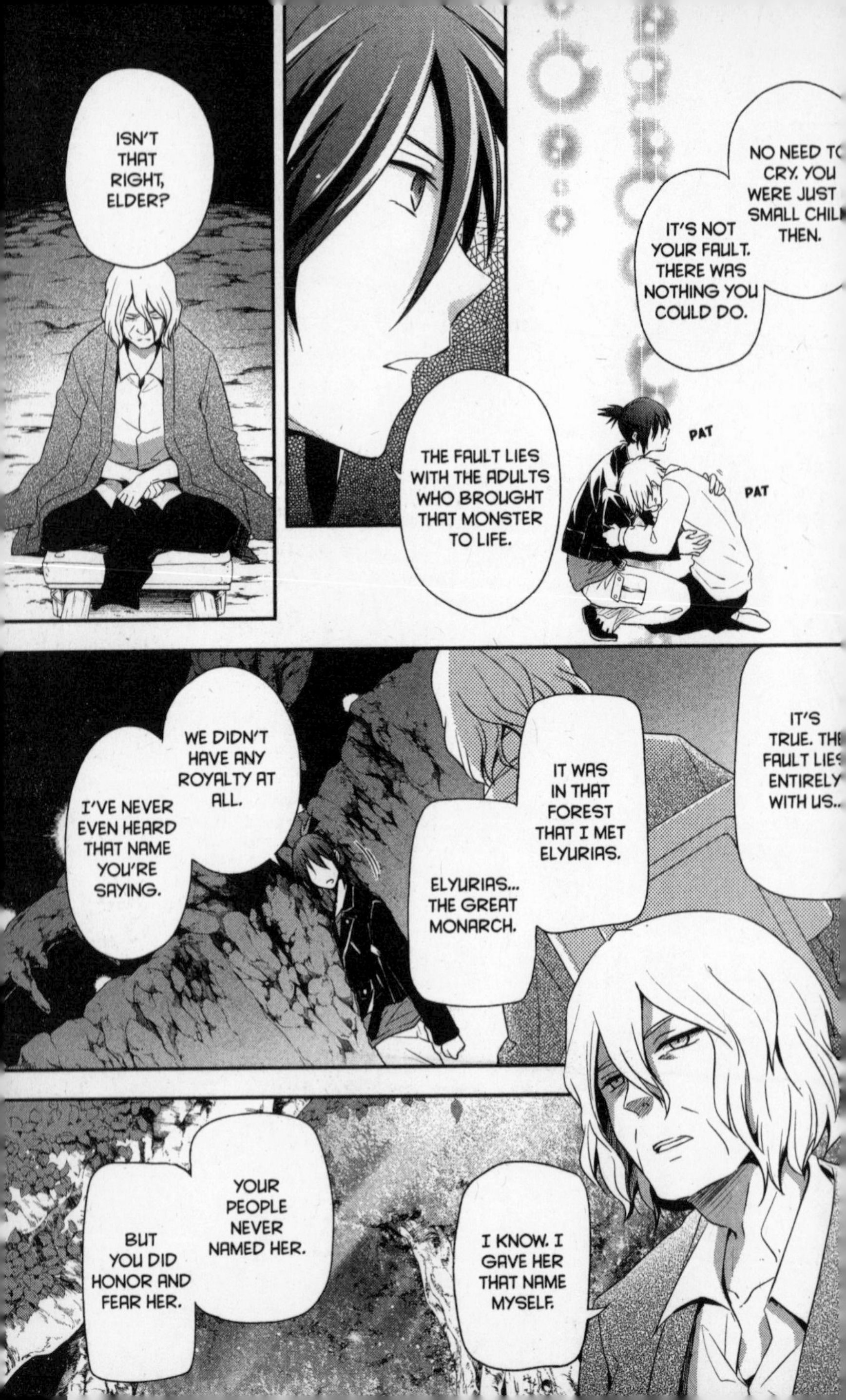
NO NEED TO CRY. YOU WERE JUST SMALL CHIL THEN.
IT'S NOT YOUR FAULT. THERE WAS NOTHING YOU COULD DO.
PAT
PAT
THE FAULT LIES WITH THE ADULTS WHO BROUGHT THAT MONSTER TO LIFE.
ISN'T THAT RIGHT, ELDER?
IT'S TRUE. THE FAULT LIES ENTIRELY WITH US...
IT WAS IN THAT FOREST THAT I MET ELYURIAS.
ELYURIAS... THE GREAT MONARCH.
WE DIDN'T HAVE ANY ROYALTY AT ALL.
I'VE NEVER EVEN HEARD THAT NAME YOU'RE SAYING.
I KNOW. I GAVE HER THAT NAME MYSELF.
YOUR PEOPLE NEVER NAMED HER.
BUT YOU DID HONOR AND FEAR HER.

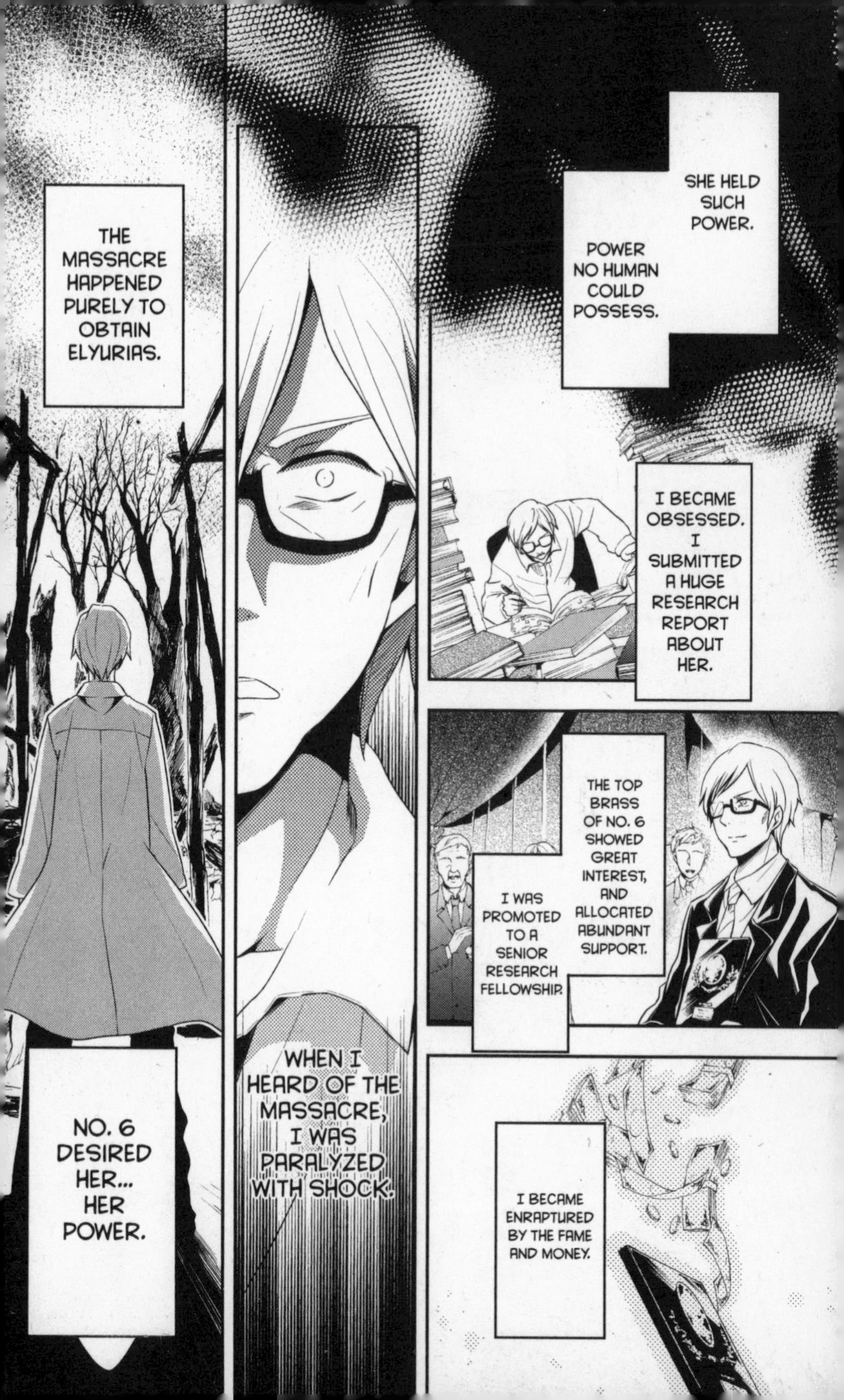
SHE HELD SUCH POWER.
POWER NO HUMAN COULD POSSESS.
I BECAME OBSESSED. I SUBMITTED A HUGE RESEARCH REPORT ABOUT HER.
THE TOP BRASS OF NO. 6 SHOWED GREAT INTEREST, AND ALLOCATED ABUNDANT SUPPORT.
I WAS PROMOTED TO A SENIOR RESEARCH FELLOWSHIP.
I BECAME ENRAPTURED BY THE FAME AND MONEY.
WHEN I HEARD OF THE MASSACRE, I WAS PARALYZED WITH SHOCK.
THE MASSACRE HAPPENED PURELY TO OBTAIN ELYURIAS.
NO. 6 DESIRED HER... HER POWER.

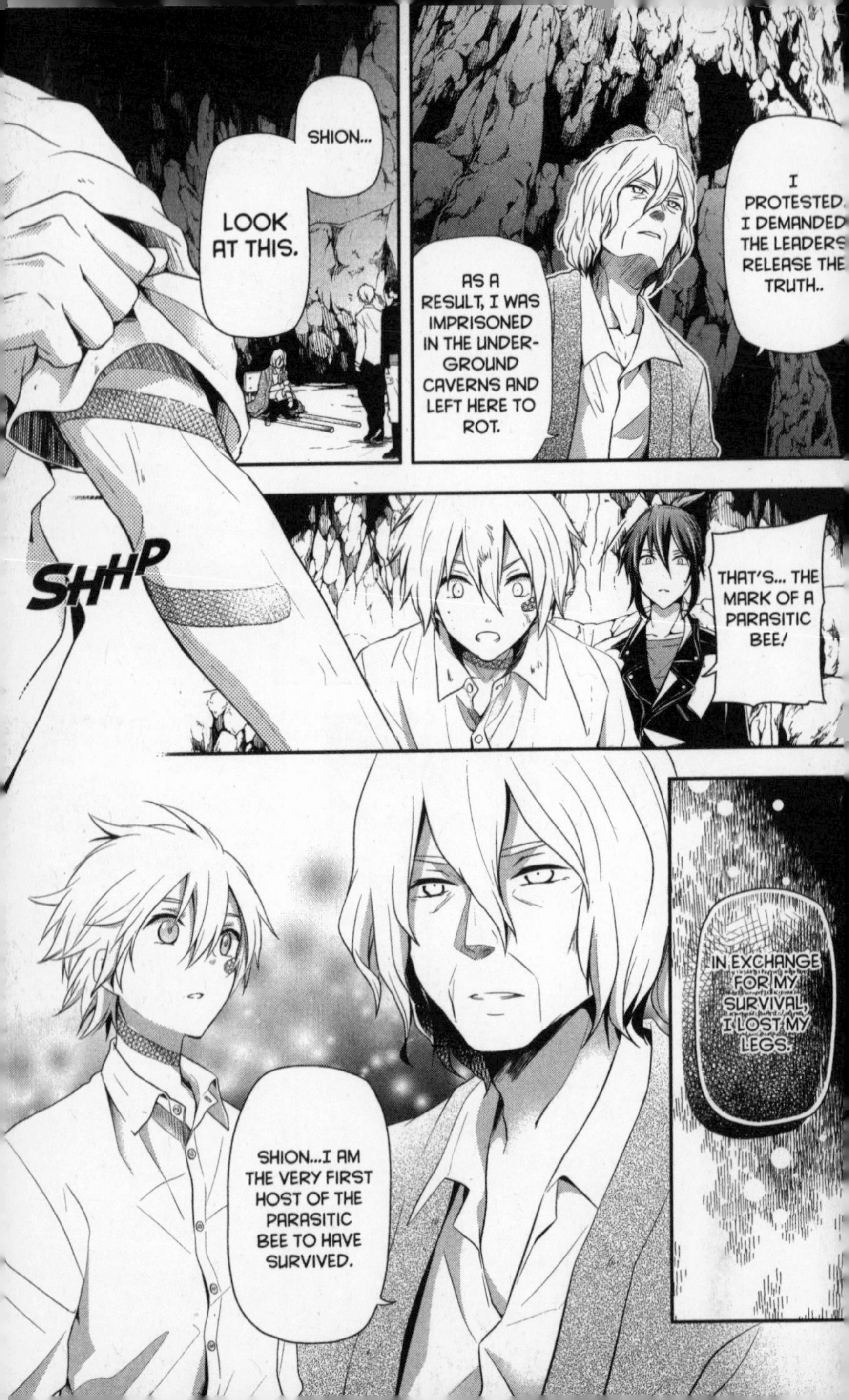
I PROTESTED. I DEMANDED THE LEADERS RELEASE THE TRUTH..
AS A RESULT, I WAS IMPRISONED IN THE UNDER-GROUND CAVERNS AND LEFT HERE TO ROT.
SHION...
LOOK AT THIS.
THAT'S... THE MARK OF A PARASITIC BEE!
SHHP
IN EXCHANGE FOR MY SURVIVAL, I LOST MY LEGS.
SHION...I AM THE VERY FIRST HOST OF THE PARASITIC BEE TO HAVE SURVIVED.

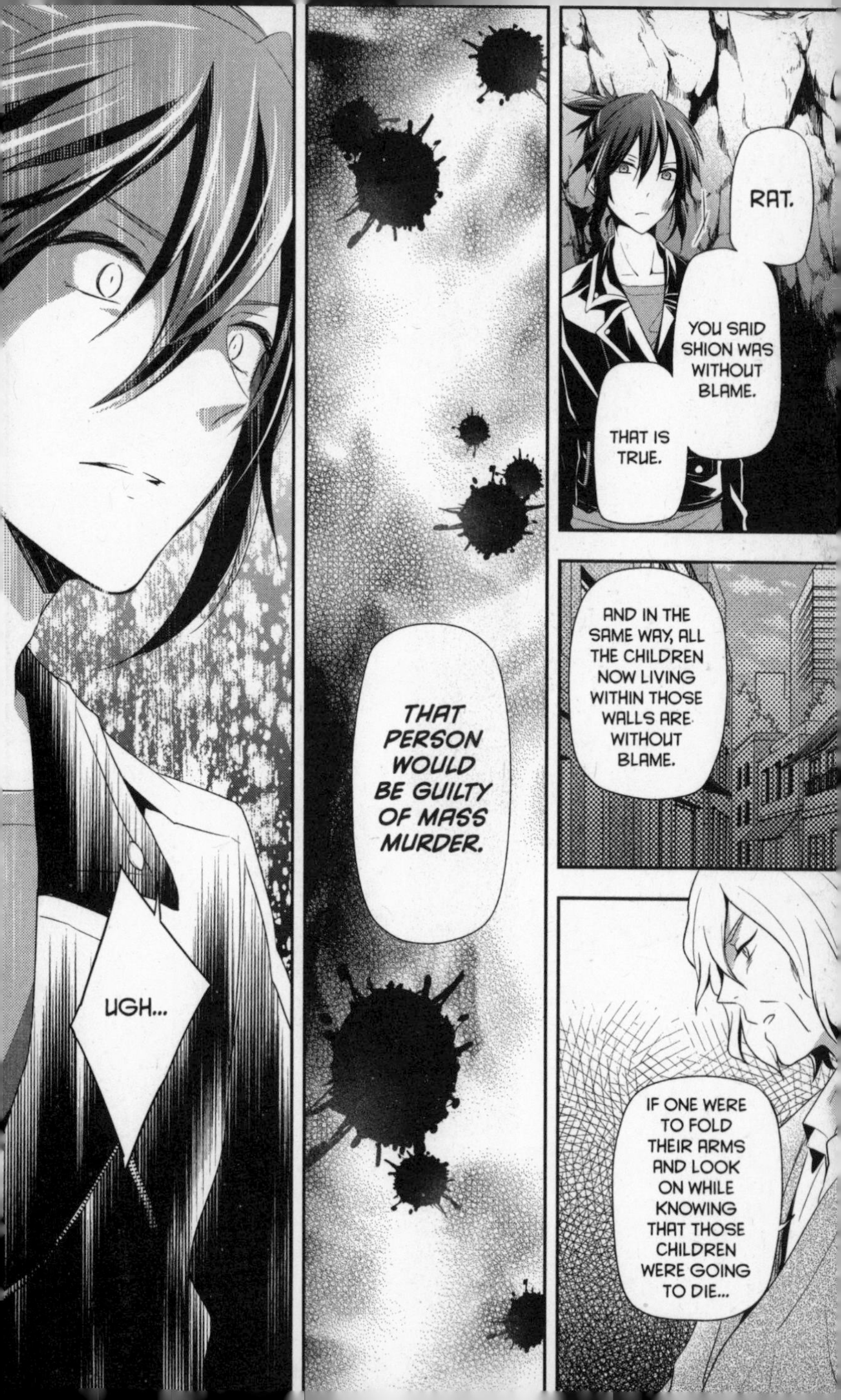
RAT.
YOU SAID SHION WAS WITHOUT BLAME.
THAT IS TRUE.
AND IN THE SAME WAY, ALL THE CHILDREN NOW LIVING WITHIN THOSE WALLS ARE WITHOUT BLAME.
IF ONE WERE TO FOLD THEIR ARMS AND LOOK ON WHILE KNOWING THAT THOSE CHILDREN WERE GOING TO DIE...
THAT PERSON WOULD BE GUILTY OF MASS MURDER.
UGH...

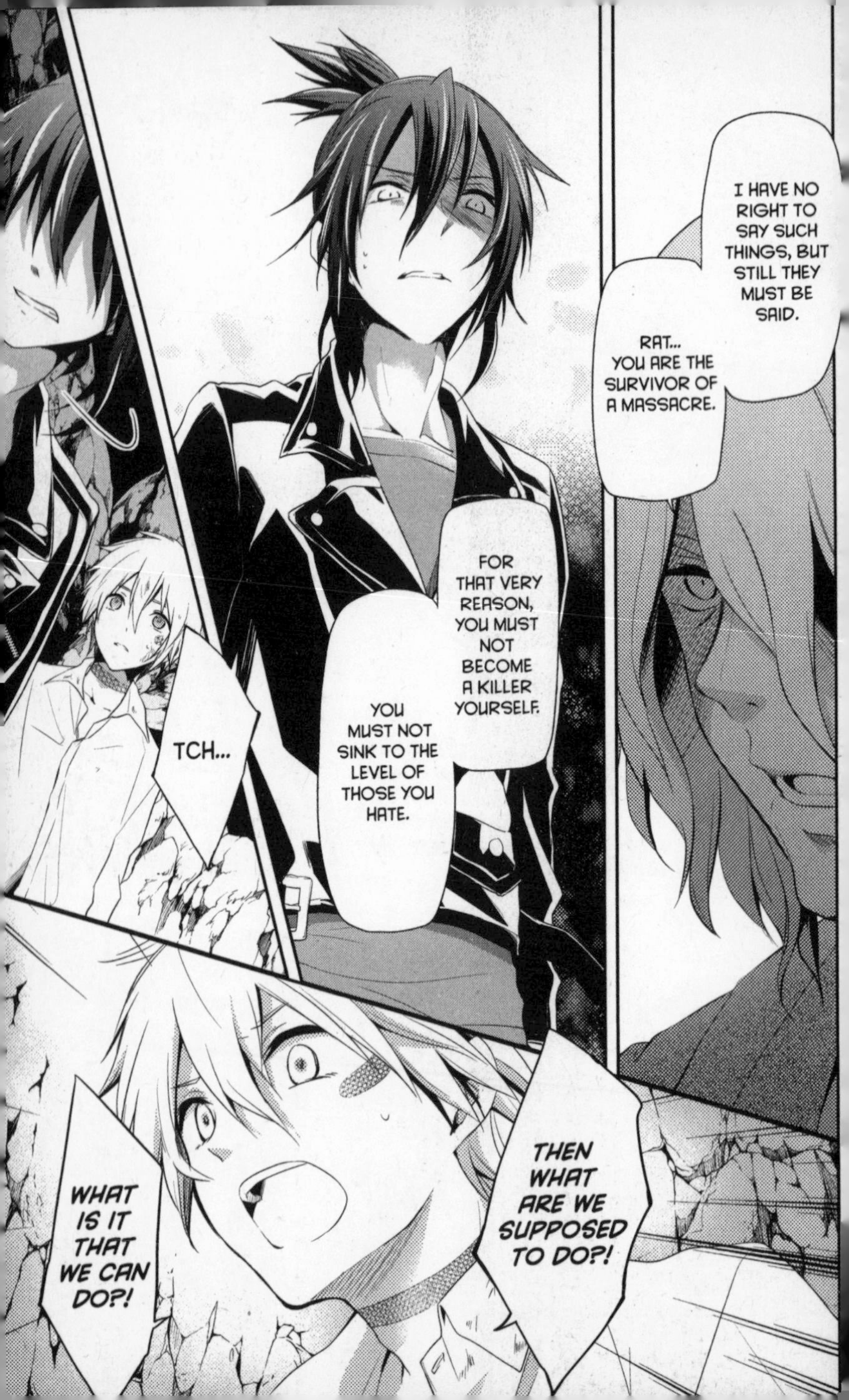

I HAVE NO RIGHT TO SAY SUCH THINGS, BUT STILL THEY MUST BE SAID.
RAT... YOU ARE THE SURVIVOR OF A MASSACRE.
FOR THAT VERY REASON, YOU MUST NOT BECOME A KILLER YOURSELF.
YOU MUST NOT SINK TO THE LEVEL OF THOSE YOU HATE.
TCH...
THEN WHAT ARE WE SUPPOSED TO DO?!
WHAT IS IT THAT WE CAN DO?!

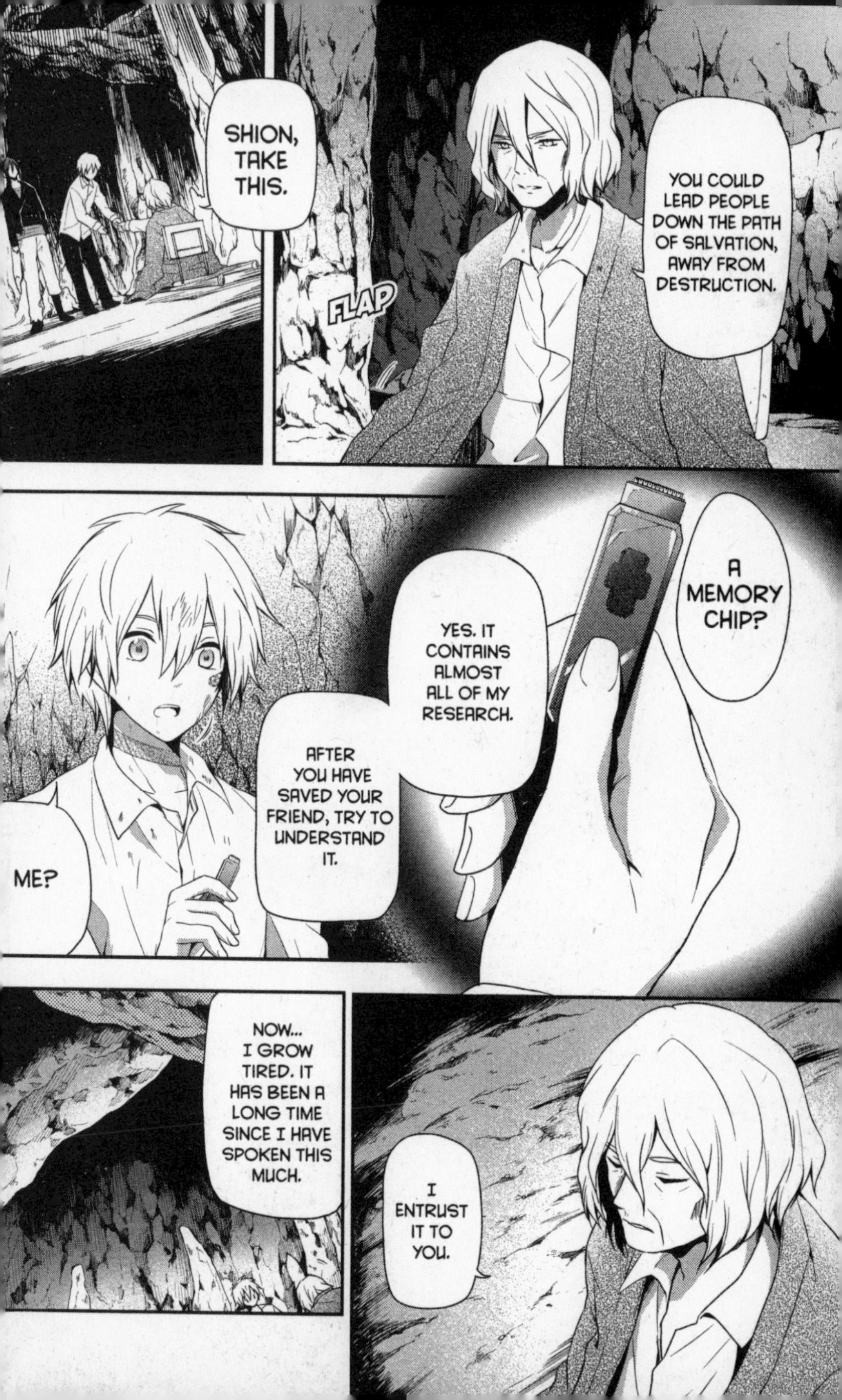
YOU COULD LEAD PEOPLE DOWN THE PATH OF SALVATION, AWAY FROM DESTRUCTION.
FLAP
SHION, TAKE THIS.
A MEMORY CHIP?
YES. IT CONTAINS ALMOST ALL OF MY RESEARCH.
AFTER YOU HAVE SAVED YOUR FRIEND, TRY TO UNDERSTAND IT.
ME?
I ENTRUST IT TO YOU.
NOW... I GROW TIRED. IT HAS BEEN A LONG TIME SINCE I HAVE SPOKEN THIS MUCH.

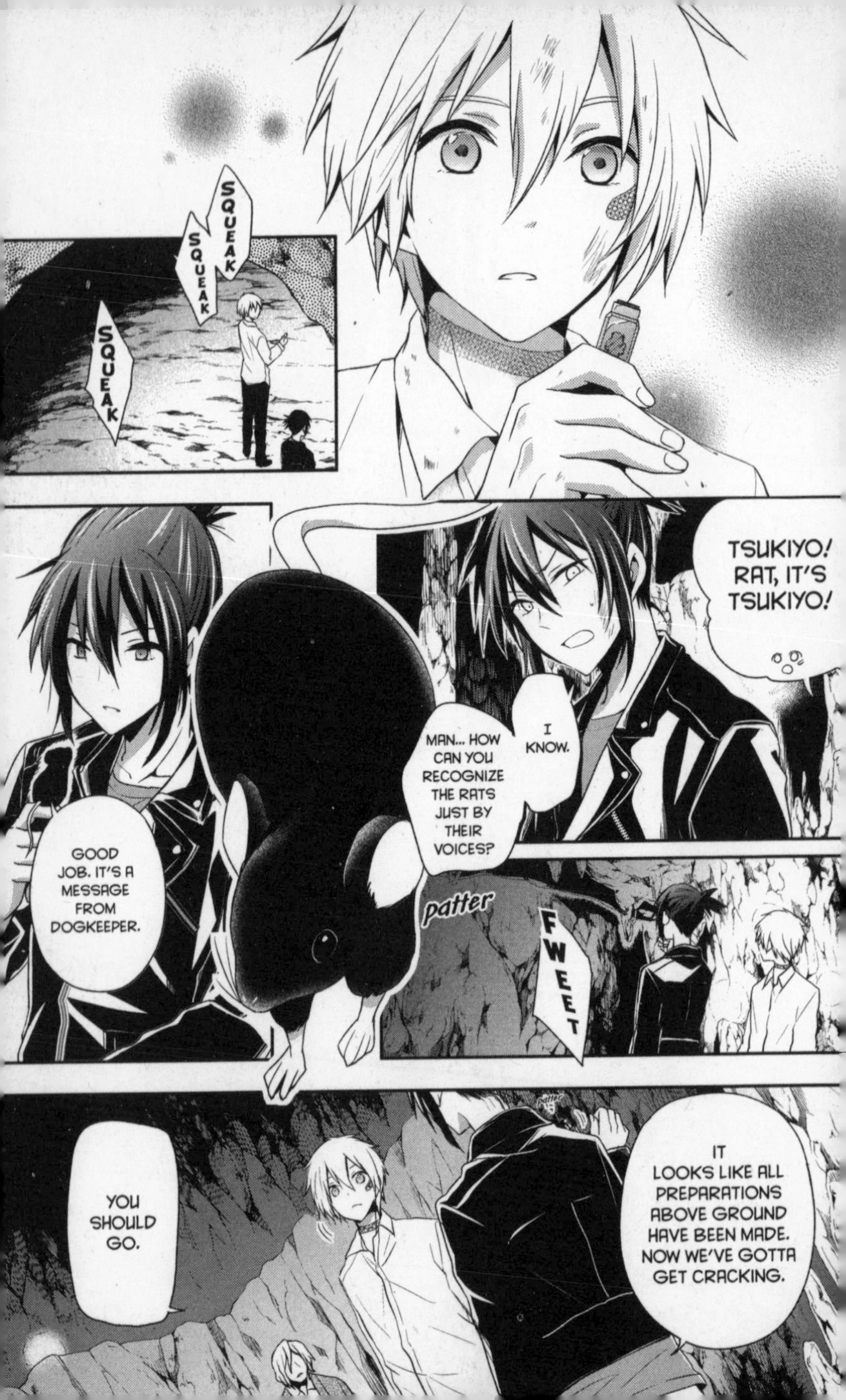

SQUEAK
SQUEAK
SQUEAK
TSUKIYO! RAT, IT'S TSUKIYO!
I KNOW.
MAN... HOW CAN YOU RECOGNIZE THE RATS JUST BY THEIR VOICES?
FWEET
patter
GOOD JOB. IT'S A MESSAGE FROM DOGKEEPER.
IT LOOKS LIKE ALL PREPARATIONS ABOVE GROUND HAVE BEEN MADE. NOW WE'VE GOTTA GET CRACKING.
YOU SHOULD GO.

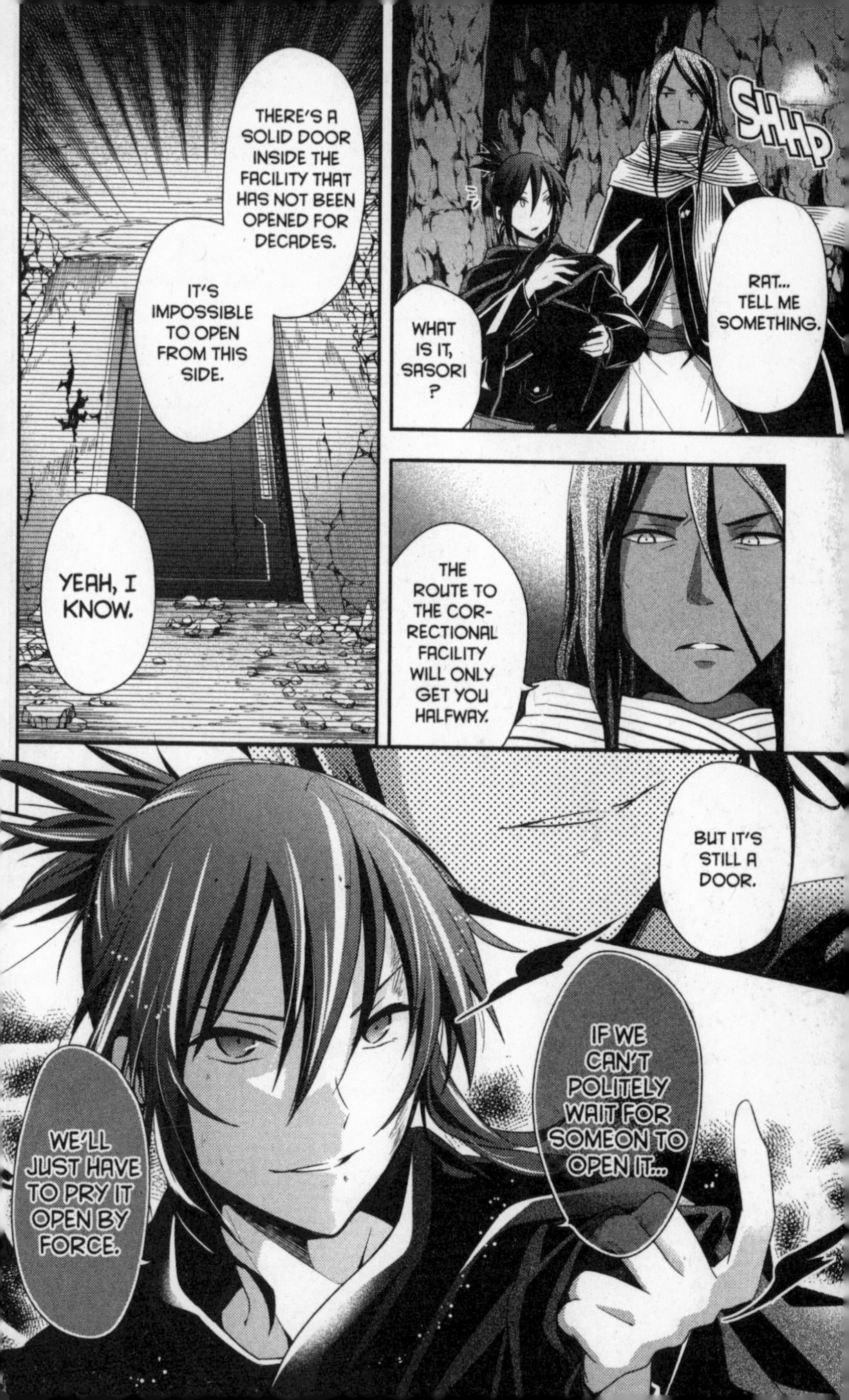
SHHP
RAT... TELL ME SOMETHING.
WHAT IS IT, SASORI ?
THE ROUTE TO THE COR-RECTIONAL FACILITY WILL ONLY GET YOU HALFWAY.
THERE'S A SOLID DOOR INSIDE THE FACILITY THAT HAS NOT BEEN OPENED FOR DECADES.
IT'S IMPOSSIBLE TO OPEN FROM THIS SIDE.
YEAH, I KNOW.
BUT IT'S STILL A DOOR.
IF WE CAN'T POLITELY WAIT FOR SOMEON TO OPEN IT...
WE'LL JUST HAVE TO PRY IT OPEN BY FORCE.

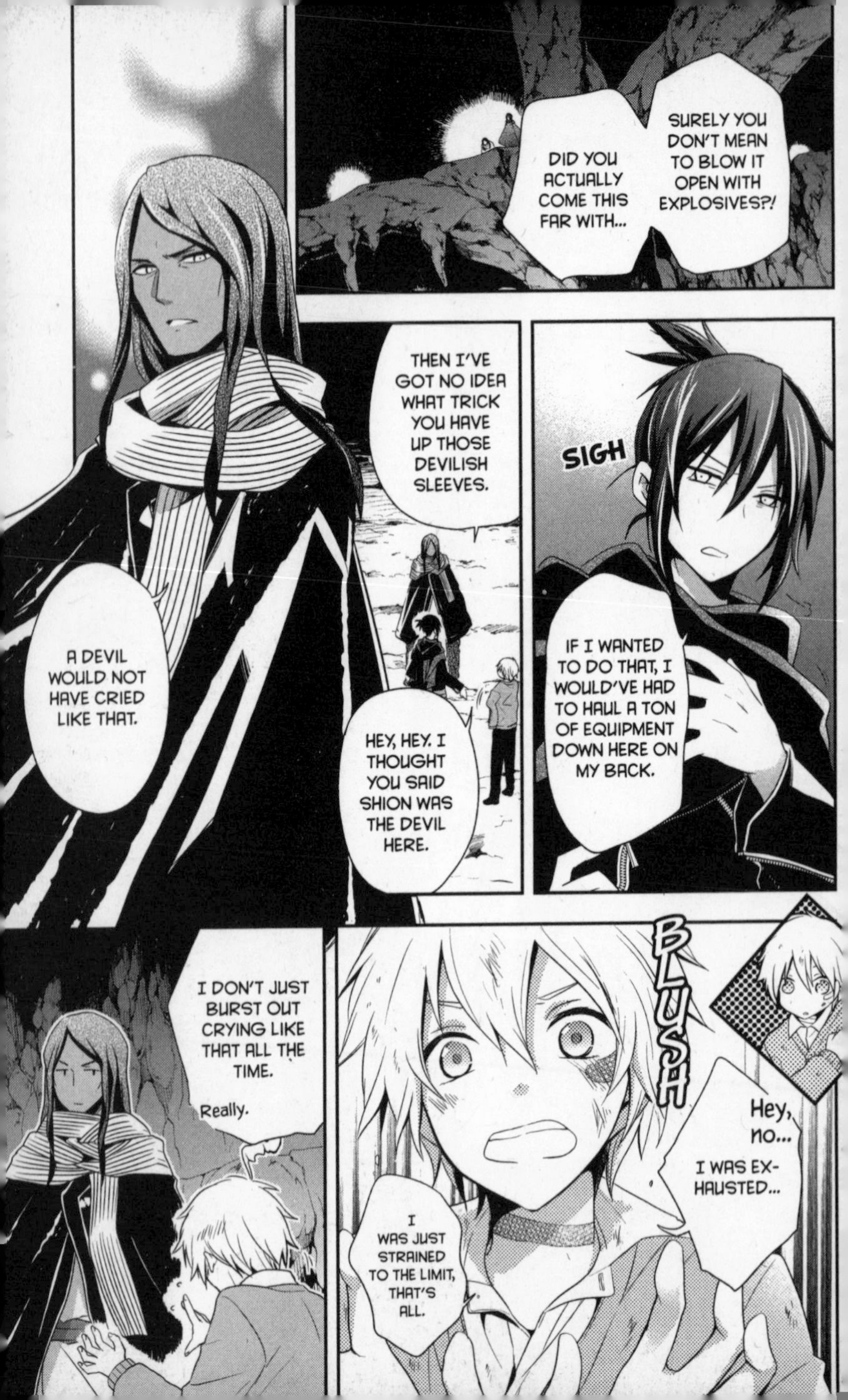
SURELY YOU DON'T MEAN TO BLOW IT OPEN WITH EXPLOSIVES?!
DID YOU ACTUALLY COME THIS FAR WITH...
SIGH
IF I WANTED TO DO THAT, I WOULD'VE HAD TO HAUL A TON OF EQUIPMENT DOWN HERE ON MY BACK.
THEN I'VE GOT NO IDEA WHAT TRICK YOU HAVE UP THOSE DEVILISH SLEEVES.
HEY, HEY. I THOUGHT YOU SAID SHION WAS THE DEVIL HERE.
A DEVIL WOULD NOT HAVE CRIED LIKE THAT.
BLUSH
Hey, no...
I WAS EX-HAUSTED...
I WAS JUST STRAINED TO THE LIMIT, THAT'S ALL.
I DON'T JUST BURST OUT CRYING LIKE THAT ALL THE TIME.
Really.

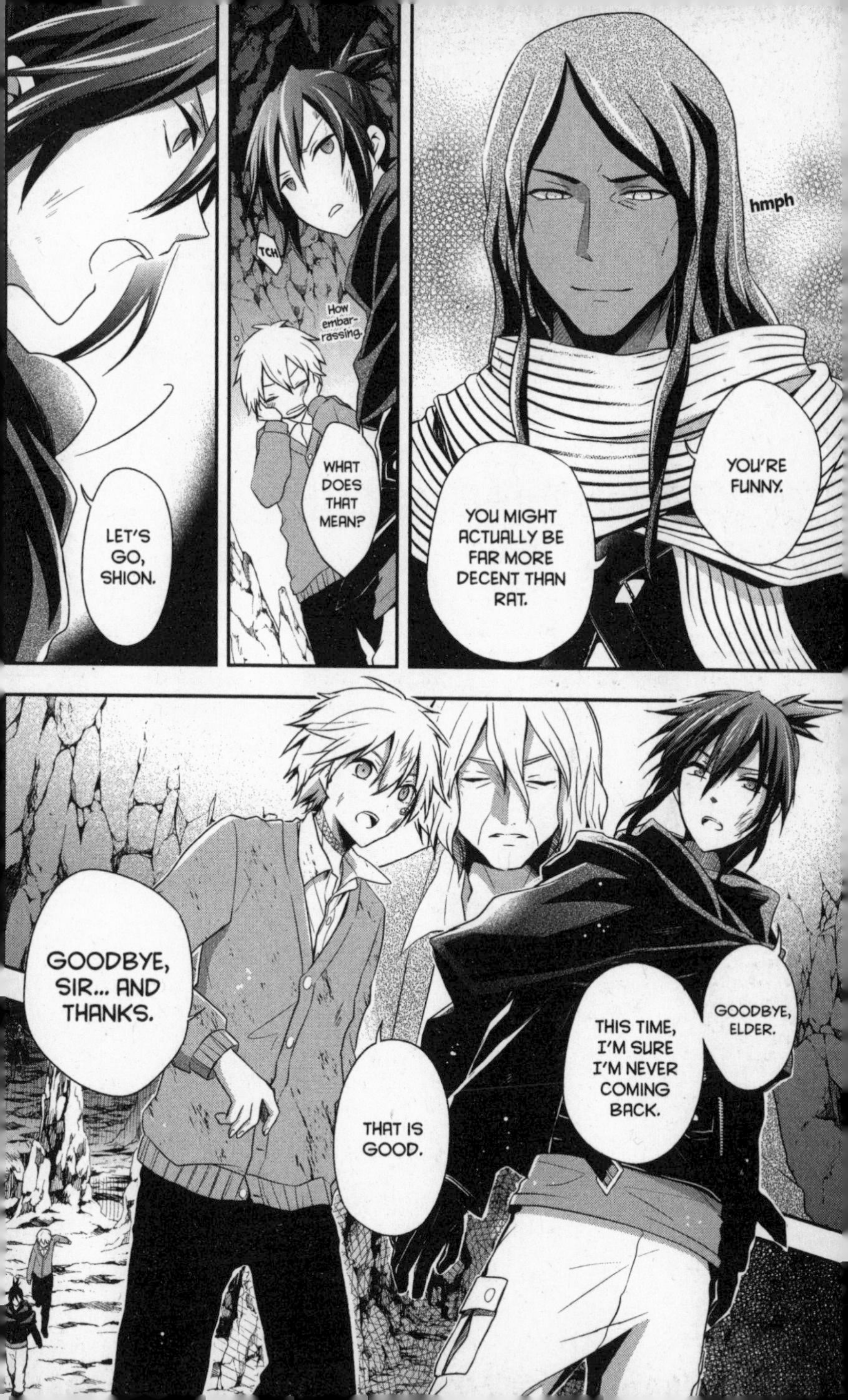
hmph
YOU'RE FUNNY.
YOU MIGHT ACTUALLY BE FAR MORE DECENT THAN RAT.
TCH
How embar-rassing.
WHAT DOES THAT MEAN?
LET'S GO, SHION.
GOODBYE, ELDER.
THIS TIME, I'M SURE I'M NEVER COMING BACK.
THAT IS GOOD.
GOODBYE, SIR... AND THANKS.

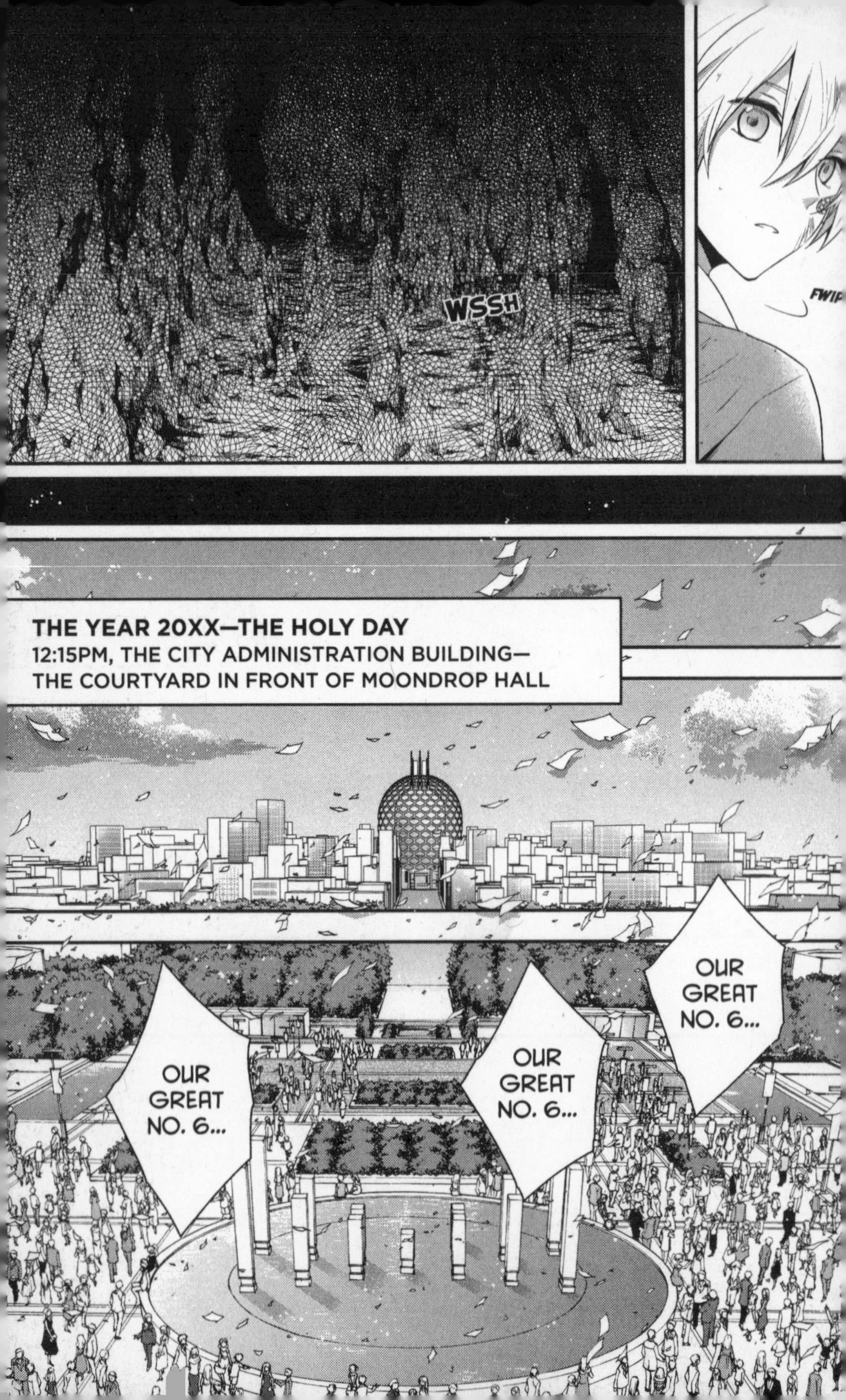
FWIP
WSSH
THE YEAR 20XX—THE HOLY DAY
12:15PM, THE CITY ADMINISTRATION BUILDING—
THE COURTYARD IN FRONT OF MOONDROP HALL
OUR GREAT NO. 6...
OUR GREAT NO. 6...
OUR GREAT NO. 6...

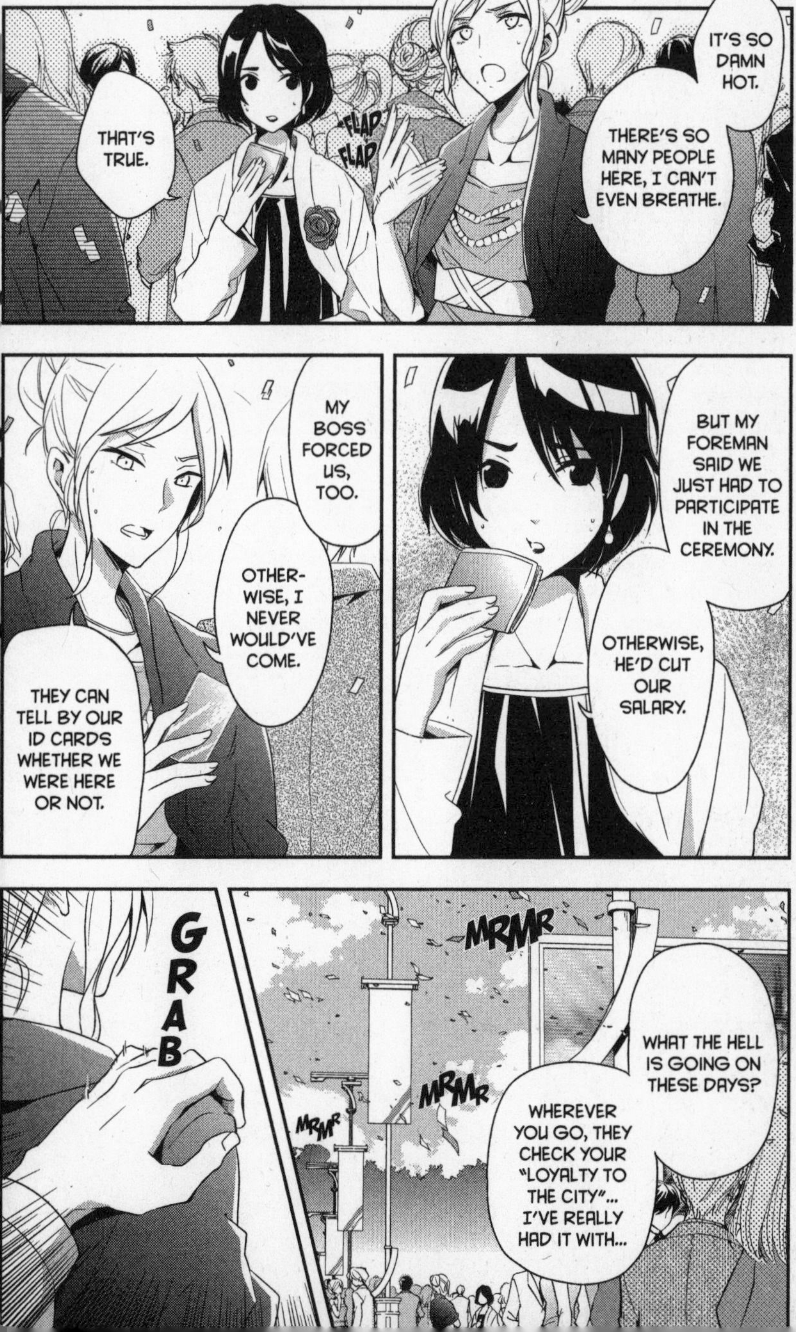
IT'S SO DAMN HOT.
THERE'S SO MANY PEOPLE HERE, I CAN'T EVEN BREATHE.
FLAP FLAP
THAT'S TRUE.
BUT MY FOREMAN SAID WE JUST HAD TO PARTICIPATE IN THE CEREMONY.
OTHERWISE, HE'D CUT OUR SALARY.
MY BOSS FORCED US, TOO.
OTHER-WISE, I NEVER WOULD'VE COME.
THEY CAN TELL BY OUR ID CARDS WHETHER WE WERE HERE OR NOT.
MRMR
WHAT THE HELL IS GOING ON THESE DAYS?
WHEREVER YOU GO, THEY CHECK YOUR "LOYALTY TO THE CITY"... I'VE REALLY HAD IT WITH...
MRMR
MRMR
GRAB

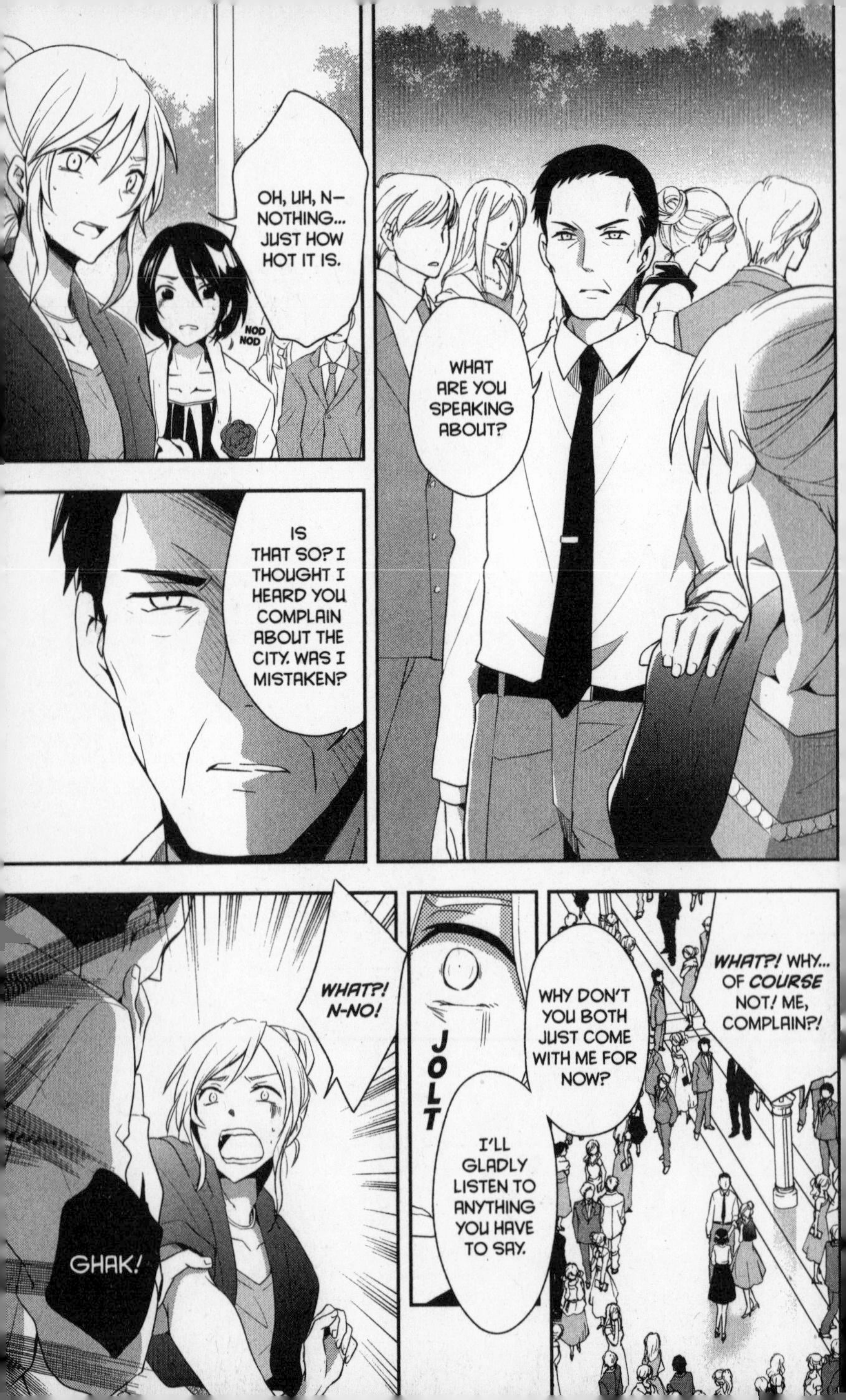
WHAT ARE YOU SPEAKING ABOUT?
OH, UH, N— NOTHING... JUST HOW HOT IT IS.
NOD NOD
IS THAT SO? I THOUGHT I HEARD YOU COMPLAIN ABOUT THE CITY. WAS I MISTAKEN?
WHAT?! WHY... OF *COURSE* NOT! ME, COMPLAIN?!
WHY DON'T YOU BOTH JUST COME WITH ME FOR NOW?
I'LL GLADLY LISTEN TO ANYTHING YOU HAVE TO SAY.
JOLT
WHAT?! N-NO!
GHAK!

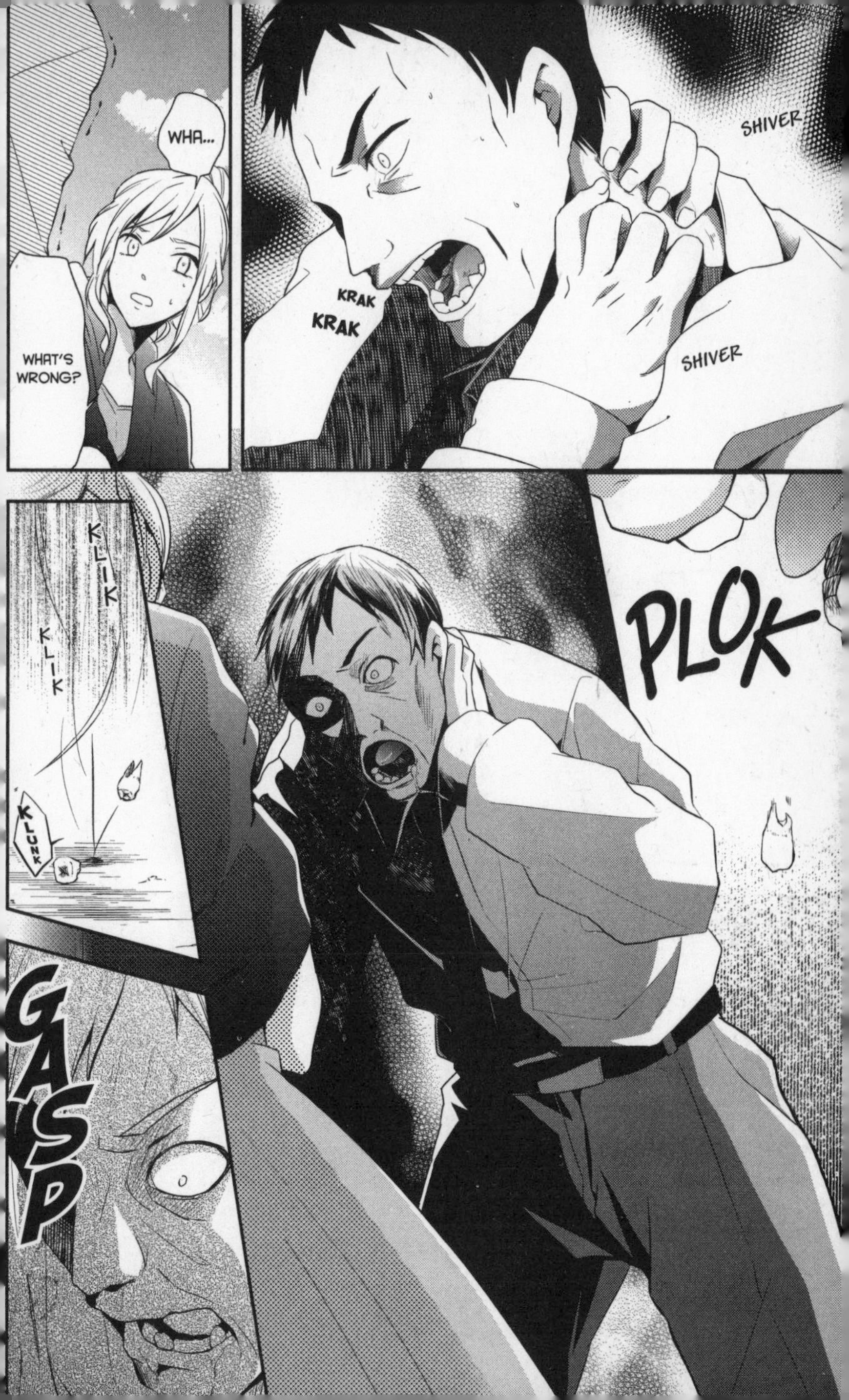
SHIVER
KRAK
KRAK
SHIVER
WHA...
WHAT'S WRONG?
PLOK
KLIK
KLIK
KLUNK
GASP

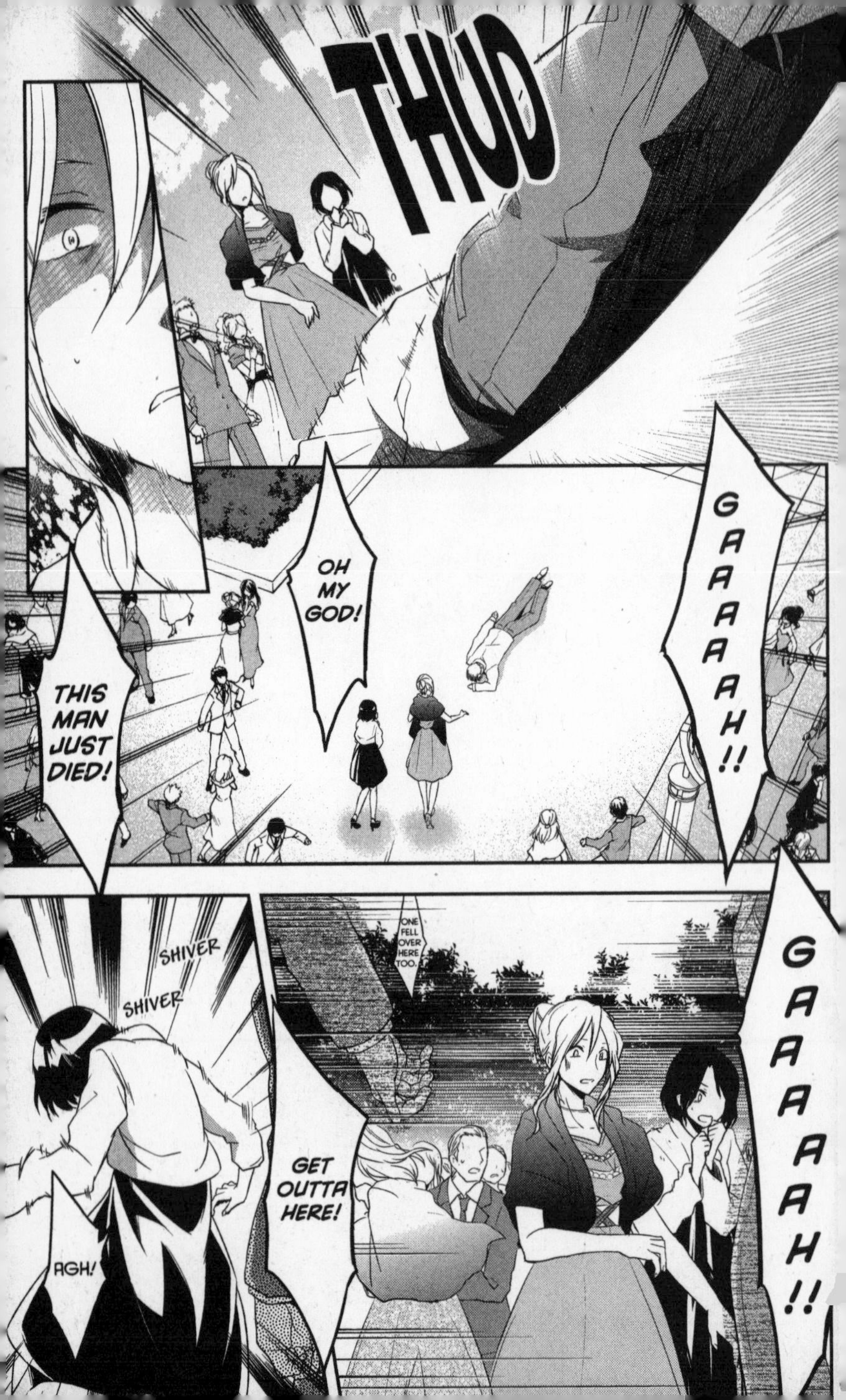
THUD
GAAAAAH!!
OH MY GOD!
THIS MAN JUST DIED!
GAAAAAH!!
ONE FELL OVER HERE TOO.
GET OUTTA HERE!
SHIVER
SHIVER
AGH!

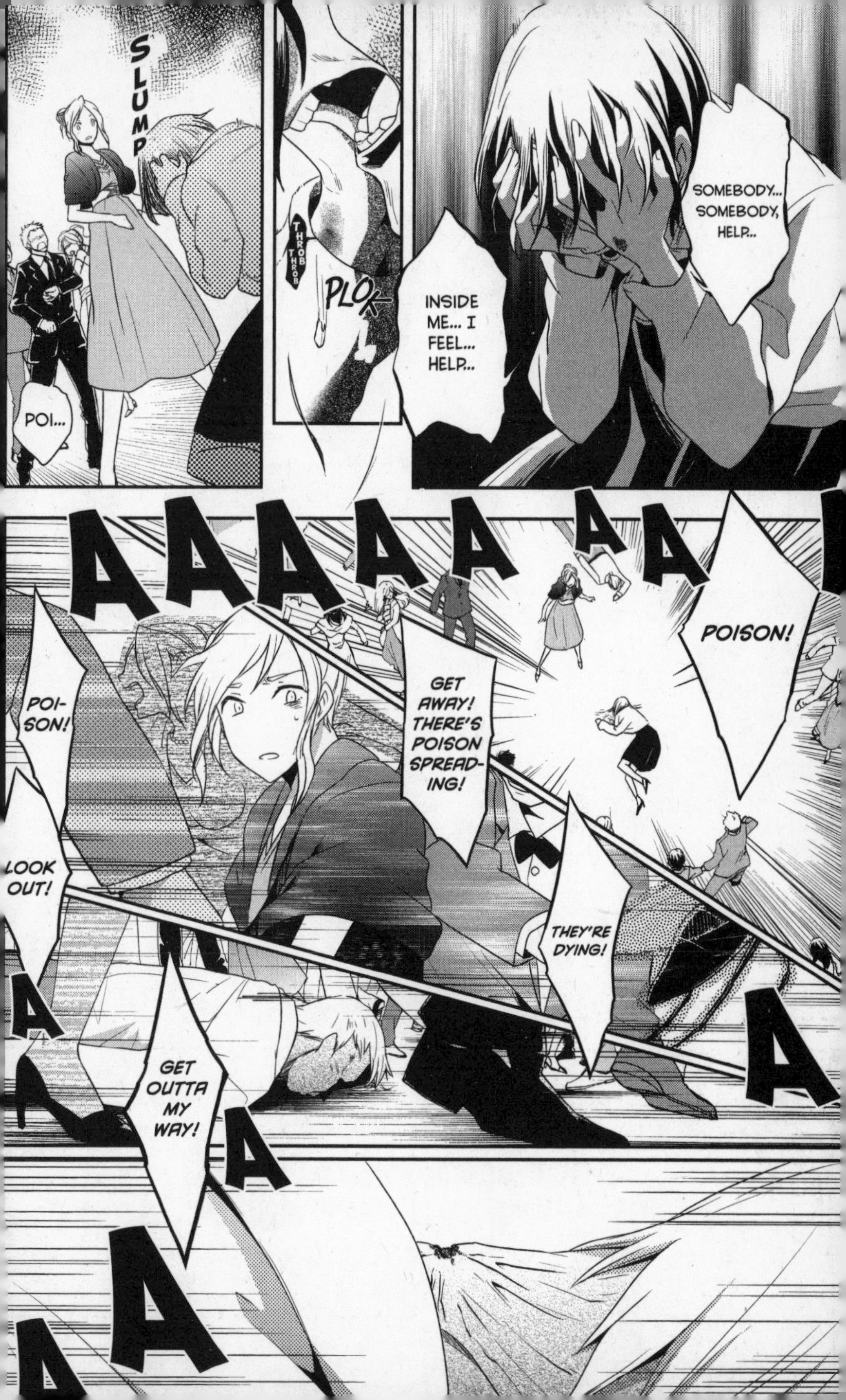
SOMEBODY... SOMEBODY, HELP...
INSIDE ME... I FEEL... HELP...
THROB THROB
PLOK
SLUMP
POI...
AAAAAAAA
POISON!
GET AWAY! THERE'S POISON SPREADING!
THEY'RE DYING!
A
POI-SON!
LOOK OUT!
A
GET OUTTA MY WAY!
AAAA

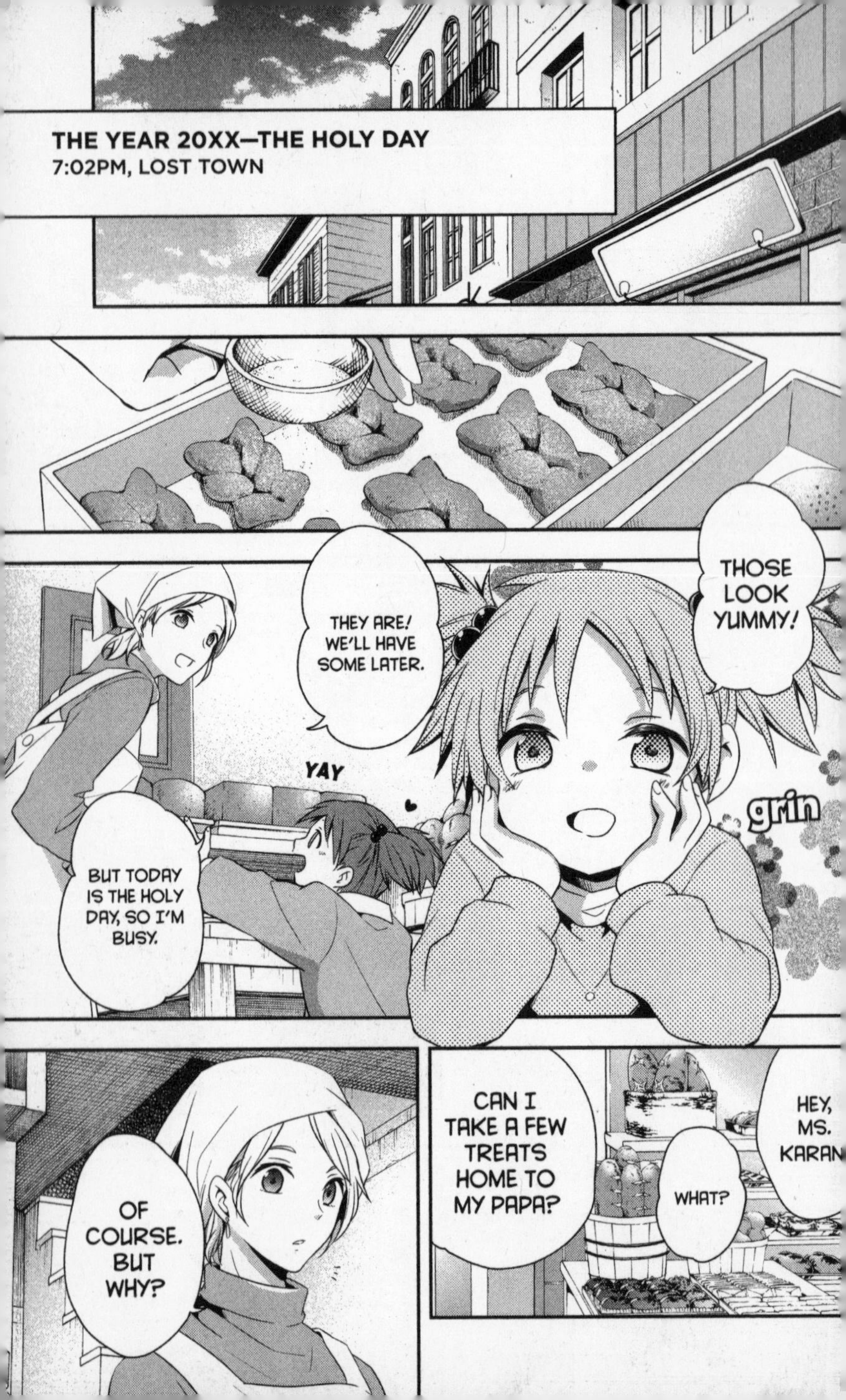
THE YEAR 20XX—THE HOLY DAY
7:02PM, LOST TOWN
THOSE LOOK YUMMY!
grin
THEY ARE! WE'LL HAVE SOME LATER.
YAY
BUT TODAY IS THE HOLY DAY, SO I'M BUSY.
HEY, MS. KARAN
WHAT?
CAN I TAKE A FEW TREATS HOME TO MY PAPA?
OF COURSE. BUT WHY?

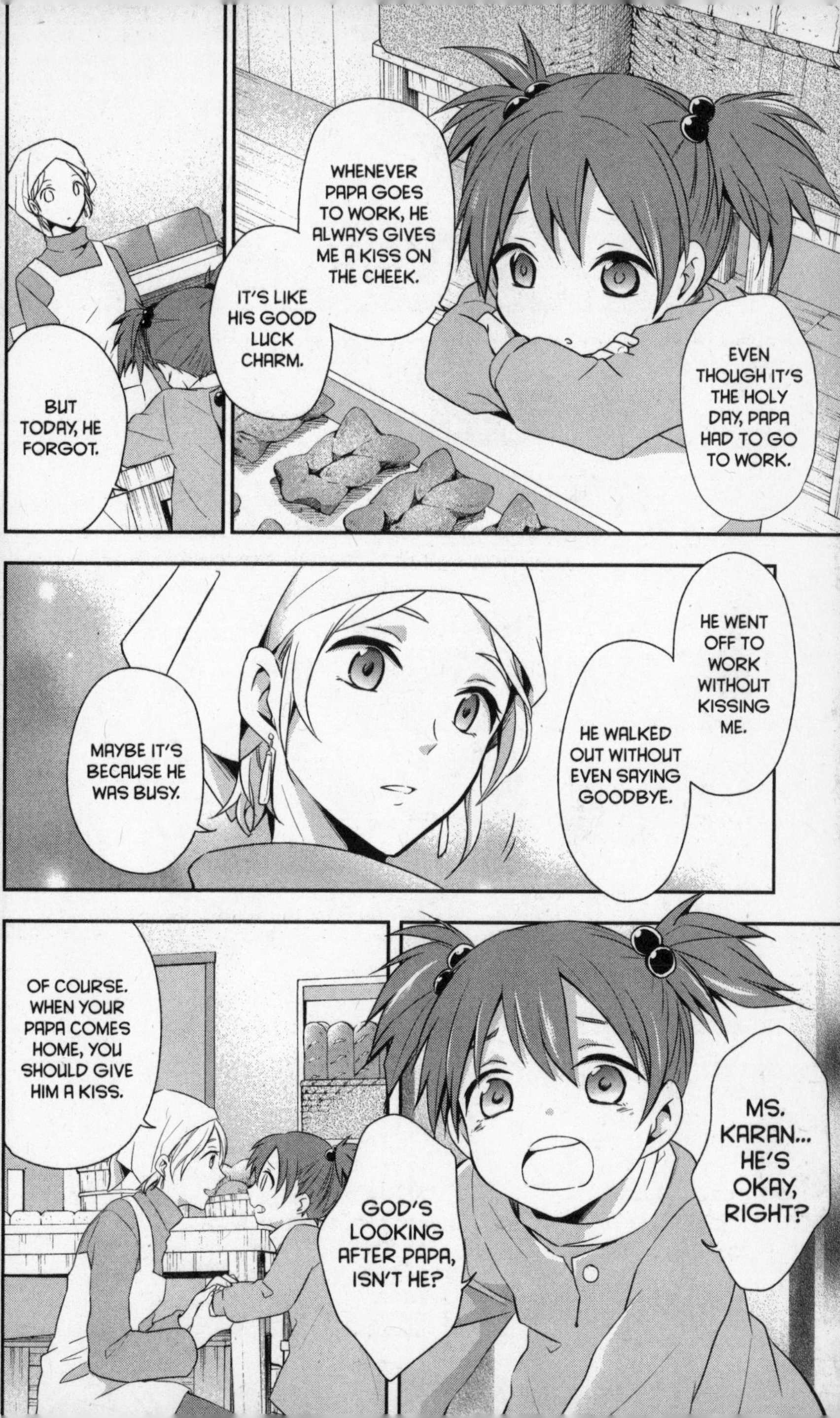
EVEN THOUGH IT'S THE HOLY DAY, PAPA HAD TO GO TO WORK.
WHENEVER PAPA GOES TO WORK, HE ALWAYS GIVES ME A KISS ON THE CHEEK.
IT'S LIKE HIS GOOD LUCK CHARM.
BUT TODAY, HE FORGOT.
HE WENT OFF TO WORK WITHOUT KISSING ME.
HE WALKED OUT WITHOUT EVEN SAYING GOODBYE.
MAYBE IT'S BECAUSE HE WAS BUSY.
MS. KARAN... HE'S OKAY, RIGHT?
GOD'S LOOKING AFTER PAPA, ISN'T HE?
OF COURSE. WHEN YOUR PAPA COMES HOME, YOU SHOULD GIVE HIM A KISS.

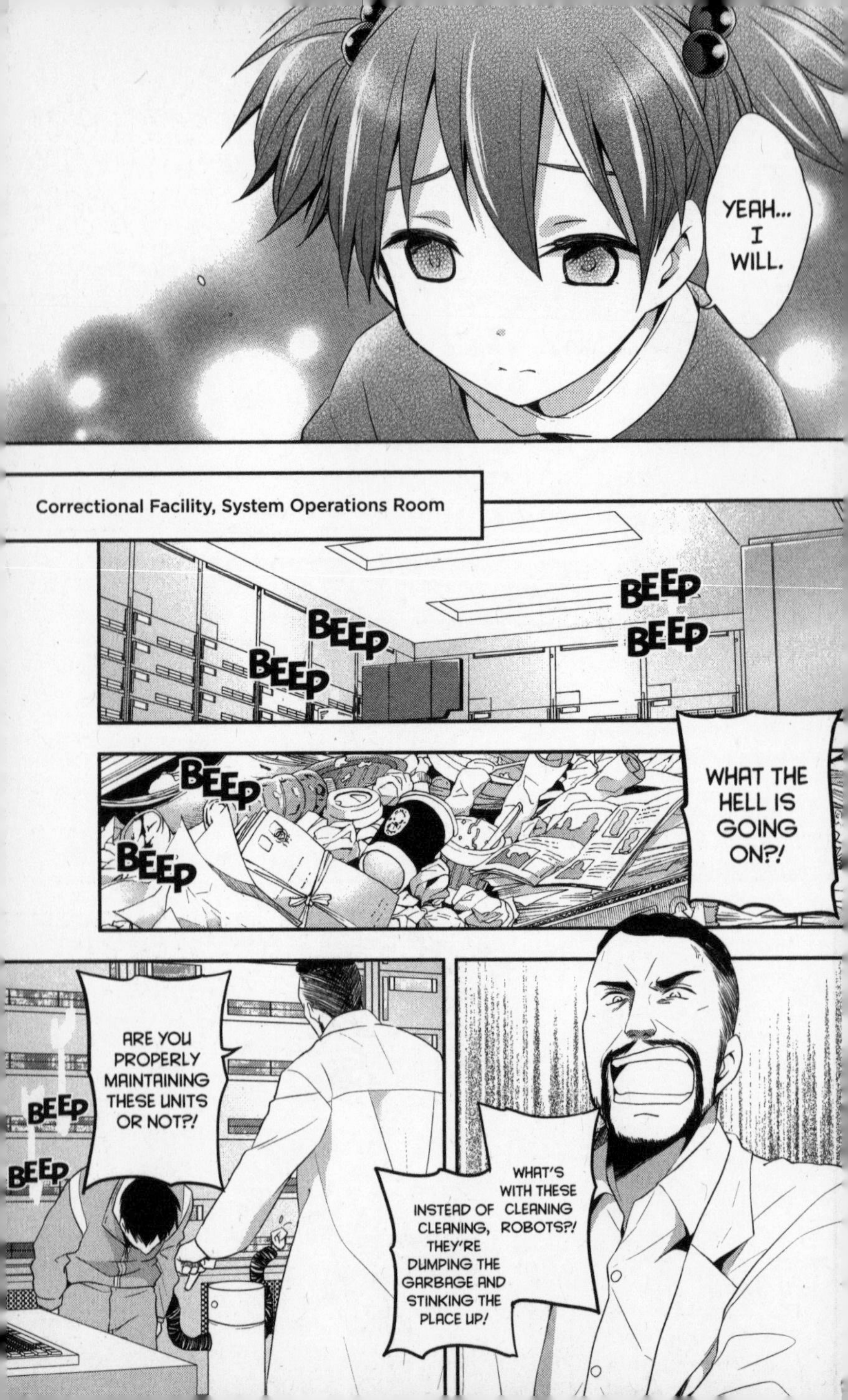
YEAH... I WILL.
Correctional Facility, System Operations Room
BEEP
BEEP
BEEP
BEEP
WHAT THE HELL IS GOING ON?!
BEEP
BEEP
WHAT'S WITH THESE CLEANING ROBOTS?! INSTEAD OF CLEANING, THEY'RE DUMPING THE GARBAGE AND STINKING THE PLACE UP!
ARE YOU PROPERLY MAINTAINING THESE UNITS OR NOT?!
BEEP
BEEP

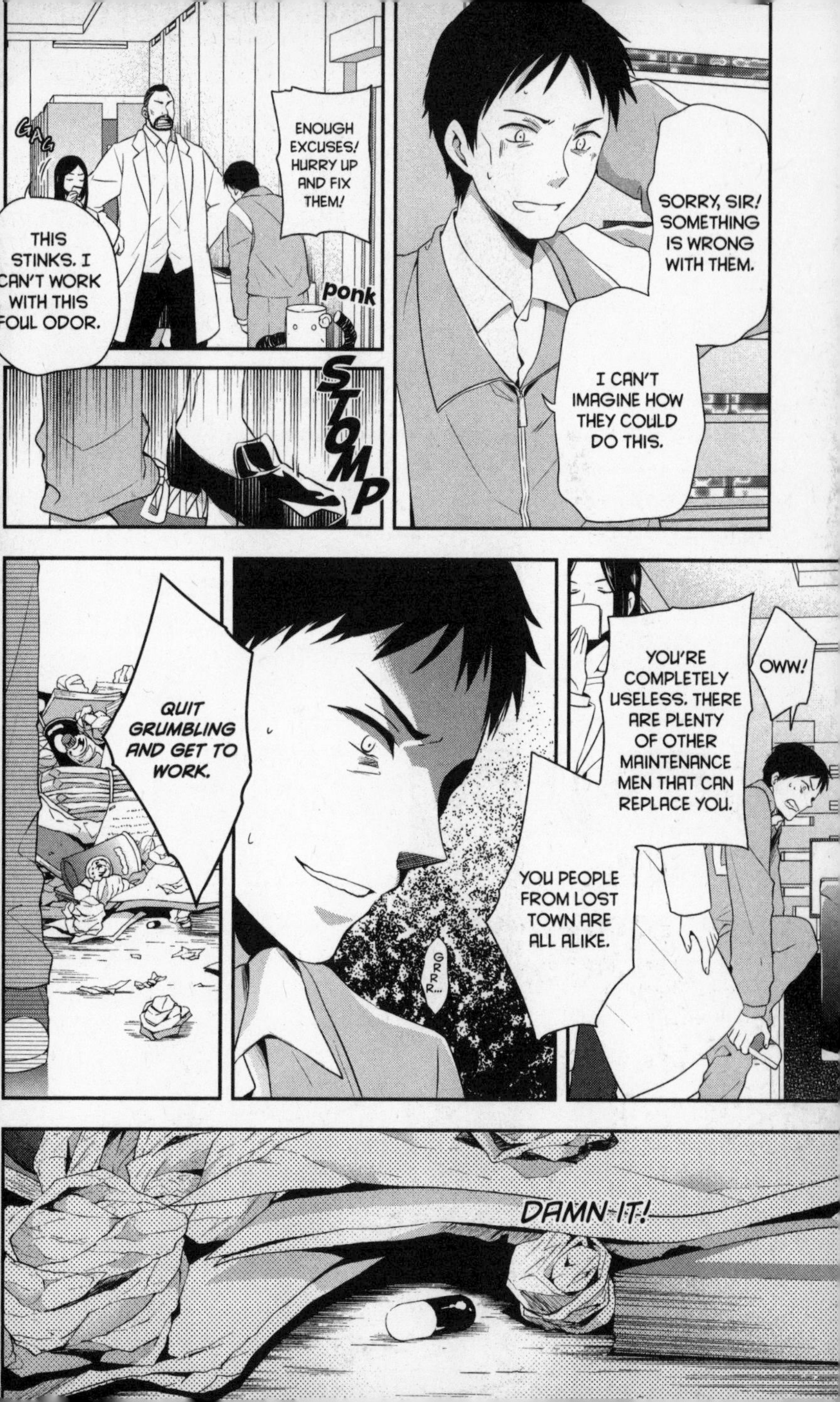
SORRY, SIR! SOMETHING IS WRONG WITH THEM.
I CAN'T IMAGINE HOW THEY COULD DO THIS.
ENOUGH EXCUSES! HURRY UP AND FIX THEM!
GAG
ponk
THIS STINKS. I CAN'T WORK WITH THIS FOUL ODOR.
STOMP
OWW!
YOU'RE COMPLETELY USELESS. THERE ARE PLENTY OF OTHER MAINTENANCE MEN THAT CAN REPLACE YOU.
YOU PEOPLE FROM LOST TOWN ARE ALL ALIKE.
GRRR...
QUIT GRUMBLING AND GET TO WORK.
DAMN IT!

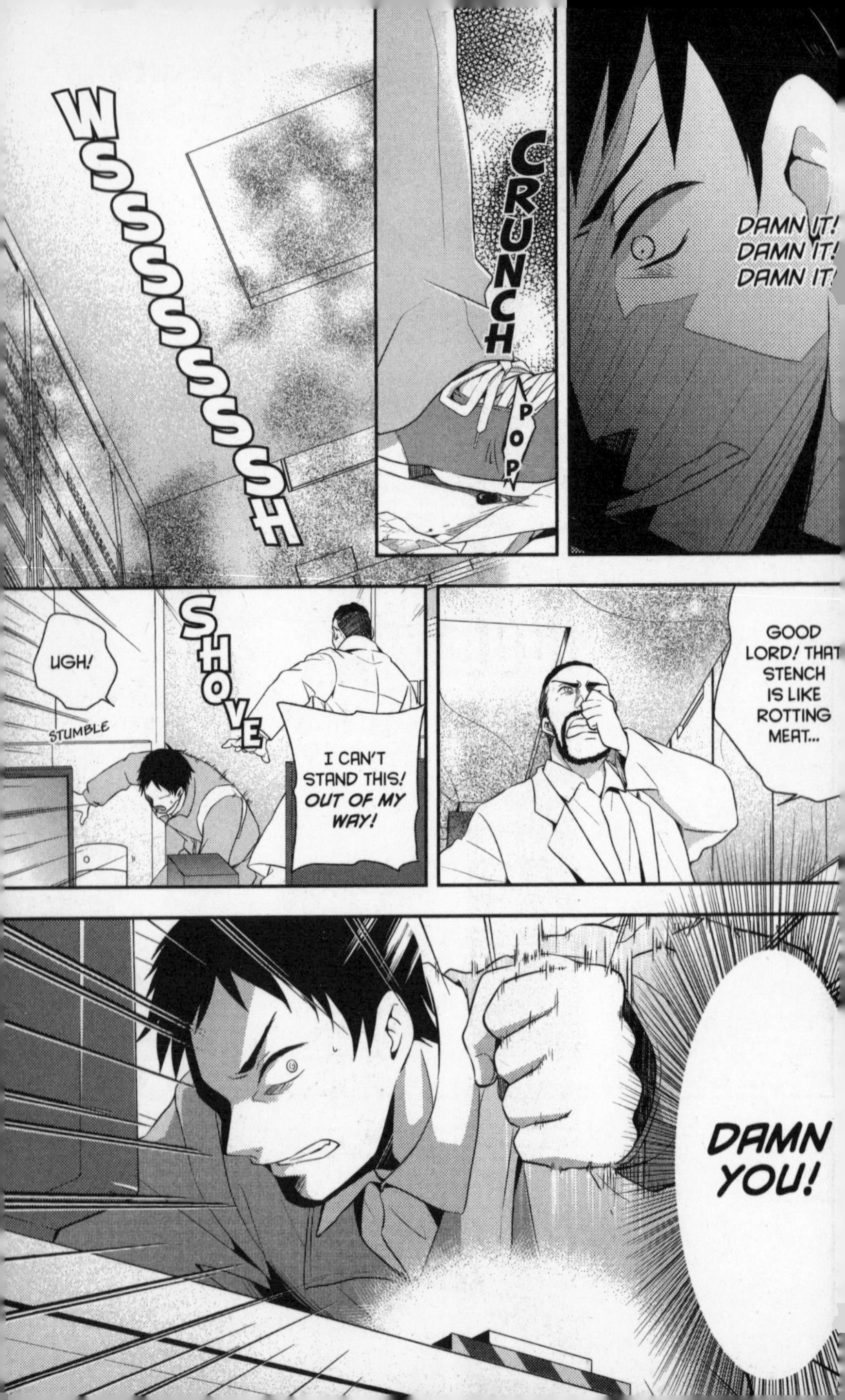
DAMN IT! DAMN IT! DAMN IT!
CRUNCH
POP
WSSSSSSH
GOOD LORD! THAT STENCH IS LIKE ROTTING MEAT...
I CAN'T STAND THIS! OUT OF MY WAY!
SHOVE
UGH!
STUMBLE
DAMN YOU!

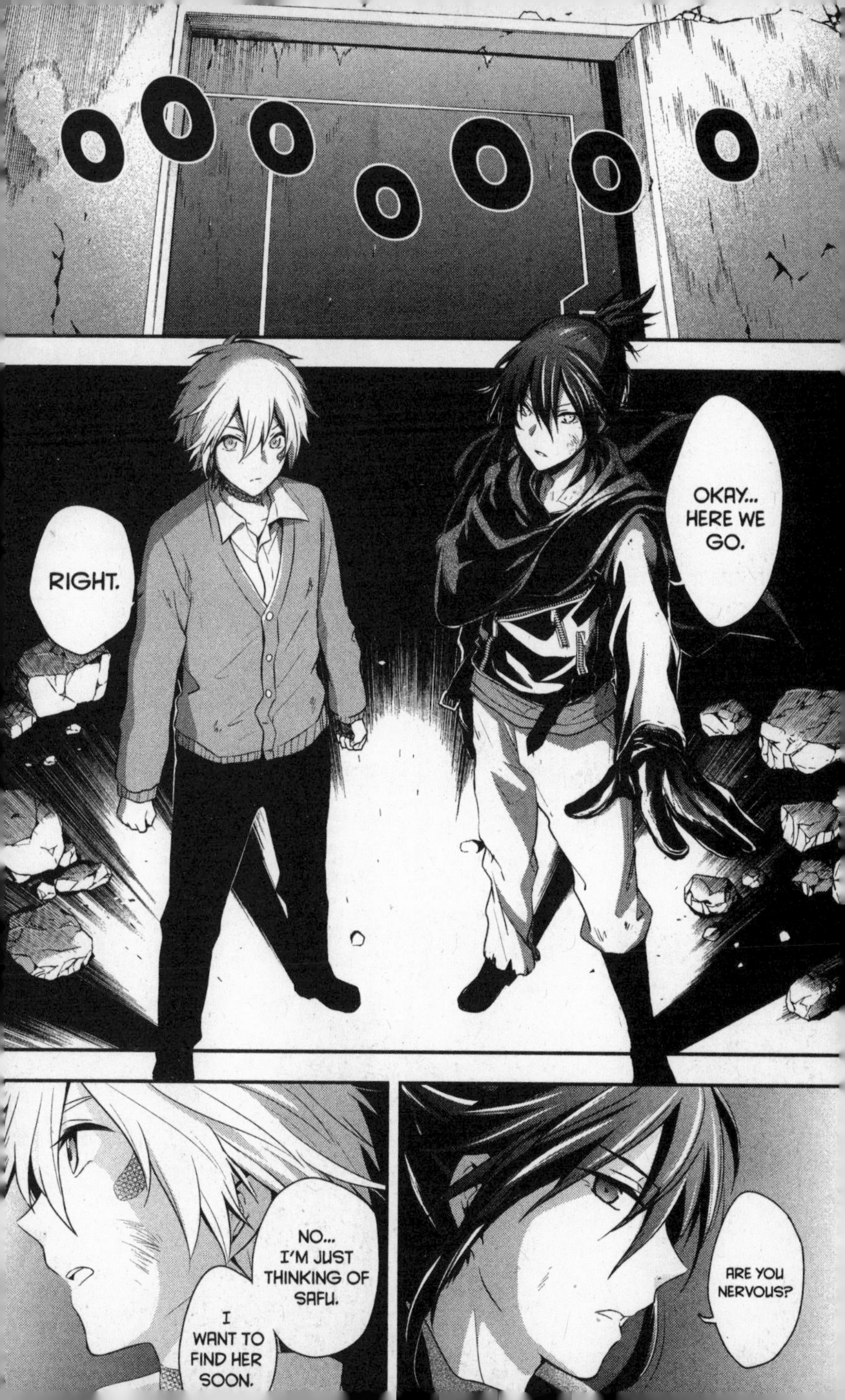
OOOOOOO
OKAY... HERE WE GO.
RIGHT.
ARE YOU NERVOUS?
NO... I'M JUST THINKING OF SAFU.
I WANT TO FIND HER SOON.

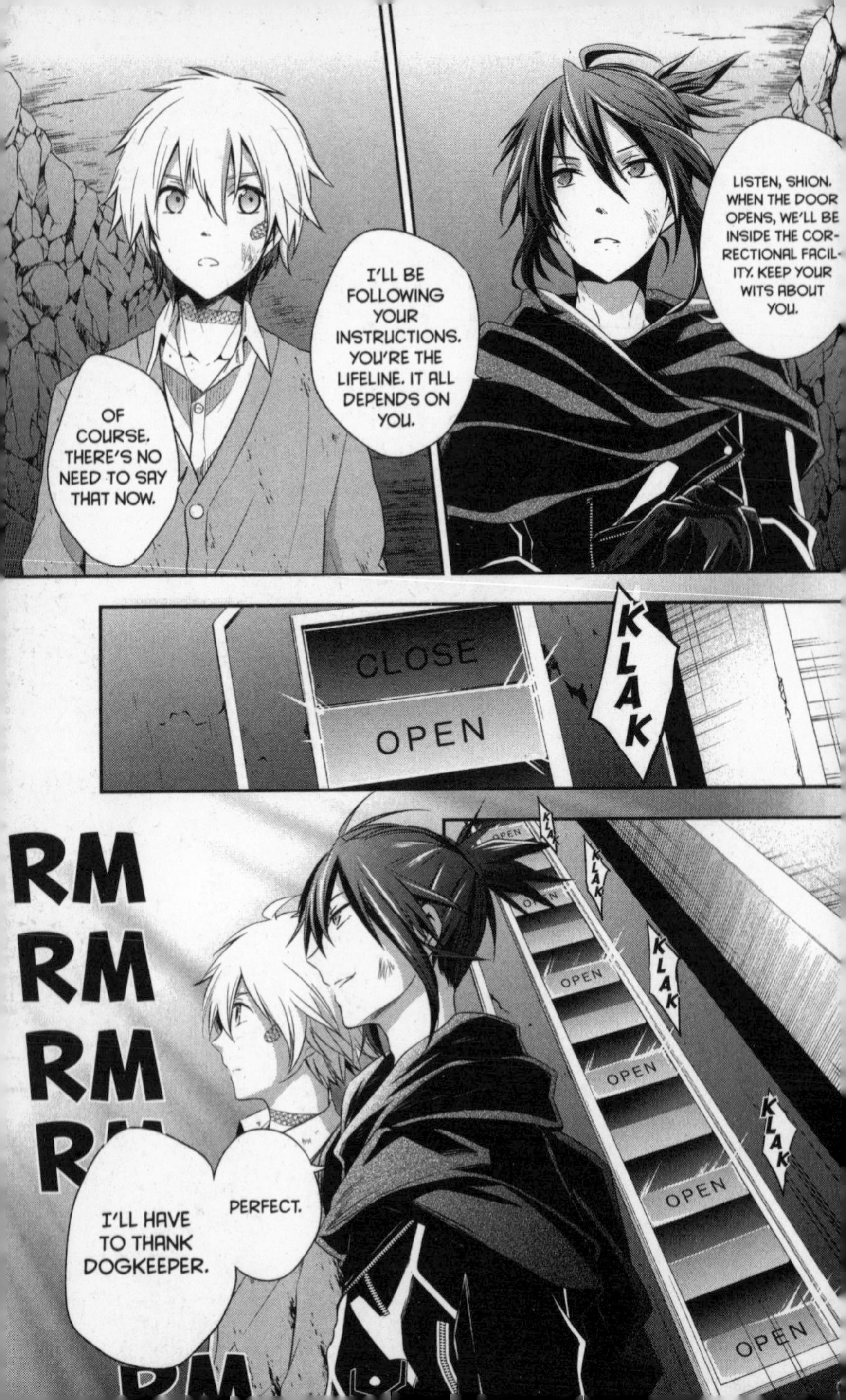

LISTEN, SHION. WHEN THE DOOR OPENS, WE'LL BE INSIDE THE CORRECTIONAL FACILITY. KEEP YOUR WITS ABOUT YOU.
I'LL BE FOLLOWING YOUR INSTRUCTIONS. YOU'RE THE LIFELINE. IT ALL DEPENDS ON YOU.
OF COURSE. THERE'S NO NEED TO SAY THAT NOW.
KLAK
CLOSE
OPEN
KLAK
KLAK
KLAK
KLAK
OPEN
OPEN
OPEN
OPEN
OPEN
OPEN
PERFECT.
I'LL HAVE TO THANK DOGKEEPER.
RM
RM
RM

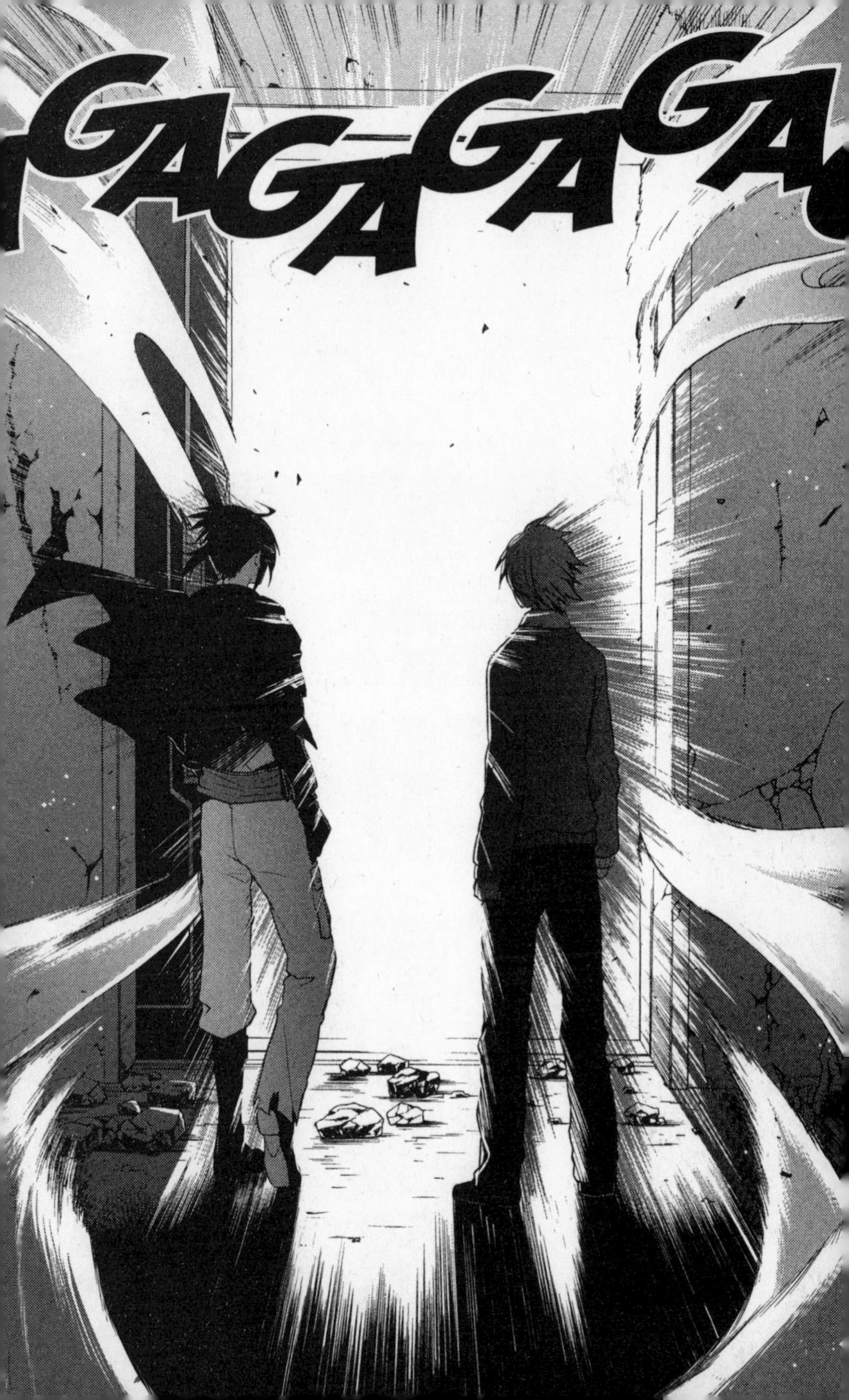
GAGAGAGAGA

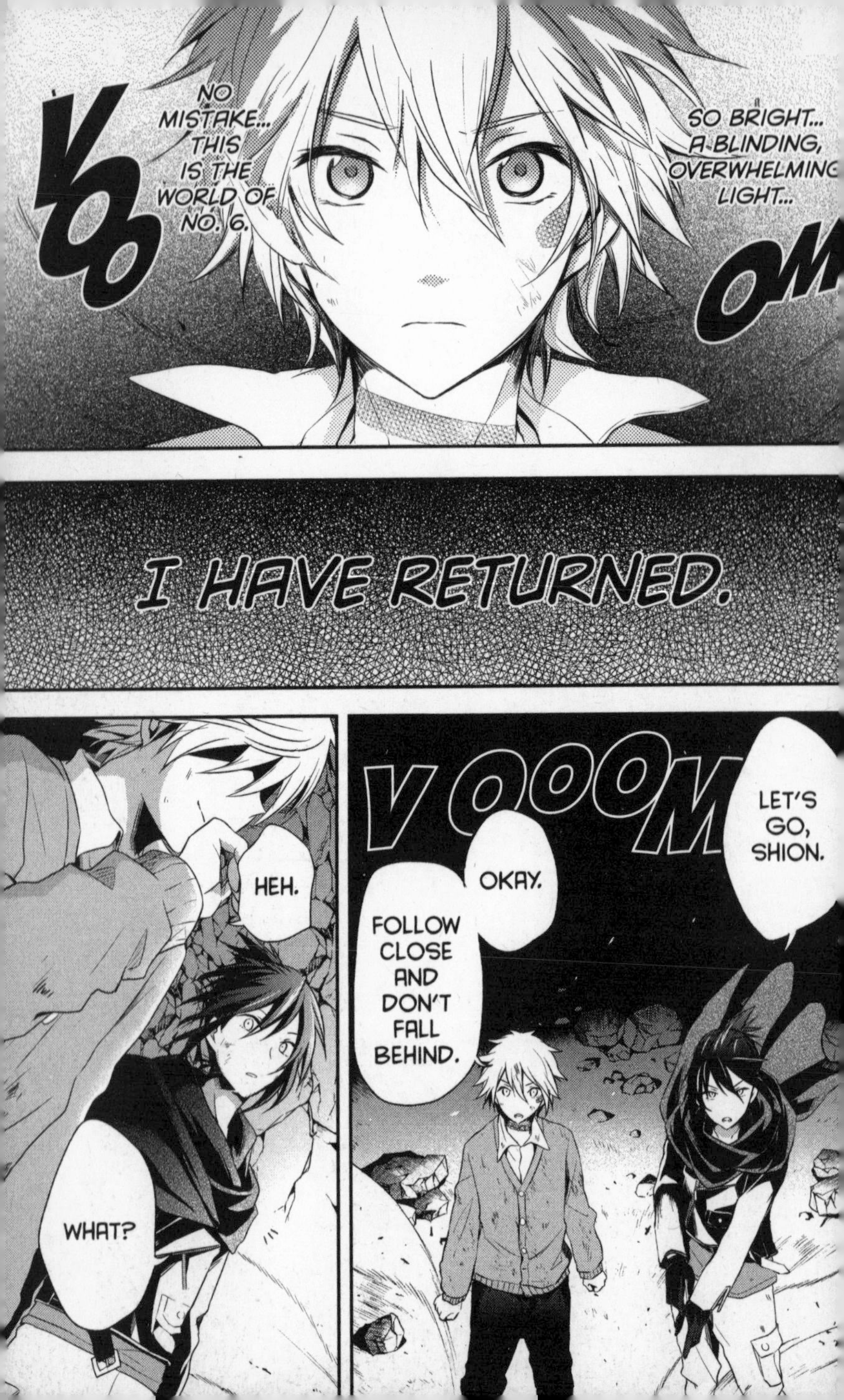
SO BRIGHT... A BLINDING, OVERWHELMING LIGHT...
OM
NO MISTAKE... THIS IS THE WORLD OF NO. 6.
VOO
I HAVE RETURNED.
LET'S GO, SHION.
VOOOM
OKAY.
FOLLOW CLOSE AND DON'T FALL BEHIND.
HEH.
WHAT?

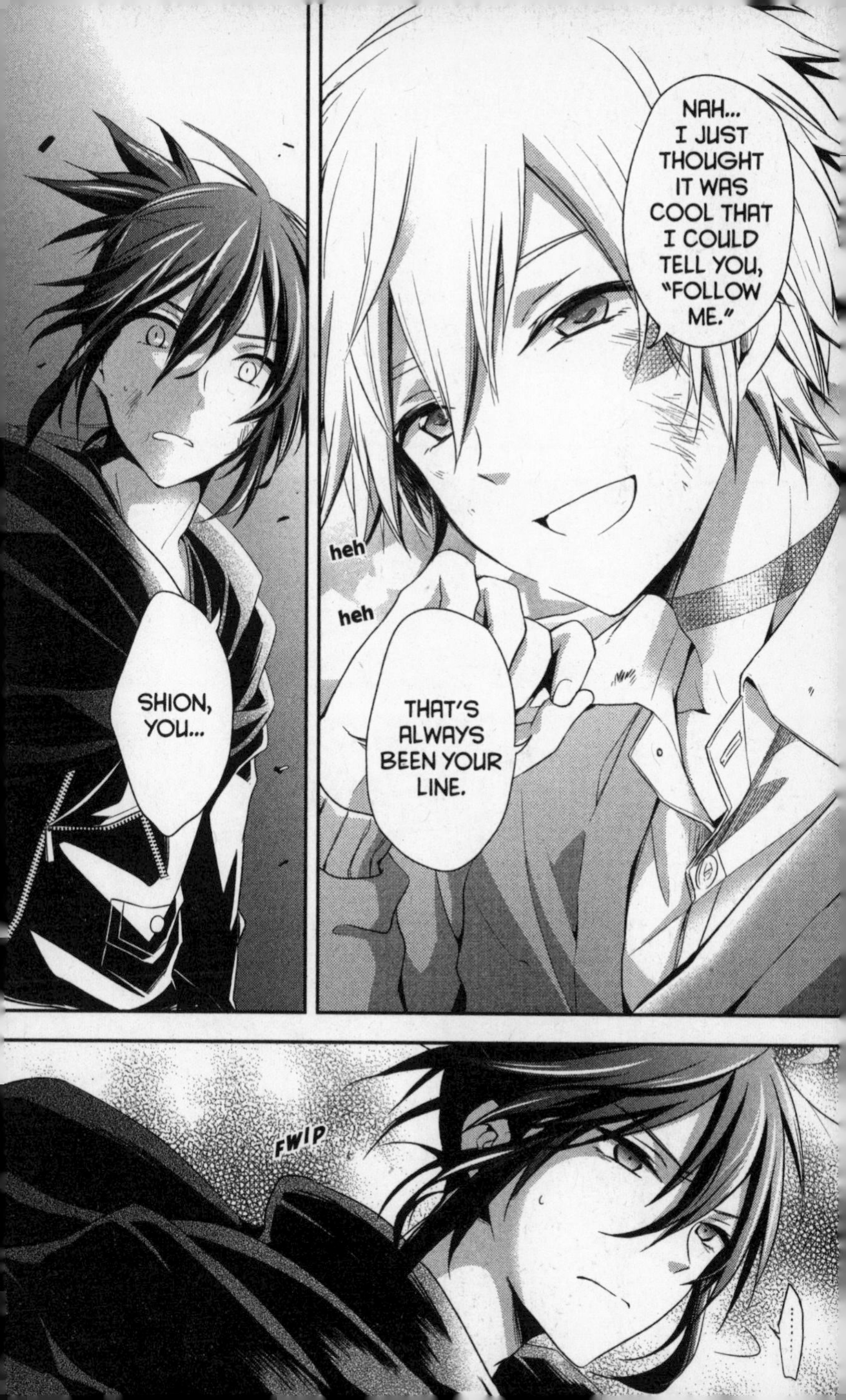
NAH... I JUST THOUGHT IT WAS COOL THAT I COULD TELL YOU, "FOLLOW ME."
heh
heh
THAT'S ALWAYS BEEN YOUR LINE.
SHION, YOU...
FWIP
......

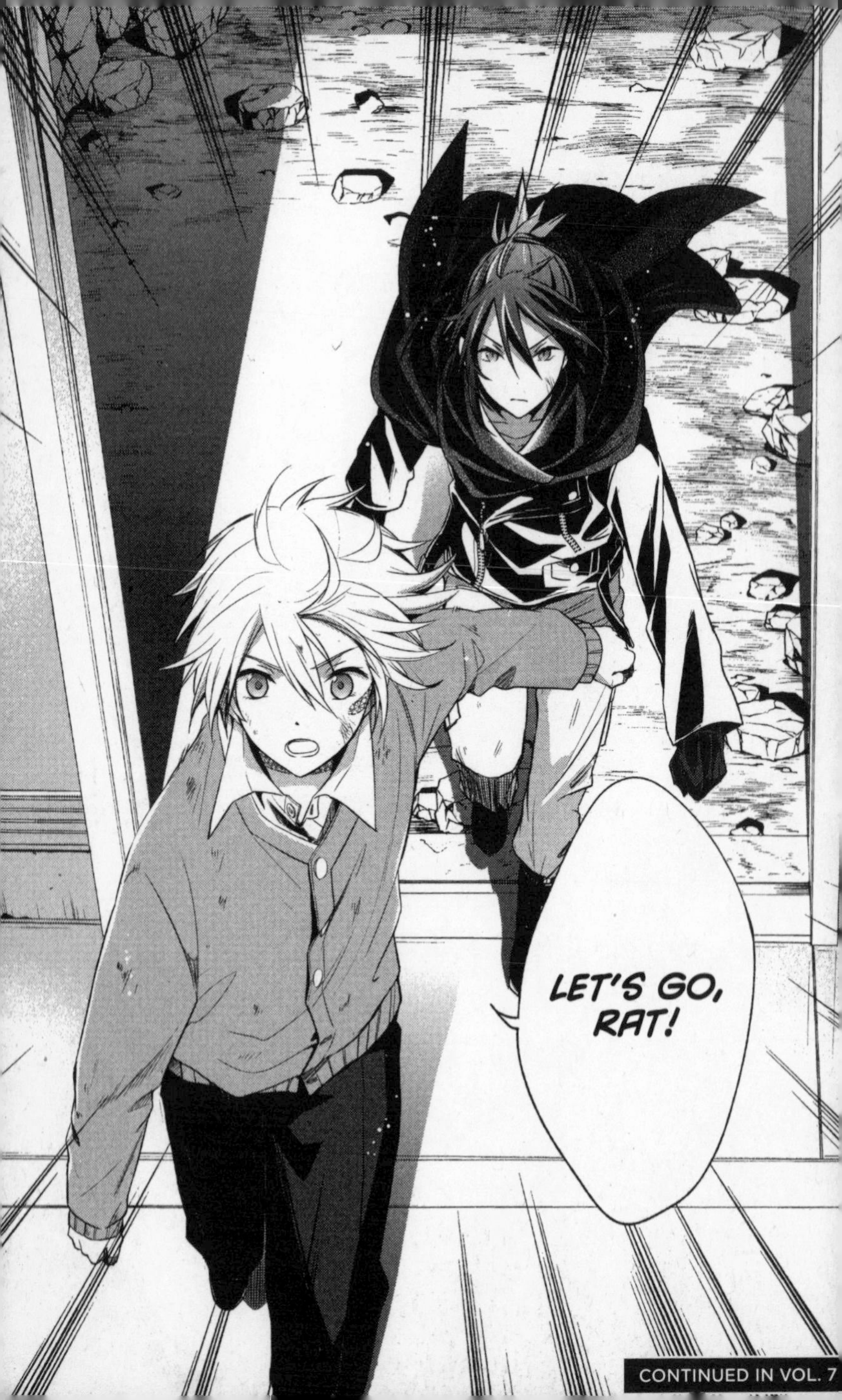
LET'S GO, RAT!

CONTINUED IN VOL. 7

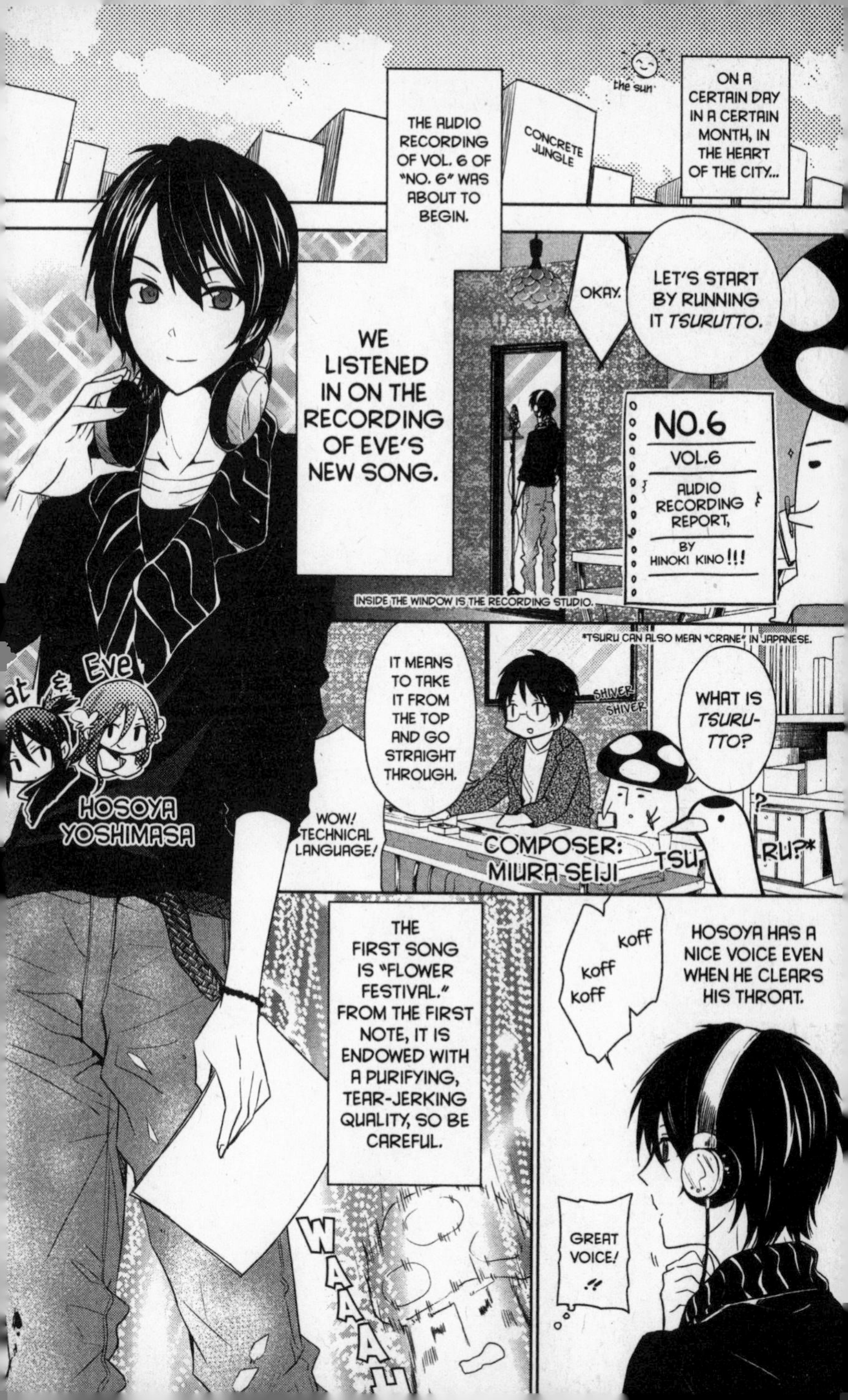

ON A CERTAIN DAY IN A CERTAIN MONTH, IN THE HEART OF THE CITY...
the sun
CONCRETE JUNGLE
THE AUDIO RECORDING OF VOL. 6 OF "NO. 6" WAS ABOUT TO BEGIN.
LET'S START BY RUNNING IT *TSURUTTO*.
OKAY.
NO.6 VOL.6 AUDIO RECORDING REPORT, BY HINOKI KINO!!!
INSIDE THE WINDOW IS THE RECORDING STUDIO.
WHAT IS *TSURU-TTO*?
TSU RU?*
SHIVER SHIVER
IT MEANS TO TAKE IT FROM THE TOP AND GO STRAIGHT THROUGH.
COMPOSER: MIURA SEIJI
WOW! TECHNICAL LANGUAGE!
*TSURU CAN ALSO MEAN "CRANE" IN JAPANESE.
HOSOYA HAS A NICE VOICE EVEN WHEN HE CLEARS HIS THROAT.
koff koff koff
GREAT VOICE!
!!
THE FIRST SONG IS "FLOWER FESTIVAL." FROM THE FIRST NOTE, IT IS ENDOWED WITH A PURIFYING, TEAR-JERKING QUALITY, SO BE CAREFUL.
WAAAAH
WE LISTENED IN ON THE RECORDING OF EVE'S NEW SONG.
at & Eve
HOSOYA YOSHIMASA

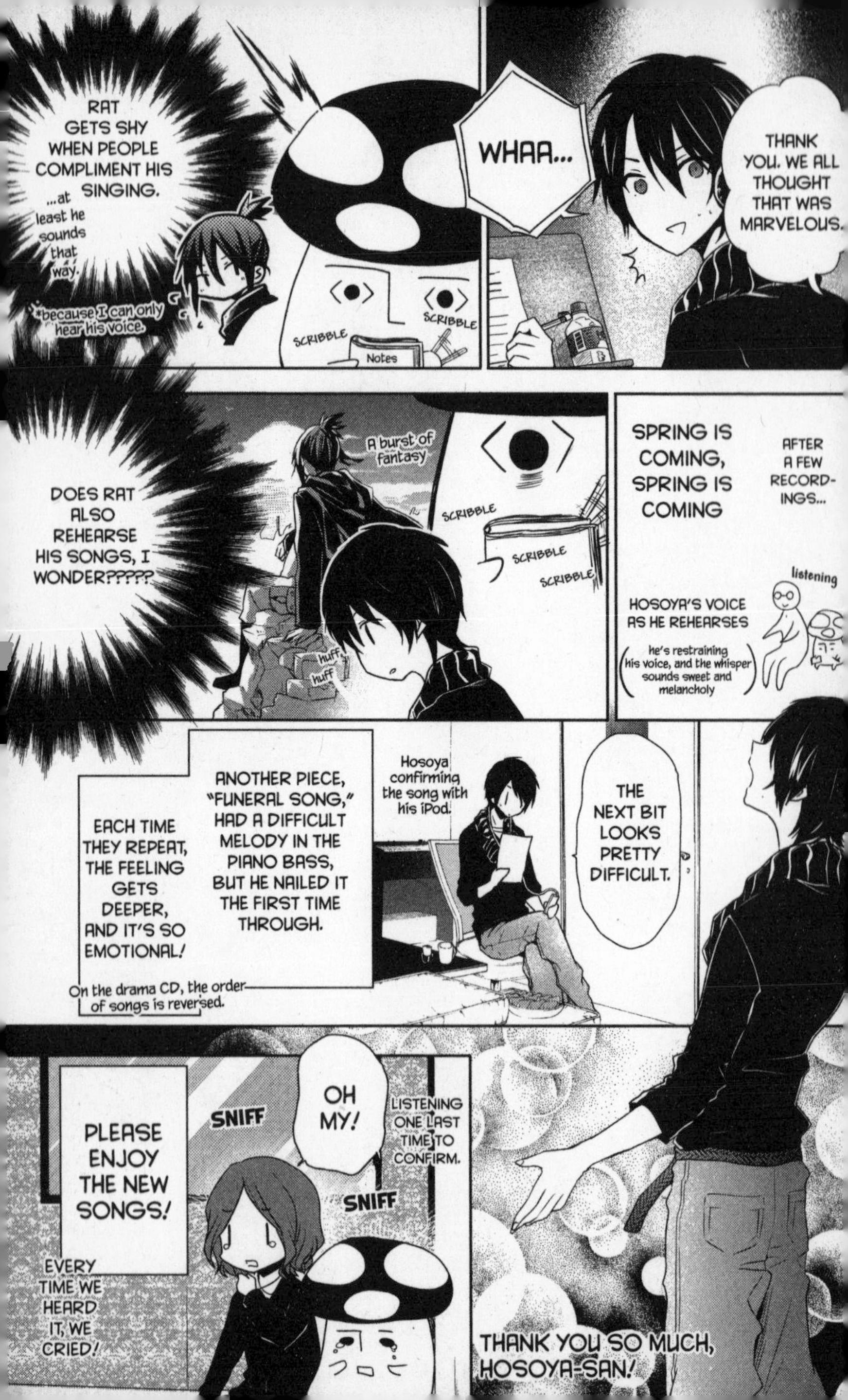
THANK YOU. WE ALL THOUGHT THAT WAS MARVELOUS.
WHAA...
RAT GETS SHY WHEN PEOPLE COMPLIMENT HIS SINGING.
...at least he sounds that way.
*because I can only hear his voice.
SCRIBBLE
SCRIBBLE
Notes
AFTER A FEW RECORDINGS...
SPRING IS COMING, SPRING IS COMING
HOSOYA'S VOICE AS HE REHEARSES
(he's restraining his voice, and the whisper sounds sweet and melancholy)
listening
A burst of fantasy
SCRIBBLE
SCRIBBLE
SCRIBBLE
DOES RAT ALSO REHEARSE HIS SONGS, I WONDER?????
huff huff
THE NEXT BIT LOOKS PRETTY DIFFICULT.
Hosoya confirming the song with his iPod.
ANOTHER PIECE, "FUNERAL SONG," HAD A DIFFICULT MELODY IN THE PIANO BASS, BUT HE NAILED IT THE FIRST TIME THROUGH.
EACH TIME THEY REPEAT, THE FEELING GETS DEEPER, AND IT'S SO EMOTIONAL!
On the drama CD, the order of songs is reversed.
THANK YOU SO MUCH, HOSOYA-SAN!
LISTENING ONE LAST TIME TO CONFIRM.
OH MY!
SNIFF
SNIFF
PLEASE ENJOY THE NEW SONGS!
EVERY TIME WE HEARD IT, WE CRIED!

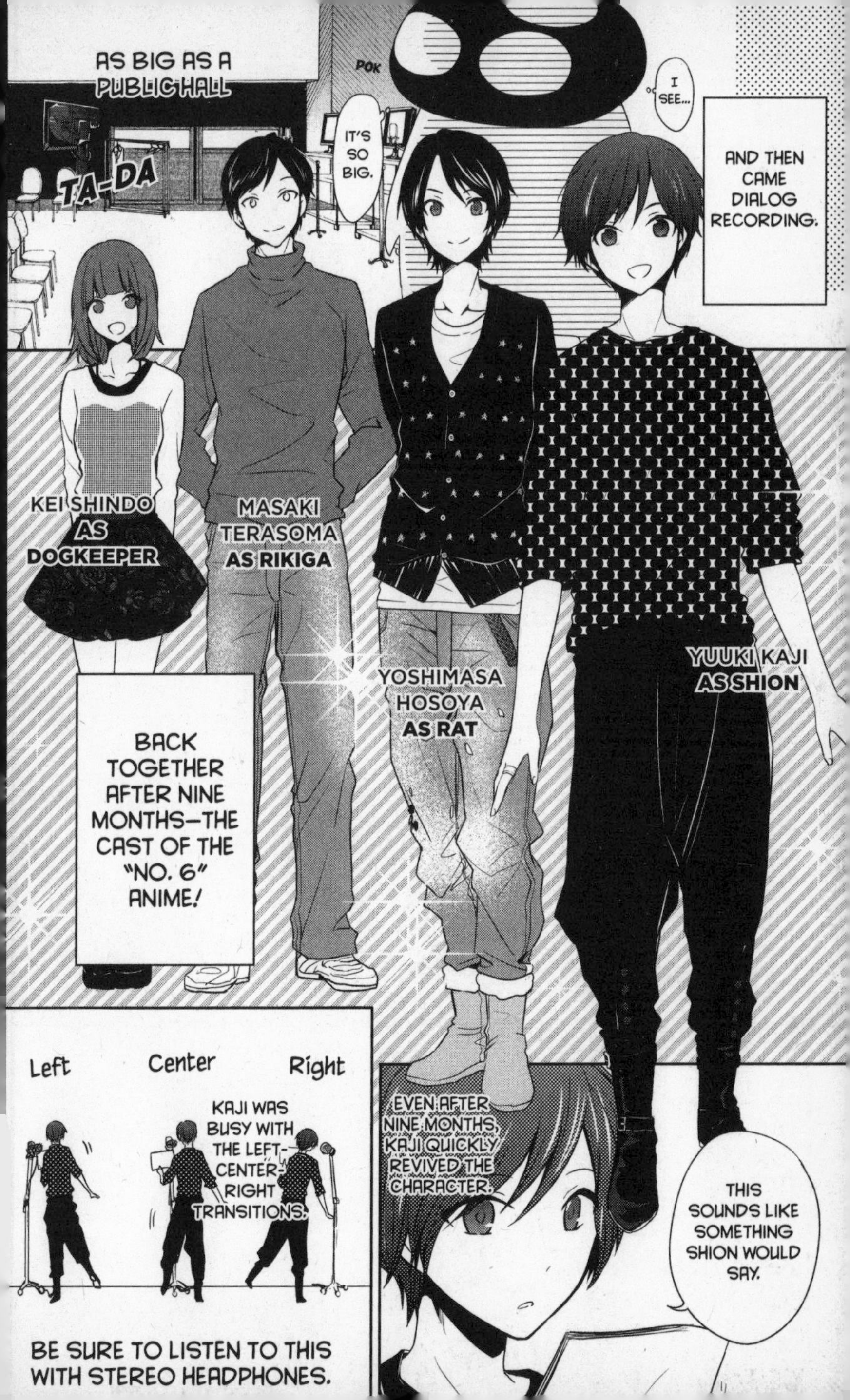
AND THEN CAME DIALOG RECORDING.
I SEE...
POK
IT'S SO BIG.
AS BIG AS A PUBLIC HALL
TA-DA
YUUKI KAJI AS SHION
YOSHIMASA HOSOYA AS RAT
MASAKI TERASOMA AS RIKIGA
KEI SHINDO AS DOGKEEPER
BACK TOGETHER AFTER NINE MONTHS—THE CAST OF THE "NO. 6" ANIME!
THIS SOUNDS LIKE SOMETHING SHION WOULD SAY.
EVEN AFTER NINE MONTHS, KAJI QUICKLY REVIVED THE CHARACTER.
Left
Center
Right
KAJI WAS BUSY WITH THE LEFT-CENTER-RIGHT TRANSITIONS.
BE SURE TO LISTEN TO THIS WITH STEREO HEADPHONES.

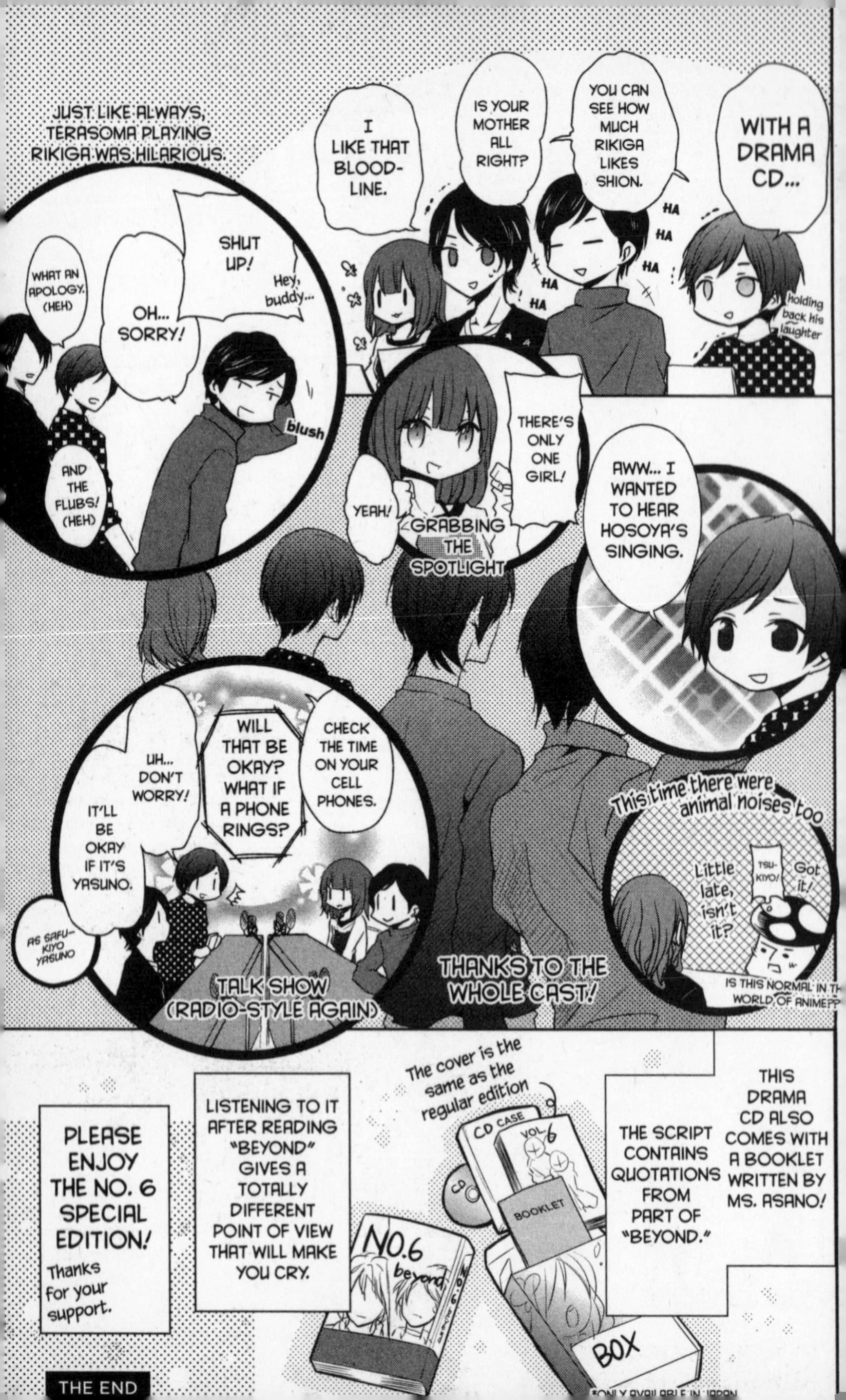
WITH A DRAMA CD...
YOU CAN SEE HOW MUCH RIKIGA LIKES SHION.
HA HA HA HA HA
holding back his laughter
IS YOUR MOTHER ALL RIGHT?
I LIKE THAT BLOODLINE.
JUST LIKE ALWAYS, TERASOMA PLAYING RIKIGA WAS HILARIOUS.
SHUT UP!
Hey, buddy...
OH... SORRY!
WHAT AN APOLOGY. (HEH)
blush
AND THE FLUBS! (HEH)
AWW... I WANTED TO HEAR HOSOYA'S SINGING.
THERE'S ONLY ONE GIRL!
YEAH!
GRABBING THE SPOTLIGHT
This time there were animal noises too
Got it!
TSU-KIYO!
Little late, isn't it?
IS THIS NORMAL IN THE WORLD OF ANIME??
THANKS TO THE WHOLE CAST!
CHECK THE TIME ON YOUR CELL PHONES.
WILL THAT BE OKAY? WHAT IF A PHONE RINGS?
UH... DON'T WORRY!
IT'LL BE OKAY IF IT'S YASUNO.
AS SAFU-KIYO YASUNO
TALK SHOW (RADIO-STYLE AGAIN)
THIS DRAMA CD ALSO COMES WITH A BOOKLET WRITTEN BY MS. ASANO!
THE SCRIPT CONTAINS QUOTATIONS FROM PART OF "BEYOND."
The cover is the same as the regular edition
CD CASE
VOL. 6
CD
BOOKLET
NO.6 beyond
BOX
LISTENING TO IT AFTER READING "BEYOND" GIVES A TOTALLY DIFFERENT POINT OF VIEW THAT WILL MAKE YOU CRY.
PLEASE ENJOY THE NO. 6 SPECIAL EDITION!
Thanks for your support.
THE END
*ONLY AVAILABLE IN JAPAN

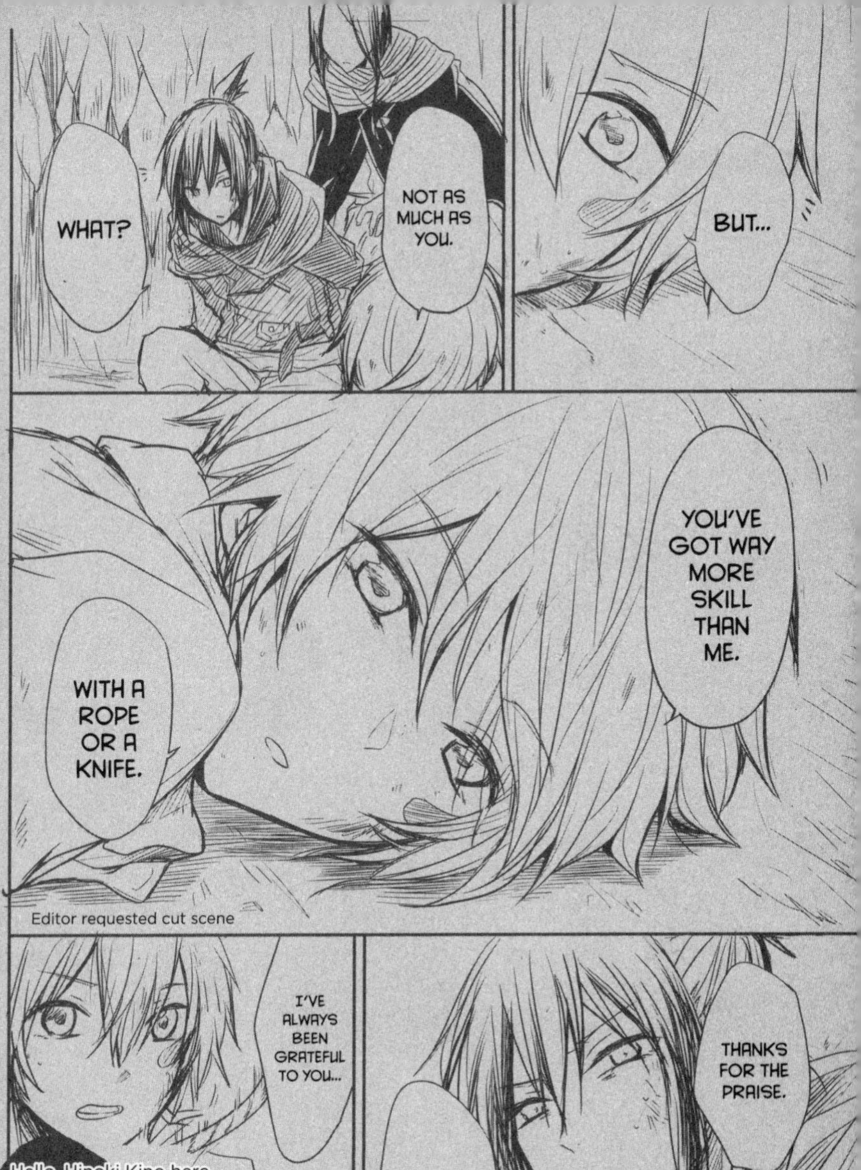
BUT...
NOT AS MUCH AS YOU.
WHAT?
YOU'VE GOT WAY MORE SKILL THAN ME.
WITH A ROPE OR A KNIFE.
Editor requested cut scene
THANKS FOR THE PRAISE.
I'VE ALWAYS BEEN GRATEFUL TO YOU...

Hello, Hinoki Kino here.
Thank you for reading vol. 6 of the "No. 6" manga. I guess this is number 6 of "No. 6"! That's why we've put out a special edition CD of volume 6 (in Japan only). Ms. Asano wrote the booklet, and the anime cast got together to record a special CD version! Including a box! Please check it out, even if you've already got the regular edition.

Volume 6 tells the story of Rat's background and the foundation of No. 6. This comes from the end of volume 5 and most of volume 6 in the novel series. Trying to cram it all in, it got a little long. In volume 7, they enter the core of the Correctional Facility. The story is packed and the panels fly by! Will Shion finally find Safu? What will Rat think about it? I look forward to seeing you in the next volume!

Hinoki Kino / March 2013

FROM CHAPTER 20

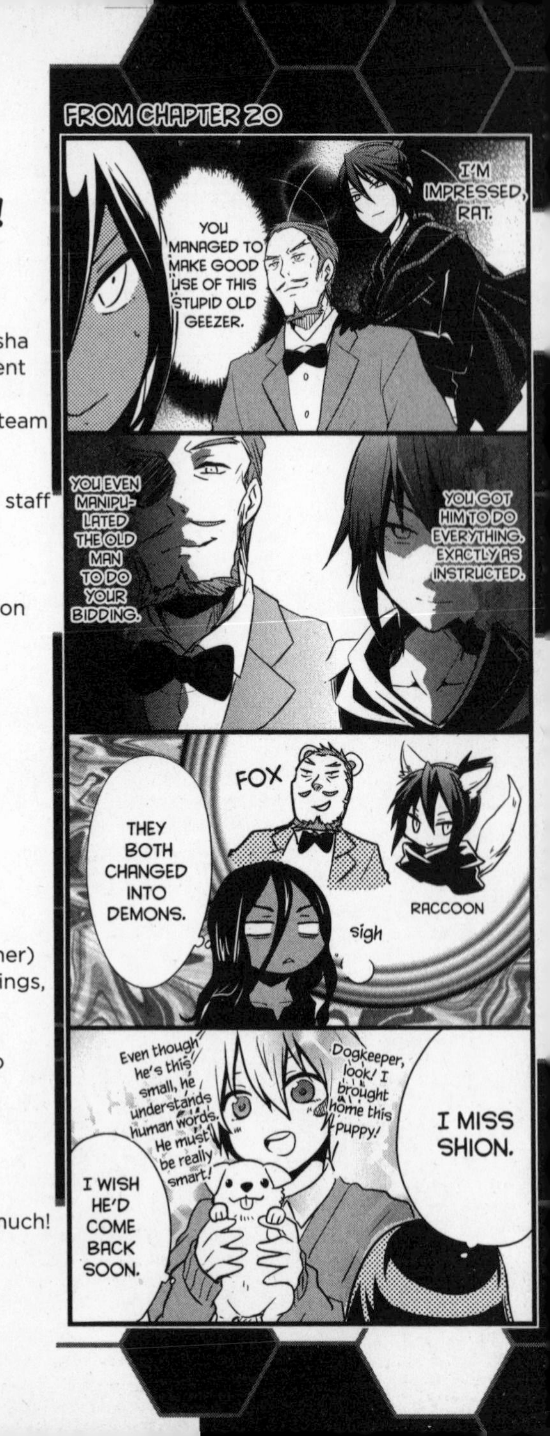
I'M IMPRESSED, RAT.
YOU MANAGED TO MAKE GOOD USE OF THIS STUPID OLD GEEZER.
YOU GOT HIM TO DO EVERYTHING. EXACTLY AS INSTRUCTED.
YOU EVEN MANIPULATED THE OLD MAN TO DO YOUR BIDDING.
FOX
RACCOON
THEY BOTH CHANGED INTO DEMONS.
sigh
I MISS SHION.
Dogkeeper, look! I brought home this puppy!
Even though he's this small, he understands human words. He must be really smart!
I WISH HE'D COME BACK SOON.

SPECIAL THANKS!

Atsuko Asano

Everyone in the Kodansha Aria Editorial Department

Everyone on the No. 6 team
Editor K
Toi8
Everyone on the anime staff
Everyone at NARTi;S
Ginkyo

* Production Cooperation
Honma
Megi
Matsugi
Noguchi Sayuri

* Finishing
Tsunocchi

* 3D
Rinkan Kei

* Color Backgrounds
Mr. dominori (Big Brother)
Family (Mom, Dad, siblings, Granny, the dog) Oda

And everyone else who helped out

Also, all you readers!

Thank you all so very much!

KC KODANSHA COMICS

Mei Tachibana has no friends — and says she doesn't need them!

But everything changes when she accidentally roundhouse kicks the most popular boy in school! However, Yamato Kurosawa isn't angry in the slightest—in fact, he thinks his ordinary life could use an unusual girl like Mei. But winning Mei's trust will be a tough task. How long will she refuse to say, "I love you"?

PRAISE FOR THE ANIME!

"This series never fails to put a smile on my face."
-Dramatic Reviews

"A very funny look at what happens when two strange and strangely well-suited peopl try to navigate the thorny path to true love together."

-Anime News Netwo

My Little Monster

OPPOSITES ATTRACT...MAYBE?

Haru Yoshida is feared as an unstable and violent "monster." Mizutani Shizuku is a grade-obsessed student with no friends. Fate brings these two together to form the most unlikely pair. Haru firmly believes he's in love with Mizutani and she firmly believes he's insane.

KC
KODANSHA
COMICS

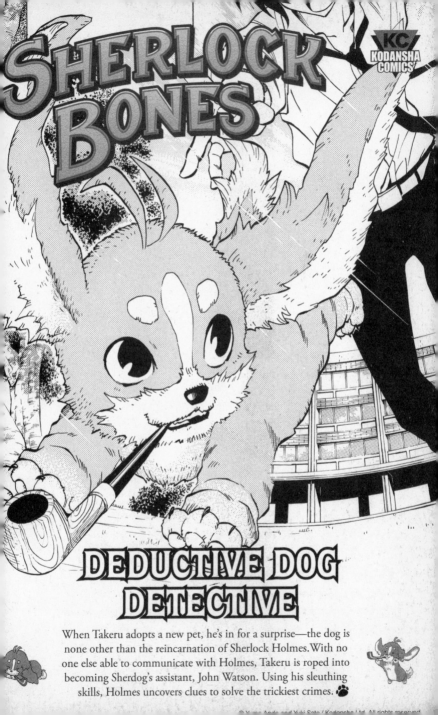

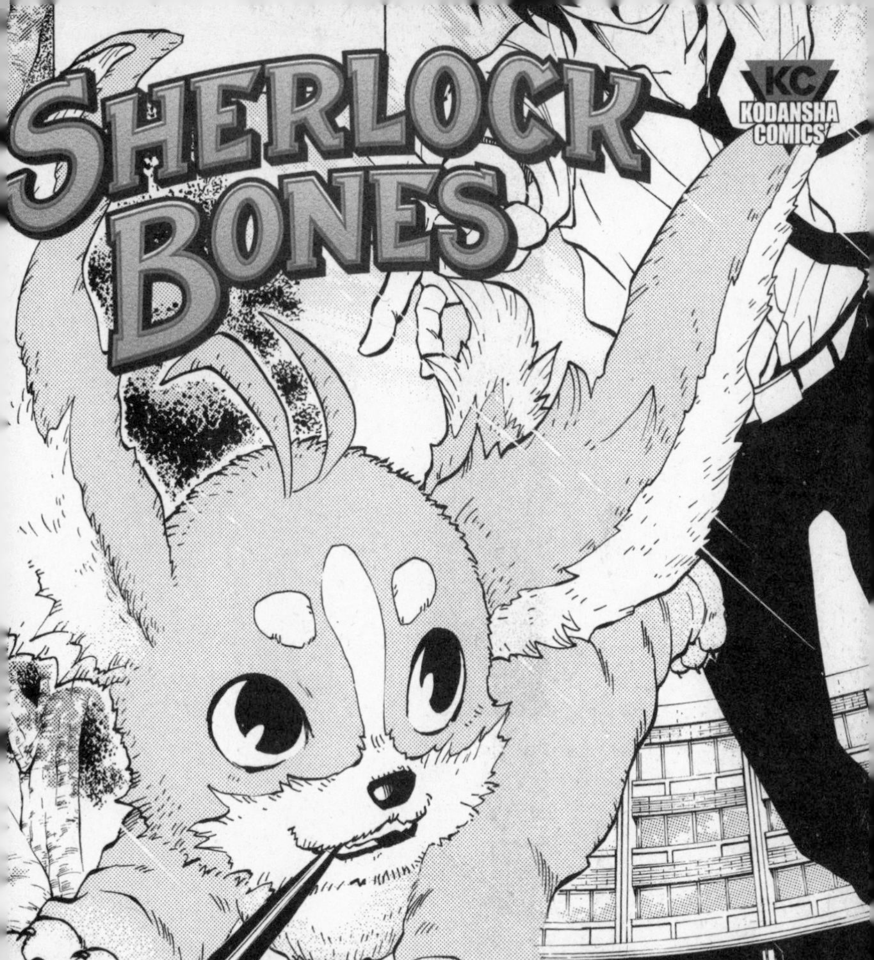
SHERLOCK BONES
KC
KODANSHA COMICS

DEDUCTIVE DOG DETECTIVE

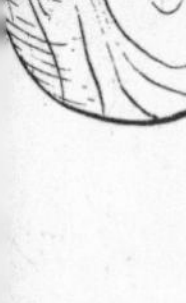

When Takeru adopts a new pet, he's in for a surprise—the dog is none other than the reincarnation of Sherlock Holmes. With no one else able to communicate with Holmes, Takeru is roped into becoming Sherdog's assistant, John Watson. Using his sleuthing skills, Holmes uncovers clues to solve the trickiest crimes.

DON'T MISS THE MOST ACCLAIMED ACTION MANGA OF 2013!

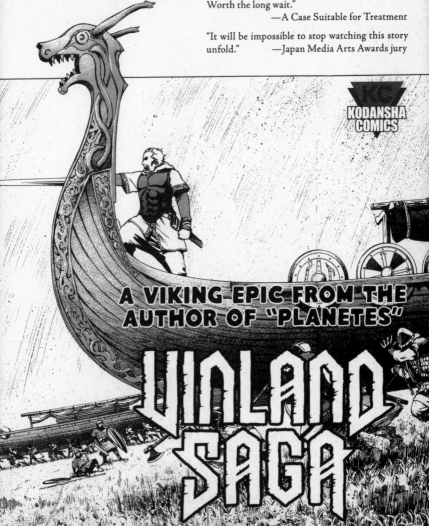

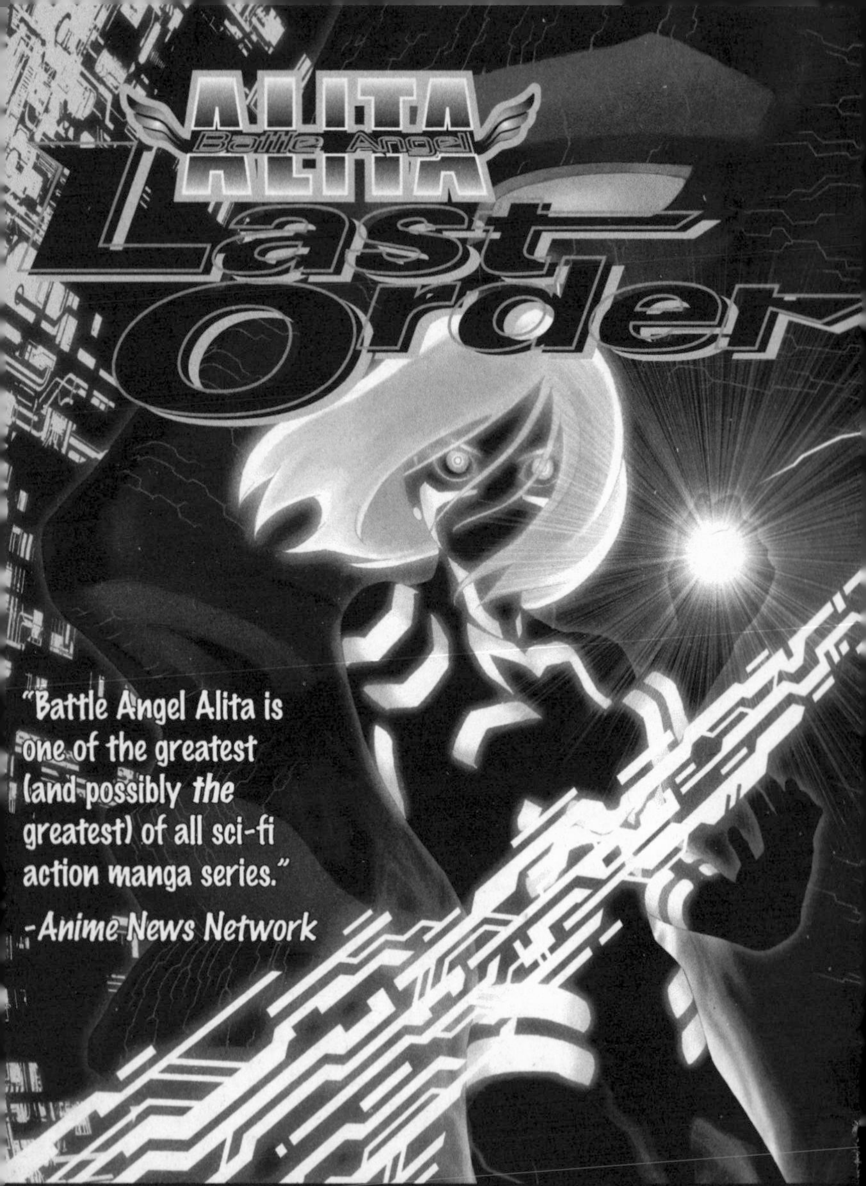
ALITA
Battle Angel
ALITA
Last Order
"Battle Angel Alita is one of the greatest (and possibly *the* greatest) of all sci-fi action manga series."
-Anime News Network

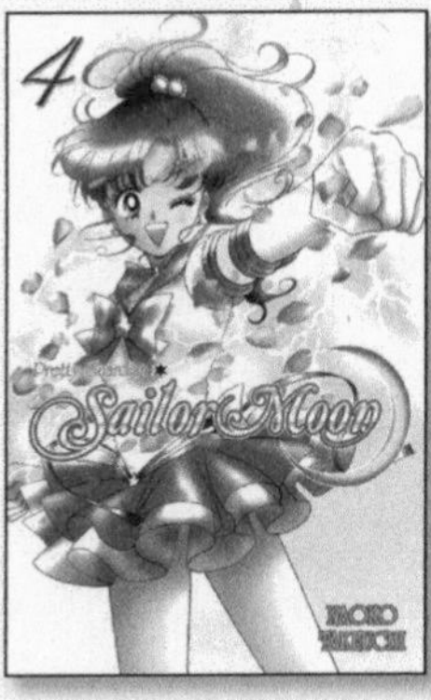
4
Sailor Moon
NAOKO
TAKEUCHI
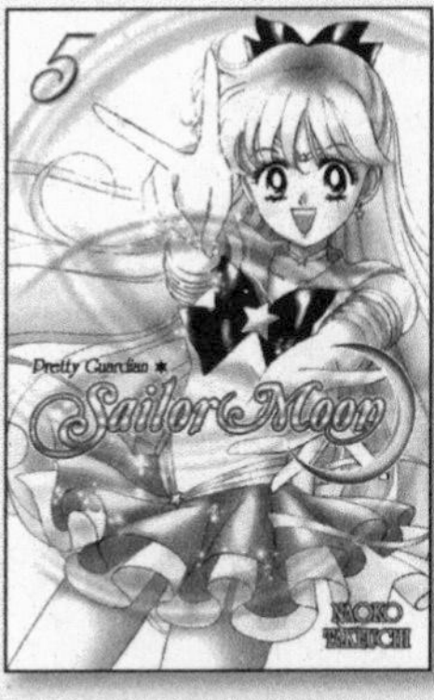
5
Pretty Guardian
Sailor Moon
NAOKO
TAKEUCHI
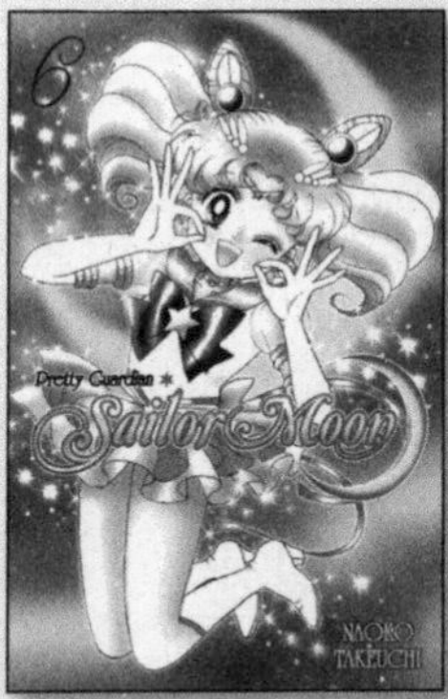
6
Pretty Guardian
Sailor Moon
NAOKO
TAKEUCHI
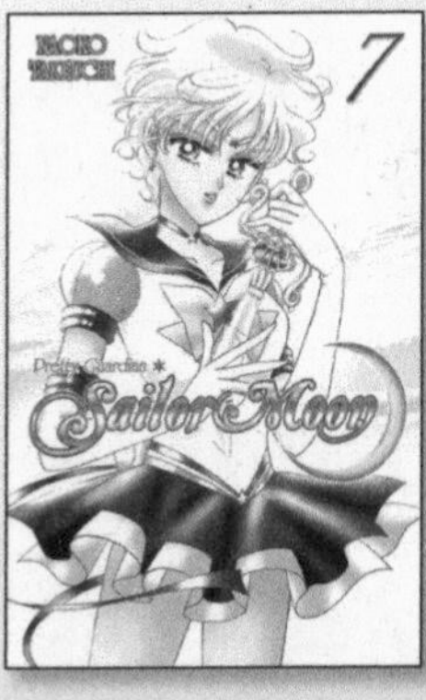
NAOKO
TAKEUCHI
7
Pretty Guardian
Sailor Moon
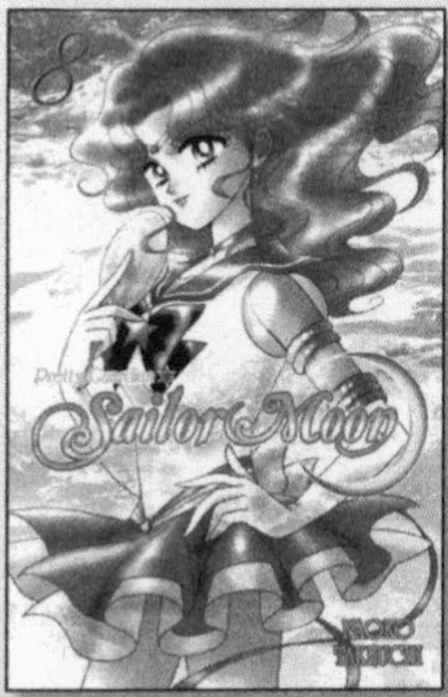
8
Sailor Moon
NAOKO
TAKEUCHI
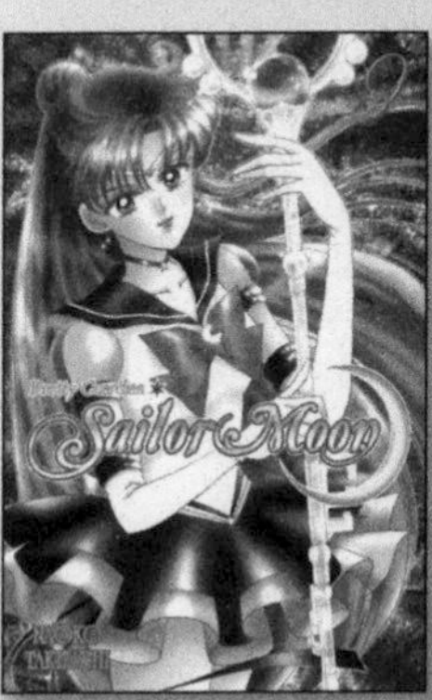
Sailor Moon
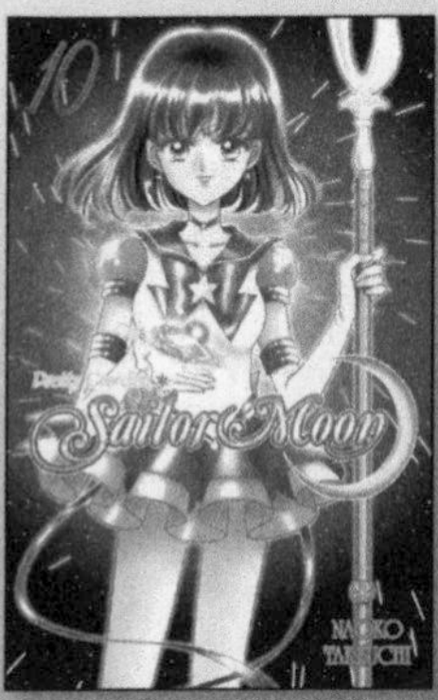
10
Sailor Moon
NAOKO
TAKEUCHI
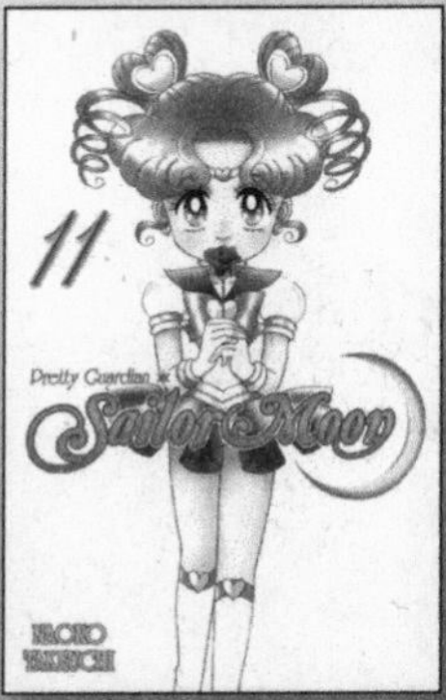
11
Pretty Guardian
Sailor Moon
NAOKO
TAKEUCHI
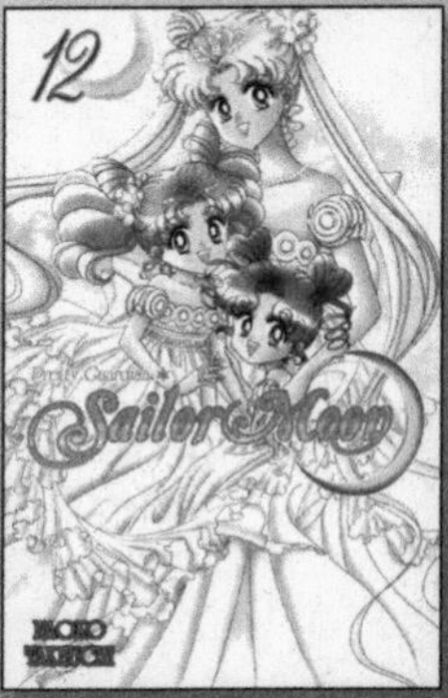
12
Sailor Moon
NAOKO
TAKEUCHI

The Pretty Guardians are back!

Kodansha Comics is proud to present *Sailor Moon* with all new translations.

For more information, go to **www.kodanshacomics.com**

THE wallFLOWER
YAMATONADESHIKO SHICHIHENGE

BY TOMOKO HAYAKAWA

It's a beautiful, expansive mansion, and four handsome, fifteen-year-old friends are allowed to live in it for free! But there is one condition—within three years the young men must take the owner's niece and transform her into a proper lady befitting the palace in which they all live! How hard can it be?

Enter Sunako Nakahara, the horror-movie-loving, pock-faced, frizzy-haired, fashion-illiterate hermit who has a tendency to break into explosive nosebleeds whenever she sees anyone attractive. This project is going to take far more than our four heroes ever expected; it needs a miracle!

1
THE wallFLOWER
YAMATONADESHIKO SHICHIHENGE
TOMOKO HAYAKAWA

Ages: 16 +

Special extras in each volume! Read them all!

KC KODANSHA COMICS

VISIT WWW.KODANSHACOMICS.COM TO:

- View release date calendars for upcoming volumes
- Find out the latest about new Kodansha Comics series

BLOODY MONDAY

Story by
Ryou Ryumon X **Art by** **Kouji Megumi**

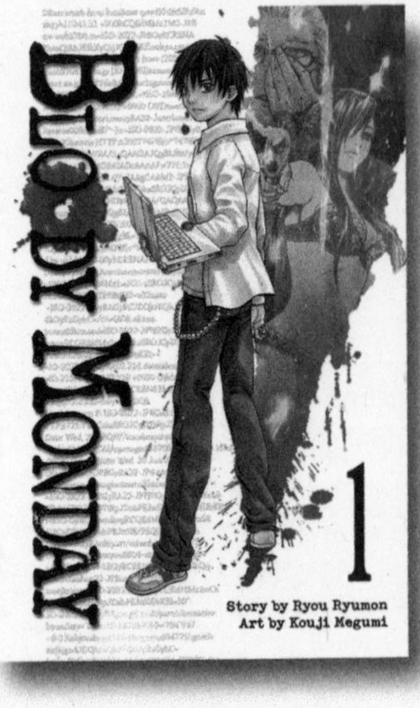
BLOODY MONDAY
1
Story by Ryou Ryumon
Art by Kouji Megumi

Takagi Fujimaru may seem like a regular high school student, but behind the cheery facade lies a genius hacker by the name of Falcon.

When his father is framed for a murder, Falcon uses his brilliant hacking skills to try and protect his sister and clear his father's name.

Special extras in each volume! Read them all!

RATING OT AGES 13+

VISIT WWW.KODANSHACOMICS.COM TO:

- View release date calendars for upcoming volumes
- Find out the latest about new Kodansha Comics series

KC KODANSHA COMICS

No. 6 volume 6 is a work of fiction. Names, characters, places, and incidents are the products of the author's imagination or are used fictitiously. Any resemblance to actual events, locales, or persons, living or dead, is entirely coincidental.

A Kodansha Comics Trade Paperback Original.

Published in the United States by Kodansha Comics, an imprint of Kodansha USA Publishing, LLC, New York.

Publication rights for this English edition arranged through Kodansha Ltd., Tokyo.

First published in Japan in 2013 by Kodansha Ltd., Tokyo
ISBN 978-1-61262-360-3

Printed in the United States of America.

www.kodanshacomics.com

9 8 7 6 5 4 3 2 1

Translation: Jonathan Tarbox/Arashi Productions
Lettering: Christy Sawyer
Editing: Ben Applegate